Fuelling the Second World War.
Deutsche Erdöl AG, 1933–1945

Manfred Grieger / Rainer Karlsch

FUELLING THE SECOND WORLD WAR

DEUTSCHE ERDÖL AG, 1933–1945

Manfred Grieger / Rainer Karlsch

societäts\verlag

In cooperation with
Gesellschaft für Unternehmensgeschichte e.V.

Typesetting: Societäts-Verlag
Cover design: Societäts-Verlag
Cover photo: Bergbrüderschaft Meuselwitz-Rositzer Braunkohlenrevier e.V./Archiv Rehfeld, „Tank wagon on the extended track system of D.P.A.G. Mineralölwerke Rositz (1936)“
Printing and finishing: Florjancic Tisk
Printed in EU

Visit us on the internet:
www.societaets-verlag.de

CONTENT

INTRODUCTION

(Manfred Grieger/Rainer Karlsch)

In this book, the authors build on their research into the history of the Wintershall AG corporation during the days of the Third Reich.[1] While the research for that project was still underway, Wintershall Holding GmbH merged with DEA Deutsche Erdoel-AG in May 2019 to form Wintershall Dea GmbH. The newly formed corporation likewise expressed the wish to have a critical study of DEA's role under the Nazi regime conducted, too. The conditions for the new appraisal were considerably more favourable than in the case of Wintershall AG, since DEA still possessed extensive, albeit by no means complete, files from the period, and these had over the last few years and with the support of the Gesellschaft für Unternehmensgeschichte e.V. (GUG) in Frankfurt/Main been prepared for academic use.[2] This meant almost all the records of Management and Supervisory Board meetings were available, as were numerous personnel and case files from DEA's various business divisions. The collections of materials in the historical archives of Deutsche Bank in Frankfurt proved to be particularly relevant to the project. As the main DEA shareholder, Deutsche Bank nominated the Chairman

---

1 Cf. Manfred Grieger et al., *Expansion at all Costs. Studies on the Wintershall AG between Crisis and War, 1929–1945*, Frankfurt 2020.

2 Cf. Friederike Steensen, *Ein Latecomer macht sich auf den Weg: Ein Firmenjubiläum als Katalysator für den Archivaufbau*, in: Archiv und Wirtschaft 1 (2024), 16–22.

and several members of the Supervisory Board and was kept thoroughly informed about the company's business operations and staff policies, and indeed was actively involved in formulating them.

Important sources on individual questions of company history were found and viewed in the collection of the Federal Archives in Berlin and Freiburg, the Lower Saxony State Archives, the Saxon State Archives in Leipzig and Freiberg, the State Archives of North Rhine-Westphalia's Westphalia section, the Bremen State Archives, the archives of the Leibniz Institute for Contemporary History in Munich, and the Austrian State Archives in Vienna. Documents from various German authorities that were transferred to Moscow after the end of the Second World War and stored in the State Archives of the Russian Federation were also appraised.

Neither at Wintershall nor at DEA did company history play much of a role before 2000, with the exceptions being celebrations for anniversaries of specific group member companies. On these occasions, the communication departments produced illustrated books and commemorative publications. Meanwhile, several DEA directors and senior executives wrote memoirs and historical accounts for internal use, but here the Nazi period was either completely ignored or glossed over for the purposes of self-justification.[3]

It was only at the end of the 1990s that a change started at DEA in the way it squared up to its own history. The impetus for this came from the public debates about the topic of forced and slave labour in the German economy during the Second World War and the establishment of the Remembrance, Responsibility and Future Foundation ("Erinnerung, Verantwortung und Zukunft", EVZ). The DEA Management Board led by Dr Dieter Dräger acknowl-

---

3 Cf. Karl Große, *Mein Leben*, Dezember 1945; Günther Schlicht, *Erinnerungen*, 2 Vol., Hamburg 1961; Rudolf Dittrich, *Aus meinem dienstlichen Leben*, Hamburg (n.d., approx. 1973); Heinz Rothbarth, *DEA – Geschichte 1899–1933*, manuscript Hamburg (n.d.); Dieter Dräger, *Von der Deutschen Tiefbohr-Aktiengesellschaft zur RWE. Zur Geschichte eines Unternehmens*, manuscript Hamburg 1989.

edged the company's historical responsibility, and RWE AG, DEA's parent company since 1988, joined the foundation initiative in May 2000 on behalf of the entire corporation. In a commemorative publication marking 100 years of DEA in 1999, Dr Dirk Bavendamm examined the company's entanglement in the Nazi war economy for the first time, albeit addressing the topic in only a few pages and without source references.[4] In light of the growing momentum of debates about the role played by businesses in the Nazi rearmament and war economy, RWE-DEA commissioned economic historians Prof. Raymond Stokes (Glasgow) and Dr Rainer Karlsch (Berlin) with compiling an overall account of the history of Germany's oil industry from its beginnings to the first oil crisis of 1973–4. This culminated in 2003 in the publication of "Faktor Öl: Die Mineralölwirtschaft in Deutschland 1859–1974" ("The oil factor: Germany's mineral oil industry 1859–1974") and in an article on Karpathen Öl AG,[5] which was a joint venture founded in 1942 by German companies to exploit the oil deposits in Galicia (now part of Poland and Ukraine). In other sets of collected essays and volumes of source material, further historians gave insights into the fates of Jewish members of DEA's Management and Supervisory Boards: One example was Georg Solmssen, Member of the Management Board of Deutsche Bank AG and Chairman of the Supervisory Board of DEA, who was forced out of office in 1938 because of his Jewish origins, as was DEA board member Fritz Haussmann.[6]

Nevertheless, these commendable and detailed studies could not hide the fact that some key themes of DEA's company history still required research. These include the company's involvement in

4 Cf. RWE-DEA AG (Ed.), *1899–1999. 100 Jahre RWE-DEA*, Hamburg 1999.

5 Cf. Rainer Karlsch, *Ein vergessenes Großunternehmen. Die Geschichte der Karpaten Öl AG*, in: Jahrbuch für Wirtschaftsgeschichte 1 (2004), 95–138.

6 Cf. Harold James/Martin L. Müller (Eds.), *Georg Solmssen – ein deutscher Bankier. Briefe aus einem halben Jahrhundert 1900–1956*, Munich 2012. Informations about Fritz Haußmann in Martin Münzel, *Die jüdischen Mitglieder der deutschen Wirtschaftselite*, Paderborn 2006, 277–280.

"aryanization", i.e. the expulsion of Jewish businesses and entrepreneurs from German economic life, as well as in the rearmament and war economy. In particular, there have been no in-depth accounts of the expansion of mineral oil production from lignite tar in the states of Saxony and Thuringia or of DEA's involvement in the exploration of oil deposits and the operation of refineries in Austria and beyond.

One particular challenge for the authors lay in the fact that DEA was a conglomerate that had lignite operations in Saxony and Thuringia, hard coal mines in the Ruhr region, oil production operations and refineries in the Hanover basin and in Schleswig-Holstein, and numerous subsidiaries, primarily in coal trading and mechanical engineering. We have therefore chosen to concentrate in the present book on the most important areas of business at DEA – hard coal mining, lignite production and processing, and crude oil production and processing. DEA's longstanding operations hub at Wietze in the district of Celle, outside Hanover, is only briefly covered. The development of the mineral oil industry in this region is being examined as part of the project "Öl aus Niedersachsen – ein Rohstoff für die nationalsozialistische Aufrüstungspolitik und Kriegführung" ("Oil from Lower Saxony – a raw material for the Nazi regime's rearmaments policy and warfare") by a team from the Institute of Didactics of Democracy at Leibniz University Hanover.[7]

The book is divided into eleven chapters. We begin by summarizing the history of DEA and its predecessor, Deutsche Tiefbohr-Aktiengesellschaft, from its foundation in 1899 up to 1933. This is followed by biographical sketches of the DEA Management Board members and the most important members of the Supervisory Board, and these reveal the decisive influence that above all

---

7 Cf. Institut für die Didaktik der Demokratie (IDD), *Öl aus Niedersachsen – ein Rohstoff für die nationalsozialistische Aufrüstungspolitik und Kriegführung*, https://www.idd.uni-hannover.de/de/forschung/projekte/projekt-detailansicht/projects/oel-aus-niedersachsen-ein-rohstoff-fuer-die-nationalsozialistische-aufruestungspolitik-und-kriegfuehrung [last retrieved on 25.7.2024].

directors of Disconto-Gesellschaft and Deutsche Bank had on the DEA Supervisory Board and to a certain extent also the DEA Management Board. The third chapter looks at the transition of the DEA operation hubs from the authoritarian management style of the interwar years to companies run under a Nazi dictatorship. In both coal mining in the Ruhr region and in the lignite mining activities in Central Germany, the Social Democratic and Communist parties as representatives of the workers as well as the trade unions were very influential before 1933. Nevertheless, there, too, the new rulers succeeded through terror and repression in breaking the resistance to the establishment of the dictatorship, whereby the pill was sweetened with social welfare provisions for the DEA workforce.

As early as 1933, the company management started to come to terms with the new balance of power. This was evident, above all, firstly in the expansion of heavy heating oil and diesel production derived from lignite tar in Rositz, and secondly in the participation in the Reich drilling programme. The company's involvement in the rearmaments and energy self-sufficiency projects was not always free of conflict, as demonstrated, among other things, by the dispute over participating in Braunkohlen-Benzin AG. DEA tried in vain to avoid having to join in this compulsory state cartel founded in 1934, as outlined in the fourth chapter and elsewhere.

The lion's share of the company's investments was funnelled into expanding its oil production facilities during the course of rearmament. The fifth chapter is therefore dedicated to the expansion of DEA's Rositz site, south of Leipzig, while the following two chapters, which focus on DEA's involvement in "aryanizations" and the development of the oil fields in Austria from March 1938, also cover new ground. We were astonished by how densely the documentation covered attempts at personal enrichment by one of the DEA Management Board members during the course of the "aryanizations" and how little of this had previously been made public.

Chapters eight, nine, and ten cover the role DEA played as an important producer of oil products for the war economy. Through both its staff and its money, the group participated in companies that exploited crude oil deposits in countries occupied by German troops, with Karpathen Öl AG in Galicia being a prime example in this regard. Over the course of the war, the DEA sites both within the borders of the original Reich and in occupied countries made increasing use of forced and slave labour, with prisoners of war, foreign civilian workers, and in 1944–5 German "Jewish half-breeds" ("jüdische Mischlinge") as well as prisoners from "work education camps" ("Arbeitserziehungslager") all deployed. The final chapter looks at the initial post-war years, which saw a high degree of continuity in DEA's personnel along with the loss of all its foreign assets and all plants in the Soviet Occupation Zone in Germany.

A WORD OF THANKS

Alongside long term CEO Mario Mehren, our sincere thanks go above all to Michael Sasse, Head of Communications at Wintershall Dea until the end of January 2024, who largely initiated and supervised the project. Managing Director of the Gesellschaft für Unternehmensgeschichte, Dr Andrea H. Schneider-Braunberger, not only helped us a great deal with her specialist expertise, but also masterfully handled the coordination of the frequently tricky research and writing work. A special thank you also goes to Friederike Steensen, Corporate History Project Manager at Wintershall Dea in Kassel, who not only prepared historical files and photos for scholarly study and carried out deeper research into certain matters, but also managed to make other documents available thanks to her persistent probing of archives and authorities. Marvin Brendel, as the Wintershall Dea corporate historian, was very helpful with file research in the early phase of the research project. Dr Stephan Lütgert, Director of the German Oil Museum in Wietze, supported the project by providing access to the testimonies of DEA Management Board members.

Parts of the manuscripts were critically appraised and commented on by colleagues, and particular thanks here go to Hendrik Altmann, Prof. Johannes Bähr, Dr Maximilian Graf, Prof. Walter Iber, Dr Karsten Linne, Dr Stephan Lütgert, and Patrick Reeb for their valuable advice on research and the manuscript. We are most grateful to the German Oil Museum in Wietze, Dr Martin Müller at the Deutsche Bank Historical Archive, Jörg Rehfeld of Bergbrüderschaft Meuselwitz-Rositzer Braunkohlenrevier e.V., the Archive of the Federal Institute for Geosciences and Natural Resources (BGR), and the Deutsches Bergbau-Museum Bochum, for their assistance in providing photographs and maps.

I. THE METAMORPHOSES OF DEA: DEEP-DRILLING COMPANY, PETROLEUM COMPANY, CONGLOMERATE

(Rainer Karlsch)

Deutsche Tiefbohr-Aktiengesellschaft (DTA) and Deutsche Erdöl-Aktiengesellschaft (DEA)

At the beginning of the 20th century, the key energy sources in Germany were hard coal and lignite, with hardly anyone talking about petroleum. It therefore caused quite a stir when on 29 May 1911 the annual general meeting of Deutsche Tiefbohr-Aktiengesellschaft (DTA; German Deep Drilling Corp.) in Berlin passed a resolution to rename itself Deutsche Erdöl-Aktiengesellschaft (DEA; German Petroleum Corporation).[1] The new company name corresponded to changes made to articles of incorporation, which now stated that the company's main object was to acquire, operate, and exploit petroleum and other mining privileges as well as acquire and sell mineral oils. This marked the temporary peak in a development that had started just under 12 years earlier with the foundation of DTA. In the space of only a decade, the corporation had grown from being a small deep-drilling company into Germany's most important petroleum corporation.

---

1 Cf. Heinz Rothbarth, *DEA – Geschichte 1899–1933*, 31.

In the year the company was renamed, DEA accounted for more than 90 percent of German crude oil extraction and processing, although the volume involved was tiny by comparison with other countries.[2] DTA/DEA had acquired petroleum operations outside Pechelbronn in Alsace (the first active oil field in Europe), and also held a stake in petroleum companies in Romania and Galicia (at the time part of Austro-Hungary, now straddling Poland and western Ukraine). During the days of the Kaiser, such an unusual development was only possible in a fledgling industrial sector.

It bears casting a glance, first of all, at DEA's predecessor company. DTA was established on 10 January 1899 by Essen-based private bank Gebrüder Laupenmühlen. The bank specialized in buying and selling mining shares, stock, and bonds and felt there were great prospects in the booming deep-drilling business.[3] To that end, first and foremost a location had to be found to set up a machine plant to manufacture drilling equipment. The site chosen was in Nordhausen – at the centre of the German Reich. The town in Thuringia, halfway between Göttingen and Leipzig, had a population of about 28,000, and points in its favour were specifically its proximity to a large potassium mine that was being set up and the high degree of industrialization in the area. Moreover, the large coal-mining regions to the east and west were both equally swiftly accessible by rail.

Wilhelm Laupenmühlen appointed young businessman Rudolf Nöllenburg (1874–1922), a native of Krefeld in the Ruhr region, to handle the set-up of the machine plant (which was made a corporate entity in its own right in 1906 as Deutsche Schachtbau GmbH) and to manage the first drilling job, whereby the company

---

2 Cf. Dietrich Hoffmann, *Die Erdölgewinnung in Norddeutschland. Von den Anfängen vor über 400 Jahren bis heute*, Hamburg 1970, 7.

3 Cf. Rothbarth, *DEA – Geschichte 1899–1933*, 1–3; Dirk Bavendamm, *1899–1999. 100 Jahre RWE-DEA*, in: RWE-DEA (Ed.), 100 Jahre RWE-DEA. 1899–1999, Hamburg 1999, 171–278, here 172–181.

would act as a subcontractor to the potassium and hard coal industry. With Nöllenburg at the helm, DTA also started drilling jobs for its own account and acquired shares in mining companies that were then sold soon after, usually at a good profit. Nöllenburg proved to have a very good eye for such speculative transactions, and in the space of only a few years DTA's capital stock was raised on various occasions and the company disbursed high dividends to its shareholders.

On 6 July 1905, the Prussian government, which ruled most of the mining regions, passed an amendment to the mining laws; the so-called "Lex Gamp" (named after parliamentarian Karl Gamp) stipulating that after only two years the state had first right to the claims to hard coal and potassium salts. This was a blow to those companies that were specialized only in deep drilling,[4] and the deep-drilling firms responded by increasing their activities in order to make best use of the time remaining until the new law on first rights came into effect. They transformed themselves into mining operations or were taken over by larger corporations. But the new law did not apply in the states of Thuringia and in the Province of Hanover, nor did the "Lex Gamp" extend to exploration for oil, and so a race began in the Province of Hanover to grab the remaining mining rights, which DTA competed in successfully. The company purchased the small Handorf oil plant in the sub-district of Steinförde, next to the village of Wietze, and merged it with three other mines in the Hanover petroleum basin in 1907 to form Vereinigte Norddeutsche Mineralölwerke AG, which was domiciled in Berlin.

Nöllenburg's most important tactical move proved to be his acquisition of all the concessions, crude oil operations, and refineries in Alsace. The new acquisitions were fused to form the

4 Cf. Erich Frenkel, *Die preußische Mutungssperre für Kalisalze und Steinkohlen (Die "Lex Gamp"). Ein Beitrag zur Frage der Aufhebung der Bergbaufreiheit*, Berlin 1913; Gerhard Dapprich, *Leitfaden des Bergrechts und anderer für den Bergbau wichtiger Rechtsgebiete mit Gesetzestexten*, Essen [4]1955, 17–19.

Betriebsgemeinschaft Pechelbronner Oelbergwerke GmbH operating company,[5] and in the years that followed, the oil extraction and processing operations in Alsace were expanded. The profitability of the firms in Pechelbronn was well above that of those in the Hanover basin, hence between 1906 and 1913 the production volume in Pechelbronn was boosted from 22,000 t to 50,000 t[6], with Pechelbronn accounting for about 60 percent of DTA's revenues at that time.[7]

Fig. 1. Oil well in Pechelbronn 1917

---

[5] Cf. on the history of the Pechelbronn oil works, in particular the dissertation by René Walther: *Pechelbronn. A la source du pétrole 1735–1970*, Strasbourg 2007.

[6] Cf. Erich Emme, *Deutschlands Mineralölindustrie und Handel. Eine Untersuchung unter Berücksichtigung des Standorts- und des Konzentrationsproblems*, PhD thesis Hamburg 1924, 169.

[7] Cf. Hubert S. Becker, *Die deutschen Erdölgebiete, ihre Entwicklung und Rentabilität*, PhD thesis Vienna 1933, 12.

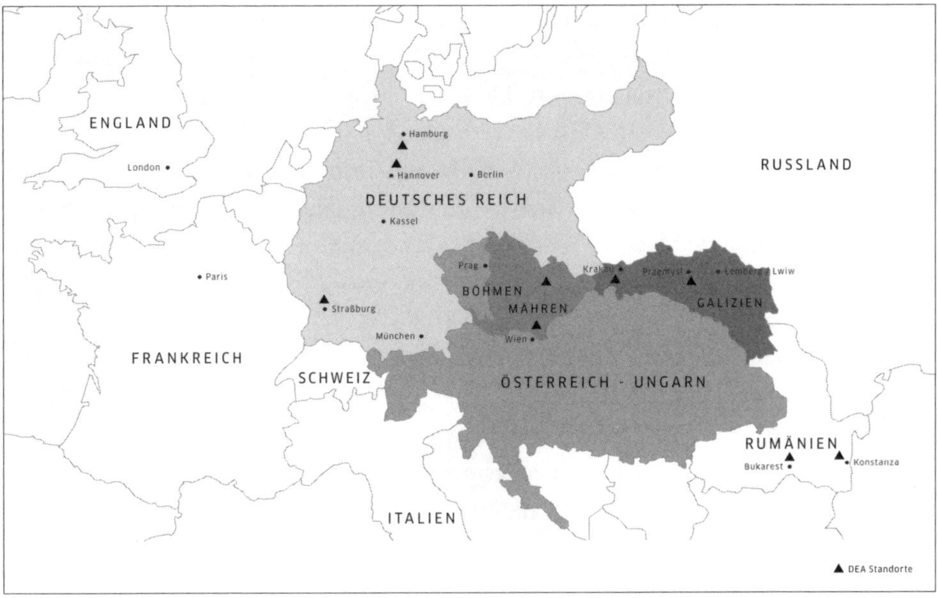

Fig. 2. DEA and DEA subsidiaries' oil producing and processing sites in Europe, around 1910

Moreover, Nöllenburg also directed that oil companies in Galicia be acquired, and he established a drilling company in Romania, meaning that DTA now had its feet on the ground in the two most important European oil production regions.

In 1910, DTA rounded out its petroleum business by acquiring the Deutsche Erdölwerke Wilhelmsburg refinery and Hannoversche Erdölraffinerie, purchasing a tar distillation plant in Grabow in Mecklenburg, and securing shares in refineries and petroleum plants in Rheinau near Mannheim and in Cologne and Hamburg.[8] Moreover, Vereinigte Norddeutsche Mineralölwerke AG was merged with Celle-Wietze AG, and the corporation's distribution system

8 Cf. Rothbarth, *DEA – Geschichte 1899–1933*, 22.

was expanded accordingly. The sales departments in Pechelbronn, in Linden near Hanover, and in Wilhelmsburg and Grabow were merged in 1911 to form Deutsche Mineralöl-Verkaufsverein GmbH (Ölkontor).

DTA also successfully expanded its petroleum interests in the Hanover basin, first by increasing its stake in Vereinigte Norddeutsche Mineralölwerke AG and in Celle-Wietze AG so that it owned them outright, and then incorporating their petroleum operations into Deutsche Mineralölindustrie AG, albeit to the exclusion of their refineries.[9] The latter company, founded by Deutsche Bank and other partners, accounted for around 70 percent of the crude oil produced in the Wietze oil field.

In order to be able to make all the above-mentioned acquisitions, DTA's capital was increased in 1911 from 5 million to 11 million Reichsmark. Furthermore, Deutsche Schachtbau GmbH was transformed into a joint stock corporation with capital of 2.5 million Reichsmark.[10]

It was thus only logical that DTA was renamed "Deutsche Erdöl-Aktiengesellschaft" (German Petroleum Corporation). At this time, there was no other company in the German Reich with a similarly strong focus on oil production and processing, but it bears noting here that the new DEA corporation was tiny compared to the large international Anglo-Dutch, American, and French oil companies.

DEA as an oil company belonging to Disconto-Gesellschaft

In order for DEA to enter the international oil business on a broader footing, lenders with deep pockets and political support were

---

9 Cf. ibid., 28.

10 Cf. ibid., 30.

Abb. 3: Georg Solmssen, DEA-Aufsichtsratsvorsitzender 1920–1936

needed. General Director Nöllenburg wanted to exploit the opportunity afforded by the fact that Deutsche Bank and its main rival, Disconto-Gesellschaft, were each trying to gain a foothold in the Romanian oil sector. He initially opted for a stake in Deutsche Petroleum-AG (DPAG), a firm founded in 1904 that pooled all Deutsche Bank's oil interests.[11] However, when in 1913 Nöllenburg came out against the Reich government's plans for a project to found a Reich petroleum monopoly, something Deutsche Bank supported, tension between DEA and DPAG grew.[12] Thereafter Nöllenburg vacillated between wooing the Disconto-Gesellschaft/S. Bleichröder banking

11 Cf. Lothar Gall, *Die Deutsche Bank von ihrer Gründung bis zum Ersten Weltkrieg*, in: id. et al., Die Deutsche Bank 1870–1995, Munich 1995, 70.

12 Cf. Fritz Blaich, *Der "Standard-Oil-Fall" vor dem Reichstag. Ein Beitrag zur deutschen Monopolpolitik vor 1914*, in: Zeitschrift für die gesamte Staatswissenschaft 126 (1970), 663–682.

group, on the one hand, and Deutsche Bank on the other. The struggle between the major Berlin banks as to who would rule the roost at DEA peaked in June 1915 at the AGM: In a forced vote, Disconto-Gesellschaft secured a majority on the DEA Supervisory Board. The meeting marked a rupture in DEA's history: The company founders, the Laupenmühlen brothers, resigned from the Supervisory Board, while Disconto-Gesellschaft and the banks allied with it placed further representatives on the board. Three of the latter's members would henceforth set the tone: Georg Solmssen (1869–1957), Richard F. Ullner (1875–1945), and Consul General Paul von Schwabach (1867–1938).[13] Georg Solmssen was to steer the affairs of DEA for more than a quarter of a century, chairing the Supervisory Board from 1920 to 1936. He was the scion of a famous banking dynasty and was the perfect example of one of the integrated German-Jewish elite.[14]

In 1900, he had opted to convert and had been baptized a Protestant. As the co-owner of the Berlin Disconto-Gesellschaft, Solmssen was able to exert a great influence on DEA's petroleum activities in Romania. After the merger of Disconto-Gesellschaft and Deutsche Bank in 1929, he was a member of the new Management Board and for a brief period in 1933 was its spokesman.

Paul von Schwabach was the owner of Bankhaus S. Bleichröder and one of Germany's most reputed bankers.[15] He was likewise born a Jew and converted to Protestantism, and in 1907 Kaiser Wilhelm II made him a member of the Prussian aristocracy. He served as an army officer in the First World War and from 1911 to 1933 was a member of the Senate of the Kaiser-Wilhelm-

13 Cf. Rothbarth, *DEA – Geschichte 1899–1933*, 37.

14 Cf. Harold James, *Georg Solmssen. Eine biographische Annäherung*, in: id./Martin L. Müller (Eds.), Georg Solmssen. Ein deutscher Bankier. Briefe aus einem halben Jahrhundert 1900–1956, Munich 2012, 11–52, here 11–32.

15 Cf. Reinhold Zilch, *Schwabach, Paul, Hermann von*, in: Neue Deutsche Biographie, Vol. 23, Berlin 2007, 776f.

Fig. 4 Richard F. Ullner, member of the DEA Supervisory Board from 1912, member of the DEA Management Board, 1933–40

Gesellschaft, the Kaiser Wilhelm Society for the Advancement of Science.

Richard F. Ullner had likewise trained as a banker and rose through the ranks to become a member of the Disconto-Gesellschaft Management Board.[16] He was a member of the DEA Supervisory Board from as early as 1912, then after the First World War he moved to become a member of the DEA Management Board, acting as its Deputy Chairman, which underscores the decisive influence the major Berlin bank had on DEA's affairs.

With Disconto-Gesellschaft on board, Nöllenburg remained DEA General Director, but he was no longer able to take decisions

16 Cf. Die Zukunft 32 (1919); Geschäftsbericht der Deutschen Erdöl-Aktiengesellschaft in Berlin über das einundvierzigste Geschäftsjahr 1939, Wintershall Dea Corporate Archive [hereafter: WD-CA], D-GB.

on his own. Disconto-Gesellschaft supported DEA's acquisition of stakes in "Concordia" Rumänische Petroleum AG, Bucharest (74 percent), in "Vega" Rumänische Petroleum-Raffinerie AG, Bucharest (60 percent), and in "Credit Petroliefer" Gesellschaft, Bucharest (50 percent).

At Solmssen's initiative, Disconto-Gesellschaft resolved to join, as lead manager, a study society for the promotion of the Edeleanu process, which was used to transform crude oils into sellable mass-market products.[17] As early as 1904, Solmssen had hired the Romanian chemist Lazăr Edeleanu to be director of the "Vega" refinery in Ploesti.[18] But application and marketing of Edeleanu's invention proved impossible there, hence the foundation of the Allgemeine Gesellschaft für chemische Industrie GmbH (Agefci), which in 1930 was renamed Edeleanu GmbH. In 1921, DEA acquired a majority of the shares in said company, and from then on, Disconto-Gesellschaft held roughly one third and DEA two thirds of the shares in Agefci and then Edeleanu GmbH.[19] The company held numerous patents inside and outside the country, and between 1910 and 1933 built a total of 41 plants worldwide worth some 24 million Reichsmark on behalf of almost all the oil majors, which brought in foreign currency and booked a profit of approx. 6.5 million Reichsmark.[20]

The Berlin big bank welcomed the strengthening of DEA sales arms when in 1912 it purchased the Aktiengesellschaft für österreichische und ungarische Mineralölprodukte ("Olex"). The Olex headquarters thereupon relocated from Vienna to Berlin. Olex was headed up by Carl Adler, a Jewish banking expert, and enjoyed

---

17 Cf. Solmssen an Kimmich, 13 April 1935, Anlage, Historisches Archiv der Deutschen Bank [hereafter: HADB], P 1658, sheet 92ff.

18 Cf. Ernst Terres, *Edeleanu, Lazăr*, in: Neue Deutsche Biographie, Vol. 4, Berlin 1959, 307f.

19 Cf. ibid.

20 Cf. ibid.

Fig. 5 Olex vehicle pool in Berlin, around 1913

excellent contacts among the authorities, which led, among other things, to it supplying petroleum to the Prussian and Saxon state railways and to the German Army through the latter's Procurement Office.[21]

After the outbreak of the First World War, DEA found itself in a wartime economy. It committed part of its profits in 1915 to building a large main administration office in Berlin's Schöneberg district which, to this day, is known as the "DEA House" or "Olex House".[22]

---

21 Cf. Rothbarth, *DEA – Geschichte 1899–1933*, 40.

22 Today, the Senate Department for Economics, Energy and Public Enterprises is housed there. Cf. Holger Hübner, *"Das Olex-Haus"*, https://www.berlin.de/sen/web/ueber-uns/historisches/artikel.58814.php [last retrieved on 20 June 2024]. On the building history of the Olex House cf. Denkmaldatenbank: *"Das Olex-Haus"*, https://denkmaldatenbank.berlin.de/daobj.php?obj_dok_nr=09066431 [last retrieved on 20 June 2024].

Fig. 6 DEA Head Office in Martin Luther Strasse 61–6 Schöneberg, Berlin, while under construction

An agreement was signed with Naval High Command in the summer of 1915, giving DEA an interest in kerosene production.[23]

However, when the production plant in Galicia and Romania was occupied by the enemy, the German war economy faced an ever more pronounced bottleneck for lubricants. DEA responded by expanding the oil extraction in Pechelbronn and in 1916 commenced experiments to use pyrolysis to extract to extract heavy heating oil, diesel, and paraffin from the lignite tar. The chemical process underlying this had been developed in Central Germany as early as the mid-19th century.[24]

Carbonization or pyrolysis involved the lignite being broken down in a vacuum at a high temperature, which led to the release of

---

23 Cf. Aufsichtsratssitzung, 9 August 1915, HADB, P 1665, sheet 37–49.

24 Cf. Fritz Welsch, *Geschichte der chemischen Industrie*, Berlin 1981, 112f.; Lausitzer und Mitteldeutsche Bergbauverwaltungsgesellschaft mbH (Ed.), *Braunkohlenveredlung in Mitteldeutschland, Teil II (Süd)*, Senftenberg 2019, 13.

Fig. 7 Aerial photo of DEA's Rositz plant (1925)

its volatile elements, although tar could only be obtained from types of coal rich in bitumen. Around 1900, in Saxony and Thuringia 12 plants were operating about 1,200 small carbonization kilns called Rolle kilns after their inventor.[25] DEA made use of these innovations and together with naval engineers developed considerably more efficient pyrolysis kilns at a test plant set up in Grabow.[26] The tar was processed to obtain heavy heating oil, diesel, machine oil, paraffin, coke, and various byproducts.

The decisive reason why DEA shifted focus and emphasized oil production on a lignite basis was the interest of the Reich Naval Office in switching the fuel for the high-sea fleet from coal to heavy heating oil. The corporation required bitumen-rich lignite reserves

---

25 Cf. Erich Grundmann, *Chemie und Technologie des Braunkohlenteers*, Berlin 1964; Welsch, *Geschichte der chemischen Industrie*, 59.

26 Cf. Rothbarth, *DEA – Geschichte 1899–1933*, 94.

in order to enter the heating oil segment in a big way, and the purchase of such stocks was prepared by a special DEA Supervisory Board sub-committee from the summer of 1916 onwards.[27] Despite considerable reservations, the Supervisory Board approved the necessary investments in October 1916.[28] Thereafter, work started on building the pyrolysis generators and a refinery in Rositz in Thuringia with an annual capacity of 120,000 t of tar.[29] It thus seemed possible to set up and expand what had hitherto been the unprofitable production of heating oil and diesel on the basis of lignite pyrolysis for years to come. However, the technology's performance was not up to expectations, as the generators used failed when it came to inputting raw lignite. The technical problems were eventually solved by the switch to briquettes.

Since the lignite pyrolysis plants in Central Germany set up by Rütgerswerke AG, Berlin, and Staatliches Kohlen- und Elektrizitätsunternehmen, Dresden, did not get beyond the pilot stage, DEA remained the technology leader in the field of heating oil production.[30]

A key figure in the collaboration between the navy and DEA was Walther Randhahn (1882–1943),[31] who had studied electrical engineering and mining and gained a PhD from TH Aachen in 1908. He then worked for various large lignite corporations before voluntarily joining the Naval Corps at the beginning of the First World War. In December 1916, at the request of the Reich Naval Office he was released from active military duty and posted to DEA in order to press the pedal on the heating oil project. Randhahn became a

---

27 Cf. Aufsichtsratssitzung, 16 August 1916, HADB, P 1665, sheet 79.

28 Cf. ibid., sheet 83f.

29 Cf. Rothbarth, *DEA – Geschichte 1899–1933*, 69f.

30 Cf. Randhahn, Memorandum betreffend Erwerb von Braunkohlewerken des Ignaz-Petschek-Konzerns durch die Deutsche Erdöl-Aktiengesellschaft, Berlin, 16 January 1939, HADB, P 1659, sheet 231–237.

31 Cf. Lebenslauf Dr. Ing. Walter Randhahn, Korrespondenz mit dem Aufsichtsratsvorsitzenden, WD-CA, D-PA-69.

member of the Management Board of Rositzer Braunkohlenwerke AG, took the helm at Oberbergdirektion Altenburg in 1921, and from 1933 onwards was also in charge of Oberbergdirektion Borna. As of that point, he was also a member of the DEA Management Board. His contemporaries described Randhahn as a strict but jovial man.[32]

Fig. 8 Dr. Walther Randhahn (around 1932)

In order to fulfil the agreement with the Reich Navy, DEA sought to acquire two large coal fields with lignite reserves of some 170 million t.[33] However, the State of Saxony issued a blocking law in November 1916 and insisted that it had first rights to any

32 Cf. Ingrid Krau, *Kohle, Öl und Krieg. Eine Biographie*, Berlin 2015, 48.

33 Cf. Randhahn, Kohlenfeld Heuersdorf-Käferhain, 24 October 1938, HADB, P 1659, sheet 180f.

claims. With the approval of the Reich Naval Office, DEA therefore acquired an interest in Rositzer Braunkohlenwerke AG (Duchy of Saxe-Altenburg) and purchased the majority of the mining rights from the neighbouring mine, Regiser Kohlenwerke (Kingdom of Saxony), from the Ignaz Petschek corporation.[34] In 1918, Aktiengesellschaft Ramsdorfer Braunkohlenwerke, Braunkohlengewerkschaft Breunsdorf, the "Saxonia" Colliery, and the shares in Duxer Kohlenverein in Großzössen (which possessed very good coal for carbonization) became the property of DEA[35], and the corporation more than doubled its lignite production as a result.[36]

The most important new acquisition was the package of shares in Duxer Kohlenverein. These were acquired from Freiherr Theodor von Liebig[37], a member of the most important family of major industrialists in Bohemia, in part for cash and in part for a stake in DEA. Liebig would later, for a short time, have a decisive influence at DEA.

En route to becoming a conglomerate

After the German defeat in the autumn of 1918, DEA faced immense business difficulties. The very substance of the company was shattered as German property was threatened with confiscation

---

[34] Cf. Randhahn, Memorandum betreffend Erwerb von Braunkohlewerken des Ignaz-Petschek-Konzerns durch die Deutsche Erdöl-Aktiengesellschaft, Berlin, 16 January 1939, ibid., sheet 231–237.

[35] Cf. Aufsichtsratssitzung, 11 September 1918, ibid., P 1665, sheet 144–148.

[36] Cf. Rothbarth, *DEA – Geschichte 1899–1933*, 74f.; Sächsisches Landesamt für Umwelt und Geologie (Ed.): *Der Braunkohlenbergbau im Südraum Leipzig*, Dresden 2003, 132–134; Ursula Bischoff, *Der Einfluss der bergbaulichen Traditionen und großindustriellen Entwicklungen auf das soziale Gefüge und die Mobilität der Braunkohlenwirtschaft von Borna*, PhD thesis Berlin 2000, 75–77.

[37] Cf. Erhard Marschner, *Liebieg, Theodor Freiherr von*, in: Neue Deutsche Biographie, Vol. 14, Berlin 1985, 495–497.

by way of reparations for the Entente Powers.[38] DEA General Director Nöllenburg and Supervisory Board Chair Ullner tried to preempt this and transferred management in Pechelbronn to a native of Alsace.[39] At the end of 1918, they assigned the drilling and shaft operation as well as the central refinery owned by DEA to Vereinigte Pechelbronner Oelbergwerke GmbH (VPO), an Alsace-based company that had been in charge of producing and distributing refined products since 1906. Nöllenburg then attempted to persuade the world market leader in the oil business, America's Standard Oil, to purchase the Pechelbronn operations and also DEA's interests in Romania. But his efforts were to no avail: When Alsace was ceded to France, the Pechelbronn petroleum factories were awarded as reparations to the French state.

DEA was more successful in camouflaging its property in Romania and Poland. To this end, in March 1919 Nöllenburg founded Terra AG in Switzerland, and all DEA's operations outside Germany were then awarded to the company, which was, in turn, assigned to Olex in Zurich and Handelsbank Basel.[40] This meant that, by all appearances, Terra AG was a purely Swiss corporation.

Given the difficult situation at DEA at the end of 1919, Ullner switched from the Supervisory to the Management Board, and as Deputy Chair of the Management Board, he concerned himself with the key financial issues relating to the company's future. Through the transactions in neutral Switzerland, Nöllenburg and Ullner succeeded in protecting DEA's foreign business from being seized by the Entente Powers and – thanks to the foreign currency raised by

---

38 Cf. Dietrich Eichholtz, *Das Versailler System. Verlust der deutschen Erdölressourcen in Europa und in Mesopotamien*, in: id. (Ed.), Deutsche Ölpolitik im Zeitalter der Weltkriege. Studien und Dokumente, Leipzig 2010, 96–187, here 109–114.

39 Cf. Rothbarth, *DEA – Geschichte 1899–1933*, 77–81.

40 Cf. Vertrag zwischen der Basler Handelsbank und der DEA über den Kauf von Aktien der "Terra"-Aktiengesellschaft, 1919, WD-CA, D-RW-00003.

selling DEA's foreign interests – managed to ensure the corporation's survival.

Although from 1919 onwards DEA only owned its German operations, Nöllenburg did not wish to withdraw completely from the international oil business. Together with partners from Switzerland, France, Czechoslovakia, and Poland, he founded the International Petroleum Union (IPU) which was domiciled in Zurich and which he hoped would gain him access to the oil fields in Galicia, which was now part of the newly founded state of Poland. The IPU also became active in Argentina and Mexico, but Nöllenburg's ambitious plans did not work out: The IPU failed both in obtaining compensation for the Pechelbronn petroleum operations from the French government and in accessing new crude oil sources in Latin or South America.

One last opportunity to keep DEA in the international oil business arose from the fact that major industrialist Freiherr Theodor von Liebig had meanwhile acquired a majority stake in DEA. The inflation caused by financing the war effort had picked up speed and accelerated the loss in the Reichsmark's external value, which encouraged speculative transactions. Liebig sought via a Dutch holding company to bundle the oil interests of Deutsche Bank and its rival Disconto-Gesellschaft – a risky undertaking, since Liebig's family was mainly invested in textile companies and did not understand much about the oil business. Nöllenburg nevertheless committed to Liebig's plan and approached Deutsche Bank, offering it lead management of the holding company. When, in the autumn of 1920, negotiations began on renewed cooperation between DEA and DPAG, these came to nothing due to the demand on the part of Disconto-Gesellschaft that it be treated on a par with its rival in the oil company that was to be founded.[41] A few months later, Nöl-

[41] Cf. Gerald D. Feldman, *Die Deutsche Bank vom Ersten Weltkrieg bis zur Weltwirtschaftskrise. 1914–1933*, in: Lothar Gall et al., Die Deutsche Bank 1870–1995, Munich 1995, 138–314, here 189.

lenburg quit the DEA Management Board owing to this difference of opinion with Disconto-Gesellschaft. He suffered from a severe illness and in July 1922 died under mysterious circumstances during a boat ride in stormy weather on Wannsee in Berlin.[42]

Nöllenburg was not able to realize his idea of anchoring DEA back in the international oil business and preserving its position as Germany's most important oil corporation for all the adverse conditions, but his name remains inseparably bound up with the swift growth of DTA and DEA prior to the First World War. He had turned DTA with its initial capital stock of 400,000 Reichsmark into a corporation (DEA) that in 1913 had a balance sheet total of some 150 million Reichsmark.[43] He was also to thank for the fact that on the basis of the sale of DEA's foreign businesses through Terra AG in Switzerland, DEA not only emerged from the years of high inflation relatively unscathed but even had foreign currency with which to enter new fields of business.

In 1922, the charismatic managing director of Deutsche Schachtbau AG, Ernst Middendorf (1874–1933) was appointed the new Chair of the DEA Management Board.[44]

He came from a mining family in Westphalia in Central Germany and, having studied in Munich, Berlin, and at the mining academy in Freiberg, had in his early career been director of Deutsche Schachtbau AG, Nordhausen. Under his direction, the company was highly successful. His expertise prompted DEA to commission him during the First World War to create the oil shafts in Pechelbronn. As General Director of DEA, thanks to the foreign currency revenue from the sale of the foreign businesses through the conduit in

---

42 Cf. Ernst Middendorf, *Rudolf Nöllenburg. Ein Lebensbild*, Berlin 1923, WD-CA, D-14-2_01602.

43 Cf. Rothbarth, *DEA – Geschichte 1899–1933*, 110.

44 Cf. Reinhold Dehnke, *Nachruf Ernst Middendorf*, in: Glückauf 41 (1933), 980; Deutsche Erdöl-Aktiengesellschaft (Ed.), *Denkschrift zum 25jährigen Bestehen der Deutschen Erdöl-Aktiengesellschaft Berlin 1899–1924*, Berlin 1924.

Fig. 9 Ernst Middendorf,
Chairman of the DEA Management Board 1922–33

Switzerland, Middendorf was above all able to strengthen DEA's coal arm by making acquisitions.

From 1925 to 1932, the DEA Management Board consisted of three ordinary members and two proxy members. Alongside Chairman Ernst Middendorf, Reinhold Dehnke (1864–1941) and Richard F. Ullner were the other members. The proxy members were Fritz Haussmann (1885–1956) and Hans Gröber (1889–1983). They all played important, albeit very different, parts in the DEA company history, as will be revealed in the following chapters.

Fritz Haussmann came from a prosperous Jewish business family in Ratibor in what is now southern Poland.[45] He studied law

[45] Cf. Personalakte Dr. Fritz Hausmann, WD-CA sowie Martin Münzel, *Die jüdischen Mitglieder der deutschen Wirtschaftselite*, Paderborn 2006, 277–280.

Fig. 10 Dr. Fritz Haussmann (around 1932),
member of the DEA Management Board, 1925–37

and economics in Munich, Freiburg, and Berlin before gaining a PhD at the University of Heidelberg in 1907 for a thesis on an aspect of civil law. He then worked as a self-employed lawyer in Berlin and in August 1916 joined DEA as its in-house lawyer. The corporation benefited in particular from his expertise in monopoly and business law. Thanks to his expert knowledge and negotiating skills, he was one of DEA's best-paid managers. Haussmann had converted to Protestantism and can be considered the prototype of a citizen firmly integrated into the German upper classes.

Hans Gröber had embarked on a career with DEA even before Haussmann. He joined the company in June 1911 immediately after completing vocational training, working initially as a member of the commercial staff in the accounts department and then in the administrative office of Raffinerie Grabow and Mineralölindus-

Fig. 11. Hans Gröber, member of the DEA Management Board, 1925–38

trie AG, Wietze.[46] During the First World War, he was in charge of materials procurement and led negotiations with the Reich Navy. In 1917, General Director Nöllenburg made him managing director of the Romanian operations and at the end of 1918 entrusted him with organizing the administration of the petroleum operations in Rositz. Karl Grosse, who followed Gröber in 1939 as DPAG Director, described him as an "*expert and big-time go-getter*".[47]

With Middendorf at the helm, DEA continued its petroleum business in the form of its subsidiary Deutsche-Petroleum Aktiengesellschaft (DPAG), although this only contributed about 25 per-

46 On the biography of Hans Gröber cf. Ullner an Solmssen, re.: Gröber, 20.6.1936; Ullner an Mojert: Bescheinigung: Hans Gröber, 23.3.1939; Kimmich: Zeugnis Hans Gröber, 16 March 1939, HDAB, P 1686, sheet 1ff.

47 Große, *Mein Leben*, 39. We would like to thank Stephan A. Lütgert of the Wietze Petroleum Museum for allowing us to inspect this unpublished manuscript.

cent of DEA's total sales during the 1920s.[48] DEA extracted itself from IPU, with its various interest groups, at the end of 1922. The majority of DEA shares thus returned to the hands of the major German banks.

The Supervisory Board was dominated by representatives of said banks, and it supported Middendorf in refocusing DEA. The petroleum corporation was transformed into a conglomerate, with coal the dominant division, and DEA thus benefited from the lignite pits it had acquired in Central Germany during the war and the pyrolysis plant it had built in Rositz. The latter's resource base was further expanded in 1920 when DEA obtained a stake in Austro-German Vereinigte Kohlen-AG, Dresden, which had mines in Witznitz and Beuna (in Saxony and Saxony-Anhalt respectively).

Dominance of the coal division

The new acquisitions were an occasion for organizational changes among the DEA lignite companies.[49] In 1921 they were assigned to two branch offices: DEA Oberbergdirektion Altenburg (Thuringia) and DEA Oberbergdirektion Borna (Saxony). Management in Altenburg was handled by Walther Randhahn, previously a member of the Management Board of Rositzer Braunkohlenwerke AG, while in Borna Director Albert Gebhardt, a member of the Management Board of Vereinigte Kohlen-AG, Dresden, took the helm.

Company documents reveal indirectly that Randhahn and even more so Gebhardt "ruled the roost" in the mining directorates (Oberbergdirektionen) they headed. Gebhardt had also created his own political power base as a member of Deutsch-Nationale Volkspartei (DNVP), as he could rely on DNVP parliamentarians and

---

48 Cf. DEA-Geschäftsberichte, lfd., WD-CA, D-GB.

49 Cf. Lausitzer und Mitteldeutsche Bergbauverwaltungsgesellschaft mbH (LMBV) (Ed.), *Mitteldeutsches Braunkohlenrevier*, Senftenberg 2013, 6f.

the leading workers to support him. The latter included longstanding workers and foremen, master artisans and controllers, whose loyalty the company bought with higher wages, company flats, and company pensions. In Thuringia, at that time a strong political left (the Social Democrats and Communists even governed for a short time in 1923) had many supporters in companies in the lignite industry.[50] Gebhardt endeavoured with some success to contain the influence of the leftist parties and trade unions in DEA firms.

In the dramatic period characterized by inflation following the First World War in Germany and attempted coups by the radical left and the Nazi Party in 1923, the DEA was busy trying to establish a sales organization for lignite and lignite briquettes. The corporation founded Brikett- und Kohlenhandel AG in Leipzig and appointed Lothar Ritter (1886–1964) to manage it. He had trained in commerce and worked as a bookkeeper for a cooperative bank and for the sales association of the Thuringian lignite mines, before moving on to Mitteldeutsches Braunkohlensyndikat in 1910. From 1913 to 1919, he held commercial power of attorney at Gasgenerator- und Braunkohlenverwertung GmbH Leipzig[51], then in 1919 he climbed the career ladder and was appointed managing director of Altenburg-Sachsen Kohlenhandelsgesellschaft mbH, Leipzig, which in 1922 was renamed Brikett- und Kohlenhandel AG (Briko). As a member of the Briko Management Board, he was responsible for unit sales of around 3-4 million tons of lignite a year and handled 14 coaling station transactions. Briko's sales by the mid-1920s totalled about 35 million Reichsmark.

DEA's establishment of Briko was emblematic of its new focus on coal, and in its 25th year DEA accounted for 4.5 percent of total German lignite output and almost 7 percent of briquette production.[52] In the 1920s, DEA acquired a series of coal trading

50 Cf. Rainer Pöhlmann, *Mein Leben. Gedanken und Erinnerungen*, Jena 2015, 18f.

51 Cf. Lothar Ritter, WD-CA, Personalakte.

52 Cf. DEA-Geschäftsbericht 1923, WD-CA, D-GB, Geschäftsberichte.

companies, among others in Magdeburg, Chemnitz, Leipzig, Halle/ Saale, Erfurt, Zeitz, Werdau (Saxony), Nordhausen, Kassel, Bayreuth, Nuremberg, and Reichenbach (Thuringia).[53]

Furthermore, the expansion of DEA's lignite pyrolysis capacity meant it was able to do more business with byproducts. In 1922, DEA acquired shares in Joseph Gautsch's long-standing wax goods business in Munich and thus gained a first bulk purchaser for the paraffin it produced in the refinery in Rositz.[54] Ceresinfabrik Compes & Cie. in Düsseldorf also soon developed into a key buyer of paraffin and montan wax, using the raw materials to produce waxes for the cable industry and to manufacture shoe polishes. Later, DEA also bought into Carl Rübsam AG in Fulda and Chemische Fabrik Eisenbüttel GmbH, Braunschweig, likewise wax goods factories, which then served as buyers of paraffin from Rositz.

Although the business with lignite and its byproducts accounted for the lion's share of DEA's sales, Middendorf did not sever all DEA's links to petroleum. He had a second shaft drilled in Wietze to boost crude oil production, expanded the refinery in Wilhelmsburg outside Hamburg, and acquired a majority in Deutsche Mineralöl-Werke, meaning DEA was able to decisively influence processing operations in Wietze and Rositz.

Middendorf bought back his former company Deutsche Schachtbau AG from the IPU, and in 1922 he also acquired a firm that had been a world leader since the early 20th century in drilling shafts using a ground freezing method, Tiefbau- und Kälteindustrie AG, Nordhausen (formerly Gebhardt & König).[55] The two firms founded Maschinen- und Apparatebau AG (Mabag), Nordhausen, in

---

53 Cf. Statuten der DEA-Beteiligungen, WD-CA, D-RW-169.

54 Cf. Rothbarth, *DEA – Geschichte 1899–1933*, 108.

55 Cf. Dietrich Hoffmann, *Acht Jahrzehnte Gefrierverfahren nach Poetsch. Ein Beitrag zur Geschichte des Schachtabteufens in schwierigen Fällen*, Essen 1962, 5; Ullrich Mallis, *Zur Geschichte der Nordhäuser Aktiengesellschaften*, in: Beiträge zur Geschichte aus Stadt und Kreis Nordhausen 40 (2015), 143–186.

1923, a company that supplied the DEA plants, among others, with petrol pumps.[56] Middendorf thus emphatically strengthened DEA's highly specialized shaft and mechanical engineering operations.

That said, the single most important new acquisition was the "Graf Bismarck" hard coal mine in Gelsenkirchen in the Ruhr region. Middendorf pulled off this masterstroke at the end of 1923, when hyperinflation prevailed, and French troops had occupied part of the region in order to enforce payment of the outstanding German reparation. Middendorf exploited the critical geographical position of hard coal mining in the Ruhr region and his personal relationship to the main shareholder in the "Graf Bismarck" Colliery, Hugo von Gahlen (1860–1933)[57], to acquire the majority of the mining rights in question for DEA.[58] Instead of a purchase contract, a 15-year leasehold agreement was concluded and a branch office opened in Gelsenkirchen named "Deutsche Erdöl-Aktiengesellschaft Zeche Graf Bismarck".[59]

In this context, DEA also secured a controlling interest in coal wholesaler Adolph Harloff GmbH, Kassel, and entered trading in hard coal and hard coal products on a significant scale. It also expanded its coal trading organization by buying up Stöck & Fischer in Bingen and Mannheim.

The general director of "Graf Bismarck", Reinhold Dehnke (1864–1941), moved to become a member of the DEA Management Board and was succeeded at the mine by mine assessor Albert Ritter (1880–1954). Dehnke's persistent efforts played an important part in ensuring that the Graf Bismarck Colliery was one of the most modern hard coal mines in the entire Ruhr region.[60] When the first shaft

---

56 Cf. Rothbarth, *DEA – Geschichte 1899–1933*, 117.

57 Cf. Peter Hüttenberger, *Düsseldorf. Geschichte von den Ursprüngen bis ins 20. Jahrhundert*, Vol. 3: *Die Industrie- und Verwaltungsstadt (20. Jahrhundert)*, Düsseldorf 1989, 194, 197.

58 Cf. Rothbarth, *DEA – Geschichte 1899–1933*, 114f.

59 Cf. DEA-Geschäftsbericht 1925, WD-CA, D-GB, Geschäftsberichte.

60 Cf. Hans Gröbel, *Mensch in Erle – Schriftenreihe zur Ortskunde*, Erle 1994.

Gaskohlenzeche

Graf Bismarck.

Kuxschein

№

des Gewerken ....

über .... Kux ...... des in Tausend Kuxe eingeteilten

Gaskohlen-Bergwerks GRAF BISMARCK,

belegen in den Regierungs-Bezirken Münster und Arnsberg, den Kreisen Recklinghausen und Gelsenkirchen und im Oberbergamts-Bezirk Dortmund.

Im Gewerkenbuche auf Pag. ...... verzeichnet. — Urkundlich unter Siegel und Unterschrift.

Zeche Graf Bismarck bei Schalke, den ....

Der Grubenvorstand.

GASKOHLENZECHE GRAF BISMARCK BEI SCHALKE.

Contrasigniert:

Fig. 12 Graf Bismarck Colliery mining share certificate

was sunk in the early 1870s, the colliery was considered to have the most valuable hard coal reserves in the field.[61] By the early 1920s a total of nine shafts had been sunk, and by 1914 a coking plant had been installed. By the time DEA took it over, the Graf Bismarck Colliery employed more than 8,100 miners and 410 white-collar workers.[62] All of the other members of the Bismarck Management Board were given positions on the DEA Supervisory Board. Meanwhile, the representatives of the banks retained their majority on that same board but now had to contend with a strong new lobby.

In 1924, the shareholders in Magdeburger Bergwerks-AG swapped their stake for shares in DEA. The "Königsgrube" Colliery, which mined hard coal near Wanne-Eickel in the Ruhr region therefore likewise became the property of DEA, and the transaction thus expanded the company's hard coal reserves in west Germany. The new addition mined especially high-grade coal,[63] although the mine's plant and technology were outdated.[64] Only one year after the takeover, DEA raised the colliery's share capital to close to 11 million Reichsmark and started to modernize it.[65]

As a major producer of lignite and hard coal, DEA was a member of Rheinisch-Westfälisches Steinkohlensyndikat (RWKS) and of Mitteldeutsche Braunkohlensyndikat, the two syndicates covering Rhineland-Westphalia and Central Germany. While companies had formed cartels voluntarily during the days of the Kaiser, after the end of the First World War the Coal Industry Act came into

---

61 Cf. Norbert Rescher, *Zeche Graf Bismarck in Gelsenkirchen 1869–1966*, www.ruhrzechenaus.de/gelsenkirchen/ge-graf-bismarck.html [last retrieved on 20.2.2023].

62 Cf. Statistiken, Zeche Graf Bismarck, WD-CA, D-RW 158.

63 Cf. DEA-Geschäftsbericht 1924, WD-CA, D-GB, Geschäftsberichte.

64 Cf. Stadtarchiv Herne, *Herne von damals bis heute. Digitales Geschichtsbuch für Herne und Wanne-Eickel*, https://herne-damals-heute.de/ [last retrieved on 20.6.2024].

65 Cf. Gerhard Gebhardt, *Ruhrbergbau. Geschichte, Aufbau und Verflechtung seiner Gesellschaften und Organisationen*, Essen 1957.

force, placing the sector under state supervision and making the formation of syndicates mandatory[66], with the intention being to avert nationalization of the coal industry called for by parts of the left and the trade unions.[67] RWKS proved to be a highly stable and exemplary organization. By contrast, Mitteldeutsches Braunkohlensyndikat was intrinsically unstable, something expressed by the fierce controversies between its members over quota regulations and the protracted negotiations on the re-enactment of the cartel agreement.[68]

The largest members of Mitteldeutsches Braunkohlensyndikat were A. Riebeck'sche Montanwerke AG (as of 1925 part of I.G. Farbenindustrie AG), the companies belonging to Czechoslovak industrialists Julius and Ignaz Petschek, the government-owned Aktiengesellschaft Sächsische Werke (ASW), and DEA. The Petscheks initially resisted the idea of a syndicate but later themselves used it as a competitive instrument. By the end of the 1920s, they controlled around 30 percent of all German lignite mines.[69]

Cartels were also formed in the petroleum market. Standard Oil and Royal Dutch Shell waged a price war in the growing German petrol market, so DEA tried to resist by teaming up with other German petroleum producers. Given the low profit expectations, in 1925 DEA incorporated the Rositz refinery into DPAG, a step connected with the so-called "Rütgers transaction": DPAG belonged to Deutsche Bank, and Rütgers Werke AG[70] had signed a joint interest

---

66 Cf. Manfred Nussbaum, *Wirtschaft und Staat in Deutschland während der Weimarer Republik*, Berlin 1978, 53–63.

67 Cf. Peter Wulf, *Die Auseinandersetzungen um die Sozialisierung der Kohle in Deutschland 1920/1921*, in: *Vierteljahrshefte für Zeitgeschichte* 1 (1977), 46–98.

68 Cf. Bischoff, *Einfluss der bergbaulichen Traditionen*, 76.

69 Cf. Gottfried Lehmann, *Das Mitteldeutsche Braunkohlensyndikat in Leipzig*, PhD thesis Greifswald 1930.

70 Rütgerswerke AG was the fourth-largest German chemical group and worked mainly in the tar and oil products sector. In 1928, the company employed around 5,000 people and achieved a turnover of RM 40–64 million. The majority of the share capital was controlled by Deutsche Bank. (Cf. Gottfried Plumpe, *Die I.G. Farbenindustrie AG. Wirtschaft, Technik und Politik 1904–1945*, Berlin 1990, 179f.).

agreement with the bank.[71] Deutsche Bank cleared its oil interests by selling its shares in DPAG, and when its plans in the Middle East came to nothing and it lost its participations in Romania, the bank initially saw no pathway to re-entering the international oil business.

DEA merged with Rütgers-Werke AG to give it the agreed majority stake in the capital stock of DPAG. DEA's petroleum interests (the production facilities in Wietze, the refineries, and the Olex sales organization) were "insulated" in DPAG,[72] and in this way the corporation intended to minimize its economic risk, especially as the petroleum business hardly turned a profit. Thanks to the transaction with Rütgers Werke AG, DEA also became the owner of Deutsche Petroleum-Verkaufsgesellschaft, of "Vaucefa" (Vereinigte Chemische Fabriken AG) in Brandenburg, "Danubia" in Regensburg, the Heider mining rights, and the "Krug von Nidda" colliery in Celle.

In the wake of the "Rütgers transaction", DPAG/DEA was rightfully able to claim to be the only, albeit small, vertically integrated German oil company.[73] Its import business was handled by "Danubia", it commanded its own small fleet of oil tankers and its own railway waggon sidings with their own boiler house, maintained its own turnaround plant and tank farm in the Port of Hamburg and in the Regensburg Danube Port, operated four refineries, and, having Olex, was the only German company with its own network of filling stations.

In order to place procurement of crude oil from abroad on a wider footing, DPAG/DEA sought a permanent arrangement with one of the oil majors. In February 1926, it signed a contract with Anglo-Persian Oil Co. Ltd. (APOC), London, the predecessor of today's British Petroleum.[74] APOC acquired 40 percent of the Olex shares at a price of 700,000 pounds sterling, after which the "new Olex" included all the oil trading companies run by DEA. APOC

---

71 Cf. Rothbarth, *DEA – Geschichte 1899–1933*, 133.

72 Cf. Memo, DEA-Vorstand, 21 December 1939, HADB, P 1659, sheet 354.

73 Cf. Titus Kockel, *Deutsche Ölpolitik. 1928–1938*, Berlin 2005, 45f.

74 Cf. Rothbarth, *DEA – Geschichte 1899–1933*, 138f.

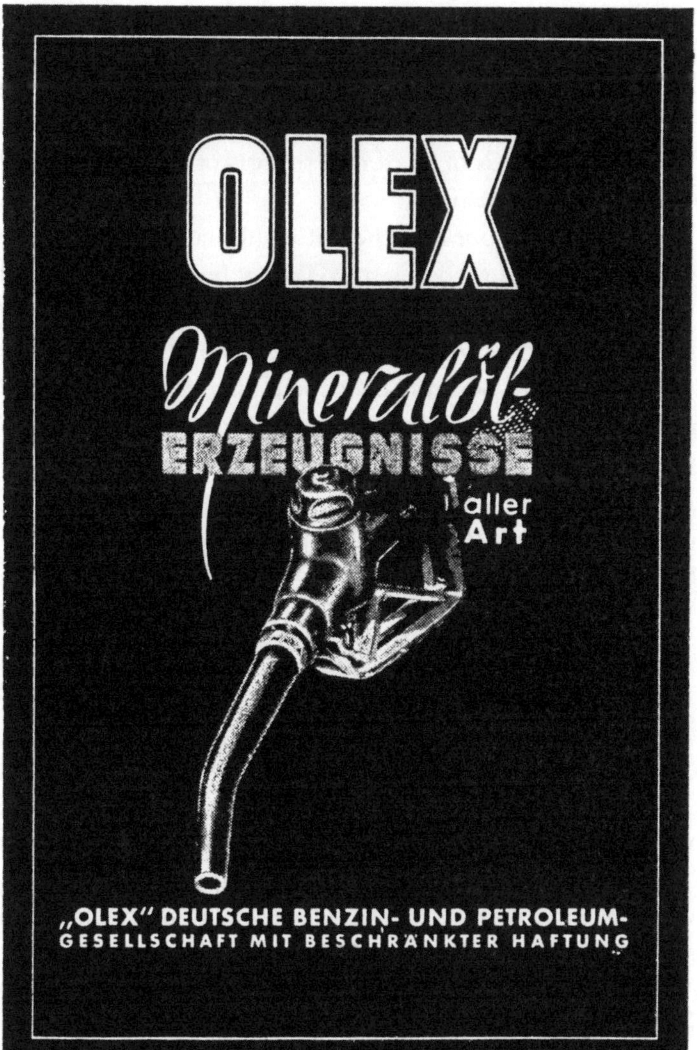

Fig. 13 Olex advertising (1944)

undertook to cover up to 70 percent of Olex's petrol and lighting oil needs and up to 60 percent of its heating oil and lubricant requirements. As at the end of 1928, DEA then started gradually selling the remainder of its Olex shares to APOC. The reasoning given was that Olex had no access of its own to sources of crude oil and the oil business was highly volatile.[75]

During this period, the DEA Management Board was increasingly sceptical with regard to the oil business. Nevertheless, DEA and Olex (from 1931 onwards completely owned by APOC) maintained a close relationship. The Olex head office was located in the DEA building in Berlin's Schöneberg district, and DPAG petroleum transactions continued to be handled through Olex.

A radical austerity strategy during the Great Depression (1929–1933)

The Great Depression (1929–1933) hit DEA hard. Companies in the coal and steel industry suffered a little less severely from the crunch in sales and prices than did the consumer goods industries, as the above-mentioned cartel agreements meant they were able to limit the slump in prices. Moreover, the coal industry depended less on exports than did mechanical engineering or the textile sector, but the Great Depression still dented the DEA's balance sheet for years to come. The volumes of lignite and hard coal mined fell annually as of 1929, reaching rock bottom in 1932.

DEA responded to the crisis by cutting payroll in all departments, cancelling shifts in the hard coal operations, temporarily discontinuing operations in some lignite pits, and completely suspending montan wax production.[76] Investments were scaled back.

---

75 Cf. Verhandlung des Geschäftsausschusses des Aufsichtsrats der DEA, 5 November 1928, HADB, P 1667, sheet 163f.

76 Cf. Rothbarth, *DEA – Geschichte 1899–1933*, 166.

Operating costs for the corporation as a whole were almost halved between 1929 and 1932. During this time, more than a third of the staff were laid off. The DEA payroll plummeted from around 16,000 in 1928 to only 9,600 in 1932.[77]

With this radical austerity strategy, DEA succeeded in still turning a profit even during the crisis years and in disbursing a dividend, reduced to four percent.[78] The petroleum business bundled in DPAG, by contrast, posted only losses after 1929, and therefore paid no dividends.

The value of the corporation's assets and interests in 1933 reflect the predominance of the lignite and hard coal division.

Value of DEA assets and interests in 1933[79]

Company	**Asset value (in million RM)**	**Share of total value (as a percentage)**
Braunkohlendirektionen Altenburg and Borna	34.2	36
Graf Bismarck Colliery	29.3	30
Mineralölwerk Rositz	3.9	4
Portfolio participations		
DPAG	21.7	22
Magdeburger Bergwerks AG	2.4	2
Deutsche Schachtbau AG	1.3	1
Tiefbau- und Kälteindustrie AG	1.4	1
Hard coal trading companies	3.8	4
Total	98.0	100

At first, it was not clear which focus the DEA Management Board would take as the economy started to turn around in 1933.

77 Cf. DEA-Geschäftsbericht für das Jahr 1938, WD-CA, D-GB.

78 Cf. file note, 15.9.1934, HADB, P 1656, no page numbers given.

79 Compiled according to: file note, 13.6.1934 über Aufsichtsratssitzung der DEA, HADB, P 1675, sheet 26–30.

The main shareholders were primarily interested in the corporation boosting its profitability, so they felt it made sense to retain the existing profile with the emphasis firmly on lignite and hard coal production. However, as early as spring 1933, the Management Board considered whether the trend emerging in the economic policy being pursued by the new Hitler/Papen government to promote a German oil industry might present an opportunity to rescue loss-making DPAG. In this situation, when the strategy was still not decided, much would depend on who held sway at the head of the corporation going forward.

II. THE MANAGEMENT AND SUPERVISORY BOARDS AT DEA

(Rainer Karlsch)

En route to dictatorship

After the DEA transferred its oil interests to its subsidiary DPAG in 1925, the Management Board was scaled back to five members, with Ernst Middendorf remaining as Chair. Richard F. Ullner, who had joined DEA from Disconto-Gesellschaft in 1919, continued in the role of Deputy Chair and maintained his decisive influence over company policy.[1] Reinhold Dehnke, General Director of the Graf Bismarck Colliery, represented the Group's coal division on the DEA board, while lawyer Fritz Haussmann and businessman Hans Gröber stayed on as deputy board members. The composition of the DEA board remained unchanged until 1933.

Following the sale of the final Olex holdings in 1931, Hans Gröber was tasked with managing all matters relating to petroleum. He then took another step up the career ladder in 1933 when he was given sole responsibility for managing DPAG. Gröber was an assertive manager who was quick to capitalize on the opportunities the Nazi regime offered a company like DEA. On the Management Board, he was the most eager advocate for expanding the petroleum

---

1 Cf. Die Zukunft 32 (1919); Geschäftsbericht der Deutschen Erdöl-Aktiengesellschaft in Berlin über das einundvierzigste Geschäftsjahr 1939, WD-CA, D-GB.

division to serve the growing demand from the Reich Navy. He also used his position on the DEA Management Board to line his own pockets through his unscrupulous participation in "aryanizations". At DPAG/DEA, he was to prove one of the biggest profiteers from the expulsion of Jews from German economic life.

All five members of the Management Board had been socialized in the burgeoning days of the Reich; all were national conservatives who had lived in Berlin's elegant Dahlem district since at least the time of their appointment to the board.[2] Despite the differences in their characters, they were united in their efforts to assert DEA's strong position in the German raw materials industry.

The appointment of Adolf Hitler as Reich Chancellor on 30 January 1933 initially appeared to have little effect on DEA, and the company's Management Board had no particular expectations of the new government. They seem to have maintained a distance from politics, and none of them belonged to the Nazi Party at that time. Like most managers of big German companies, they accepted the destruction of democracy – the overturning of fundamental rights enshrined in the Weimar Constitution, the abolition of all other parties apart from the Nazi Party, the dissolution of the trade unions, and the persecution of opponents of the regime – without passing comment.

From the history of its foundation, DEA had always been closely associated with the internationally oriented banking world, and its management bodies included several prominent representatives of the assimilated and integrated German-Jewish elite. Even long before the Nazis took power, völkisch-nationalist circles had already called for boycotts of Jewish businesses, with the aim being to drive Jews out of economic life and society.[3] What changed after

---

2 Cf. Personalakten DEA-Vorstand, WD-CA, D-PA.

3 Cf. Frank Bajohr, *"Arisierung" und wirtschaftliche Existenzvernichtung im Nationalsozialismus*, in: Andrea Bambi/Axel Drecoll (Eds.), Alfred Flechtheim. Raubkunst und Restitution, Berlin 2015, 29–36.

1933, however, was that anti-Semitism was elevated to state doctrine. The boycott of Jewish businesses organized across the Reich on 1 April 1933 and the "Law for the Restoration of the Professional Civil Service" enacted on 7 April 1933, according to which officials of "non-Aryan descent" were to be retired, clearly demonstrated the intentions of the new rulers. In public companies, too, and in the banks that remained under state control after the banking crisis of July 1931 – which included Deutsche Bank and Dresdner Bank and thus the two main shareholders of DEA – efforts began to expel Jews from management functions.

Georg Solmssen, Spokesperson for the Board of Deutsche Bank and Chairman of the Supervisory Board at DEA, had the foresight to see what would follow. On 6 April he and Franz Urbig, Chair of the Supervisory Board at Deutsche Bank, were urged by Reichsbank President Hjalmar Schacht to remove several Jewish members from the bank's board.[4] Three days later, Solmssen wrote to Urbig: "*The expulsion of Jews from the civil service, which has now been implemented by law, raises the question of the consequences still to come for the private sector from these measures, which have been accepted unquestioningly even by the educated section of the population. I fear we are only at the beginning of a development that is aimed purposefully, according to well-laid plans, at the economic and moral annihilation of all members of the Jewish race living in Germany in a way that is completely indiscriminate. The utter passivity of those classes not belonging to the National Socialist Party, the lack of any sense of solidarity on the part of those who have hitherto worked shoulder to shoulder with Jewish colleagues in the factories in question, the ever more apparent urge to benefit themselves from the vacant posts, and the silence about the shame and disgrace that are being inflicted irremediably on all those who, although blameless, are seeing the foundations of their honour and existence destroyed from one*

4 Cf. Harold James, *Die Deutsche Bank und die Diktatur*, in: Lothar Gall et al. (Eds.), Die Deutsche Bank 1870–1995, Munich 1995, 315–408, here 336.

day to the next – all this shows a situation so hopeless that it would be wrong not to look things in the face avoiding any attempt to gloss over them. I must gain clarity as soon as possible about what is to happen, and I refuse to endure a tolerated existence as a marked man waiting until the day when I am myself dismissed."[5]

Few were as clear-headed and far-sighted as Solmssen. DEA, like all privately managed businesses, was unaffected by the "Law for the Restoration of the Professional Civil Service". Nevertheless, at the DEA's Annual General Meeting on 22 June 1933, defamatory accusations were brought against Solmssen. Lawyer Rudolf Schmidt, who represented a small group of shareholders, accused Solmssen of exaggerated expense claims and also criticized the consultancy contracts concluded with Ernst Springer, who likewise came from a Jewish family. With these attacks, Schmidt aimed to undermine the positions of the Jewish members of the Supervisory Board, but Solmssen defended himself against the "*unscrupulous behaviour*",[6] and since the accusations proved unfounded, there were no consequences. Yet they reflected the increasingly anti-Semitic mood among a section of the DEA shareholders.

The first personnel changes were made in the Works Council. Since the National Socialist Factory Cell Organization (*Nationalsozialistische Betriebszellenorganisation, NSBO*) failed to resonate with employees in the industry, Hitler's government passed a law suspending works council elections and abolishing co-determination in companies. The two representatives elected by the Works Council before 1933 had thereupon to quit the DEA Supervisory Board,[7] which meant there were no longer any representatives of the workers and employees on said board. In the authoritarian atmosphere of the Third Reich, the "Law for the Organization of National

5 As cited in: ibid., 337.

6 Cf. Solmssen an Vorstand der DEA, 19.7.1933, HADB, P 1656, sheet 62–67.

7 Cf. Geschäftsbericht der Deutschen Erdöl-Aktiengesellschaft zu Berlin über das fünfunddreißigste Geschäftsjahr, 1933, WD-CA, D-GB, DEA-Geschäftsberichte.

Labour" passed in January 1934 and the "leader and follower principle" enshrined within it gave so-called "company leaders" even more power.[8]

The Management Board under Richard F. Ullner (1933–1940)

At the end of 1933, Richard F. Ullner took over as Chair of the Management Board. With him as CEO, the DEA management adapted to the economic policy of the new Hitler-Papen government. As urged by the government, DEA took on several hundred new workers in their coal plants to help combat unemployment and also contributed to the "Adolf Hitler Fund" and to the "Winter Relief" organization.[9] The company also began to pool its petroleum interests, the background to which was *"the increased attention recently paid to this sector of the economy by widely varying circles."*[10] The Rositz oil refinery was transferred to DPAG, while the merger of DEA and DPAG was put back.

In place of General Director Reinhold Dehnke, who moved to the Supervisory Board on account of his age, mining assessor Albert Ritter joined the DEA Management Board at the end of 1933. Since Ritter also represented the Graf Bismarck Colliery, this shored up the strong position of the Bismarck shareholders at DEA.

The lignite companies were able to increase their influence even further. As part of a restructuring at the DEA lignite companies, the mining administrative offices ('directorates') in Altenburg (Thuringia) and Borna (Saxony) were merged. From January 1934, the lignite operations for central Germany were controlled solely from Borna, with management of the new DEA lignite administra-

---

8 Cf. Adam Tooze, *Ökonomie der Zerstörung. Die Geschichte der Wirtschaft im Nationalsozialismus*, Munich 2006, 130.

9 Cf. Aufsichtsratsprotokoll, 13.10.1933, HADB, P 1663, sheet 22.

10 Cf. Aufsichtsratsprotokoll, 12.12.1933, ibid., sheet 23.

Fig. 14 The complete DEA Management Board in December 1933

tion falling to Walther Randhahn. He was co-opted onto the DEA Management Board and thus reached the peak of his career. Randhahn joined the Nazi Party in April 1936.[11]

In DEA's subsidiary companies, exclusion of Jewish members of the Management and Supervisory Boards proceeded more quickly than at the parent company, with DPAG particularly hard hit. Three out of four Management Board members – Carl Adler, Bela Szilasi, and Ernst Lehner – were forced to step down in 1933. They were among the pioneers of the petroleum trade and had set up Olex, DPAG's functioning sales company. Following the sale of initially 40 percent of the Olex shares in 1926, Adler remained active as

11 Cf. NSDAP-Gaukartei, Bundesarchiv Berlin [hereafter: BArch Berlin], R 9361-IX Kartei/33710828.

General Director of Olex, while Szilasi likewise joined Olex slightly later, and Lehner continued as a member of the DPAG management board.[12]

In 1933, the Anglo-Persian Oil Company, now the sole owner of Olex, terminated all contracts with Jewish employees in Germany, including those of Adler and Szilasi,[13] as the parent company feared its German business might otherwise be disadvantaged. In October 1933, Lehner stepped down as Director of DPAG.[14] He withdrew from public life but remained a member of the Olex Supervisory Board until the end of 1937. Upon his retirement, Olex Supervisory Board Chair, Richard Ullner, described him as a "*petroleum expert of international standing*".[15] Shortly afterwards, Lehner left Germany, as did Szilasi.[16] Adler remained active as a consultant for another oil firm until 1935, fled to Vienna that same year, to Switzerland in March 1938, and eventually to Cuba, where he died in Havana on 13 October 1945.[17]

Mining assessor Hermann Bruch was the only member of the old DPAG board to remain in his post until October 1933, when he moved to become chairman of the management board of Bergbau-AG Lothringen. At the end of 1933, Hans Gröber became the new sole director of DPAG and a full member of the DEA Supervi-

---

12 Cf. Niederschrift über die Verhandlungen des Aufsichtsrates der DPAG am 23.11.1926, WD-CA, D-PA-110.

13 Cf. Rainer Karlsch/Raymond G. Stokes, "*Faktor Öl*". *Die Mineralölwirtschaft in Deutschland 1859–1974*, Munich 2003, 162.

14 Cf. Niederschrift über die Verhandlungen des Aufsichtsrates der DPAG am 12.12.1933, WD-CA, D-PA-110.

15 Ullner, Bescheinigung für Dr. Ernst Lehner, 11.4.1938, WD-CA, D-PA-0007, Personalakte Ernst Lehner.

16 Cf. Günter Schlicht, *Erinnerungen*, Vol. 1, Hamburg 1961, 74.

17 Cf. Übermittelter Auszahlungsentscheid zu Gunsten der Ansprechpartnerin Marie Leighton betreffend das Konto des Carl Adler, Claims Resolution Tribunal, 4.4.2003.

sory Board, gaining considerable power as a result of these developments.[18]

Exclusion of Jews from the Supervisory Board

From 1920 to 1931, the composition of the 25-member Supervisory Board at DEA remained virtually unchanged. Banker Georg Solmssen was its pre-eminent figure as Supervisory Board Chair. His First Deputy was Consul General Paul von Schwabach, owner of Bankhaus S. Bleichröder. The role of Second Deputy was filled by mine owner Hugo von Gahlen from Düsseldorf, while the Third Deputy was Ernst Springer, who was Privy Chief Finance Councillor in the Reich Debt Administration. Like Paul von Schwabach, Springer, who was the son of the publisher and bookseller Julius Springer, came from a Jewish family but remained a staunch Protestant throughout his life.

In response to the global economic crisis (1929–1933), in 1932 the Supervisory Board was cut to 17 people. From 1934, retired cavalry captain Alhard von Burgsdorff took the position of Deputy Chairman in place of Ernst Springer, which shifted the balance on the Supervisory Board in favour of the Bismarck Colliery shareholders. Burgsdorff joined the Nazi Party in April 1933.[19]

On 15 September 1935, the Nazi Party's 7th Party Congress resolved to pass three laws that were adopted by the German Reichstag on the very same day and went down in history as the "Nuremberg Laws".[20] The "Reich Citizenship Law" created a two-race soci-

---

18 Cf. Kimmich, Zeugnis Hans Gröber, 16.3.1939, HADB, P 1686, sheet 1ff.

19 Cf. NSDAP-Gaukartei, BArch Berlin, R 9361-IX Kartei/5221380.

20 Cf. Cornelia Essner, *Die "Nürnberger Gesetze" oder die Verwaltung des Rassenwahns 1933–1945*, Paderborn 2002; Magnus Brechtken et al. (Eds.), *Die Nürnberger Gesetze – 80 Jahre danach: Vorgeschichte, Entstehung, Auswirkungen*, Munich 2017.

ety in which only citizens of the Reich had full civil rights, while those deemed members of "foreign races" did not. The creation of a privileged Reich citizenry enabled the gradual disenfranchisement of other, supposedly inferior citizens.

Even more important than the Reich Citizenship Law itself were the ordinances issued in accordance with it, which translated the monstrous racial law into bureaucratic practice. An initial ordinance issued on 14 November 1935 included a Nazi definition of the term "Jew". In the absence of a demonstrable characteristic, the religious affiliation of a person's ancestors was used as the criterion to classify them as belonging to the "Jewish race", regardless of whether those involved were Jews, Christians, or atheists. The law was aimed primarily at the exclusion and disenfranchisement of Jews.

The "Nuremberg Laws" came as a shock to all those who had converted to Christianity and now suddenly found themselves assigned to the "Jewish race". The consequences of the new laws were yet to become clear in terms of their sheer brutality, but the continued spread of anti-Semitism in German society indicated that worse was to come. Many of those affected did not want to accept that they were now to be considered second-class citizens and tried in vain to obtain an "Aryan certificate" or a "Reich citizenship certificate".[21]

Fritz Andreae, Managing Director of Hardy & Co. bank in Berlin and a member of the DEA Supervisory Board, likewise endeavoured to obtain full civil rights. In early May 1936, having realized the futility of his attempts, he did not seek re-election to the DEA Supervisory Board.[22] The Andreae family eventually obtained

---

21 Cf. Ingo von Münch, *Die deutsche Staatsangehörigkeit. Vergangenheit, Gegenwart, Zukunft*, Berlin 2007, 65.

22 Cf. Fritz Andreae an Ullner, Vorstand der DEA, 4.5.1936, Korrespondenzen mit Aufsichtsratsmitgliedern, WD-CA, D-PA-0065; Vorstandssitzung 22.4.1936, ibid., D-PA-29.

permission to leave the country in 1939 and emigrated to Switzerland.[23]

Following the enactment of the 1st Ordinance to the Reich Citizenship Act, it became likely that there would be other demands for resignations by Jewish members of the Management and Supervisory Boards and battles for positions at DEA. While the main shareholders, Deutsche Bank and Dresdner Bank, did not yet make any moves, the Bismarck shareholders, whose leading figures had joined the Nazi Party in the spring of 1933, went on the offensive in May 1936. They held around 17 percent of DEA shares and sought to increase their influence,[24] criticizing, among other things, the high remuneration of the DEA Management Board and excessive royalties from the contracts with Edeleanu GmbH. They more or less openly demanded that Jews be expelled from both the Management and Supervisory Boards, whereby the reference to the "Nuremberg Laws" was unmistakable. The Bismarck Colliery shareholders demanded "*that the management of the company (DEA – the authors) be taken over this very day by men who, through generations of tradition, are most closely bound up with the fortunes of the company for themselves and their descendants, and that the board assume an unassailable position in relation to the present state for now and the future.*"[25]

Their efforts were aimed primarily at Solmssen, as Supervisory Board Chair, without it being openly stated. Solmssen still had strong backing at Deutsche Bank and on the DEA Management Board. When the new composition of the DEA Supervisory Board came up for discussion in early 1936, Deutsche Bank and DEA

---

23 Cf. Ingo Köhler/Dieter Ziegler, *Heirats- und Verkehrskreise als Instrument wirtschaftsbürgerlichen Aufstiegs. Die Familie Andreae*, in: Genealogie 1/2 (1997), 385–402.

24 Calculated according to: Generalversammlungs-Protokoll, 30.6.1938, WD-CA, DRW-269 sowie Ullner an Burgsdorff, 9.5.1938, ibid., D-PA-0065.

25 Cf. Einschreiben der Herren von Waldthausen, von Burgsdorff, von Berghes, Mellinghoff, Poensgen an Solmssen, 19.5.1936, HADB, P 1658, sheet 140.

board member Ullner reached a verbal agreement.[26] Whether this was in anticipation of moves by the critics remains unclear, but the agreement with Ullner was that he should use all means available to him to ensure that a member of the board at Deutsche Bank would continue to chair DEA's Supervisory Board in future. As a respected banker, Ullner was to remain loyal to Deutsche Bank, into which Disconto-Gesellschaft had been absorbed. In return, he was offered the prospect of joining the Deutsche Bank Supervisory Board from April 1936. The Graf Bismarck Colliery shareholders, meanwhile, had the weaker hand, yet their attack was intended to accelerate the exclusion of Jews from the Supervisory Boards of DEA and its subsidiaries.

The Bismarck shareholders did not attack Solmssen head-on; instead, they emphasized his outstanding competence, but with a subtext in their letter that was abundantly clear. Solmssen and Ullner reacted to the attack by focusing primarily on Deutsche Bank's interest in the position of the Supervisory Board chair at DEA in their argumentation and at the same time preparing for changes of personnel.[27] It was undoubtedly no coincidence here that these were to affect the Supervisory Board members who had been declared Jews by law, namely Paul von Schwabach, Ernst von Springer, and Fritz Andreae. Ullner proceeded tactically. He pointed to the good cooperation thus far between the Management Board and the Chairman of the Supervisory Board,[28] but he did concede that the members of the Supervisory Board were free to elect a new chairman. An open dispute within the Supervisory Board over the chairmanship was nevertheless to be avoided.

Once Solmssen had received the backing of the Management Board, he offered the Bismarck Colliery shareholders the pros-

---

26 Cf. Aktenvermerk Kimmich, Geheim, 27.3.1936, ibid., sheet 132.

27 Cf. Aktenvermerk, Geheim, 27.5.1936, ibid., sheet 142f.

28 Cf. Thesenpapier (vermutlich von Ullner im Mai 1936 verfasst), Aufsichtsrat DEA, Allgemeines, WD-CA, D-PA-0066.

pect of a fifth mandate. Since a representative of Dresdner Bank was now also to be added, parity between the banks and the mining shareholders was ensured. A request by Burgsdorff to become Deputy Chairman of the Management Board was rejected by Solmssen, although he nevertheless agreed to the promotion of his long-time employee Karl Kimmich at Disconto-Gesellschaft (now Deutsche Bank) to the position of Deputy Chairman in place of von Schwabach, a banker.[29] The Bismarck shareholders then agreed to accept Kimmich as a new Supervisory Board Chair in the event of Solmssen's resignation.[30]

Karl Kimmich had been a member of the Management Board at Deutsche Bank AG since 1933.[31] He had started his career as a banker in 1906 as an employee of A. Schaffhausenscher Bankverein, but after it merged with Deutsche Bank and Disconto-Gesellschaft he had been taken on by Deutsche Bank AG and worked in the syndicate business.

The changes to the Supervisory Board were settled in a final meeting between Solmssen and Burgsdorff on 24 June 1936.[32] Solmssen stepped down as Chairman of the Supervisory Board,[33] swapping roles with Kimmich, but nevertheless hoped to maintain a certain influence as First Deputy Chairman. It was a withdrawal in stages. Von Burgsdorff became Second Deputy Director.

Shortly after the changes to the Supervisory Board, Dresdner Bank attempted to expand its position at DEA and demanded that one of its representatives be installed as Deputy Chairman or appointed to the DEA Supervisory Board's executive committee.[34] Ullner turned the request down in a meeting with Supervisory Board

---

29 Cf. Aktennotiz, 28.5.1936, HADB, P 1658, sheet 145–148.

30 Cf. ibid.

31 Cf. Feldman, *Die Deutsche Bank*, 265.

32 Cf. Aktennotiz Solmssen, 24.6.1936, HADB, P 1658, sheet 155–157.

33 Cf. Aktenvermerk 26.6.1936, ibid., sheet 158; Geschäftsbericht der Deutschen Erdöl-AG für 1936, 2.

34 Cf. Schippel an Solmssen, 13.7.1936, HADB, P 1658, sheet 198.

Fig. 15 Karl Kimmich, Chairman of the DEA Supervisory Board 1936–45

member Hans Schippel, but did signal his agreement to awarding a second seat on the Supervisory Board to another member of the Dresdner Bank board, namely Alfred Busch,[35] who was eventually elected in June 1937.[36]

The final exclusion of Jews from the Supervisory Board took place in May 1938, shortly before which the Stock Corporation Act had been amended to exclude Jews from Management and Supervisory Board mandates. If the legal definition of "Jews" had been a contradictory construction to begin with, then the difficulties in determining what were "Jewish companies" inevitably increased.[37]

---

35 Cf. Aktennotiz Ullner vom 25.8.1936, Aufsichtsrat DEA, Allgemeines, WD-CA, D-PA-0066; Aktenvermerk Kimmich, 4.8.1936, HADB, P 1658, sheet 213.

36 Cf. Kimmich an Busch, 11.6.1937, HADB, P 1658, sheet 263.

37 Cf. Benno Nietzel, *Die Vernichtung der wirtschaftlichen Existenz der deutschen Juden 1933–1945. Ein Literatur- und Forschungsbericht*, in: Archiv für Sozialgeschichte 49 (2009), 561–613.

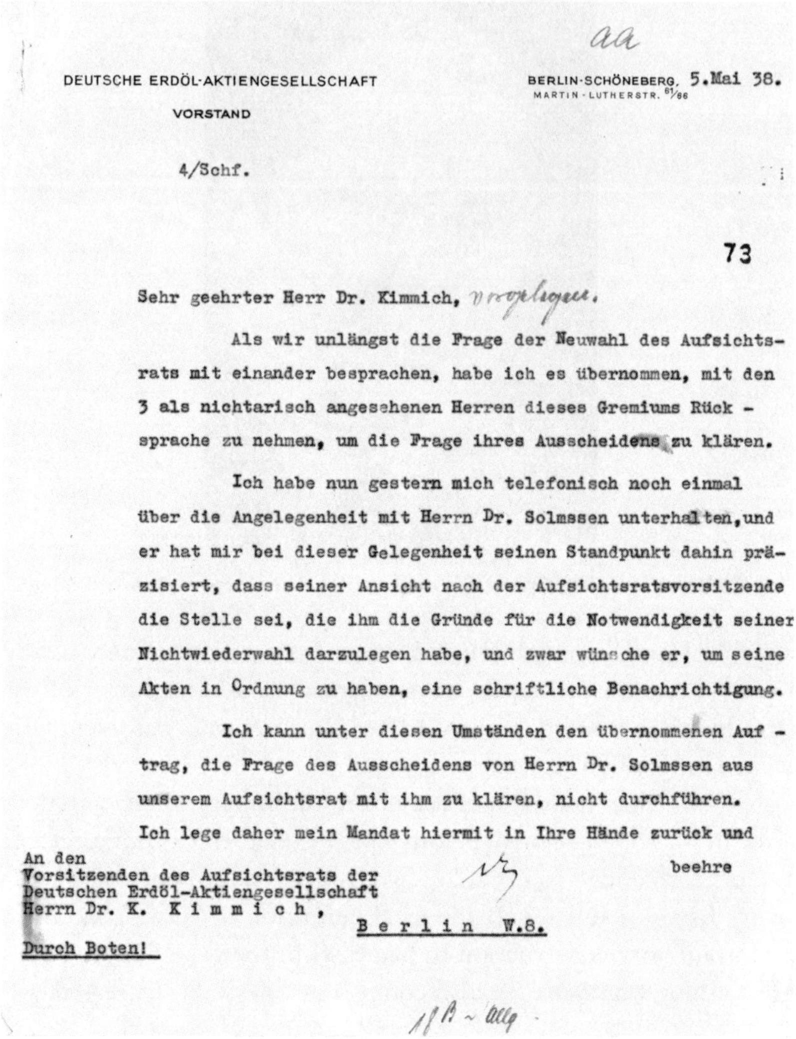

DEUTSCHE ERDÖL-AKTIENGESELLSCHAFT

VORSTAND

BERLIN-SCHÖNEBERG, 5.Mai 38.
MARTIN-LUTHERSTR. 61/66

4/Schf.

73

Sehr geehrter Herr Dr. Kimmich,

Als wir unlängst die Frage der Neuwahl des Aufsichtsrats mit einander besprachen, habe ich es übernommen, mit den 3 als nichtarisch angesehenen Herren dieses Gremiums Rück - sprache zu nehmen, um die Frage ihres Ausscheidens zu klären.

Ich habe nun gestern mich telefonisch noch einmal über die Angelegenheit mit Herrn Dr. Solmssen unterhalten,und er hat mir bei dieser Gelegenheit seinen Standpunkt dahin präzisiert, dass seiner Ansicht nach der Aufsichtsratsvorsitzende die Stelle sei, die ihm die Gründe für die Notwendigkeit seiner Nichtwiederwahl darzulegen habe, und zwar wünsche er, um seine Akten in Ordnung zu haben, eine schriftliche Benachrichtigung.

Ich kann unter diesen Umständen den übernommenen Auf - trag, die Frage des Ausscheidens von Herrn Dr. Solmssen aus unserem Aufsichtsrat mit ihm zu klären, nicht durchführen. Ich lege daher mein Mandat hiermit in Ihre Hände zurück und

beehre

An den
Vorsitzenden des Aufsichtsrats der
Deutschen Erdöl-Aktiengesellschaft
Herrn Dr. K. K i m m i c h ,
B e r l i n W.8.

Durch Boten!

Fig. 16 Letter from Ullner to Kimmich, 5 May 1938

The DEA Management Board aimed to persuade "*three gentlemen regarded as non-Aryan*" to resign their mandates before the annual general meeting scheduled for June 1938. The man charged with conducting the talks was Kimmich, the Chairman of the Supervisory Board.[38] The letter on the matter read: "*The Aryan question, generally speaking, has recently taken on a fundamentally different aspect. (…) At a works meeting, our company was denounced by the workforce as being Judaized, and in response to the protest of the works manager concerned, 'Solmssen' was repeatedly shouted from the crowd. We have reason to assume that similar events will also play out at the general meeting, which would be detrimental to the image of the company and which all those involved have an interest in avoiding. However, the decisive factor for our opinion is the circumstance (…) that the field issue* (acquisition of a new coal field in Saxony – the authors) *cannot be resolved in our favour without us providing proof that the three gentlemen considered to be non-Aryan are no longer members of the Supervisory Board. And yet the issue of acquiring the field is the basis for the entire further development of our company.*"[39]

Richard F. Ullner was therefore less concerned with possible anti-Semitic protests than with hard-nosed, economic calculation. In the race to acquire new coal fields in Saxony, DEA would only have a chance, he believed, as a "*purely German company*". It was therefore imperative that Solmssen and the two other members of the Supervisory Board be dismissed, regardless of their great contribution to the company's development.

Kimmich was embarrassed to have to suggest to his former boss, whose achievements he admired, that he should refrain from seeking re-election to the Supervisory Board of DEA and its subsidiaries.[40] Solmssen chose not to attend the Supervisory Board

---

38 Ullner an Kimmich, 5.5.1938, HADB, P 1659, sheet 73–75.

39 Ibid.

40 Cf. Kimmich an Solmssen, 6.5.1938, ibid.

meeting and resigned his seat.[41] He also had to allow a consultancy contract with Edeleanu GmbH, Berlin, which was still ongoing, to expire at the end of 1938.[42] Solmssen had maintained a second home in Switzerland since August 1934, so he moved there and took Swiss citizenship. Paul von Schwabach and Ernst Springer were likewise forced to resign their seats – a humiliation for all three, who had long before converted to the Protestant faith.

Kimmich prepared a short speech for the Supervisory Board meeting on 30 June 1938, paying tribute to the resigning members.[43] He praised Solmssen's outstanding achievements, particularly in relation to DEA's petroleum interests. Schwabach had worked more "*in the background*", while Springer, as DEA Supervisory Board Chair at a time of world war, had "*guided DEA through all the storms*".[44] Solmssen's departure was officially announced at the DEA Annual General Meeting on 30 June 1938, and Alhard von Burgsdorff was appointed Deputy Chairman.[45]

It was evidently very important to the Management Board that the DEA be outwardly perceived as a "purely German company", and the names of Paul von Schwabach, Ernst Springer, and Georg Solmssen were already omitted from the 1937 annual report published at the end of June 1938. Paul von Schwabach died of a pulmonary embolism in 1938.[46] Ernst Springer, meanwhile, was dismissed from the Reich Debt Administration after the Nuremberg Race Laws came into force in 1935. In January 1944, he was arrested

41 Cf. Solmssen an Kimmich, 11.5.1938, ibid.

42 Cf. Schreiben Terres an Solmssen, 23.8.1939, WD-CA, D-PA-0039 Solmssen.

43 Cf. Ungezeichneter Aktenvermerk: "Herrn Dr. Kimmich", ibid., sheet 95.

44 Ibid.

45 Cf. Geschäftsbericht der Deutschen Erdöl-AG für 1937, 2.

46 Cf. Reinhold Zilch, *Schwabach, Paul Hermann von*, in: Neue Deutsche Biographie, Vol. 23, Berlin 2007, 776f.

by the Gestapo and deported to Theresienstadt concentration camp, where he died in June 1944.[47]

In early October 1938, Ullner sent a questionnaire from the Reich Ministry of the Interior to all the members of the DEA Supervisory Board, in which respondents were required to declare their denomination and that of their spouses.[48] This "Aryan certificate" was essential if they were to remain active on the Supervisory Board.

Fritz Haussmann is dismissed from the Management Board

It was during Ullner's time in office that Fritz Haussmann was also excluded from the Management Board. Haussmann was one of the veterans of the company, having joined DEA in 1916 as an in-house lawyer, and he had earned himself a reputation as an authority in the fields of corporate, antitrust, and tax law.[49] In early October 1935, Haussmann, who was then 50, asked Solmssen, the Chairman of the Supervisory Board, if he could retire *"for health reasons"* but offered to continue working for DEA on the basis of a consultancy contract.[50] In fact, Haussmann's illness was merely a pretext, and the real reason for his request to leave the board was the "Nuremberg Laws" that had been passed just a few days earlier. Solmssen discussed the next steps with Haussmann in private and once again proved to be a clever tactician. He proposed that Haussmann retire as of 1 April 1936 and at the same time offered him a three-year consultancy contract in order to secure Haussmann's expertise for DEA.[51] He hoped that this would at least provide the invaluable manager with material

---

47 Cf. Hildegard Frisius, *Dr. Ernst Gotthelf Springer*, https://www.stolpersteine-berlin.de/de/boothstr/33/ernst- gotthelf-springer [last retrieved on 10.10.2023].

48 Cf. Ullner an Kimmich, 4.10.1938, HADB, P 1659, sheet 171f.

49 Cf. Kimmich an Haußmann, 1.1.1938, HADB, P 1687.

50 Cf. Haußmann an Solmssen, 5.10.1935, handwritten, ibid.

51 Cf. Solmssen an Haußmann, 14.10.1935, ibid.

security. In the meantime, though, Haussmann had regained hope, as he was confident that the company was reliant on his expertise for upcoming tax audits. In January 1936 he asked to postpone the date of his retirement.[52] While Solmssen was open to the idea, von Burgsdorff disagreed and sought a meeting with Ullner to discuss the matter.[53] But the Chairman of the DEA Supervisory Board did not succumb to the pressure from Burgsdorff, and when the board contracts came up for renewal in October 1936, Haussmann's contract was also extended by four years and four months.

Haussmann trusted that his colleagues on the board, with whom he had worked for so many years, would not leave him in the lurch. Yet after an unpublished decree issued on 4 January 1938, in which the Reich Ministry of Economics defined the term "Jewish commercial enterprise" for the first time (a company was considered a "*Jewish commercial enterprise*" if it had a Jewish owner, if it was "controlled" by a Jewish partner or board member, or if a quarter of the Supervisory Board members were Jewish), the new chairman of the DEA Supervisory Board, Karl Kimmich, retroactively set Haussmann's retirement to 1 January 1938.[54] Haussmann subsequently emigrated to Switzerland in May,[55] and the consultancy contract that had been agreed for the period after his retirement back in 1936 thus came into force. Yet this brought no consolation for Haussmann, who wrote bitter letters to Ullner from Switzerland: "*Regardless, I don't know whether the DEA can be indifferent when it sends one of its most valuable people, who has rendered it loyal and valuable service for 23 years, away overnight and bars him from the premises, and then, when he is forced to go abroad completely destitute, declares:*

---

52 Cf. Haußmann an Solmssen, 20.1.1936, ibid.

53 Cf. Burgsdorff an Solmssen, 14.2.1936, ibid.

54 Cf. Kimmich an Haußmann, 31.12.1937, ibid.

55 Cf. AG Erinnern und Bewahren (Ed.), *Jüdische Schicksale in der Havelstadt Werder. Fritz Haußmann,* https://www.juedische-schicksale-werder.de/fritz-haussmann/ [last retrieved on 10.10.2023].

Now we regret that we can do nothing more, as we cannot and do not wish to expose ourselves or to swim against the tide, and for us the files are closed."[56]

Ullner tried to help. One plan involved placing Haussmann at a subsidiary of Edeleanu GmbH in the Netherlands, which had been set up to secure drilling contracts abroad, acquire oil fields, and participate in the construction of refineries. Ullner and Gröber wrote to the Chief Finance President of Berlin to acquire the necessary foreign exchange permit: "*Dr Haussmann who, as a non-Aryan, has resigned his position as a member of the board at our company, is able to devote himself to this activity in an adequate manner. He is an internationally recognized expert in the area of domestic and foreign commercial, stock corporation, tax, mining, and patent law.*"[57] Yet the plan failed, as did the efforts to find Haussmann a position with a foreign company.[58]

The Foreign Exchange Control Office of the Chief Finance President was critical of the contract with Haussmann and the severance arrangements. The officials wanted to know "*why such a far-reaching contract was concluded as late as 23 October 1936 – at a time when other companies were already distancing themselves from Jewish management and supervisory board members*".[59] The DEA Management Board defended its actions, referring to the legal situation that applied at the time.[60] In autumn 1938, the consultancy contract was terminated: "The implementation of the consultancy contract agreed with Mr Haussmann is no longer tenable for us for the known rea-

---

56 Haußmann an Ullner (n.d., approx. spring 1938), WD-CA, Personalakte, D-PA-009, Dr. Haußmann.

57 Cf. Ullner und Gröber an Oberfinanzpräsidenten Berlin, 23.5.1938, WD-CA, ibid.

58 Cf. Ullner an Haußmann, 14.8.1939, WD-CA, D-PA-010, Dr. Haußmann.

59 Cf. Oberfinanzpräsident Berlin, Devisenstelle, 26.9.1938, betr.: Abfindungszahlungen an den jüdischen Auswanderer Dr. Fritz Haußmann, ibid.

60 Cf. DEA-Vorstand an Oberfinanzpräsidenten Berlin, Devisenstelle, 17.9.1938, ibid.

sons and due to the developments that have occurred in the meantime, and it is objectively entirely impossible."[61]

In the meantime, a dispute ensued concerning severance payments. The Reich Ministry of Economics and the Foreign Exchange Control Office of the Chief Finance President in Berlin accused DEA of incorrect behaviour in its dealings with Jewish members of the Management and Supervisory Boards and demanded that payments be stopped. The DEA Management Board defended itself with the assertion that service contracts with "*non-Aryans*" were not prohibited in 1936. Haussmann had not only rendered the company "*valuable service*" but had also enjoyed an "*outstanding reputation*" among employees.[62]

The stricter foreign exchange regulations introduced in the German Reich meant that Haussmann received only a fraction of the money to which he was entitled. He appealed to Ullner repeatedly, reminding him of his promise that DEA would stand by him and asking for a meeting either in Switzerland or London.[63] Ullner reacted with irritation and accused him of misjudging reality: "*You seem to have completely forgotten that it would have been more convenient for us to draw a clear line of separation in 1935 and that it was only out of camaraderie that we refrained from doing so.*"[64] Nevertheless, he did travel to London to meet Haussmann in August 1939.[65] Although their conversation was tense, Ullner arranged a money transfer to Haussmann in the days that followed with the help of the German-South American Gold Discount Bank.[66] Barely had the first payment been made when the outbreak of war prevented further transfers. Ullner and his successor Karl Schirner did manage

---

61 Ullner und Gröber an Kimmich, 9.9.1938, ibid.

62 Cf. Ullner/Randhahn an Kimmich, 7.3.1939, ibid.

63 Cf. Haußmann an Ullner, 23.3.1939, ibid.

64 Ullner an Haußmann, 3.5.1939, WD-CA, D-PA-013, Dr. Haußmann.

65 Cf. Ullner an Kimmich, 2.8.1939, WD-CA, D-PA-010, Dr. Haußmann.

66 Cf. Ullner an Haußmann, 18.8.1939; Ullner an Haußmann, Genf, 28.8.1939, ibid.

to support Haussmann's mother in Berlin financially to the extent that she was able to leave for Geneva in early 1940,[67] and in mid-1940 Haussmann left Switzerland for Venezuela to take up a consultancy contract there.[68]

It bears noting that the DEA Management Board had held onto Haussmann's employment for a long time despite growing pressure and had also been willing to fulfil its financial obligations towards him. Neither the aloof-seeming Ullner nor Schirner were anti-Semites; indeed, they helped to ease Haussmann's situation and that of his mother.[69] After the war ended, the new DEA Management Board, under the leadership of Schirner, acknowledged that Haussmann had been wrongly treated and reached a settlement with him in May 1949.

The Management Board under Karl Schirner (1940–1945)

In 1938, the new Chairman of the Supervisory Board, Karl Kimmich, who was a member of the board at Deutsche Bank, wanted to see a younger, dynamic man at the helm of DEA rather than the aging board members.[70] The man he chose was Karl Schirner (1885–1973), who was to replace Hans Gröber on the board and take over as Chairman from April 1940. Kimmich praised Schirner as *"an outstandingly capable businessman with extensive industrial knowledge, an energetic, clear-cut personality of the finest calibre, a man with tremen-*

---

67 Haußmann an Schirner, 15.4.1940, ibid.

68 Cf. Haußmann an Kimmich, 15.4.1940, ibid.

69 Bavendamm's assessment that Ullner behaved "insensitive and uncooperative" towards Haussmann reflects Haussmann's perspective (Cf. Bavendamm, *1899–1999,* 210). The sources do not provide complete support for this thesis. Furthermore, Haussmann's trace was not lost in South America, but he returned to Switzerland and reached a settlement with DEA in 1949.

70 Cf. Aufsichtsratssitzung, 26.10.1938, HADB, P 1663, sheet 59.

dous capacity who is particularly well known in industrial circles in western Germany".[71]

Schirner had completed a commercial apprenticeship in Berlin with the firm Arthur Koppel, then went to England for three and a half years to undergo further training; he then became Commercial Director of AEG's Mannheim branch in 1909. During the First World War, he was an officer in charge of a company and was wounded. From 1913 to 1922, he worked at the Siemens-Schuckert head office in Berlin and then joined the board at Deutsch-Luxemburgische Bergwerks- und Hütten AG. After the business was taken over by Vereinigte Stahlwerke AG (VESTAG), a company managed by Fritz Thyssen, he became a member of its board. From May 1933 he was Chairman of the Supervisory Board at Vereinigte Aluminiumwerke (VAW) and from 1935 a member of the board at Vereinigte Industrieunternehmungen AG (VIAG), a holding company for industrial holdings of the German Reich.[72]

In 1938 Schirner, by his own admission, was seeking "*a position that involves getting my hands dirty*" and made it a condition that he would be made Chairman of the Board at the new firm.[73] Having grown up in the home of a Protestant pastor, Schirner was more distanced from the Nazi Party and chose not to join, as he stated in his biographical notes for the denazification committee after the war. As the VAW increasingly came under the influence of the Nazi Party, he decided to take up Kimmich's offer and moved to DEA in November 1938.[74] He initially joined the Management Board of DPAG, replacing Hans Gröber who left DEA on 1 January 1939.[75] Even before Schirner was officially put in charge of the board, he

---

71 As cited in: Manfred Pohl/Andrea H. Schneider, *VIAG-Aktiengesellschaft 1923–1998. Vom Staatsunternehmen zum internationalen Konzern*, Munich 1998, 130.

72 Cf. ibid., 129–131, 190f.

73 Cf. Karl Schirner, Curriculum Vitae, 1946. Biographische Notizen für den Entnazifizierungsausschuss, WD-CA, D-14-2/1381.

74 Cf. Karl Schirner, ibid.

75 Cf. Urkundenrolle-Nummer 57, RA Bruno Hüls, D-RW-271.

Fig. 17 Karl Schirner, DEA Chairman of the DEA Management Board 1940–5

had already received DEA's audit reports, reports on the lignite operations, and detailed information on the naval contract from Kimmich.[76]

Schirner was an outstanding businessman who appeared unapproachable and was therefore also known in the company as "der Eisheilige" (the "Ice Saint" after those of German folklore).[77] He succeeded in finalising the long-disputed acquisition of the Heuersdorf-Käferhain lignite field near Leipzig in the summer of 1939 and in arranging the purchase of the "Nova" refinery in Schwechat, just outside Vienna. It was a brilliant start. Schirner then officially replaced Ullner as Chairman of the Management Board at the annual general meeting in 1940.

---

76 Cf. Kimmich an Schirner, 28.12.1938, HADB, P 1659, sheet 216–224.

77 Cf. Bavendamm, *1899–1999*, 211.

Kimmich and Schirner were united in their agreement to maintain the greatest possible entrepreneurial scope in relation to the state. They made the most of the opportunities offered by the Nazi state to expand their business with coal and petroleum. They also had no qualms about exploiting the predicaments of Jewish entrepreneurs and foreign companies in order to strengthen DEA's market position, as demonstrated most significantly by their efforts to take over parts of the Petschek Group.[78]

With Schirner's appointment and the beginning of the war, DEA's business policy came to focus primarily on oil production and processing.[79] This was not so much down to the personal intentions of the new Chairman of the Board as to the new framework for DEA's activities dictated by rearmament and the war economy. Added to this were the unexpected oil discoveries in Austria and in Heide in Holstein.

The five-member board was still dominated by its mining faction, with Walther Randhahn (Borna), mining assessor Albert Ritter (Gelsenkirchen) and, from 1942, former mining assessor Max Grotowsky (Gelsenkirchen), but as Chairman of the Board Schirner, who was not a trained oil expert but an economist, pushed ahead with oil production. The actual petroleum experts, for whom the new focus was advantageous, had been based in Wietze since the merger of DPAG and DEA on 1 April 1940. However, management of the oil companies was subsequently moved to Schöneberg in Berlin. Karl Grosse, Erich Greiser, and Günther Schlicht now acted as directors there. While Greiser was less prominent, Grosse and Schlicht had a decisive influence on the petroleum division in the period that followed and would play important roles in the German wartime economy.

---

78 Cf. Chapter 3 and for the role of Kimmich: James, *Deutsche Bank*, 348f.

79 Cf. Schlicht, *Erinnerungen*, 81.

Fig. 18 Karl Grosse (3rd from l.), member of the DEA Management Board, 1935–42; General Director of Karpathen Öl AG, 1942–45. Photo from the 1936 May Day celebrations in Wietze, with Fritz Teuter (from l. to r.), Hans Hubrig, and Günther Schlicht

Karl Grosse, who was born in 1886 in the mining town of Klostermannsfeld, trained as a miner in his hometown from 1902 and volunteered for military service between 1905 and 1907. He then attended the mining college in Senftenberg as well as the Higher Mining Academy in Eisleben from 1909 to 1911. In March 1911, Grosse took up a position as a foreman at the Salzmünde potash plant, later moving to the Ellers potash trade union in 1913.[80] He was drafted just a few days after the outbreak of the First World War, seriously wounded in September 1914, and discharged from the army in June 1915. He resumed work in potash mining before joining DEA in September 1917. His mining training meant he was ideally

80 Cf. Personalbogen Karl Große, 1921, WD-CA, Personal-Abteilung DEA; Große, *Mein Leben*.

suited to work on construction of the world's first oil shaft in Pechelbronn, where DEA put him in charge of operations. After the war ended, he was forced to leave Pechelbronn on 9 November 1918, and a year later he wrote to General Director Nöllenburg: "My career has been completely cut short."[81] He considered the appointment he had been given in the meantime, at DEA's Rositz lignite works, as merely a stopgap measure. Nöllenburg eventually secured Grosse's appointment as DPAG's Deputy Director of Operations in Wietze from December 1920, where his experience in oil shaft mining was to be hugely beneficial from then on. Nevertheless, DPAG, a DEA subsidiary, was by no means a priority for the Group at that time, and further advancement seemed unlikely until the early 1930s.

Grosse was power-conscious and set the tone in Wietze as Technical Director. In May 1933 he joined the Nazi Party, which gave his career a boost,[82] and he was appointed to the board of DPAG in 1935 together with Eugen Bauer (Wilhelmsburg refinery) and Max Heyne (Rositz refinery). Grosse was a member of the German Society for Mineral Oil Research and in 1937, as an experienced practitioner, was appointed head of the petroleum extraction section of the Fuel Industry Economic Group, an organisation of the Reich's Industry Group. He thus assumed a key position in the German petroleum industry.

His position in the Group was further enhanced following the "Anschluss" of Austria in 1938, when he proved adept at acquiring concessions in the new territories. After war broke out, he was involved in the establishment of the Beskid companies in occupied Poland and took charge of them himself. In June 1940, he led a commando unit to occupy the Pechelbronn oil works in Alsace and was

81 Große an Generaldirektor Nöllenburg, 12.12.1919, ibid.

82 Cf. NSDAP-Gaukartei, BArch Berlin, R 9361-IX Kartei/12131156.

appointed trustee there.[83] It was following this event, at the latest, that Grosse was also regarded to a certain extent as an expert in the takeover of oil companies in occupied countries

In February 1942, there were initial discussions with Göring's State Secretary Erich Neumann about establishing a large oil company in occupied Poland and Ukraine.[84] Representatives of several firms put Grosse forward for the post of General Director of Karpathen Öl AG. The Chairman of the Board at DEA, Karl Schirner, agreed.

Grosse took up his new position in July 1942, and his employment contract with DEA was suspended until the end of the war. As General Director of Karpathen Öl, he was in charge of a company employing more than 30,000 people, while his salary, including bonuses, amounted to around 100,000 Reichsmarks a year and was therefore well above the remuneration paid to managers at most armament firms.[85] He was at the peak of his career. As General Director of Karpathen Öl, Grosse ensured that certain key positions in the company were filled by DEA colleagues. Yet his rise to become General Director and thus his closer involvement in the business of armaments and occupation came at a price, as became apparent after the end of the war.

---

83 Cf. Bericht des Beauftragten des OKW und des Reichswirtschaftsministeriums zur Wiederinbetriebnahme der früheren Vereinigten Pechelbronner Ölbergwerke, Bundesarchiv Freiburg [hereafter: BArch Freiburg], Rüstungsinspektion V, Stuttgart, RW 20-5/41.

84 Cf. DEA an Karl Große, 24.2.1942, WD-CA, Personal-Abteilung DEA.

85 Cf. Konti Öl (Karl Blessing) an Große, 16.6.1942, ibid.

No less ambitious was the other director of DEA's petroleum operations, Günther Schlicht.[86] He studied mining engineering from 1921 to 1924, initially in Munich and then at the Technical University in Berlin. In between his studies, he took part in battles in Upper Silesia in 1921 as a member of the Freikorps Oberland. He graduated as a mining engineer at the end of 1924 and joined the state mining administration, becoming a mining assessor in April 1928. Up to this point, Schlicht had specialized in coal and ores. When Ernst Middendorf, General Director of DEA and a fellow member of the Berg- und Hüttenmännischer Verein, offered him the management of DPAG's mining division, Schlicht left the civil service and switched to the private sector. In 1932 he married the daughter of DEA board member Reinhold Dehnke. The next year, he became an authorized signatory at DPAG and in February 1936 the Second Technical Director in Wietze under Karl Grosse. Their relationship was amicable, but at times also tense.

Politically, Schlicht was a German nationalist. By his own admission, he tended towards the DNVP and joined the "Stahlhelm" in January 1933,[87] an organization of former front soldiers that was taken over by the Sturmabteilung in mid-1933. In November 1937 he applied to join the Nazi Party and was accepted with retroactive effect from 1 May.[88] After the merger of DEA and DPAG, Schlicht was transferred from Wietze to Berlin-Schöneberg to the

86 Cf. Günther Schlicht, biografische Angaben, WD-CA, 3000–01265; An extensive biographical tribute has been published by Stephan A. Lütgert, *"Ein Bergmann ging ins Öl". Zur Erinnerung an Bergassessor Dr. Ing. E. h. Günther Schlicht (1901–1962)*, in: EEK 9 (2022) 34–46; Karsten Linne critically examines Schlicht's role in the National Socialist war economy, *Der Krieg als Chance. Ein deutscher Manager auf "Expedition" in den Kaukasus*, in: Zeitschrift für Geschichtswissenschaft 5 (2024), 398–418.

87 Cf. Schlicht, *Erinnerungen*, 76.

88 NSDAP-Gaukartei, BArch Berlin, R 9361-IX Kartei/37700385.

newly established administration of all the DEA petroleum operations, which he managed together with Karl Grosse.[89]

Schlicht gradually became DEA's most important petroleum expert. He took part in Göring's oil conferences and, following his success in expanding oil production in Heide, was named a "Wehrwirtschaftsführer", or "war industry leader", in 1942. In August 1942, Schlicht was assigned to the Mineral Oil Technical Brigade (TBM) and entrusted with its technical management. After the failure of the Caucasus venture, Schlicht returned to Berlin. In April 1943 he was appointed a deputy member of the DEA Management Board and succeeded Grosse as head of the petroleum extraction unit. Schlicht willingly allowed himself to be integrated into state functions of the Nazi war economy.

---

89 Cf. Schlicht, *Erinnerungen*, 85.

III. DEA COMPANIES BETWEEN THE AUTHORITARIAN CORPORATE REGIME AND THE NAZI DICTATORSHIP

(Manfred Grieger)

The DEA hard coal mines in the 1920s

The coal division became even more dominant in the DEA group with the successful entry into hard coal mining in the Ruhr region in 1924. DEA sought to boost output at the Graf Bismarck colliery in Gelsenkirchen by deepening the shafts and sinking the new mineshaft at pithead IX while expanding the pithead at VII/VIII. It likewise tried to further rationalize operations by introducing technology into coal mining wherever possible. Given the strong rivals in the market, however, coal prices were low, and this, combined with rising wage costs, put pressure on the profit margins. DEA tried to counteract dwindling profits at the Graf Bismarck colliery as early as 1928 by cutting 1,300 members of the workforce. Meanwhile, the adoption of jackhammers in all facework pushed the output per man per shift to a new record high of 1.26 tonnes, so these two measures combined to keep hard coal mining in the black.

Managers at the DEA mines was distanced from the Works Councils Act (Betriebsrätegesetz), which had been passed by the Reichstag in 1920 as a late result of the November Revolution and had introduced democratization into relations between employers and employees. Just how much they were adverse to it can be seen from a statement the company was asked to submit on the occasion of the 10th anniversary of these legal regulations: The head of the legal department at DEA's Graf Bismarck colliery wrote to the Buer Mining Office (Bergrevier) on 25 February 1930, which then reported to the state supervisory authority for mining, the Senior Mining Office (Oberbergamt) in Dortmund, that the worker representatives in the colliery had "either completely become firm followers of the trade unions" or " had morphed into "a primarily political fighting organ [...] of the Communist Party intended to pursue its party goals". Instead of "nurturing company interests", or so the company said, the representatives of the works council allowed themselves to be guided "by trade union or purely political aspirations that have nothing to do with company operations". As a result, they were not fulfilling the "sense and purpose" of worker representatives as stated in the Works Councils Act. The mines management rejected this form of in-company co-determination because it was, as a rule, "not possible" to conduct "objective negotiations based on the interests of the company". For, according to the company management, the workers' representatives primarily exhibited an "agitator approach" instead of acting as the "intermediary body between employers and workforce".

The legal department at DEA's Graf Bismarck colliery went so far as to claim that the works council members considered it their "primary task" to "expand their own powers wherever possible and reduce the independence of the operations managers and supervisory staff". The works council as an institution, it said, did not even bring any real benefit on issues of accident prevention. With the exception of the suggestion that the election term be extended from one year to several years, the company was not prepared to make any other statements as, in its opinion, what was needed first was "a key change in the interpretation of the law by the works council members and the circles of employees behind them".[1]

For its part, the works council at pitheads II/VI/IX in the Graf Bismarck colliery emphasized that it had not been able to find a basis for cooperation with management. The latter had, over the last ten years, "left no stone unturned in its efforts to disadvantage the works council in its legal activities".[2] The works councils had, moreover, been prevented from exercising their co-determination rights as regards works housing and welfare institutions, in which context the Mining Office had simply supported the company, it said. The works council chairman, August Lippek, gave a more balanced judgement, pointing out that the Works Councils Act had "proved its worth" and "had fulfilled its purpose". However, he said, the stipulations had at times not sufficed, so he advocated the "works councils being accorded more rights" in order to ensure "equal rights between employers and employees".[3]

At the Königsgrube colliery, where operations underground and on the surface were beefed up until 1930, the daily output per man per shift was 1.22 tonnes.[4] Owing to the Great Depression, however, demand dipped, and in 1930 the company slashed the Königsgrube colliery workforce by 459 and cut back production by around 20 percent by imposing 52 idle shifts. The reduction in output continued unabated in 1931, dropping almost ten percent at the Graf Bismarck colliery and by 14 percent at the Königsgrube colliery. In 1932, production output and unit sales fell to new lows with-

---

1 DEA-Zeche Graf Bismarck, Rechtsabteilung, Mitter, an Bergrevierbeamten des Bergreviers Buer, 25.2.1930, 1ff., Landesarchiv Nordrhein-Westfalen [hereafter: LAV NRW], dept. Westfalen, Bergämter No. 8067.

2 Betriebsausschuss des Schachts II/VI/IX der Zeche Graf Bismarck, Sperling, an Bergrevieramt Buer, 25.2.1930, 1, ibid.

3 Betriebsratsvorsitzender August Lippek an Bergrevier Buer, 20.2.1930, ibid.

4 Geschäfts-Bericht der Deutschen Erdöl-Aktiengesellschaft zu Berlin über das 30. Geschäftsjahr 1928, Berlin 1929, 2f.

out the mines therefore operating at a loss.[5] The DEA executives had assumed, when entering the hard coal mining segment, that they would see a clear rise in output volumes, and this initially occurred from 1924 onwards, but in 1932 output had dropped back to below the 2-million-tonnes mark. Given the increases made in capacity and the greater use of technology and more effective mining techniques, the hard coal division essentially ran on standby at the nadir of the Great Depression, waiting for demand to pick up. Progress was made in consolidating the operations at the Graf Bismarck colliery in 1932, but only pithead I/IV ran two shifts. Pitheads VII/VIII and II/VI/IX had been switched over to single-shift operations, while the wheels at pithead III/V were motionless.[6]

Hard coal output at DEA mines (in tonnes)[7]

Year	Graf Bismarck	Königsgrube	Total output
1923	535,457	111,497	646,854
1924	1,742,477	286,142	2,028,619
1925	1,856,985	437,266	2,294,251
1926	2,324,778	542,069	2,866,846
1927	2,198,973	557,641	2,756,614
1928	2,109,523	550,882	2,660,495
1929	2,326,194	608,053	2,934,247
1930	1,901,378	488,087	2,389,465
1931	1,722,031	418,689	2,140,720
1932	1,553,914	392,056	1,944,970

In order to present his achievements on behalf of the DEA group in a good light, Reinhold Dehnke, the colliery's director who

5 Geschäfts-Bericht der Deutschen Erdöl-Aktiengesellschaft zu Berlin über das 34. Geschäftsjahr 1932, Berlin 1933, 1.

6 Jahresbericht des Bergreviers Buer für das Jahr 1932, 5, LAV NRW, dept. Westfalen, Bergämter No. 8089.

7 Statistiken Graf Bismarck und Königsgrube, WD-CA, D-RW-128.

had since been made a member of the DEA Management Board, focussed on the surplus of 28.6 million Reichsmark the Graf Bismarck colliery had generated in the years 1925 to 1931. This compared, he continued, to DEA expenditure of 7.8 million Reichsmark. He therefore estimated the "gross profit" made at 20.7 million Reichsmark. After deducting amortization, the net profit came to just short of nine million Reichsmark, which translated into average net annual income of 1.28 million Reichsmark.[8] From his viewpoint, taking over the Graf Bismarck colliery had thus been a good bit of business for DEA. In the opinion of the Supervisory Board Chairman, though, expectations had been somewhat dashed by the general performance, and the diversification strategy had therefore not on balance achieved the desired results.

The DEA lignite mines

In 1923, a year of hyperinflation, the lignite operations mined just under 5.4 million tonnes of lignite and produced 1.8 million tonnes of briquettes – 4.5 and 6.7 percent respectively of the total German output.[9] In the lignite plants, DEA continued to mechanize opencast operations, for example by opting for large excavators in the Dora and Helene mines, something that reduced production costs.[10] As labour costs rose, so the mining management in Altenberg and Borna sought to reduce overall expenses by introducing large-scale machinery for stripping, coal production, and coal processing operations. Demand was only brisker for a few years, until prospects

8 Reinhold Dehnke, Auswirkung des Erwerbs der Gewerkschaft Graf Bismarck von 1925–1931, 17.3.1933, 1ff., WD-CA, D-PA-36.

9 Geschäfts-Bericht der Deutschen Erdöl-Aktiengesellschaft zu Berlin über das 25. Geschäftsjahr 1923, Berlin 1924, 1.

10 Geschäfts-Bericht der Deutschen Erdöl-Aktiengesellschaft zu Berlin über das 30. Geschäftsjahr 1928, Berlin 1929, 3.

dimmed with the onset of the Great Depression after 1929. Sluggish sales in 1930 led to temporary discontinuation of activities at the Breunsburg colliery and Altenburger Kohlenwerke. Countless idle shifts were introduced for all the mines, and production sagged as a consequence by about 21 percent.[11] Max Heyne, as Director of Erdölwerke Rositz, stated in a letter to the group head office dated 17 August 1931: "Our pit now runs two idle shifts a week, payroll in the briquette factory is down to 45 percent."[12] In fact, lignite output hit a new record high in 1928 at 7.2 million tonnes. From the viewpoint of many DEA managers, the decrease in output volumes up to 1932 – a drop of almost one third to 4.9 million tonnes – ran parallel to the decline of the inter-war republic in Germany.

Lignite output at DEA mines (in 1,000 tonnes)[13]

Year	Raw coal	Briquettes
1928	7,209	2,605
1929	7,111	2,598
1930	5,593	2,051
1931	5,589	2,040
1932	4,954	1,827

The majority of the Rositz operations managers rejected the republic as a system and, most of all, the in-company codetermination involving works councils and labour councils. In spring 1930, Mineralölwerke Rositz attacked the works council members by assigning them unfavourable jobs and cutting their wages in the hope of prompting them to give notice. Moreover, the chairman of both the works council and the labour council, Christian Schoch,

11 Geschäfts-Bericht der Deutschen Erdöl-Aktiengesellschaft zu Berlin über das 32. Geschäftsjahr 1930, Berlin 1931, 2.

12 DEA-Mineralölwerke Rositz, Direktion, Max Heyne an Dr. Lossen, 17.8.1931, 3, StA Leipzig, Bestand 20684, DEA-Mineralölwerke Rositz, No. 2.

13 Figures based on DEA annual reports for the years 1928 to 1932.

was sacked with no warning and without the approval of the works council. The company accused him of engaging in trade with condoms on the company grounds and of having left his workstation early, but it lost the lawsuit that then went before the Reich Labour Court (Reichsarbeitsgericht) and was therefore forced to re-employ Schoch.[14] DEA's intention of ridding itself of the trade unionists and works council members whom the employees held in high regard was evident in all these steps that it took.

In order to adapt operations to lower output volumes, management halted work at the Breuneburg, Mariengrube, Neuglück, and Ramsdorf briquette factories. Lignite mining operations were concentrated in pit II at the Regis open-cast mine once large-scale strip mining had gone turnkey there.

Business recovery after the Nazis took power

The DEA annual report for 1933 describes the formation of a government under Reich Chancellor Adolf Hitler as a "national uprising". Unlike other sectors of the economy, the demand for fuels did not pick up as a direct result, but the company nevertheless interpreted the political watershed as heralding an economic turnaround. In order to be ready for the upturn, DEA increased its investment in new plant and equipment. Fully in line with the Party's strong emphasis on high-profile labour procurement for public infrastructure projects such as autobahn construction,[15] the Nazi regime also expected that new hirings would reduce mass unemployment.

---

14 Reichsarbeitsgericht (RAG 591/1930), Beschluss, 25.4.1931, StA Leipzig, Bestand 20684, DEA-Mineralölwerke Rositz, No. 43; Reichsarbeitsgericht (RAG 26/1930), Beschluss, 6.12.1930, StA Leipzig, Bestand 20684, DEA-Mineralölwerke Rositz, No. 43; see too Verfahren vor dem Reichsarbeitsgerichts Paul Deglow, BArch Berlin, R 3010, No. 1080, and Christian Schoch, BArch Berlin, R 3010, No. 1712.

15 Detlev Humann, *"Arbeitsschlacht". Arbeitsbeschaffung und Propaganda in der NS-Zeit 1933–1939*, Göttingen 2011, 85ff.

Hence, DEA played to the new government gallery in the interest of fostering social peace, engaging new workers beyond the numbers required to boost production, and thus the payroll rose by nine percent in 1933 alone.[16] Brighter economic activity and, most significantly, the Nazis' rearmament policy offered the prospect of domestic demand for oil products growing. DPAG therefore expanded its oil production and processing operations, while DEA strengthened its upstream lignite works, above all, in order to be able to provide the necessary raw materials.

The upturn in coal mining in the Ruhr region

The corporation exploited the economic upturn emerging in the second half of 1933 in order to guide its hard coal mining operations out of the doldrums. In 1933, the renewal work and construction of a new office, shower, and locker building at pithead VII at the Graf Bismarck colliery presaged renewed growth. Production edged up to 1.606 million tonnes, which the Management Board rated as a positive sign, although unit sales were still not up to the mark, resulting in higher coal and coke inventories of 64,000 and 133,000 tonnes respectively.[17] DEA's net profit for the year fell by around RM 175,000, and the syndicate levy, which increased by around 14 percent to around RM 5.8 million, also resulted in losses of almost RM 1 million. Nevertheless, the hard coal division booked pre-tax profits of a massive 1.685 million Reichsmark.[18]

In spring 1933 the Supervisory Board set out to bring a breath of fresh air into the hard coal division management and there-

---

16 Geschäftsbericht der Deutschen Erdöl-Aktiengesellschaft in Berlin über das 35. Geschäftsjahr 1933, Berlin 1934, 1.

17 Ibid.

18 Niederschrift über die Verhandlungen des Aufsichtsrats der DEA, 13.6.1934, 2f. and 7, WD-CA, D-PA-0120.

fore wanted one of the DEA Management Board members, 69-year-old Reinhold Dehnke, to retire so that they could replace him with someone younger. The former General Director of the Graf Bismarck colliery protested, however, in a lengthy letter to Management Board Chairman Ernst Middendorf on 18 March 1933, claiming that DEA had not given him the recognition that was his due. If he were to retire, Dehnke wanted to receive some sort of compensation of his forfeited income in the form of either a long-term consultancy contract or positions on several supervisory boards. Middendorf responded quite coldly, reminding him that it was a real exception for men of his age "to still receive emoluments of over 100,000 Reichsmark".[19] Middendorf indicated that if Dehnke retired as of 1 April 1933, he would be paid in full until the end of the year and after that receive a monthly pension of 2,000 Reichsmark. Supervisory Board Chairman Georg Solmssen excluded Dehnke being given a position on the DEA Supervisory Board; instead, the board pressed ahead with its strategy of younger men, appointing Mining Assessor Albert Ritter to direct the hard coal division and making him a member of the DEA Management Board to enable him to represent the division's interests at the group level.

The change at the DEA helm as regards the hard coal division occurred for reasons of age and economics. The political sea-change caused by the Nazis taking power also led to Communist Party members and trade unionists being expelled from companies, and the mine managers had already used various waves of firings during the Great Depression to remove politically unwelcome members of the Communist Party or grassroots trade union officers from the payroll. The elections to the works council at the Königsgrube colliery conducted on 10 March 1933 in line with the still valid legal regulations had resulted in three of the nine seats going to

19 Reinhold Dehnke an Ernst Middendorf, 18.3.1933, WD-CA, D-PA-36; Ernst Middendorf an Reinhold Dehnke, 23.3.1933, ibid.

"National Workers' Associations" such as the Nationalsozialistische Betriebszellen-Organisation (the Nazi Factory Cell Organization, NSBO).[20] However, the Communists were just as strong, while the mining association grabbed two seats and the Christian trade union one.[21] Since the Nazi regime was aiming to consolidate its power in companies, too, and trying to eliminate all remnants of Communist influence, on 4 April 1933 it passed its Law on Company Representations and on Business Associations. This provided regulations for "eliminating" the membership in company representative bodies of persons deemed to have an outlook inimical to the state or the economy. Henceforth, employment contracts could be terminated "on suspicion of an outlook inimical to the state".[22] On 12 April 1933, the Reich Minister of the Interior instructed the state police forces (Landespolizeibehörden) to initiate the "necessary investigations and removals" of such persons with the goal of ensuring "company representations that have a national outlook and are willing to work". "Marxist members of company representative bodies" could even be removed if there was only suspicion, but no actual proof, of "activity in a manner inimical to the state and economy (membership of a Communist organization, aspirations for a 'united front'

20 Magdeburger Bergwerks-AG, Zeche Königsgrube an Bergrevier Herne, 9.5.1933, LAV NRW, dept. Westfalen, Bergämter No. 7458; see Dieter Mullay, *Von der NSBO zur Deutschen Arbeitsfront (DAF)*, in: Politische Macht und Gewaltausübung im 20. Jahrhundert. Zeitgeschichte, Zeitgeschehen und Kontroversen, Wien 2011, 193–214; Tobias Mulot, *Von der Betriebszelle zur Arbeitsfront. Die Hamburger NSBO auf dem Weg in die "Leistungsgemeinschaft" des "Dritten Reiches"*, in: Frank Bajohr/Joachim Szodrzynski (Eds.), Hamburg in der NS-Zeit. Ergebnisse neuerer Forschungen, Hamburg 1995, 203–230; Gunther Mai, *Die Nationalsozialistische Betriebszellen-Organisation. Arbeiterschaft und Nationalsozialismus 1927–1934*, in: Detlev Heiden/Gunther Mai (Eds.), Nationalsozialismus und Thüringen, Weimar 1995, 165–188.

21 Magdeburger Bergwerks-AG, Zeche Königsgrube an Bergrevier Herne, 9.5.1933, LAV NRW, dept. Westfalen, Bergämter No. 7458.

22 Oberbergamt Dortmund, Karl Hatzfeld, an Bergämter, 26.4.1933, 1, LAV NRW, dept. Westfalen, Bergämter No. 8111.

between the Social Democrat and Communist workers, abuse as a functionary of a political party, etc.)".

After the dismantling of free trade unions on 2 May 1933, the District President (Regierungspräsident) in Arnsberg directed in mid-May 1933 that five of the 11 elected works council members at pithead VII/VIII of the Graf Bismarck colliery be removed from office and replaced with new members loyal to the Nazi Party. In this way, the composition of the works council was changed to conform with the interests of the company and the regime, which meant ipso facto the suspension of the prior Works Councils Act.[23] Seven of the 13 members of the works council of pithead I/IV, among them tusker Wilhelm Plewka, were replaced in the same way.[24] Yet there were still "discrepancies", so the new Nazi Party Gelsenkirchen Lord Mayor (Oberbürgermeister) of Gelsenkirchen Carl Engelbert Böhmer, in agreement with the NSBO district head, applied to have another worker excluded. After being pressurized, two members of the works council withdrew, ostensibly "voluntarily", and from July 1933 onwards the new "labour council" also included two pit foremen, meaning white-collar workers.[25] On 3 July 1933, the composition of the company representation for pithead II/VI/IX was also changed,[26] and two other works council members were also excluded from the body as of the end of August 1933.[27] As in countless other companies with elected works councils, but also in many areas of (local) politics, within the space of six months the democratically

---

23 Regierungspräsident Arnsberg, Dr. Punder, an Zeche Graf Bismarck, 19.5.1933, ibid.

24 Regierungspräsident Arnsberg, Bachem, an Zeche Graf Bismarck, 26.5.1933, ibid; Jahresbericht des Bergreviers Buer für das Jahr 1933, 11, LAV NRW, dept. Westfalen, Bergämter No. 8089; Klaus Wisotzky, *Der Ruhrbergbau im Dritten Reich. Studie zur Sozialpolitik im Ruhrbergbau und zum sozialen Verhalten der Bergleute in den Jahren 1933 bis 1939*, Düsseldorf 1983, 26ff.

25 Regierungspräsident Arnsberg, Bachem, an Zeche Graf Bismarck, 9.7.1933, LAV NRW, dept. Westfalen, Bergämter No. 8111.

26 Regierungspräsident Arnsberg, Bachem, an Zeche Graf Bismarck, 3.7.1933, ibid.

27 Regierungspräsident Arnsberg, Täglich, an Zeche Graf Bismarck, 26.8.1933, ibid.

elected representatives were replaced by people loyal to the Nazi Party and the participatory structures thus transformed into a pliant board.[28]

At the Königsgrube colliery, the pattern was the same: With reference to the law on company representations and to the "Reich Presidential Ordnance to Maintain Peace and Order", Social Democrats / Communists Karl and Wilhelm Frontzek, Gruber, Konarski, Rogowski, and Wuttke – as the colliery management informed the Mining Office quite openly – were "forced to withdraw from the works council" by Nazi and nationally minded representatives of the company. Their places were taken by "three Nazis and three Deutschnationale (German nationalists)" respectively, something the District President in Arnsberg decreed retrospectively on 4 May 1933.[29] The NSBO's Röhlinghausen District Group proposed in mid-July 1933 that its loyal members be appointed to both the Supervisory Board of Magdeburger Bergwerks-AG and to the company committee (Betriebsausschuss) and the workers council (Arbeiterrat).[30] Moreover, that same day the NSBO Röhlinghausen District Group also nominated the members of the new council of salaried employees at the Königsgrube colliery,[31] and the District President in Arnsberg formally appointed said persons on 27 July 1933.[32]

---

28 Werner Milert/Rudolf Tschirbs, *Die andere Demokratie. Betriebliche Interessenvertretung in Deutschland 1848 bis 2008*, Essen 2015, 244ff.; Peter Steinbach, *Die Gleichschaltung. Zerstörung der Weimarer Republik – Konsolidierung der nationalsozialistischen Diktatur*, in: Michael Kißener (Ed.), Der Weg in den Nationalsozialismus 1933/34, Darmstadt 2009, 66–99.

29 Magdeburger Bergwerks-AG, Zeche Königsgrube an Bergrevier Herne, 9.5.1933, LAV NRW, dept. Westfalen, Bergämter No. 7458.

30 NSBO, Ortsgruppe Röhlinghausen, Ortsgruppenbetriebswart Klostermann, an Bergrevier Herne, 14.7.1933, ibid.

31 Ibid.

32 Regierungspräsident Arnsberg an Zeche Königsgrube, 27.7.1933, ibid.; Zweijahresbericht des Bergrevierbeamten des Bergreviers Herne als Gewerbeaufsichtsbeamter für die Jahre 1933 und 1934, 8, LAV NRW, dept. Westfalen, Bergämter No. 7593.

Tusker Wilhelm Plewka had hitherto been the staff representative on the DEA Supervisory Board and was now removed from that position and replaced by a miner called Paul Lubowitzki, who was nominated by the Nazi Party. On 20 November 1933, DEA Management Board member Richard F. Ullner then contacted his fellow Management Board member Albert Ritter, who was responsible for the hard coal division, to find out more about Lubowitzki.[33] Ritter did not know the Nazi nominee for the Supervisory Board in person and therefore had, for his part, to request information from local pit officials. A native of Gelsenkirchen, Lubowitzki (born in 1895) had been employed at the Graf Bismarck colliery since 1909 and therefore for his entire working life, as had his brother Franz. He was married and the father of four children, was of Polish-Catholic origin, and had originally been a member of the Zentrum (Centre) Party. However, years before 1933 he had switched to the Sturmabteilung (Storm Troopers, SA),[34] the Nazi Party's paramilitary combat and terror organization, and to the NSBO, which had held a majority of the works council seats at some of the pitheads even before 1930. In 1933, Lubowitzki had been voted company superintendent of pithead VII. His superiors termed him "calm", reporting that he "hardly contributed a word" at the meetings of the works council. They otherwise knew of nothing "disadvantageous" about his "behaviour and conduct". While his company superiors drew an overall picture of Lubowitzki as a harmless man, Ritter added that, according to other sources, Lubowitzki's "great strength" lay in his ability to "consume considerable amounts of alcohol in conc. form".[35] Ullner, who always wanted to be kept abreast of such external members of the Supervisory Board, instructed his secretary to include this answer in the correspondence with the Management Board, evidently feeling this discrediting information was of value. Lubowitzki

33 Richard F. Ullner an Albert Ritter, 20.11.1933, WD-CA, D-PA-62.

34 Daniel Siemens, *Sturmabteilung. Die Geschichte der SA*, Berlin 2019, 79ff.

35 Albert Ritter, Vermerk, 21.11.1933, WD-CA, D-PA-62.

did not take part in the very next regular meeting of the Supervisory Board because the Law on the Order of National Labour enacted on 20 January 1934 terminated any employee representation on such a board. The company's annual report for 1933, which was published on 4 July 1934, therefore no longer included any employee representatives.[36] The company management kept the persons nominated by the Nazi regime at arm's length because they felt the men were likewise not suited to participate.

The end of trade union co-determination was a welcome development for the DEA Management and Supervisory Boards, having been a nuisance to them since its statutory introduction in 1920. Now they could once again unrestrictedly lord it over their employees as minions. Yet this did not completely eventuate, as the "Vertrauensrat" (consultative council) system established in 1934 under the control of the Deutsche Arbeitsfront (DAF) also insisted on the council having a say in discussions of accidents and being empowered to inspect accident sites on its own.[37] Line manager Meyer at pithead II/VI/IX, who wanted to tell the DAF company administrator Heinrich Klöcker to refrain from taking part in retrospective inspections to clarify the causes of "accidents" in future, was forced in his statement of 7 December 1934 to the Buer Mining Office to give ground.[38] The colliery management believed that Klöcker's complaint had "most probably stemmed from some personal annoyance".[39] In summer 1935, at the Graf Bismarck colliery representatives of the consultative council participated in works inspections by the mining authorities on average 16 times a month.[40]

---

36 Geschäftsbericht der Deutschen Erdöl-Aktiengesellschaft in Berlin über das 35. Geschäftsjahr 1933, Berlin 1934, 2.

37 Betriebswalter Heinrich Klöcker an Kreisamtsleitung der NSBO und DAF, 16.11.1934, LAV NRW, dept. Westfalen, Bergämter No. 8111.

38 Betriebsführer Meyer, Erklärung, 7.12.1934, ibid.

39 Bergassessor Whennan, Stellungnahme, 28.11.1934, 3, ibid.

40 Bergrevier Buer an Oberbergrat Bickhoff, 6.9.1935, ibid.

In the first half of 1934, production and unit sales rose 20 percent thanks to participation in the sales of the coal syndicate, which the DEA Supervisory Board judged as a positive sign of a nascent upturn in the company.[41] A syndicate levy down almost five percent created greater financial scope, since the surplus increased again by 180,000 Reichsmark, yet the increased demand also meant there were new hirings, and this slowly started to offset the reduction in jobs in Gelsenkirchen during the Great Depression.[42]As a sign of symbolic support of Nazi regime, the DEA Management Board of the Graf Bismarck colliery donated 500 Reichsmark for the erection of a monument to fallen miners in the Senior Mining District (Oberbergamtsbezirk) of Dortmund.[43]

The number of idle shifts at the Königsgrube colliery climbed in 1933 to 63, up 46 on the year, only to fall to 29 in 1934. However, the payroll increased steadily from the end of 1932 to the end of 1933 from 1,086 to 1,108 persons. At the end of 1934, the figure had risen to 1,163, which led to a clear improvement in the mood among mining families.[44] The Luise pithead at the Königsgrube colliery was given a new conveyor machine building in 1933, and this served to boost production to 415,000 tonnes. Yet the economic situation remained tense, to the extent that Magdeburger Bergwerks-AG, as in the prior year, forewent payment of a dividend.[45] In terms of business administration, 1934 was the turning point, as production at the Königsgrube colliery rose to 485,000 tonnes.

---

[41] Niederschrift über die Verhandlungen des Aufsichtsrats der DEA, 13.9.1934, 2, WD-CA, D-PA-0120.

[42] Ibid., 3 and 6.

[43] DEA-Vorstandssitzung, 23.1.1934, 3, WD-CA, D-PA-24.

[44] Zweijahresbericht des Bergrevierbeamten des Bergreviers Herne als Gewerbeaufsichtsbeamter für die Jahre 1933 und 1934, 6, LAV NRW, dept. Westfalen, Bergämter No. 7593.

[45] Geschäftsbericht der Deutschen Erdöl-Aktiengesellschaft in Berlin über das 35. Geschäftsjahr 1933, Berlin 1934, 3.

Although DEA was the dominant shareholder in Magdeburger Bergwerks-AG with its stake of 91.3 percent, for fiscal reasons on 18 July 1935, it acquired the lease to the Königsgrube colliery as at the beginning of the year. The lease agreement was initially signed for three years up to 31 December 1937, as approved by the Reich Economics Ministry and envisaged Magdeburger Bergwerks-AG "replacing the amortization and the interest on the loan capital". Moreover, DEA assumed the dividend guarantee to the external shareholders on a scale of a DEA dividend, and at least of four percent.[46] The administration of the Königsgrube colliery took over the far larger Graf Bismarck colliery.[47] Magdeburger Bergwerks-AG was integrated into the DEA group as well as various lignite mining operations subsidiaries in 1936 in the course of reorganization.[48]

In early 1935, the DEA Management Board retained its cautious stance on new investments in hard coal plant with a view to prioritizing production of tar oil from lignite, and waited to see whether demand for hard coal would rise enduringly. For the time being, only the "deserved average amortization" of about 1.5 million Reichsmark would be available for new buildings.[49] At any rate, in the first half of 1935 demand indeed became brisker, such that the Graf Bismarck and Königsgrube mines for hard coal started to move "on a gradually upward course".[50] On this basis, the payroll at the

---

46 Pachtvertrag der DEA mit der Magdeburger Bergwerks-AG, 18.7.1935, 1ff., WD-CA, D-RW-186.

47 Geschäftsbericht der Deutschen Erdöl-Aktiengesellschaft in Berlin über das 37. Geschäftsjahr 1935, Berlin 1936, 2; Niederschrift über die Verhandlungen des Aufsichtsrats der DEA, 1.10.1935, 2ff., WD-CA, D-PA-0120.

48 Niederschrift über die Verhandlungen des Aufsichtsrats der DEA, 20.11.1936, 2ff., ibid.

49 Niederschrift über die Verhandlungen des Aufsichtsrats der DEA, 4.3.1935, 6, ibid.

50 Niederschrift über die Verhandlungen des Aufsichtsrats der DEA, 1.10.1935, 8, ibid.

Königsgrube colliery remained on a steady level, with 1,173 employees at year-end 1936.[51]

Formally speaking, the Nazi Party had firmly established itself in the driving seat. Since reports on sentiment at the collieries did not include statements on the company parades carried out on 30 January 1935, which were held to mark the second anniversary of the Nazis coming to power, on 12 February 1935 the Senior Mining Office in Dortmund instructed the Mining Offices to submit special reports. At the Königsgrube colliery, a company parade had been held after the end of the morning shift, and all the "loyal comrades" took part in it, with the exception of a few machine operators who had to ensure works safety.[52] The frequent parades, marches, and addresses during the period when the Nazi rulers were still consolidating their positions served to prove their power for all to see and to indoctrinate those miners who were initially more reserved towards the Party. Once parades had long since become routine, they ceased to have any special significance.

Beneath the surface, however, there were cracks in the Nazified company community (Betriebsgemeinschaft). A vote conducted in April 1935 among the 90 employees in the main administration office for the Gelsenkirchen collieries to choose who would be appointed "trusted representatives" saw a turn-out of 87.7 percent, which was below the usual participation and approval scale during the Nazi dictatorship.[53] Admittedly, turnout among the 2,109 members of staff at pithead I/IV was 88.5 percent, and the company superintendent and the DAF company cell superintendent polled

---

51 Zweijahresbericht des Bergrevierbeamten Rudolph des Bergreviers Herne als Gewerbeaufsichtsbeamter für die Jahre 1935 und 1936, 14.1.1937, 8, LAV NRW, dept. Westfalen, Bergämter No. 7593.

52 Magdeburger Bergwerks AG, Zeche Königsgrube, Max Fröhlich an Bergrevier Herne, 16.2.1935, LAV NRW, dept. Westfalen, Bergämter No. 7441.

53 Abstimmungsleiter Stichmann, Ergebnis über die Abstimmung zu der Liste der Vertrauensmänner am 12. April 1935 für die Hauptverwaltung, 12.4.1935, LAV NRW, dept. Westfalen, Bergämter No. 8111; Wisotzky, *Ruhrbergbau*, 104ff. and 273ff.

Fig. 19 The "Graf Bismarck" colliery complex around 1930

1,357 and 1,363 respectively and duly took their places on the consultative council. Yet of the total votes of 1,867, no fewer than 402 persons or 21.5 percent rejected the "entire list of candidates".[54] Just short of a further 100 voted against the candidates on the list, while at pithead II/VI/IX, 223 or 14.8 percent of the 1,502 participants rejected the entire list.[55] Indeed, a minority of those eligible to poll used their votes to demonstrate opposition to the institution of a consultative council controlled by the Nazis, and one could sense the

54 Abstimmungsleiter Meyer, Ergebnis über die Abstimmung zu der Liste der Vertrauensmänner am 12./13. April 1935 für Schachtanlage I/IV, 15.4.1935, LAV NRW, dept. Westfalen, Bergämter No. 8111.

55 Abstimmungsleiter Meyer, Ergebnis über die Abstimmung zu der Liste der Vertrauensmänner am 12./13. April 1935 für Schachtanlage II/IV/IX , 13.4.1935, ibid.; a similar result was also achieved at the pit VII/VIII; Abstimmungsleiter Bruch, Ergebnis über die Abstimmung zu der Liste der Vertrauensmänner am 12./13. April 1935 für Schachtanlage VII/VIII, 13.4.1935, ibid.

rejection of the Nazi regime among a remaining set of employees.[56] At pithead III/V, where 97.9 percent of the employees cast a vote, 23 of the 91 ballot papers were illegible. One member of staff opposed the Nazis' insistence on uniformity by rejecting the entire list of candidates. Meanwhile, the 45 votes that went to the mine deputy standing for the DAF contrasted with the no less than 22 votes (or one third) that expressly turned him down.[57]

DEA's profits rose in 1935 thanks to lower operating costs, with the number of idle shifts remaining at a low level. Although demand continued to pick up, the Graf Bismarck colliery again imposed an idle shift on 19 February 1936,[58] but the payroll size remained constant: Ongoing rationalization of mining operations as well as the new building and expansion work meant that daily output had been boosted to such a point that if orders were not called down the interim storage facilities swiftly became overflowed. DEA planned in 1936 initially to invest a total of 1.5 million Reichsmark in the two pitheads, and in the years that followed a further three million Reichsmark were to be committed to them.[59] Production in the pitheads at the Königsgrube colliery likewise increased significantly between 1933 and 1937. What were now greater production costs were offset by higher revenue owing to the greater demand and the reduced syndicate levy. Unit sales via the Rhineland-Westphalian Coal Syndicate rose from 50.42 to 64.26 percent, which can be read

---

56 See Rüdiger Hachtmann, *Industriearbeit im "Dritten Reich". Untersuchungen zu den Lohn- und Arbeitsbedingungen in Deutschland 1933–1945*, Göttingen 1988, 31ff.; Detlev Peukert, *Die KPD im Widerstand. Verfolgung und Untergrundarbeit an Rhein und Ruhr 1933–1945*, Wuppertal 1980, 204ff.; Milert/Tschirbs, *Die andere Demokratie*, 272ff.

57 Abstimmungsleiter Wagener, Ergebnis über die Abstimmung zu der Liste der Vertrauensmänner am 12. April 1935 für Schachtanlage III/V, 12.4.1935, LAV NRW, dept. Westfalen, Bergämter No. 8111.

58 DEA-Vorstandssitzung, 18.2.1936, 3, WD-CA, D-PA-2.

59 Niederschrift über die Verhandlungen des Aufsichtsrats der DEA, 4.3.1936, 5, WD-CA, D-PA-0120.

as an indicator of how strongly networked both collieries were with the Ruhr-region industry.

Mine hard coal output (in tonnes) 1933–1938[60]

Year	Graf Bismarck	Königsgrube	Total output
1933	1,606,378	414,584	2,020,962
1934	1,868,683	485,363	2,354,046
1935	1,996,268	522,813	2,519,081
1936	2,143,325	525,107	2,668,432
1937	2,697,774	600,533	3,298,307
1938	2,708,589	584,486	3,293,075

The Graf Bismarck colliery came to the attention of the state police office in Recklinghausen, which was responsible for operations in the Münster government area, when in July 1935 the "Manchester Guardian" reported on "workers' unrest" and a strike there. There were also rumours in Münsterland that the poor economic situation was leading to the miners not going down into the pits but going on hunger strike instead. Another claim was that a delegation from the Gelsenkirchen Graf Bismarck and Consolidation collieries "had been sent to the Führer".[61] According to the Gestapo, there was no substance to the rumours, and miner Heinrich Jansen, who lived in Holsterhausen outside Recklinghausen and had been a member of the Communist Party-affiliated "Kampfbund gegen den Faschismus" (Combat League against Fascism) in 1932, was detained at the end of July 1935 for spreading the rumour and was sentenced in November 1935 to three months in jail for this "malice". Jansen was released from the court prison in Recklinghausen on 23 December

60 Statistiken Graf Bismarck und Königsgrube, WD-CA, D-RW-128.

61 Staatspolizeistelle Recklinghausen (II/3-172/35 No. 2130/35), Dr. Fischer, an Oberpräsident Münster, 3.8.1935, LAV NRW, dept. Westfalen, Oberpräsidium, No. 5030.

1935.[62] In other words, a single person lent expression to the dissatisfaction of many miners with their social situation, but such actions no longer stirred up the masses.[63]

Like mining in the Ruhr region as a whole, after 1936 DEA intensified its in-company social welfare programme at its pitheads.[64] DEA's annual report for 1937 boasts of extensive in-company social welfare provisions totalling 2.5 million Reichsmark. These also included a "bonus" of a total of 325,000 Reichsmark granted to the staff of the Graf Bismarck colliery as a thank-you for the increase in coal production per head.[65] In the same vein, two percent of the miners' annual income was shelled out on top of their agreed wages. DEA allocated 750,000 Reichsmark to the reserves for social support and pension commitments, to the extent that the former grew to just short of 1.9 million Reichsmark. Assuring staff loyalty was also the intention behind providing works apartments and granting building loans, so that no less than 43 percent of the staff in the hard coal operations lived in company housing or in flats the company helped finance. Particular attention was paid to the teaching workshops intended to "train suitable young men", and by the end of 1937 375 "young miners" had been trained there ready to serve in the coal mines.[66] Moreover, in 1936 DEA hired a "works care-worker" for the Graf Bismarck colliery, who was meant to address the social needs of the mining families but applied völkisch-racist criteria in doing so.

---

62 Karteikarten von Gefangenen des Gerichtsgefängnisses Recklinghausen, 6.10.1932-31.1.1956, http://collections.arolsen-arcjhives.org/de/document/12161436 [last retrieved on 1.7.2024].

63 Wisotzky, *Ruhrbergbau*, 139ff.

64 Ibid., 179ff.

65 DEA-Vorstandssitzung, 7.7.1937, 4, WD-CA, D-PA-29.

66 Geschäftsbericht der Deutschen Erdöl-Aktiengesellschaft in Berlin über das 39. Geschäftsjahr 1937, Berlin 1938, 7.

At the same time, a "school for infants" (Kleinkinderschule) was set up at Graf Bismarck pithead I/IV.[67]

In the context of the DAF "Schönheit der Arbeit" (beauty of work) programme, the interior of the social rooms was improved; moreover, the company supported participation in events held by Nazi organizations such as the "Kraft durch Freude" (strength trough joy, KdF) programme by providing free tickets or subsidies for KdF trips. In order to establish a Nazi "company community", the mining operations arranged "company parades, evenings for comrades, joint outings, company celebrations" and the like.[68] Political indoctrination took place, for example, through collective sessions listening to radio broadcasts of speeches by Nazi politicians. Moreover, the company provided financial support for staff members delegated to attend the Nazi Party "Reich Party Conference" and other Party and DAF events. According to the DEA, there was "good cooperation" with the DAF company superintendent and the consultative council members formed for the pitheads.[69] The DAF was also active in the field of accident protection measures, and from February 1936 onwards the Mining Office official responsible regularly lectured at the consultative councils of the various pitheads at the Graf Bismarck colliery.[70] One member of the latter and two DAF company superintendents were correspondingly trained at Party Ordensburg Erwitte (Castle of the Order in Erwitte) and assumed

67 Jahresbericht des Bergreviers Buer für das Jahr 1936, 15, LAV NRW, dept. Westfalen, Bergämter No. 8089.

68 Geschäftsbericht der Deutschen Erdöl-Aktiengesellschaft in Berlin über das 39. Geschäftsjahr 1937, Berlin 1938, 8.

69 Geschäftsbericht der Deutschen Erdöl-Aktiengesellschaft in Berlin über das 39. Geschäftsjahr 1937, Berlin 1938, 8; Jahresbericht des Bergreviers Buer für das Jahr 1937, 17, LAV NRW, dept. Westfalen, Bergämter No. 8089.

70 Arbeitsschutz-Vortrag für die Vertrauensmänner der Schachtanlagen Graf Bismarck, 17.2.1936, LAV NRW, dept. Westfalen, Bergämter No. 8111; Besprechung über Maßnahmen zur Verhütung von Unglücksfällen auf der Schachtanlage Graf Bismarck 1/4, 18.1.1937, ibid.

the office of "work protection administrator".[71] The completion of additional "shelter installations" erected as part of the air-raid protection measures gave a foretaste of the increasing militarization of company life.[72]

Even if the DEA mines management invested in the infrastructure for a Nazi "company community", the relations between the mines in the Ruhr region and the Nazi Party remained ambivalent with regard to in-company social welfare policies. The Gau Economic Adviser (Gauwirtschaftsberater) in the Nazi Party Gau in North Westphalia, Christian Franke, sought to establish a housing society with capital of 100,000 Reichsmark to promote housing in the Nazi Party Gau that he represented, but in 1937 his idea was not particularly welcomed by the management of the Graf Bismarck colliery. In order to avoid becoming directly allied with a Nazi Party functionary and undertaking a joint venture with the Nazi Party in the form of a public-private project, the Management Board member responsible for the hard coal division, Albert Ritter, with the full agreement of the other coal industrialists, proposed instead that a "disposable fund" be made available to Nazi Party Gauleiter Alfred Meyer and said he would make suggestions as to what it should include.[73] Efforts were made by the Nazi Party Gau in South Westphalia (whose ambit covered the Königsgrube colliery) to provide political "training for the senior gentlemen", something that the head of the District Group Coal Mining Ruhr attached to the Mining Economic Group, Ernst Buskühl, declined on behalf of the

71 DEA, Zechen Graf Bismarck und Königsgrube an Bergrevier Buer, 8.11.1937, ibid.

72 Geschäftsbericht der Deutschen Erdöl-Aktiengesellschaft in Berlin über das 39. Geschäftsjahr 1937, Berlin 1938, 7.

73 DEA-Vorstandssitzung, 28.6.1937, 3, WD-CA, D-PA-29; see Gerhard Kratzsch, *Das wirtschaftspolitische Gauamt der Gauwirtschaftsberater*, in: Jürgen John (Eds.), Die NS-Gaue. Regionale Mittelinstanzen im zentralistischen "Führerstaat", Munich 2007, 218–233; zu Gauleiter Meyer see Heinz-Jürgen Priamus, *Meyer. Zwischen Kaisertreue und NS-Täterschaft. Biographische Konturen eines deutschen Bürgers*, Essen 2011, 236ff.

industry, citing the executives' complete concentration on boosting output.

The management of the Graf Bismarck colliery intended to increase the volume of lower-quality coal it mined and then use it itself. This was linked to the renewal of the electricity generation facilities at the mine, which was necessary anyway, since it sought to become the provider of electricity to the city of Gelsenkirchen.[74] Moreover, it was willing in principle to participate more intensively in supplying the Ruhr region with power in the context of the Rhineland-Westphalian Coal Syndicate.[75] Even if the detailed arrangements still needed to be made, at pithead I in the Graf Bismarck colliery, a power station was set up at a cost of 4 million Reichsmark with three modern high-pressure boilers and turbogenerators, with the plan being to operate them with low-quality coal from the company's own mines. Alongside providing electricity to the works, the power station, when commissioned in 1938, could also provide electricity to third parties. The integration of Ruhr mining into the general power grid was handled by Steinkohlen-Elektrizitäts AG (Steag), in whose equity capital, now raised to 25 million Reichsmark, DEA acquired 653,000 Reichsmark in early 1939 in line with its stake in the syndicate.[76]

Possibly the DEA mines' greatest contribution to integrating their staff into the Nazi system was the growth in output and payroll. In 1937 at the Graf Bismarck colliery, pithead I/III went back into

---

[74] Niederschrift über die Verhandlungen des Aufsichtsrats der DEA, 25.5.1936, 6f., WD-CA, D-PA-0120.

[75] DEA-Vorstandssitzung, 11.2.1937, 1f., WD-CA, D-PA-29; Jahresbericht des Bergreviers Buer für das Jahr 1936, 10f., LAV NRW, dept. Westfalen, Bergämter No. 8089; Jahresbericht des Bergreviers Buer für das Jahr 1937, 11, ibid.

[76] Geschäftsbericht der Deutschen Erdöl-Aktiengesellschaft in Berlin über das 39. Geschäftsjahr 1937, Berlin 1938, 1; Niederschrift über die Verhandlungen des Aufsichtsrats der DEA,14.3.1939, 4, WD-CA, D-PA-0120; Dietmar Bleidick, *Die Energieregion Ruhrgebiet, Eine historisch-statistische Studie*, Baden-Baden 2023, 135ff.

operation after five years of suspension, with coal cutting starting again. Coal production then commenced in autumn 1938. Although only 220 tonnes were mined a day, the fact that all the pitheads were back producing was an important symbolic act, showing that the former crisis had been overcome once and for all.[77] In 1937-8, however, mechanization of mine operations came up against initial limits as, for example, highly volatile coal still had to be mined by hand using jackhammers. Only a small portion of the coal was loosened with mechanical cuts or blasting.

Total output of the two DEA collieries stagnated in 1937-8 at a little over 3 million tonnes. Compared to the figure of just under 2 million tonnes in 1932, this meant an improvement of over 50 percent. In 1938, the set of pitheads at Graf Bismarck was producing more than 2.7 million tonnes and was placed third in the Ruhr mine league tables. Königsgrube was, by contrast, in the lower ranks, turning out 586,000 tonnes.[78] The economic upturn continued to drive a clear increase in staffing levels. While the Graf Bismarck colliery had 5,051 staff on the books in 1936, by 1938 the figure had climbed by more than a third to 6,913. At that point in time, the Königsgrube colliery employed 1,600 persons.[79]

From 1938 onwards, however, it became clear that willingness among 14-16-year-olds to choose mining as a profession was sharply declining, so there were concerns about how to recruit a sufficient number of duly qualified new miners.[80] All in all, mining in the Ruhr region was heading for structural difficulties in economic and social terms, and this caused concern for the Nazi Party about

77 Jahresbericht des Bergreviers Buer für das Jahr 1938, 2f. and 12, LAV NRW, dept. Westfalen, Bergämter No. 8089.

78 Hans-Christoph Seidel, *Der Ruhrbergbau im Zweiten Weltkrieg. Zechen – Bergarbeiter – Zwangsarbeiter*, Essen 2010, 574 and 578.

79 Jahresbericht des Bergreviers Buer für das Jahr 1937, 2, 5 and 12, LAV NRW, dept. Westfalen, Bergämter No. 8089; Seidel, *Ruhrbergbau*, 574 and 578.

80 Jahresbericht des Bergreviers Buer für das Jahr 1938, 17, LAV NRW, dept. Westfalen, Bergämter No. 8089; Wisotzky, *Ruhrbergbau*, 243ff.

whether the energy base required for armaments and the war could be secured. The crisis in sales of the early 1930s had morphed into a production crisis in 1938-9. The high demand for coal could no longer be met with the given staff levels, and only by extending working hours and making it harder to change jobs could companies foresee overcoming the problems. While the bitter pill of longer working hours could be sweetened with the offering of higher wages, disciplinary measures and conflicts – for example over food provisions – led to a rise in unexcused absenteeism, a trend that undermined the expected rise in output.[81] The issue of a lack of workers remained unsolved.

---

81 Seidel, *Ruhrbergbau*, 73ff. and 128ff.; see too Dieter Ziegler, *Kriegswirtschaft, Kriegsfolgenbewältigung, Kriegsvorbereitung. Der deutsche Bergbau im dauernden Ausnahmezustand (1914–1945)*, in: id. (Ed.), Rohstoffgewinnung im Strukturwandel. Der deutsche Bergbau im 20. Jahrhundert, Münster 2013, 15–182, esp. 146ff.

The Nazis assert their power, and the expansion of the DEA lignite production hubs around Rositz

As was the case in many other companies, when the coalition of the Nazi Party and the Deutschnationale Volkspartei (German Nationalist People's Party, DNVP) took power on 30 January 1933, the local management in Rositz led by Max Heyne and Hans Hase started to hope that the crisis would soon be overcome. It is possible that when the navy called down a modest volume of 1,600 tonnes of heating oil at the end of February 1933, this was considered a favourable sign that the remaining order sum of 2,000 tonnes would soon be increased by new orders.[82] To promote "the provision of work", a coal rail track was installed from the Waltersdorf pit to the briquette factory at the Altenburger Kohlenwerke, and the Ramsdorf underground mine went back into operation. Moreover, the Waltersdorf II open-cast mine was re-opened, and productivity was boosted with more intense large-scale open-cast mining at the Regis and Witznitz pits.[83]

It would be overly simplistic, however, to assume that the Rositz management were resolute Nazi Party members or sympathizers. For Director Heyne informed his colleague Hans Hase that the DNVP held an election event at the Concordia colliery on 26 February 1933 featuring Walther Rademacher, DEA Director of the Senior Mining Directorate Borna, who was campaigning to be elected to parliament. Citing DEA authorized signatory Robert Hanke, who was present at the event, Heyne reported that Rademacher "performed very well" in the Concordia Hall, which

---

82 Max Heyne an Hans Hase vom 27.2.1933, 1, StA Leipzig, Bestand 20684, DEA-Mineralölwerke Rositz, No. 2.

83 Geschäftsbericht der Deutschen Erdöl-Aktiengesellschaft in Berlin über das 35. Geschäftsjahr 1933, Berlin 1934, 1f.

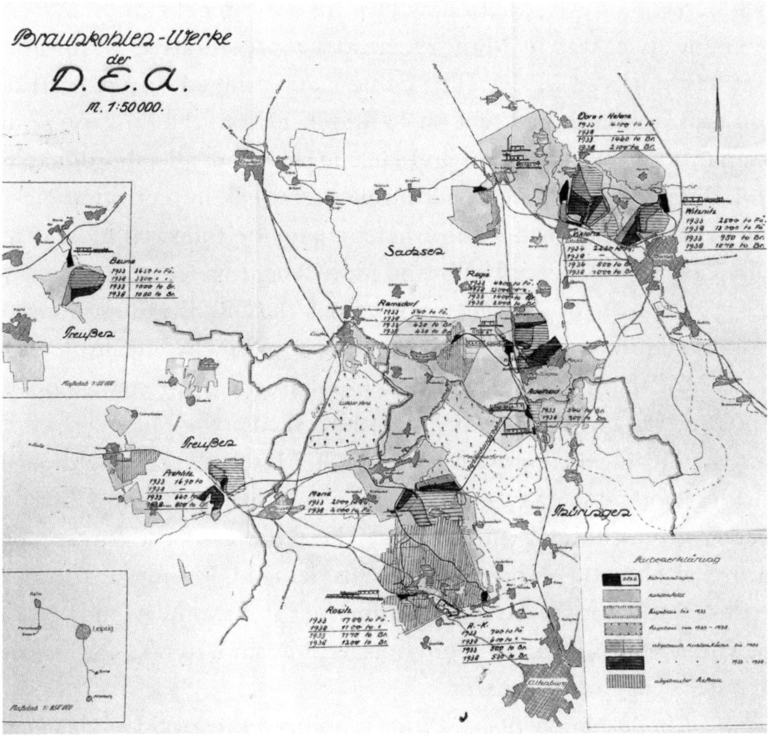

Fig. 20 The DEA Lignite mines in Saxony and Thuringia (1938)

was fairly full and noticeably attended by many DEA staff members.[84]

Exuberant following the election of the new government, the Nazi Party District Head (Kreisleiter) in Borna, Friedrich Munde, sought to curtail the local claims to power by the director of the DEA Senior Mining Directorate (Oberbergdirektion) Borna, Albert Gebhardt. Gebhardt, who made no bones about his DNVP

84 Max Heyne an Hans Hase, 27.2.1933, 3, StA Leipzig, Bestand 20684, DEA-Mineralölwerke Rositz, No. 2.

membership and was well-known for his patriarchal corporate management style, was to Munde's mind a representative of an order that had outlived its day. The controversy hinged on the instruction that Gebhardt had sent on 14 March 1933 to the directorates in Bauna, Witznitz, and Dorn and Helene that were all subordinate to him, directing that "great caution be exercised" in recruiting Nazis and "that Nazi efforts within the company be followed most carefully". He would, he said, allow no more "disturbance of in-company peace" from them than he would from the "Red trade unions".[85] Munde said that by refusing to hire Nazis and by his insulting comparison of them with "Marxists", Gebhardt was the one who was "most endangering" public "calm and security". The Nazi Party District Head called on Gebhardt on 20 March 1933 "to relinquish within the course of this day" the helm to his deputy and "immediately go on holiday and to leave the region for the foreseeable future".[86] Should Gebhardt ignore this demand, Munde, as the local representative of the State Commissioner in Saxony, would call on the Amtshauptmannschaft (provincial leadership) to take the "necessary steps" against Gebhardt.

On 22 March 1933, Munde mobilized the local Gendarmerie in order to force Gebhardt to remain in the Senior Mining Directorate office until the Kreishauptmannschaft Leipzig (district leadership) had issued instructions to Theodor Mittasch as the Amtshauptmann in Borna, a status equivalent to a state councillor (Landrat) in Prussia. Gebhardt did not allow himself to "be pushed around and robbed of his freedom", whereupon Munde prohibited him in writing from leaving his home "in the interests of his integrity". That the Nazi Party functionary usurped the official powers of the Amtshauptmann was something he asked Mittasch to excuse when asking

---

85 Albert Gebhardt an Betriebsdirektion Bauna, Wirtnitz, Dora & Helene, 14.3.1933, BArch Berlin, R 1501, No. 5023, sheet 19.

86 NSDAP-Kreisleiter Borna, Friedrich Munde, an Günther Gebhardt, 20.3.1933, ibid., 17f.

the latter to retrospectively approve the act. At the same time, he encouraged Mittasch to use his personal contact with Director Gebhardt to prompt the latter "to give in".[87]

With the approval of the Borna Amtshauptmann, Gebhardt, whom the Nazi Party District Head had threatened with "detention", was placed under police guard in his home, ostensibly in order to ensure that "no attacks on him were possible".[88] On 23 March 1933, the Reich Ministry of the Interior wired an instruction to the Reich Commissioner (Reichskommissar) for Saxony Manfred von Killinger, who had been appointed by the Reich government, that the measures be discontinued. District Head Munde emphasized in his statement that Gebhardt had been "ruthless and overbearing in his treatment" of the employees and had therefore ensured that "Marxism had gained the upper hand in the company's operations" and was a "prominent representative" of the DNVP.[89] Munde continued to try and persuade Gebhardt to leave Borna and encouraged the Reich Ministry of the Interior to prompt DEA to immediately post Gebhardt to a position elsewhere.

For his part, Gebhardt mobilized support: According to Munde, he had been accused by the lawyer of the Leipzig DNVP of himself disturbing the public peace and order, whereby the lawyer had threatened that the staff at the lignite works would go on strike and assemble in Borna to proclaim their confidence in Gebhardt. Moreover, the Stahlhelm League of First World War veterans was considering violent intervention, which Munde rated as an attempt to agitate. Amtshauptmann Mittasch, he said, prevented any escalation. According to District Head Munde, 90 percent of the offi-

87 Ibid.

88 Friedrich Munde, Vertrauensmann des Staatskommissars im Bezirk der Amtshauptmannschaft Borna, an den Herrn Reichsminister des Innern, 28.3.1933, 1, ibid, 1.

89 Friedrich Munde, Vertrauensmann des Staatskommissars im Bezirk der Amtshauptmannschaft Borna, an den Herrn Reichsminister des Innern, 28.3.1933, 2, ibid., 3.

cials and salaried staff at DEA's Dora and Helene works in Gross Zossen thereupon "defiantly" joined the Nazi Party, which he interpreted as a sign of the staff rejecting the mining director.[90] Walther Rademacher, who, as a DNVP politician and DEA manager, had until then enjoyed the support of his superiors, by no means stood loyally at Gebhardt's side. But his lack of political spine did not in the end pay off for him. In March 1933 he took his seat in the Reichstag for the DNVP, but at the combined vote for the "people's referendum" in November 1933 on the foreign policy course Nazi Germany should take and the new Reichstag, he was no longer put up for election and lost his seat.

Like other local and regional Nazi Party politicians, Nazi Party District Head Munde sought to gain direct influence over companies in order to assert himself against the long-standing hegemony of the economic elites. Evidently, the self-confident dominance of Mining Director Gebhardt, whom Munde termed an "autocrat", was a source of annoyance for the Nazi Party. Given that the Nazi Party wanted to make certain that business activity proceeded as smoothly as possible and therefore insisted that the lower Party echelons should desist from spontaneous intervention, Munde had to keep himself in check for the time being in the interest of smoothly acquiring and consolidating political power. Alternating radicalization and restraint were the maxim to prevent the DNVP and its supporters from opposing the "Government of National Concentration", as it was called.

The DEA senior executives, for their part, were not interested in escalating the conflict with the Nazi Party in Saxony and attempted to retire Gebhardt as quietly as possible. The DEA board wanted to avoid upsetting the apple cart and therefore to remove the politically controversial figure of Gebhardt from sight. "In order to

---

90 Friedrich Munde, Vertrauensmann des Staatskommissars im Bezirk der Amtshauptmannschaft Borna, an den Herrn Reichsminister des Innern, 28.3.1933, 6, ibid.

arrange his personal affairs once and for all", the DEA Management Board ordered him to appear before them in Berlin on 25 November 1933.[91] In December 1933, further negotiations were held on the best approach to take.[92] The DEA heads were not prepared to grant him a seat on the Supervisory Board or to give him a consultancy contract for four years, and instead they wanted Gebhardt to simply agree to the one or other Supervisory Board seat in group member companies.[93] Here, the DEA Management Board tried to de-escalate things, not out of political motives but solely in pursuit of their material interests, which they felt they could assert more easily under the new rulers. This made it imperative to reach a consensus with the new form of politics, so the idea was to make Gebhardt's farewell sweeter by gifting him a car. The Management Board was not prepared to make any further concessions to Gebhardt, and no agreement had been reached on the details of his pension by the autumn of 1934.[94] The conflict with Albert Gebhardt, who had put his finger on the initially limited reach of the powers of the local Nazi Party elite, was something the latter remembered for a long time to come. As the Nazi Party proceeded to shore up its power base, the dispute over the primacy of politics as opposed to that of business continually flared up.

Over and above the Gebhardt case, the local Nazi politicians had fundamental reservations about the DEA corporation. On 8 August 1933 the DEA Senior Mining Directorate in Altenburg, which managed all the mining operations the group owned in Thuringia, wrote an extensive letter to the Altenburg Lord Mayor (Oberbürgermeister) Franz Reible, who had been pushed into office

---

91 DEA-Vorstandssitzung, 23.11.1933, 1, WD-CA, D-PA-24.

92 DEA-Vorstandssitzung, 8.12.1933, 1, ibid.

93 DEA-Vorstandssitzung, 23.1.1934, 1, ibid.

94 DEA-Vorstandssitzung, 13.2.1934, 2, ibid.; DEA-Vorstandssitzung, 20.2.1934, 1; DEA-Vorstandssitzung, 2.3.1934, 1; DEA-Vorstandssitzung, 5.4.1934, 3, ibid; DEA-Vorstandssitzung, 27.6.1934, 1; DEA-Vorstandssitzung, 25.9.1934, 1, ibid.

in spring 1933.[95] In it, they sought to dispel the claim that DEA was a major corporation interested solely in its profits during a time of great social need, and pointed to its broad activities to reduce unemployment. However, the Altenburg Nazi Party started to spread the rumour that in DEA companies there were a "large number of Communists and Marxist leaders among the workforce". In order to refute all claims that the company supported the Nazis' political enemies in any way, Walther Randhahn, since 1923 head of the DEA Senior Mining Directorate Altenburg, offered to "fire those persons" who could be proven to have been conducting Communist or Social Democratic activities, "and hire in their place suitable persons from the nationalist camp".[96]

However, the Altenburg Lord Mayor and the Party "Alter Kämpfer" Bernhard Giesselmann, who had joined the Nazi Party on 1 March 1930 and was Chairman of the City Council and, from 15 August 1933 onwards, head of the local welfare office,[97] refused to let up. They claimed that DEA was ostensibly "working against the interests of the city and the Nazi Party", and Reible even threatened Randhahn "with dismissal, detention, and concentration camp".[98] Both Nazi Party politicians may have had a fundamental dislike of the DEA corporation, internally and publicly – for example, at the Nazi Party District Congress in September 1933 (attended by 3,000 people), they created the impression that DEA systematically disadvantaged unemployed inhabitants of Altenburg when it came to new

---

95 Franz Reible, Parteikorrespondenz und Parteiunterlagen, BArch Berlin, R 9361-I/2807; R 9361-II/1050000.

96 DEA-Oberbergdirektion Altenburg, Walther Randhahn/Lampe, an Oberbürgermeister Franz Reible, 8.8.1933, 5, WD-CA, D-PA 90.

97 DFG-VK Darmstadt, Giesselmann, Bernhard, https://dfg-vk-darmstadt.de/Lexikon_Auflage_2/GiesselmannBernhard.htm [last retrieved on 1.6.2024]; see too BArch Berlin, R 1501/206616; R 9361-II/294297.

98 DEA betr. Beschwerde gegen den Stadtvorstand Altenburg (Entwurf) o.D. [26.9.1933), WD-CA, D-PA-90; DEA-Oberbergdirektion Altenburg, Walther Randhahn, DEA-Vorstand, 26.9.1933, WD-CA, D-PA-90.

recruits for the Regis works. The local Nazi Party simply ignored the fact that, at the end of July 1933, of the total payroll of 1,135, 150 of the employees already lived in Altenburg, whereas six months earlier the figure had been 118. They also carefully omitted to mention that new hirings were only possible with the express approval of the Borna Labour Office. Above all Bernhard Giesselmann, who until 15 August 1933 had spent 13 years working for the company, reaching the position of head of the Legal and Land department at DEA Senior Mining Directorate Altenburg, clearly still had a bone to pick with his former employer. With contrafactual claims, he mobilized opposition to it, particularly among the unemployed.

On 20 September 1933, Giesselmann discredited Randhahn in person at a public assembly on the occasion of the winter support campaign against hunger and cold that Hitler had launched seven days earlier; it was framed as the "Winterhilfswerk des Deutschen Volkes" (Winter Support Programme of the German People) and came under the jurisdiction of the Nationalsozialistische Volkswohlfahrt (Nazi People's Welfare) scheme.[99] Giesselmann criticized that a magnate who had an income of more than 50,000 Reichsmark only donated 20 Reichsmark a month to the Welfare Office and had said he would only double the amount if he received an "income tax exemption" for the sum. Mining Director Randhahn issued a formal complaint on 27 September 1933 against the "worst possible form of slander". He opened a lawsuit for "gross breach of confidence" committed by Giesselmann, who had sent an official request to the Inland Revenue office to obtain information on Randhahn's private income and had then, with slanderous intention, deliberately completely understated the donations Randhahn made, as from January to September 1933 his donations were not a monthly 20 but a total of no less than 716.30 Reichsmark. Randhahn listed 189.30 Reichsmark

---

99 Florian Tennstedt, *Wohltat und Interesse. Das Winterhilfswerk des Deutschen Volkes. Die Weimarer Vorgeschichte und ihre Instrumentalisierung durch das NS-Regime*, in: Geschichte und Gesellschaft 2 (1987), 157–180.

for the "Reichstagswahl, Partei und Stahlhelm", 37 Reichsmark for the "Winterhilfswerk 1932-3", 200 Reichsmark as a "Spende zur Förderung der nationalen Arbeit", 250 Reichsmark as a "Sauckel-Marschler-Spende", and 40 Reichsmark for the "Altenburger Wohlfahrtsspende". He clearly felt he was on the back foot, as he designated the sum of 807.98 Reichsmark he had paid for improvements to the grounds of his house as "in the interests of creating jobs and in pursuit of the calls repeatedly made by the Reich and state governments".[100] Declaring the purchase of a "compact car" for his son for 2,300 Reichsmark, in place of a planned holiday abroad, as a measure to stabilize the German economy hardly attested to a great feel for the social reservations that were running riot in a region in crisis against "fat cats" employed in large corporations.

Randhahn called on the DEA Management Board the same day to approach the Minister President of Thuringia, Willy Marschler, in writing, and to send a copy of the missive to State Secretary Paul Stolze in the State of Thuringia Ministry of Finance and Economic Affairs.[101] The Management Board believed that Randhahn's insistence on a public retraction went too far, although feelers put out to former Finance Minister Stolze (a former member of the right-wing Deutsche Volkspartei DVP), who had joined the Nazi Party on 1 May 1933 and was an administrative expert, revealed that Lord Mayor Reible was showing "an exaggeratedly fierce approach toward other offices, too" and this had already come to the attention of the government. Stolze was guiding Minister President Marschler in this regard, who sought to take care of "the matter within the state's jurisdiction".[102]

---

100 DEA-Oberbergdirektion Altenburg, Walther Randhahn, Beschwerde über den Stadtvorstand Altenburg wegen öffentlicher Beleidigung und Verleumdung von 27.9.1933, 3, WD-CA, D-PA-90.

101 DEA-Oberbergdirektion, Walther Randhahn, an DEA-Vorstand vom 27.9.1933, ibid.

102 DEA-Oberbergdirektion, Walther Randhahn, an DEA-Vorstand Richard F. Ullner, 28.9.1933, 1, ibid.

At the end of September 1933, again overshooting their powers, Altenburg Lord Mayor Reible and Nazi Party District Head of Borna, Friedrich Munde, agreed that for all future new hires at the Regis works, which lay in Saxony, half of those considered should be men living in Altenburg in Thuringia. This prompted Randhahn to activate the Treuhänder für Arbeit für Mitteldeutschland (Custodian of Labour in Central Germany), Senior Government Councillor (Oberregierungsrat) Karl Heinrich Wiesel, in Weimar in October 1933.[103] Minister President Marschler was not interested in any further escalation of the matter, and State Secretary Stolze and the Minister President of the State of Thuringia agreed that "they wanted to create the necessary calm to allow business to flourish", to which end, all "attacks influenced by envy and cantankerousness" needed to be rejected most firmly.[104]

The formal relationship between DEA and the local Nazi Party was quite simply ambivalent. For in the midst of these public conflicts, DEA made 5,000 Reichsmark available to the City of Altenburg on 24 August 1933 for the construction of an outdoor pool.[105] Then, by way of symbolic rapprochement, in early December 1933 Walther Randhahn encouraged the DEA Management Board to make a financial contribution to a "Monument to National Uprising" planned in Altenburg, although the board as a whole reserved the right to decide.[106] A resolution was taken in mid-December 1933 to provide support of 300 Reichsmark to the local Stahlhelm organization "at its urgent request" and immediately before the subsequent

---

103 DEA-Oberbergdirektion, Walther Randhahn, an DEA-Vorstand Richard F. Ullner, 5.10.1933, 1f., ibid.; Rüdiger Hachtmann, *Vom Wilhelminismus zur neuen Staatlichkeit des Nationalsozialismus. Das Reichsarbeitsministerium 1918–1945*, Göttingen 2023, 631ff. and 722 et passim; zu Wiesel, ebd., 722 et passim.

104 DEA-Oberbergdirektion, Walther Randhahn, an DEA-Vorstand, 18.10.1933, WD-CA, D-PA-90.

105 DEA, Beschwerde gegen den Stadtvorstand Altenburg (Entwurf) o.D. [26.9.1933], 2, ibid.

106 DEA-Vorstandssitzung, 8.12.1933, 2, WD-CA, D-PA-24.

merger of the former DNVP defence league with the Storm Troopers in the context of the policy of "Gleichschaltung" (submission by enforced conformity with the Nazis). This underscores the illusions the DEA Management Board had as regards the political future of its former preferred party in the inter-war parliamentary system.[107] At the same time, the DEA Management Board also wanted to grant the community at its Rositz site financial support to build an outdoor pool, although on this occasion the sum was only 3,000 Reichsmark.[108]

In March 1934, news leaked of the company's decision to merge the two mining management offices, the one in Altenburg in Thuringia, the other in Borna in Saxony – in Leipzig. This caused quite a stir and once again brought the structural reservations many a Nazi had toward the "oil corporation" back out into the open.[109] The efforts by the State of Thuringia government to reach out and get the Führer's Commissioner for Economic Issues Wilhelm Keppler to intervene at the level of the DEA Central Management Board did not get through. While Altenburg Lord Mayor Reible and the Thuringia state government prioritized avoiding a public dispute given the great economic importance of the major corporation and thus the hope that the two sides would coexist beneficially, Bernhard Giesselmann, as the Altenburg Nazi Party local politician and Chair of the City Council, went on the offensive in mid-March 1934. He stated all his reservations, as he was closely familiar with Walther Randhahn from his many years working at the DEA Senior Mining

107 DEA-Vorstandssitzung, 18.12.1933, 4, ibid.; Dennis Werberg, *Der Stahlhelm – Bund der Frontsoldaten. Eine Veteranenorganisation als politischer Akteur und ihr Verhältnis zum Nationalsozialismus*, Berlin 2023, 277ff.; Hermann Beck, *Konflikte zwischen Deutschnationalen und Nationalsozialisten während der Machtergreifungszeit*, in: Historische Zeitschrift 3 (2011), 645–680.

108 DEA-Vorstandssitzung, 23.1.1934, 5, WD-CA, D-PA-24.

109 "Die Dea will nach Leipzig, Ein schwerer Schlag für Altenburgs Wirtschaft", Altenburger Beobachter, 7.3.1934, Bergarchiv Freiberg, Bestand 40051, No. 1057; DEA-Vorstandssitzung, 22.3.1934, 1, WD-CA, D-PA-24.

Directorate Altenburg, and characterized Randhahn as a reactionary who had, he said, caused Nazis such as himself, a Party member since 1929, a true "time of suffering" by "harassing" them. In 1932 Randhahn had, he claimed, provided all associations and organizations other than the Nazi Party with coal. He also claimed Randhahn had declared to the head of the Nazi Women's Group that "he would not give a penny to that movement, whose Führer will at some point end up in the dirt".[110]

Randhahn had, he continued, like DEA Director Gebhardt, issued the instruction that "no Storm Troopers" be hired". While the latter had at least been "overthrown as of 30.1.1933", Randhahn continued to act, he said, as "just as awful a reactionary" and "went unpunished for it". Giesselmann criticized Randhahn publicly as "antisocial and despicable". The company cell superintendent of the Altenburg DEA mining management also tried in mid-April 1934 to undermine Randhahn by accusing him of only sticking to his personal interests instead of serving the will of the staff, since he had refused to award a Christmas bonus. The man claimed that Randhahn wanted to show the Altenburg citizens that "money still means power" and that "Nazis must also be shown to be subjects".[111] Such assertions did not do anything to calm the situation.

At the end of the day, DEA reached a compromise with the state agencies and concentrated its mining management in Borna instead of, as had at one time been intended, in the city of Leipzig.[112] While Altenburg Nazi Party politicians called for action against Randhahn in "the sharpest of forms",[113] the State of Thuringia gov-

---

110 Bernhard Gießelmann an Staatsminister Fritz Wächtler, 15.3.1934, 3ff., Bergarchiv Freiberg, Bestand 40051, No. 1057.

111 Betriebszellenobmann Johannes Geisler an Staatsminister Wächtler, 16.4.1934, 4, ibid.

112 Wilhelm Keppler an Ministerpräsident Fritz Marschler, 23.3.1934, ibid.; DEA-Vorstandssitzung, 5.4.1934, 1, WD-CA, D-PA-24; DEA-Vorstandssitzung, 25.4.1934, 1, ibid.

113 Vermerk, 16.4.1934, Bergarchiv Freiberg, Bestand 40051, No. 1057.

ernment felt it needed to continue to "set store" in a good relationship with DEA in order to avoid an even greater relocation of production from there to Saxony. One strong indication of the efforts by the DEA senior executives to establish good terms with those now in political power was the fact that on 21 March 1934, in the various DEA plants Adolf Hitler's radio broadcast proclaiming a "spring battle for work" was taken as the occasion for "duly and properly" held company parades.[114] Randhahn also did his bit personally, when on 1 April 1936 he joined the Nazi Party.[115]

---

114 DEA-Vorstandssitzung, 22.3.1934, 1, WD-CA, D-PA-24; Humann, *Arbeitsschlacht*, 679ff.

115 Parteikorrespondenz Dr.-Ing. Walther Randhahn, BArch Berlin, R 9361-I/2776.

IV. REICH DRILLING PROGRAMME, BUYING INTO BRABAG, AND THE NAVY CONTRACT

(Rainer Karlsch)

Consolidating DPAG

In January 1933, Solmssen and Ullner travelled to London to negotiate a settlement with the Chair of APOC, Sir John Cadman. The background to this was DEA's gradual sale between 1926 and 1931 of the shares in "Olex" Deutsche Benzin- und Petroleum-Gesellschaft mbH to APOC, in which the British government held the majority. The purchase price had not been completely paid to DEA when, on 3 September 1931, Great Britain abandoned the gold standard.

For all the warnings by experts, the gold standard had been reintroduced in Britain in 1925 and had led to an over-valuation of pound sterling, which made exports more expensive and intensified the structural crises in the British economy.[1] Pound sterling floated freely after the country left the gold standard and had by year-end shed some 40 percent in value. The question of how to offset the losses resulting from the devaluation of the currency was a long-standing bone of contention between APOC and DEA. After tough negotiations, the two parties agreed that DEA would shoul-

---

[1] Cf. Burkhardt Röper, *Die drei Abwertungen in Großbritannien*, Econstor Wirtschaftsdienst, Vol. 29 (1949), 9–15.

der 60 percent and APOC 40 percent of the losses resulting from the devaluation of pound sterling. In return, APOC committed to pay all purchase price instalments due later immediately.[2] After this settlement, DPAG booked an inflow of some 613,000 pounds sterling, which corresponded to approx. 14.1 million Reichsmark.[3] It was a deal that, in such times of crisis, could probably only be achieved by such internationally experienced bankers as Solmssen and Ullner.

For DEA, despite the write-offs, the deal was a stroke of good fortune. Its DPAG subsidiary now had a great deal of liquidity. During the days of the Great Depression and the foreign exchange quotas introduced by the Reichsbank in July 1931, a strong stock of foreign exchange constituted a real business advantage. This was used firstly to acquire Rositzer Mineralölwerke from the parent corporations in order to improve DEA's treasury chest. Meanwhile, a lignite field in the Breitingen region was also purchased for 192,000 pounds sterling from ASW, a corporation that belonged to the State of Saxony – the field lay next to the open-cast mine that DEA ran in Regis and contained roughly 50 million tonnes of high-quality lignite. The negotiations to procure the field had been on the table for years, and DEA was now in a position to pay in foreign exchange, which enabled ASW to cover a debt it owed in US dollars.[4] Moreover, the income from the Olex sale also enabled DEA to provide financing for its Magdeburger Bergwerks-AG subsidiary.

The hard currency generated by the OLEX sale thus enabled DEA not only to steady the ship at its DPAG subsidiary, but also strengthen its lignite base in Central Germany. When the economy slowly started to show signs of recovery in spring 1933, the DEA management board betted on the hard coal and lignite mining sector picking up. In order to do justice to the objectives of the new Reich government and the various state governments to reduce high unem-

---

2 Cf. Aufsichtsratsprotokoll, 13.1.1933, HADB, P 1666, sheet 95f.

3 Cf. Heinz Rothbarth, *DEA. Geschichte 1899–1933*, 171.

4 Cf. ibid., 172.

ployment, for the first time in some years it hired several hundred new miners, even though demand for coal was only picking up slowly.[5]

The petroleum business still did not turn any meaningful profit. For that reason, since the end of the 1920s DPAG had not disbursed any dividends. The Reich Navy, once the main buyer of the heavy heating oil produced in the Rositz refinery, was subject to the restrictions of the Treaty of Versailles and therefore constrained in what it could purchase. Although DEA remained the main domestic supplier to the navy, it was only able to sign short-term supply contracts for limited amounts of heating oil, with the ceiling in the early 1930s being between 18,000 and 26,000 t per year.[6]

Deutsche Bank therefore considered DEA's majority stake in DPAG to be the "*Achilles heel of the DEA balance sheet*".[7] It seemed almost inevitable that the "*interest would need to be written down*", especially as the opportunities to streamline DPAG operations appeared to have been as good as exhausted.[8] Only in the event of stronger customs protection for German petroleum products would the business situation improve, so the Supervisory Board thought.

The Reich drilling programme

In 1933, it was not yet clear what strategy the Reich government would take as regards petroleum and the oil industry. There were contradictory signals, with various groups of players pursuing their own respective interests and trying to push their projects through. The international petroleum corporations, meaning Royal Dutch Shell, Standard Oil, and APOC, indicated that they were in a position to cover the growing German demand for crude oil. They sug-

---

5 Cf. DEA-Geschäftsbericht für 1933, WD-CA, D-GB-DEA.

6 Cf. Marine-Verträge, 23.10.1929, WD-CA, D-RW-373.

7 Memo 15.9.1934, HADB, P 1675, sheet 37.

8 Ibid.

gested various refinery programmes to the Hitler government and also proposed that oil imports be made without resort to foreign currency. I.G. Farbenindustrie AG and the petroleum and chemical industries in the Ruhr region in general both had great ambitions. They had high hopes for the new technologies they had developed to synthesize liquid fuels from coal. The German petroleum companies, by contrast, advocated stronger government support for the domestic petroleum industry. A "petroleum alliance" emerged, membership of which included Preussische Geologische Landesanstalt (State of Prussia Geological Institute) and the German petroleum companies. On behalf of DPAG/DEA, its chief geologist Alfred Kraiss supported the idea of a state-supported drilling programme,[9] and the latter was in fact put in place very quickly.

On 10 January 1934, a meeting was held at the Reich Economic Ministry with the major German petroleum companies,[10] at which Günther Schlicht participated for DEA. The Reich government announced that it would make loans available for the development of new oil fields. It declared that it was prepared to assume half of the pure drilling costs within the framework of a plan (later called the "Reich drilling programme") to be elaborated by Geologische Landesanstalt. To the extent that drilling proved successful, the company in question would then repay the Reich loan using the profits from the field.

The Reich drilling programme paved the way for incisive changes in the legal basis for petroleum extraction. At the end of 1934, Prussia introduced pre-emptive rights for the state for petroleum and thus created the very first basis for applying modern mine development methods. Until then, mining had relied mainly on land ownership, and this had led to strong fragmentation of the sites,

---

9 Cf. Kockel, *Deutsche Ölpolitik*, 78.

10 Cf. Bericht über die geplanten Reichsdarlehen für Erdölaufschlüsse, 11.1.1934, Archiv der BGR Hannover, No. 5893, on the Reich`s drilling programme in general: Kockel, *Deutsche Ölpolitik*, 108–117 and 135–177.

meaning that it was difficult for the oil industry to acquire rights to closed complexes. The new regulations enabled the government to award uniform concession agreements, usually limited in time to five years, whereby at least one prospective drilling had to have taken place during that period. Should the drilling be successful, mining rights were then granted for 30 years against a 5 percent extraction charge. This meant that deposits could be developed uniformly.[11]

The Act on Mineral Deposits of 4 December 1934 obliged all companies and state geological agencies to forward their geological and geophysical documents to the Geologische Landesanstalt. Material that had hitherto been kept secret was then used to compile maps and thus brought to bear for future exploration. DEA responded to the Reich drilling programme by restructuring its mineral oil business unit and put the idea of a merger with DPAG on the backburner for fiscal reasons. Instead, the corporation sold its tar refinery to DPAG. Schwelwerke Rositz, which supplied the crude tar produced from the lignite to the refinery, continued to be a DEA portfolio company.[12]

The Reich drilling programme was not intended to give Germany oil independence, as geological conditions in the German Reich were insufficient for that. The intention was to boost domestic oil production through the exploration for and development of new fields, and thus take the sting out of the Reich's foreign exchange balance.[13] Another frequently voiced argument was the effect of the state-supported drilling programme as an economic fillip.

The Reich drilling programme was indeed state-driven but did not exclusively rely on state planning. Rather, it was up to the individual companies to take the initiative on drilling, to file the relevant

11 Cf. Hanns-Heinz Kasper, *Die Erdölgewinnung Deutschlands*, PhD thesis Freiberg 1977, 317.

12 Cf. Geschäftsbericht 1934, WD-CA, D-GB-DEA.

13 Cf. Alfred Bentz, *Die deutschen Erdöllagerstätten*, Archiv der BGR Hannover, No. 87993.

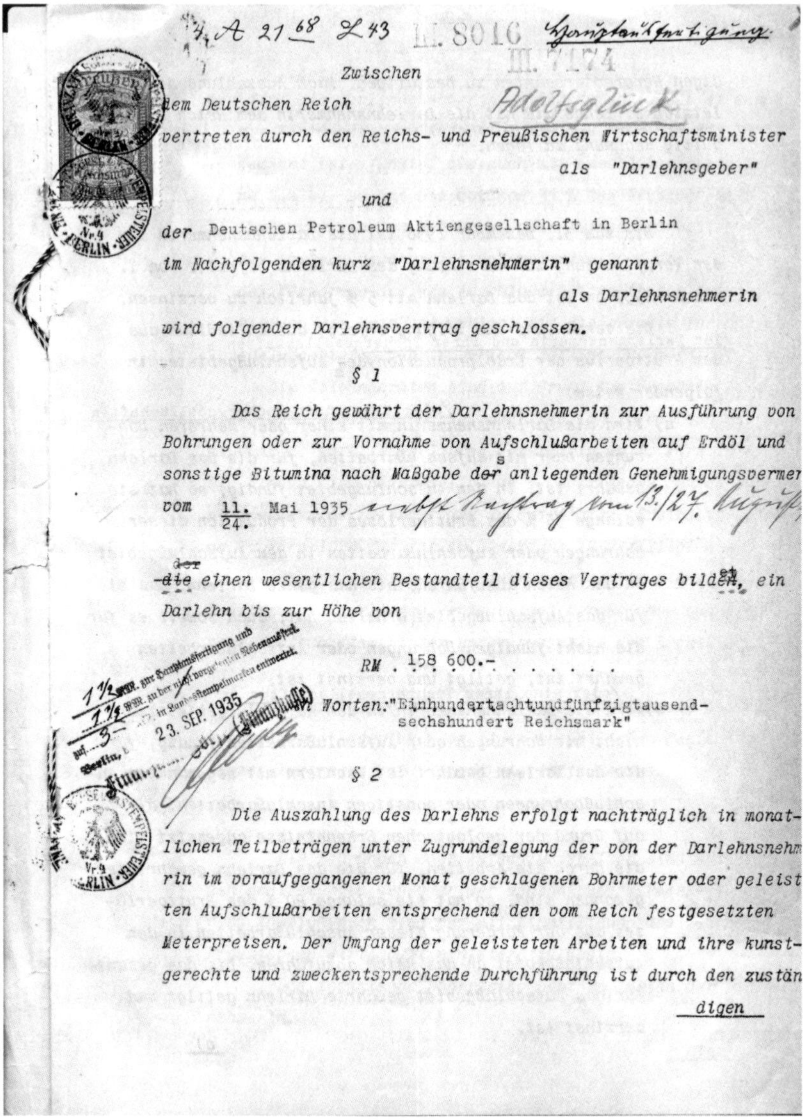

Zwischen

dem Deutschen Reich

vertreten durch den Reichs- und Preußischen Wirtschaftsminister

als "Darlehnsgeber"

und

der Deutschen Petroleum Aktiengesellschaft in Berlin

im Nachfolgenden kurz "Darlehnsnehmerin" genannt

als Darlehnsnehmerin

wird folgender Darlehnsvertrag geschlossen.

§ 1

Das Reich gewährt der Darlehnsnehmerin zur Ausführung von Bohrungen oder zur Vornahme von Aufschlußarbeiten auf Erdöl und sonstige Bitumina nach Maßgabe der anliegenden Genehmigungsvermer vom 11. Mai 1935 die einen wesentlichen Bestandteil dieses Vertrages bilden, ein Darlehn bis zur Höhe von

RM . 158 600.- . . . . . .

in Worten:"Einhundertachtundfünfzigtausend-sechshundert Reichsmark"

§ 2

Die Auszahlung des Darlehns erfolgt nachträglich in monatlichen Teilbeträgen unter Zugrundelegung der von der Darlehnsnehmerin im voraufgegangenen Monat geschlagenen Bohrmeter oder geleisteten Aufschlußarbeiten entsprechend den vom Reich festgesetzten Meterpreisen. Der Umfang der geleisteten Arbeiten und ihre kunstgerechte und zweckentsprechende Durchführung ist durch den zustän digen

Fig. 21 Agreement between DPAG and the Reich and Prussian Economics Minister covering a loan of 158,000 Reichsmark for drilling the "Adolfsglück" well in Lower Saxony, (1935)

applications, and then draw up their own drilling programmes. Geologische Landesanstalt, the 1934 successor to the Institut für Erdölgeologie, identified the drilling areas that offered the greatest prospect of success,[14] and the state recouped its outlays for the exploration work in the form of the extraction charge and increased tax revenues.

Within the borders of the German Reich, excluding Austria, a total of 643 "Reich trial drillings" were made between 1933 and 1945. DPAG/DEA and Wintershall AG, the two major German oil players, accounted directly for 286 of the trial drillings. Roughly one tenth of these drillings found oil and led to nine mainly smaller oil fields going into production. Moreover, DEA benefited from further successful drilling projects as a member of various consortiums.[15] One initial focus of the Reich drilling programme was drilling in the Hanover basin. However, DPAG/DEA did not make major finds there, but in the neighbouring zone of Gifhorn and in Heide (Holstein). By the end of the Second World War, a total of 21 trial drillings had been made near Gifhorn as part of the Reich programme. The Gifhorn 7 (RB 201a) hole hit oil, with initial production some 6–7 t/day. DPAG/DEA succeeded in 1939 in being exempted from repaying the exploration grants totalling almost 1 million Reichsmark,[16] arguing that the drilling project had taken place during the first stage of the programme.

While the Gifhorn find was a smaller field, the one outside Heide was to prove more important as of 1939.[17] The second exploratory drilling at "Holstein 2" hit oil at a depth of 400 metres on 13 September 1935. "Holstein 3 and 4" followed, with two low-level boreholes both likewise striking black gold, but these were not subsidized by the Reich, as the Reich drilling programme only covered

---

14 Cf. Kockel, *Deutsche Ölpolitik*, 161f.

15 Cf. Marvin Brendel, *Über 1945 hinaus: DEA und Wintershall als Nutznießer des Reichsbohrprogramms*, manuscript Kassel 2023.

16 Cf. Kockel, *Deutsche Ölpolitik*, 170.

17 Cf. chapter VIII.

Fig. 22 Oil field outside Gifhorn (1936)

deep drilling.[18] By 1939, additional trial drilling proved that the field near Heide was a significant find and one that was swiftly tapped during the war years. This can be seen from the production figures which shot up swiftly, only to dwindle from 1942 onwards, as well as from the swift growth in payroll.

New oil finds in commercial quantities by DPAG/DEA in the 2nd and 3rd phases of the Reich drilling programme[19]

Structure	Ordnance map	Date	Region
Heide	Heide-490	5 September, 1935	Schleswig
Gifhorn	Meinersen 1890	20 September, 1935	Hanover
Weingarten	Weingarten	1936	Baden
Hope/Adolfsglück	Schwarmstedt	12 December, 1936	Hanover
Wiessee	.	1937	Bavaria

18 Cf. DEA-Vorstandssitzung, 28.1.1936, WD-CA, D-PA-29, part 1.

19 Compiled according to: Kockel, *Deutsche Ölpolitik*, 176.

Development of the new oil fields in Gifhorn and Heide in 1935–6 did not immediately lead to production volumes being boosted. In 1937, DPA's oil production volume actually dipped,[20] and it was only after the outbreak of war – and above all thanks to new fields found in Austria – that petroleum gained a greater status in the company's portfolio and led to a change in perspective.

For DEA, the Reich drilling programme laid the foundations for a renewed stronger focus on oil production inside the Reich's territory. The corporation was to benefit from the results of the programme for many decades after the Second World War.[21]

Payroll trends at the DEA oil companies 1939–1945[22]

	1939	1940	1941	1942	1943	1944
Head Office Berlin	0	31	.	35	48	4
Wietze	1,037	1,053	1,135	1,276	1,218	1,366
Holstein	463	843	981	1,735	1,889	2,264
Sand-lime brick factory	39	36	34	.	.	.
Ostmark region	147	339	369	1,181	2,339	2,690
Wilhelmsburg Refinery			573	630	625	519
"Nova" Refinery			385	628	685	688
Service	176	97				
Consortium Slovakia	0	597	648	668	620	
Pechelbronn		1,489	2,269	2,384	2,366	2,339
Total		**4,486**	**5,402**	**8,537**	**9,792**	**10,907**

20 Cf. DEA-Geschäftsbericht für 1937, WD-CA, WD-DEA D-Geschäftsberichte.

21 However, Titus Kockel's assessment that the Reich's drilling program was a "gigantic flop" (Kockel, *Deutsche Ölpolitik*, 176) must be clearly contradicted.

22 Compiled according to: Jahresberichte Erdölbetriebe, WD-CA, 4112–1274/1275.

A mandatory cartel: Braunkohle-Benzin AG (BRABAG)

As early as 1933, DPAG Director Gröber had anticipated that general demand for petroleum would pick up. Even more important were enquiries from the Reich Navy, which he felt gave grounds to hope for an expansion in heating oil and diesel sales.[23] In 1934, total German consumption of heating oil came to 580,000 tonnes, but domestic output was only about 200,000 tonnes. The situation was even more dramatic when it came to diesel fuel, with less than 10 percent of total German consumption originating inside the country.[24]

Gröber correctly forecast that the country would soon opt for rearmament and managed to overcome his Supervisory Board's sceptical outlook toward DPAG by suggesting profits would turn around soon. In the summer of 1934, signs pointed to a pending long-term contract with the navy. The contract would ensure DPAG sound profits and restore the corporation's profitability.[25] With the expansion of its lignite-based petroleum production, DPAG/DEA sought, as in 1917–8, to gain special status as the main supplier to the Reich Navy.

Negotiations between DPAG/DEA and the Reich Navy were making good headway when Reich Economics Minister Hjalmar Schacht decided to take a surprising step. He invited the members of the Management and Supervisory Boards of Germany's major lignite producers to a meeting in Berlin on 21 September 1934.[26] Schacht told the surprised captains of industry that they would be obliged to participate in a company that would run two

---

23 Cf. note (Rothbarth), Marinemappe, 16.8.1934, WD-CA, D-RW-373.

24 Cf. Hans-Jürgen Zetzsche, *Logistik und Operationen. Die Mineralölversorgung der Kriegsmarine im Zweiten Weltkrieg*, PhD thesis Kiel 1986, 49.

25 Cf. Memo for Solmssen re.: DEA, 25.8.1934, HADB, P 1675, sheet 36ff.

26 Cf. Wolfgang Birkenfeld, *Der synthetische Treibstoff* 1933–1945, Göttingen 1964, 37f.

factories, which would together produce a total of 500,000 tonnes of synthetic petrol from lignite each year.[27] All lignite producers who mined more than 400,000 tonnes a year were obliged to take out an equal stake in the project. In return, Schacht offered to procure the petrol obtained from coal liquefaction at prices that covered the companies' costs.

The industrialists present were open to the project but did not agree when it came to the technology to be used.[28] Schacht favoured the Bergius-Pier method developed by I.G. Farben which, unlike the Fischer-Tropsch method, enabled the production of aircraft fuel, which was expensive and otherwise had to be imported.[29] While the Bergius-Pier method had not at the time reached industrial-scale profitability, the chemists at I.G. Farben were banking on synergies by using secondary products.

The lignite company managers felt the Bergius-Pier method was not yet sufficiently mature and shied away from the licence fees that I.G. Farben demanded. They instead championed the Fischer-Tropsch method of producing synthetic fuels as developed by Ruhrchemie AG, yet this approach produced neither airplane fuel nor diesel, so for the military the main fuels produced using Fischer-Tropsch synthesis were not really viable. The Reich Economics Minister responded swiftly. Only a week after the meeting, on 28 September 1934, he issued the "*Decree on Establishing Mandatory Joint Ventures in the Lignite Industry.*"[30]

---

27 Cf. Protokolle der DEA-Vorstandssitzungen, 25.9. und 20.10.1934, WD-CA, D-PA-24.

28 While Wolfgang Birkenfeld's pioneering work on the development of synthetic fuel argues that the lignite companies flatly refused to voluntarily participate in the project, more recent historical research calls this into question. On the contrary, RAG, ASW, EWAG, Bubiag, Flick and I.G. Farben were interested in the project and profited from it. (Cf. Jonas Scherner, *Die Logik der Industriepolitik im Dritten Reich*, Vol. 174, part 4, 2008, 108f.)

29 Cf. Sabine Brinkmann, *Das Dritte Reich und der synthetische Treibstoff: Eine Kritik der Forschung aus chemietechnischer Sicht*, in: Akkumulation 15 (2001), 16–23.

30 Cf. Reichsgesetzblatt 1934 [hereafter: RGBl], part 1, 863f.

The foundation of the mandatory joint ventures spelled difficulties for both DEA and the navy. At the end of 1933, the corporation had already committed initial investments to liquefaction of lignite in order to boost DPAG's heavy heating oil and diesel output.

The navy's specialist for oil supplies was Ministerial Councillor Friedrich Fetzer.[31] In the words of Admiral Ernst Raeder, Fetzer had "*familiarized himself with almost all the world's oil fields in the course of his travels*" and also had superb connections both inside and outside Germany.[32] Fetzer was DEA's key opposite at the negotiating table when it came to heating oil procurement, and he criticized the establishment of BRABAG as he considered it a decision taken against the navy's interests.[33]

At a DEA Management Board meeting of 20 October 1934, it was likewise the voices sceptical of the BRABAG project that predominated.[34] The board was troubled by the government intervention in the lignite industry:[35] While it viewed participation in the project initiated by Schacht to be basically inevitable, it wanted to be exempted from a contribution to BRABAG's founding capital, or at least to only have to put up a reduced amount.

The Reich Economics Ministry scheduled the meeting to sign the articles of incorporation of the mandatory joint venture for the afternoon of 26 October 1934. When the DEA Management

---

31 Friedrich Fetzer (17.9.1896–23.1.1985): Volunteer in the First World War, seriously wounded; studied chemistry and law in Munich. Numerous study trips to oil-producing countries; Ministerialrat in the OKM, expert on oil supply; resigned in 1942 and returned to Lindau, played a key role in saving the town of Lindau from destruction at the end of April 1945; Head of Department in the Federal Ministry of Economics, OECD in Paris (cf. Zetzsche, *Logistik und Operationen*, 61–65; Karl Bachmann, *Dr. Friedrich Fetzer von Schloss Moos: ein verdienter Lindauer unserer Zeit*, in: Jahrbuch des Landkreises Lindau 1993).

32 Ernst Raeder, *Mein Leben*, Vol. 2, Tübingen 1957, 59.

33 Cf. Manfred Rasch, *Zur Mineralölpolitik der Kriegsmarine*, in: Militärgeschichtliche Mitteilungen 1 (1985), 71–101.

34 Cf. Protokoll der DEA-Vorstandssitzung, 20.10.1934, WD-CA, D-PA-24.

35 Cf. Abstract of Memo Dr. Paul Mojert, 25.9.1936, HADB, P 1658, sheet 215.

Board learned of this, on the morning of the day in question a phone conference was arranged, something quite unprecedented at the corporation.[36] Gröber, as Chair of the DPAG Management Board, registered his objections to participation in the mandatory joint venture. He then hurried to the Reich Economics Ministry, where he had been granted an audience with Schacht only a few minutes prior to the decisive meeting; there he again stated DEA's reservations. The minister promised relief, whereupon the DEA Management Board sent Gröber into the funding meeting with a formula in his pocket: This suggested that companies which, as of 1935, would have already boosted mineral oil and paraffin products to a level above that of 1933 would be exempted from making a capital contribution. This applied only to DEA.

The evening of 26 October 1934 saw the official foundation of Braunkohle-Benzin AG (BRABAG), domiciled in Berlin. Participants in the equity were: I.G. Farbenindustrie AG; Ilse-Bergbau AG (from 1938 onwards, VIAG); Deutsche Erdöl AG (DEA); Werschen-Weissenfelser Braunkohlen AG (WW); Braunkohlen- und Brikettindustrie AG (Bubiag); Aktiengesellschaft Sächsische Werke (ASW); Elektrowerke Aktiengesellschaft (EWAG); Rheinische Aktiengesellschaft für Braunkohlenbergbau und Brikettfabrikation (RAG); Mitteldeutsche Stahlwerke AG (Mittelstahl); and Anhaltische Kohlenwerke AG (AKW).[37] Each company was awarded 10 percent of the BRABAG shares and was meant to pay 10 million Reichsmark in tranches to create the 100 million Reichsmark capital stock that had been decided. The government guaranteed the shareholders an annual dividend and that it would procure a fixed volume of lignite and synthetic petrol at fixed prices.

BRABAG constituted a hybrid of state capitalism and private entrepreneurialism and was subordinated to the Reich Economics

---

36 Cf. Protokoll der DEA-Vorstandssitzung, 26.10.1934, WD-CA, D-PA-24.

37 Cf. RGBl. 1934, part 1, 1068.

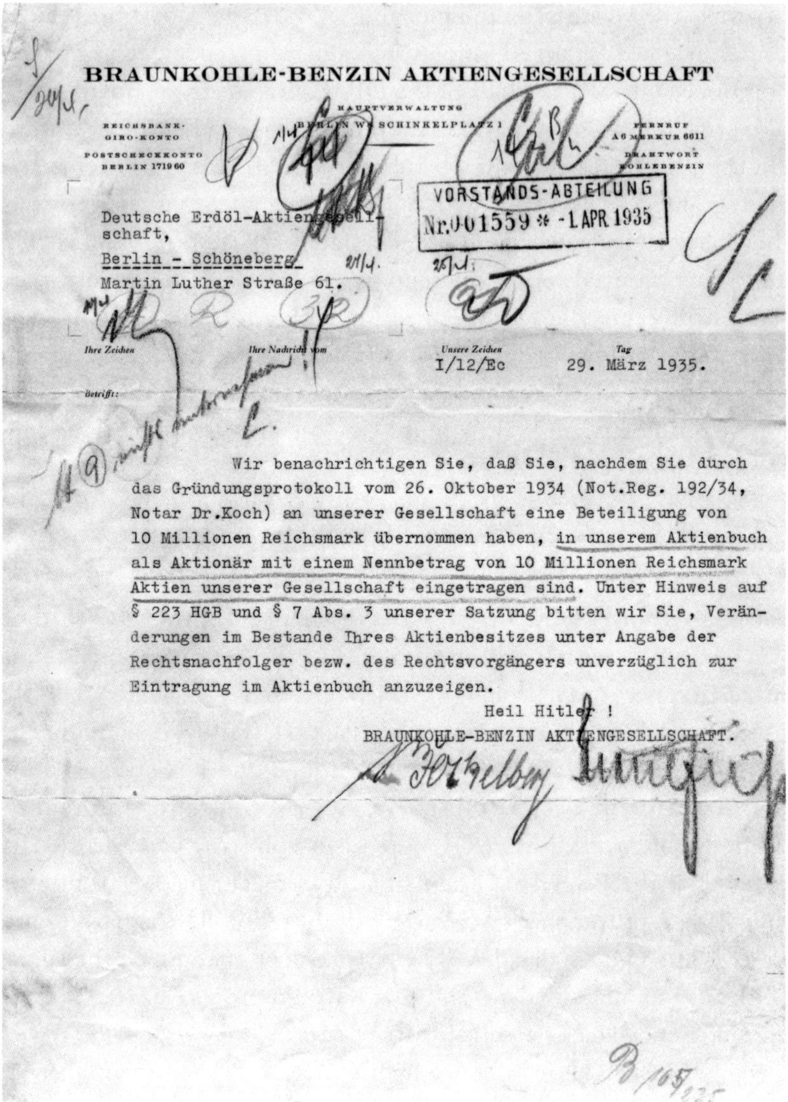

BRAUNKOHLE-BENZIN AKTIENGESELLSCHAFT

HAUPTVERWALTUNG
BERLIN W 8 SCHINKELPLATZ 1

REICHSBANK-GIRO-KONTO
POSTSCHECKKONTO BERLIN 171960

FERNRUF A 6 MERKUR 6611
DRAHTWORT KOHLEBENZIN

VORSTANDS-ABTEILUNG
Nr. 001559 * - 1 APR 1935

Deutsche Erdöl-Aktiengesell-
schaft,

Berlin - Schöneberg
Martin Luther Straße 61.

Ihre Zeichen | Ihre Nachricht vom | Unsere Zeichen I/12/Ec | Tag 29. März 1935.

Betrifft:

Wir benachrichtigen Sie, daß Sie, nachdem Sie durch das Gründungsprotokoll vom 26. Oktober 1934 (Not.Reg. 192/34, Notar Dr.Koch) an unserer Gesellschaft eine Beteiligung von 10 Millionen Reichsmark übernommen haben, in unserem Aktienbuch als Aktionär mit einem Nennbetrag von 10 Millionen Reichsmark Aktien unserer Gesellschaft eingetragen sind. Unter Hinweis auf § 223 HGB und § 7 Abs. 3 unserer Satzung bitten wir Sie, Veränderungen im Bestande Ihres Aktienbesitzes unter Angabe der Rechtsnachfolger bezw. des Rechtsvorgängers unverzüglich zur Eintragung im Aktienbuch anzuzeigen.

Heil Hitler !

BRAUNKOHLE-BENZIN AKTIENGESELLSCHAFT.

Fig. 23 Confirmation of the registration of DEA as a BRABAG shareholder (1935)

Ministry. The state avoided any financial risk but exerted considerable influence over the corporate policy. The four-man Management Board included Heinrich Koppenberg of Junkers-Werke and Carl Krauch of I.G. Farben – both men were in charge of the technical management of the BRABAG factories, and both were influential captains of industry, government officials, and later important representatives of the Nazi Party – along with General (retd.) Alfred von Vollard-Bockelberg and businessman Fritz Kranefuss.[38] The latter had joined the Nazi Party as early as 1932 and then the SS in 1933, and was in close contact with Reichsführer SS, Heinrich Himmler.[39] Government official and SS Oberführer Wilhelm Keppler was appointed Chairman of the Supervisory Board, a man who in 1933–4 had a strong influence on Hitler as regards economic issues.[40]

After the argument over the details of founding BRABAG, the lignite industrialists reached a compromise. Alongside the Bergius-Pier method, the mandatory joint venture would also use the Fischer-Tropsch method of synthesis, which they favoured. Moreover, the scale of the capital contributions, the production sites, and other questions were still undecided. In the final instance, the major lignite producers (RAG, ASW, EWAG, Bubiag, and I.G. Farben) all benefited from the joint venture. They succeeded in boosting their production volumes and locked into state-guaranteed profits.

DEA opposed a participation in BRABAG for purely business reasons. It had nothing against booking orders from government, as its negotiation with the Reich Navy shows, but wanted to focus on expanding production of heating oil and diesel. In the naval

---

38 Cf. Tobias Bütow/Franka Bindernagel, *Ein KZ in der Nachbarschaft. Das Magdeburger Außenlager der BRABAG und der Freundeskreis Himmler*, Weimar 2003, 31–33.

39 From the end of the 1930s, Kranefuß dominated the executive committee of BRABAG. He also organized the "Freundeskreis Himmler" (Himmler's Circle of Friends). Cf. ibid., 41–57.

40 Cf. Birkenfeld, *Der synthetische Treibstoff*, 40ff.

project, DEA bore sole entrepreneurial responsibility, whereas at BRABAG it had no influence over the management and was supposed to be a passive financial backer. As a result, the DEA Management Board, citing ongoing talks with the navy, tried to ensure that DEA "*was as far as possible released from Braunkohle-Benzin A.G.*".[41] The arguments were summarized in an official memo that referenced, amongst others, the creation of a lignite tar factory in Rositz during the First World War and "*maintaining the loss-making German oil production*".[42]

The Reich Economics Ministry responded indignantly. Although the ministry had pledged to keep the DEA memoir confidential, civil servants leaked it to the competition and at the same time made it clear there would be no concessions.[43] The competition responded to the DEA memoir unequivocally: Since no one could duck membership of the mandatory joint venture, all the major lignite producers should at least have a stake in it.

In the months that followed, DEA tried on several occasions to make submissions to get an "*exemption*" from the liquefaction project,[44] but in spring 1936 it was forced to concede that its efforts had no chance of success.[45] It did, however, manage to get its contribution to the founding capital reduced from 10 to 5.86 million Reichsmark,[46] and the ink was put to the paper of the licence agreement between BRABAG and I.G. Farben on 22 August 1935.[47] A few weeks earlier, construction had started on two liquefaction

---

41 Protokoll der DEA-Vorstandssitzung, 13.11.1934, WD-CA, D-PA-24.

42 Cf. Hans Gröber, Darlegung zur Stellung der DEA im Rahmen der deutschen Mineralölversorgung vom 24. Oktober 1934, Nationalarchiv (NA) Washington, T-83, Roll 53.

43 Cf. ibid.

44 Note, 9.11.1934, HADB, P 1658, sheet 68.

45 Cf. Niederschrift über die Verhandlungen des Aufsichtsrats der Deutschen Erdöl-Aktiengesellschaft, 4.3.1936, HADB, P 1663, sheet 45.

46 Cf. ibid.

47 Cf. Birkenfeld, *Der synthetische Treibstoff*, 45.

plants, one near Böhlen, outside Leipzig, the other near Magdeburg.[48] Building work started almost simultaneously on a third plant that made use of the Fischer-Tropsch process in Schwarzheide, near Ruhland, in South Brandenburg. From spring 1937 onwards, a further plant using the Bergius-Pier method patented by I.G. Farben was constructed near Zeitz, outside the city of Halle. At the beginning of the war, all four BRABAG plants were up and running and made an important contribution to German fuel supplies.

The Reich Navy Programme and the Four-Year Plan

Despite the additional financial strain caused by the participation in BRABAG, the Management Boards of neither DPAG nor DEA wished to change the strategy they had embarked on of boosting petroleum production from lignite tar. They maintained their investment programme of 18 million Reichsmark in DPAG operations, initially scheduled for three years, and planned to allocate a further 18 million Reichsmark for the period 1937 to 1942. DEA sought to *"gain a special status in German oil production"* and, as CEO Ullner put it, in the process *"to retain a free hand in technological, financial, and business terms"*.[49] His words reflect the corporate philosophy: DEA wanted to finance its own growth going forward, to lock into government contracts, but not to become dependent on the state.[50]

The project to expand lignite-based oil production was based on experiences made in the First World War. It was meant to animate lignite production, which had been stagnating for years, and

---

48 Cf. Protokoll der Aufsichtsratssitzung der Brabag am 31.10.1935, NA Washington, T-83, Roll 53.

49 Niederschrift über die Verhandlungen des Aufsichtsrats der Deutschen Erdöl-Aktiengesellschaft, 6.11.1934, HADB, P 1666, sheet 117.

50 Cf. Memo, 18.5.1935, ibid., P 1675, sheet 67.

"*meet the need to create broad-based German oil production*".[51] However, at a Management Board meeting of 4 March 1935, Ullner called for caution "*given the poor experiences we made with war-time contracts in the period just before the war broke out*".[52] He advocated proceeding very carefully.

The corporation wanted to finance the investment programme by drawing on hidden reserves (including the "savings sacrifices" Middendorf had put aside) and later floating a bond.[53] Ullner sought to structure heating oil prices charged to the Reich Navy in war-time in such a way that the new plant could be amortized completely in five years in each instance.[54] The corporation also wanted to always be in a position to put the programme on hold, and Ullner hoped that the navy would succeed in having DEA "*released from the obligations of the government's so-called Brabag Action*".[55]

The Supervisory Board approved Ullner's circumspect strategy, with the aim of achieving growth financed without recourse to loans.[56] Given sub-par utilization of the mining capacities of DEA's lignite operations, the corporation felt that after years in crisis the "oil programme" had the potential to offer longer-term profitability.

The tempo of talks between DPAG/DEA and the Reich Navy was upped with conclusion of the Anglo-German Naval Agreement on 18 June 1935.[57] The treaty allowed the German Reich to rearm its navy, and shortly thereafter a new supply contract between the Reich Navy and DPAG/DEA was signed covering the

---

51 Niederschrift über die Verhandlungen des Aufsichtsrats der Deutschen Erdöl-Aktiengesellschaft, 4.3.1935, ibid., P 1666, sheet 123.

52 Ullner an Solmssen, 7.3.1935, ibid., P 1658, sheet 84.

53 Cf. Aktenvermerk Kimmich, 24.3.1937, ibid., sheet 242–247.

54 Cf. Aktenvermerk 15.3.1935, ibid., P 1656, no page numbers given.

55 Ibid.

56 Ibid. Sitzung des Geschäftsausschusses des Aufsichtsrats, 4.3.1935, ibid., P 1667, sheet 198–201.

57 Cf. Norbert Theodor Wiggershaus, *Der deutsch-englische Flottenvertrag vom 18. Juni 1935 und die geheime deutsche Aufrüstung 1933–1935*, Bonn 1972.

supply of 300,000 tonnes of heating oil over four years.[58] The navy's annual procurement volume would thus rise by a factor of over three compared to the previous highest figure supplied. The contract not only ensured full capacity utilization of DPAG's pyrolysis plants in Central Germany and its refinery but also meant the "*lignite operations were able to book the ultimate in profits*".[59] DPAG/DEA thus now had its cash cow to milk. Operations were profitable as early as the end of 1935, and for the first time in five years DPAG was able to disburse a dividend of 3 percent.[60]

Commensurate with the increase in DPAG's importance, the prior sole director of DPAG Hans Gröber was now assigned three deputy directors Karl Grosse (Wietze), Max Heyne (Mineralölwerk Rositz), and Eugen Bauer (Erdölwerke Wilhelmsburg)[61], all three long-standing technical directors.[62]

In August 1936, with the Olympic Games already underway in Berlin, Adolf Hitler penned a secret memo. He believed that war with the Soviet Union was unavoidable and demanded that new "living space in the east" be obtained. In the main part of the memo, Hitler insisted that the German Army be fit to roll within four years

58 Cf. Aktenvermerk re.: Deutsche Erdöl AG, 5.10.1935, HADB, P 1675, sheet 76.

59 Ibid.

60 Cf. Niederschrift über die Verhandlungen des Aufsichtsrats der Deutschen Erdöl-Aktiengesellschaft, 1.10.1935, HADB, P 1666, sheet 123ff.

61 Eugen Bauer (1.2.1878–16.7.1957): Born in Roädestvenko (Moscow governorate), 1896–1901 studied theology and chemistry in Dorpat; 1902–07 industrial chemist at Naphta Gesellschaft and Gebr. Nobel in Baku; 1908–1916 director of Campina petroleum refinery (Romania), from 1916 Berlin, 1924 technical director of DPAG Berlin, 1926–1945 director of Deutsche Erdöl AG Wilhelmsburg, retired in Hamburg (Cf. Baltisches biografisches Lexikon, digital: https://www.bbld.de [last retrieved on 20.6.2024].

62 Cf. Niederschrift über die Verhandlungen des Aufsichtsrats der Deutschen Erdöl-Aktiengesellschaft, 1.10.1935, HADB, P 1666, sheet 123ff.

and the German economy likewise be ready for war.[63] He ordered the maximum possible expansion of the synthetic production of petroleum, rubber, and fats, as well as an increase in domestic iron ore mining and processing. Göring read out some of the memo at a cabinet meeting on 4 September 1936, and on 18 October 1936 Hitler appointed him "Plenipotentiary of the Four-Year Plan".

Göring then proceeded to establish a "Raw Materials and Foreign Currency Staff Unit" consisting of Luftwaffe officers and representatives of industry and destined to gear German business more strongly to producing more arms and to becoming independent of imports. This spelled a turn away from the economic policy pursued by Schacht up until then. Göring also used his new powers to clip the wings of the Reich Economics Ministry.[64]

The "Raw Materials and Foreign Currency Staff Unit" morphed into the "Office for German Raw Materials and Production Materials", that in 1938 was renamed "Reich Agency for Economic Expansion" and in 1939 became the "Reichsamt".[65] This authority was the "heart of the entire Four-Year Plan organization" and organized the mobilization of German raw materials and the manufacture of substitutes.[66] It was, moreover, assigned the duty of coordinating and financing the R&D efforts this required. The research department at the Reichsamt für Wirtschaftsaufbau (Reich Agency for Economic Growth; RAW) ran countless working groups and expert sections, and, with former I.G. Farben Management Board member

---

63 Cf. Wilhelm Treue, *Dokumentation: Hitlers Denkschrift zum Vierjahresplan 1936.* in: Vierteljahrshefte für Zeitgeschichte 2 (1955), 184–210; Dietmar Petzina, *Autarkiepolitik im Dritten Reich. Der nationalsozialistische Vierjahresplan*, Stuttgart 1968.

64 Cf. Ingo Loose, *Das Reichswirtschaftsministerium und die nationalsozialistische Judenverfolgung 1933–1945*, in: Albrecht Ritschl, Das Reichswirtschaftsministerium im Dritten Reich, Berlin 2016, 357–532.

65 Cf. Sören Flachowsky, *Das Reichsamt für Wirtschaftsausbau als Forschungsbehörde im NS-System*, in: Technikgeschichte 3 (2015), 185–224.

66 Cf. Petzina, *Autarkiepolitik*, 61f.

Carl Krauch at its helm, was to emerge as one of the most important armaments industry research establishments. When Krauch was appointed "Plenipotentiary of Special Issues in Chemical Production" (GBChem) in August 1938, it made him one of the most influential armaments managers in the Nazi regime. One month earlier, the Director of the Institut für Erdölgeologie (Institute for Oil Geology) attached to Preussische Geologische Landesanstalt, Prof. Dr Alfred Bentz, had been appointed "Officer in Charge of Oil Production".[67] Bentz was the main architect of the Reich drilling programme.[68]

DEA's management had to adapt to the swiftly changing roles and responsibilities in the tiers of government economic management. Contacts in the Reich Economics Ministry and the navy remained important, but the Four-Year Plan and the "Bentz Office" increasingly took a front seat.

After public announcement of the Four-Year Plan, DEA found itself needing to beef up the expansion programme it had already resolved. Ullner explained to his Supervisory Board on 24 September 1936 that "*there can be no doubt that we must take the announcement into account*".[69] Compared to its original plans, the DEA would henceforth only produce an additional 40,000 tonnes of tar a year. The additional tar volume would be processed in the company's own refineries in Rositz, Wilhelmsburg, and Wietze. To achieve this, the ongoing investment programme would need to be increased by 14.5 million Reichsmark. Ullner justified this with the "*imperatives of state*" communicated to DEA.[70]

---

67 Cf. Vierjahresplanorganisation, BArch, R 26 I, sheet 6.

68 Cf. Eugen Seibold/Ilse Seibold, *Alfred Bentz – Erdölgeologe in schwieriger Zeit 1938–1947*, in: International Journal of Earth Sciences 6 (2002), 1081–1093.

69 Niederschrift über die Verhandlungen des Aufsichtsrats der Deutschen Erdöl-Aktiengesellschaft 24.9.1936, WD-CA, D-PA-29, part 1.

70 Ibid.

Fig. 24 Wilhelmsburg refinery (before 1944)

In the months that followed, the Four-Year Plan Authority raised its target figures on several occasions. DEA in turn adjusted its investment plans, with a shortage of materials increasingly making itself felt, leading to delays realizing construction projects.

As of spring 1937, negotiations with the Reich Navy entered their critical stage. Since the authority for the Four-Year Plan made no effort to sufficiently consider the navy's needs, in May 1937 Admiral Raeder sent an urgent letter straight to Göring and essentially demanded an independent programme just for the navy.[71] The navy pressed for the largest possible pyrolysis plants to be built and for the pedal to be pressed immediately to boost oil production in Heide. DPAG Director Gröber had to dampen the expectations of those on the other side of the negotiating table, as the immediate erection of plant that was scaled up entailed too great a technical

71 Zetzsche, *Logistik und Operationen*, 55.

risk.[72] Nevertheless, Gröber made no bones of the fact that DPAG had to swiftly expand its refinery capacities to at least 275,000 tonnes in order to operate profitably.

A company fronting for the navy abroad?

For all the efforts to boost local heating oil and diesel production, the navy did not think "oil independence" was possible.[73] For that reason, the navy leaders also sought to raise oil imports and acquire oil concessions outside the country. As early as 1935, the navy concluded an agreement to procure 35,000 tonnes a year of heating oil derived from oil shale from Estonia.[74]

The Four-Year Plan Authority, the Reich Economics Ministry, and the Reich War Navy teamed up with industrial companies for projects that imported crude oil from Iraq and elsewhere without foreign currency being required, and in order to acquire oil concessions. In early 1936, steel corporation Otto Wolff entered into talks for an oil concession in Ecuador.[75] A military dictatorship ruled there, and the Third Reich had a good relationship with it. Whether the Otto Wolff corporation was only interested in orders for steel or was contemplating entering the oil business is not really clear. At any rate, the Cologne-based corporation also tried to get a toehold in Venezuela and Brazil.

In the summer of 1936, the Ecuador project had made such progress that the award of the concession was imminent. At that point the Raw Materials and Foreign Currency Staff Unit got

---

72 Cf. DPAG-Vorstandssitzung, 16.4. und 26.5.1937, WD-CA, D-PA-29, part 1.

73 Cf. Anand Toprani, *"The Navy`s success speaks for itself": The German Navy`s Independent Energy Security Strategy 1932–1940*, in: Naval War College Review, 3 (2015), 91–118.

74 Cf. Rasch, *Zur Mineralölpolitik der Kriegsmarine*, 71–101.

75 Cf. Kockel, *Deutsche Ölpolitik*, 230–251.

involved and proposed a consortium be founded consisting of German banks and oil and steel companies. The unit suggested DPAG/DEA join the consortium and also intended to provide a grant of 10 million Reichsmark for the project. In autumn 1936, oil geologist Alfred Bentz toured Ecuador and Venezuela on a mission to establish whether and where German industry should get involved in oil exploration in South America. Unlike the international oil experts, he favoured Ecuador, especially as the oil majors did not dominate the sector there.

After Bentz's return, talks were held in Berlin with the potential consortium members on 1 October 1936. Schlicht was sceptical of the project and considered Ecuadorian mining laws to be a major hindrance.[76] He insisted that of the German oil industry only DPAG/DEA be allowed to join the consortium. When Bentz and others rejected this, he torpedoed the talks. Director Siedersleben of Otto Wolff AG noted, looking back, that DPAG "*commented very shabbily, indeed pejoratively about the Ecuador plan*".[77]

The Wolff corporation thereupon tried to woo Gewerkschaft Elwerath and Wintershall AG into signing up to the Ecuador project. Elwerath was, however, already working to full capacity and hardly had any cash in its treasury.[78] There were also concerns on the part of machine and drilling plant company Alfred Wirth & Co. that should DPAG/DEA be excluded, the latter might cancel contracts that were indispensable to it.

The Wolff corporation tried again. DPAG's Director Grosse was invited to meet Bentz in Berlin on 13 October 1938.[79] The Wolff corporation's Director Siedersleben began by describing the early

---

76 Cf. ibid., 240.

77 Direktor Siedersleben, Otto Wolff AG an Direktor Müller, Maschinen- und Bohrgerätefirma Alfred Wirth & Co. in Erkelenz, 7.7.1937, Rheinisch-Westfälisches Wirtschaftsarchiv, Otto Wolff AG, Stahlhandel Cologne, 72-143-6.

78 Cf. Müller an Siedersleben, 5.7.1937, ibid.

79 Cf. Otto Wolff AG: Aktenvermerk über eine Besprechung betreffend ecuadorianische Ölkonzession, 13.10.1938, ibid.

days of the Ecuador project and stated that Gewerkschaft Elwerath and Texas Oil, with whom it had links, had turned their backs on the undertaking. Siedersleben therefore offered DPAG a stake in the Ecuadorian oil concession business. The Wolff corporation wanted to involve Standard Oil or another US oil corporation once the time was ripe, and talks had already been held in this regard, he said.

To finance the undertaking, foreign currency equivalent to almost 1.25 million Reichsmark in total had been promised. Since such a sum would hardly suffice for more protracted exploration activities, an agreement needed to be made with a "major foreign-currency holder among the oil companies", with the choice being Standard Oil, as the latter was friendly toward Germany. Grosse, so the plan, would in October join Bentz and Director Werner Müller of Maschinen- und Bohrgerätefirma Alfred Wirth & Co. in Erkelenz and depart on a trip to Ecuador that would last several months.[80] The trio of experts was to assess the economic viability of the concession areas and optional fields that the Wolff corporation had acquired. In the concession area, DPAG would then make three trial drillings for oil. Grosse expressed interest but needed to first consult with his fellow DPAG/DEA board members.

Yet the project continued to rest on wobbly foundations, as above all there was a shortfall in dollars, and also without a strong US oil-industry partner at your side nothing could be achieved in South America. There was also resistance to the enterprise inside Germany, with the Fuel Industry Economic Group, where representatives of I.G. Farben set the tone, rejecting it.

After a brief consultation, DPAG/DEA withdrew: "*We are forced by the new conditions that have now arisen in the Ostmark and the neighbouring countries to commit all our resources in order to develop these regions. However much we are ourselves interested in the Ecuador project, we regret that we at present discern no way in which we could partici-*

---

80 Cf. Otto Wolff AG an Direktor Große, DPAG Wietze, 10.12.1938, ibid.

pate in the same."[81] The strong reference to the "Ostmark" was not an excuse, as in November 1938 specifically there had been a breakthrough there in the search for oil. DPAG/DEA thus resolved to go for the bird in hand rather than two that might be hidden in a bush in Ecuador and focus its limited capacities on European oil fields.

Mexico came into play as another potential partner for oil deals for the Reich Navy. The leftist Mexican government sought to nationalize its oil industry and was looking for a counterbalance to the dominant US and Anglo-Dutch oil corporations. It therefore did not shy away from stronger economic links to the Third Reich.

Initially, the navy tried to gain a foothold in Mexico with the help of US oil magnate William Rhodes Davis, who sympathized with Hitler.[82] Davis' company "Crusader" operated the third-largest refinery in Germany, the "Eurotank" in Hamburg. However, one of Davis' companies was so embroiled in a bribery scandal in Mexico that the Reich Navy took a different avenue, enquiring whether DPAG would be able to handle drilling jobs on behalf of the Mexican government. DPAG's Gröber said in June 1936 that the project was undergoing an "*initial assessment*".[83] A good year later, the Naval High Command instructed Dresdner Bank to set up a "Gesellschaft für überseeische bergbauliche Unternehmungen mbH" (company for overseas mining enterprises; Überseeische). This company would then prepare a concession agreement with the Mexican government.[84] From the outset, the Überseeische had a government face and was essentially a front for the navy. It took its cue here from the Anglo-Persian Oil Corporation (APOC, later British Petroleum), the

---

81 DPAG, Wietze an Otto Wolff AG, Köln, Abt. Ausland Berlin, 24.11.1938, ibid.

82 Cf. Dale Harrington, *Mystery Man: William Rhodes Davis, Nazi Agent of Influence*, New York 2001.

83 Cf. DEA-Vorstandssitzung 26.6.1936, WD-CA, D-PA-29, part 1.

84 Cf. Wilhelm Meier-Dörnberg, *Die Ölversorgung der Kriegsmarine 1935 bis 1945*, Freiburg 1973, 40; Johannes Bähr, *Die Dresdner Bank in der Wirtschaft des Dritten Reiches*, München 2006, 420.

foundation of which was prompted by the Admiralty in London, and the British government remained its main shareholder.

The navy intended to grant DPAG/DEA a key role as its strategic partner in Überseeische.[85] DPAG/DEA was expected to act as the oil mining company, and the navy command requested that it devise a financial plan for the Mexico project.

Alfred Bentz estimated that some 8–10 million tonnes of crude oil could be obtained without foreign currency from Mexico only a year after the project started. DPAG/DEA thereupon attempted to squeeze Dresdner Bank out of the deal and position itself as sole lead manager.[86]

A concession agreement with the Mexican government was ready for signature in spring 1938, only for the Reich Economics Ministry to get cold feet.[87] The civil servants feared that the US and British oil corporations might completely discontinue their oil supplies to Germany if the navy insisted on acquiring oil concessions in Mexico, since the Mexican government had nationalized its oil fields on 18 March 1938,[88] prompting the international oil companies to impose a procurement and transport boycott on the nationalized Mexican oil industry. The German navy exploited the situation to procure crude oil from Mexico, but the large-scale plan to produce oil in Mexico, in which DPAG/DEA played a key role, was confined to the wastebin the moment Big Oil threatened to immediately stop supplies to Germany. Such a boycott would have hit the German rearmament efforts hard.[89]

The DEA board members had not really identified with the navy's far-reaching overseas plans anyway. For good reason, they felt

---

85 Cf. Titus Kockel, *Zickzackkurs in den Krieg. Deutsche Ölpolitik von Achnacarry Castle bis Karinhall (1928–1938)*, in: Dietrich Eichholtz, Deutsche Ölpolitik im Zeitalter der Weltkriege, Studien und Dokumente, Leipzig 2010, 256f.

86 Cf. Bähr, *Die Dresdner Bank*, 421.

87 Cf. Kockel, *Zickzackkurs in den Krieg*, 269–274.

88 Cf. Kockel, *Deutsche Ölpolitik*, 312.

89 Cf. Bähr, *Die Dresdner Bank*, 422.

DPAG was too weak to be able to compete with the oil majors – DPAG had neither the know-how nor the staff to do that. Moreover, the DEA executives were well aware of how Deutsche Bank's ambitious oil projects before the First World War had come a cropper. They continued to believe the corporation's key business activity was coal mining and processing.

The December 1937 navy contract

Even before the projects in Latin America were declared to have definitively failed, DPAG/DEA's German heating oil project came under pressure as the navy started asking what was, in principle, the best procedure to adopt.[90] The reason behind this was that Stinnes GmbH had successfully trialled a new process for producing heat oil from hard coal. The Essen-based company had carefully studied the Bergius-Pier method and developed its own preliminary stage, an extraction method it named the Pott-Broche process. Stinnes founded Ruhröl GmbH, which in early 1937 turned the key on a liquefaction plant in Welheim in the northern Ruhr region that was dedicated to liquefying hard coal to produce synth-fuels.[91] Since other companies were also eying an entry into producing synth fuels from hard coal, and the focus in the Four-Year Plan was on I.G. Farben's liquefaction process, DPAG/DEA was in danger of lagging behind in terms of technology. DPAG/DEA had to quickly explain

---

90 Cf. DEA-Vorstandssitzung, 1.6.1937, WD-CA, D-PA-29, part 1.

91 Cf. Günther Ibing, *Über die Extraktion von Steinkohle in Kombination mit der Druckhydrierung von Pech (Arbeitsweise der Ruhröl GmbH von 1938 bis 1944)*, in: Deutsche Gesellschaft für Mineralölwissenschaft und Kohlechemie (Ed.), Compendium (1974/75), 311–318; Manfred Rasch/Alfred Pott, 287–290, in: Günter Bayerl (Ed.), *Braukohlenveredelung im Niederlausitzer Revier. 50 Jahre Schwarze Pumpe*, Münster 2009.

Fig. 25 DEA's Fichtenhainichen refinery (1936)

how its method was technically mature. Once it had done so, the negotiations with the navy picked up speed again.[92]

In autumn 1937, the broad strokes of a long-term supply contract with the Navy were apparent. DEA would commit from April 1939 to deliver a total of 1.5 million tonnes of heavy heating oil over the next 5–12 years in annual instalments of 125,000–150,000

92 Cf. DEA-Vorstandssitzung, 2.6.1937, WD-CA, D-PA-29, part 1.

tonnes.[93] A price of 130 Reichsmark/t of heating oil was agreed for the first deliveries. The price factored in the start-up costs for a new plant was well above the previous price of 85 Reichsmark/t of heating oil.[94] The supply obligations referred only to heating oil, but the navy was accorded the right, in line with new plant DEA might erect, to procure a certain quantity of diesel oil instead of heating oil.

As a first step toward reaching the production targets, the capacity of the old pyrolysis factory in Rositz would be expanded to 175,000 tonnes p.a. In the next step, capacity would be expanded at the pyrolysis plant in Rositz and the refinery in Fichtenhainichen in Thuringia, in both cases to 275.000 tonnes p.a.[95] To this end, a total of some 120 million Reichsmark would be invested, with a further 50-60 million in expenditure to acquire new lignite fields and expand lignite production.

Planned capacity expansion for the Navy Programme (status: September 1937)[96]

Date	Heating oil (in tonnes)	Diesel (in tonnes)	Cumulative investments (in million Reichsmark)
1 April 1938	100,000	10,000	10
1 April 1941	150,000	30,000	28
1 April 1943	220,00	70,000	45
1 April 1945	290,000	110,000	120

There were reservations on the part of the DEA Management Board as some felt that the commitments went too far and

93 Cf. Schreiben des Oberbefehlshabers der Kriegsmarine an die DPAG, 13.12.1937, HADB, P 1659; Verpflichtungen gegenüber der Kriegsmarine, 8.12.1938, WD-CA, D-RW-127.

94 Cf. Marinewerft Wilhelmshaven an DEA, 7.8.1933, WD-CA, D-RW-373.

95 Cf. Kimmich: Aktenvermerk 6.12.1937, HADB, P 1659, sheet 16–19.

96 Cf. Kimmich: Aktenvermerk über ein Gespräch mit Herrn Ullner am 6.9.1937, ibid., sheet 2f.

the pace of expansion was too fast.[97] Randhahn wanted to undertake the third expansion stage together with a third-party company, while Ullner worried about the quality of product, and Ritter asked whether the ring presses were fully functional and wanted to have a withdrawal clause included in the contract. In the final instance, DPAG Director Gröber managed to dispel the concerns.

On 13 December 1937, the Commanding Officer of the Reich Navy signed the new supply contract with DEA. It included the words: "*This contract is part of an overall supply contract still to be agreed*", in the framework of which DEA was to supply the navy with a total of 6 million t of heating oil.[98] That was the kicker in the contract. The high production volume could only be achieved under the condition that the corporation acquired a large new lignite field adjacent to its existing fields. Otherwise, expansion of the oil plant would not have made economic sense. The contract with the navy therefore included the clause that DEA was to acquire a predefined lignite field from ASW. The field would then be mined only with navy approval and primarily for its ends.

The problem innate in this stipulation was that it was to the detriment of third parties. Despite verbal agreements in December 1937, no contract had yet been signed with ASW. DEA was therefore not firmly obliged to further expand its plant, although it intended by the end of December 1942 at the latest to declare whether additional plant could be erected to process tar in order to achieve the expected delivery target volume of 6 million tonnes of heating oil and diesel.[99]

At the end of 1937, Hans Gröber reported in a letter to the Authority for German Raw Materials and Production Materials what

---

97 Cf. DEA-Vorstandssitzung, 6./7.10.1937, WD-CA, D-PA-29, part 1.

98 Schreiben des Oberbefehlshabers der Kriegsmarine an die DPAG, 13.12.1937, HADB, P 1659, sheet 222; Verpflichtungen gegenüber der Kriegsmarine, 8.12.1938, WD-CA, D-RW-127.

99 Cf. DEA-Vorstands-Abteilung: Vertrag DPAG-Kriegsmarine 13.12.37/20.1.1938, ibid.

capacities DEA intended to establish in the long term under the terms of the Navy Programme and the Four-Year Plan.

DEA undertakings for the Four-Year Plan[100]

1. Expansion of the Wilhelmsburg refinery
2. Expansion of the pyrolysis plants in Regis to produce 175,000 tonnes of tar
3. New mines developed in Regis
4. Drilling programme in Wietze

Gröber estimated the total investment required to be 50 million Reichsmark.

DEA undertakings for the Navy Programme

1.	Acquisition of a lignite field from ASW	26.5 million Reichsmark
2.	Development of the mine	30.0 million Reichsmark
3.	Construction of new pyrolysis plants	110.0 million Reichsmark
4.	Expansion of the Fichtenhainichen refinery	10.0 million Reichsmark
5.	New-build refinery for 300,000 tonnes of tar from pyrolysis	30.0 million Reichsmark
	Sum total	206.5 million Reichsmark

In other words, DEA intended to make immense investments in the period from 1937 to year-end 1942 for the Navy Programme and the Four-Year Plan. While the capital requirement to acquire the ASW coal field in 1938 was to be covered by a bond, in subsequent years DEA intended mainly to finance investments from the high write-downs. In March 1938, with help from Deutsche

100 Compiled according to: Aktenvermerk: Besprechung mit Gröber, 22.12.1937, BArch Berlin, R 3101/20139, sheet 34.

Bank, Dresdner Bank, and Bankhaus Hardy & Co., DEA floated a bond for 25 million Reichsmark.[101]

By then, the corporation had new opportunities outside coal. After the discovery of oil reservoirs in Holstein, outside Gifhorn, and first and foremost in Austria in autumn 1938, the corporate policy shifted back to focus on oil.

---

101 Cf. Zeichnungsantrag für eine Anleihe in Höhe von 25 Mio. Reichsmark, HADB, P 1656, sheet 249–252.

V. EXPANDING THE DEA HUB AT ROSITZ, 1933–8

(Manfred Grieger)

Boosting lignite mining and taking over new coal fields

The year 1933 was also one of transition for the lignite industry, with mining growing by only two percent and briquette making by only three. Nevertheless, DEA managed to acquire lignite mining rights close to the Regis, Witznitz, and Waltersdorf plants, rounding out its portfolio of valuable and favourably positioned lignite fields.[1] As at 1 January 1934, Mineralölwerke Rositz was sold to Deutsche Petroleum AG and the pyrolysis plants in Regis and Rositz leased to it – although this was only of operational importance to the extent that lignite mining and heavy heating oil production now had to be coordinated between the two corporations. The merger of the management at the Altenburg and Borna mining directorates, by contrast, focussed on ensuring responsibility came under one roof for the mining administration, which had been expanded to include Gewerkschaft Viktoria in 1934.[2]

1 Geschäftsbericht der Deutschen Erdöl-Aktiengesellschaft in Berlin über das 35. Geschäftsjahr 1933, Berlin 1934, 2.

2 DEA-Vorstandssitzung am 23.1.1934, 4, WD-CA, D-PA-24; DEA-Vorstandssitzung am 5.4.1934, 4, ibid.; Geschäftsbericht der Deutschen Erdöl-Aktiengesellschaft in Berlin über das 36. Geschäftsjahr 1934, Berlin 1935, 2; Jahresbericht der Deutschen Petroleum-AG, Mineralölwerke Rositz für das Jahr 1934 vom 5.5.1935, StA Leipzig, 20684, DEA-Mineralölwerke Rositz, No. 5.

Fig. 26 The head office of DEA's Mining Operations in Borna (1938)

The main task of the lignite operations in Central Germany was to secure the raw materials needed to produce heating oil. As early as January 1934, DEA learned from offices in Berlin that the "authorities" were definitely favourably inclined with regard to "better capacity utilization" of Mineralölwerk Rositz.[3] The DEA Management Board was also "very gratified" by the fact that the Nazi government was interested in covering all paraffin demand from inside the country. To this end, in 1934 the lignite operations converted Open-Cast Mine I in Waltersdorf, where 150 men had been fired at the end of 1933,[4] to large-strip mining. The Dora-Helene and Viktoria open-cast mines were pooled in order to enable better utilization of the heavy machinery and achieve better performance. Moreover, an expansion of the plant and equipment boosted pro-

3 DEA-Vorstandssitzung am 23.1.1934, 2, WD-CA, D-PA-24.

4 DEA-Vorstandssitzung am 11.1.1934, 1, ibid.

duction at the Regis and Viktoria briquette factories, while the new power station at Dora-Helene significantly improved power supplies.

The DEA Management Board and Supervisory Board both intended to lock into the Nazi government's insistence that domestic production of heating oil be boosted in order "to extract ourselves from the ongoing stagnation in the lignite segment".[5] After all, the production of heating oil from lignite, which had been tried and tested for over a decade and where there was significant upward potential, also offered an opportunity to really boost operations in Rositz by linking lignite mining, briquette production, and heating oil distillation. In actual fact, coal mining and briquette production rose steadily after 1933, and the increase in output also influenced payroll levels so that cancelled shifts were soon a thing of the past. The drop in unemployment and the increased disposable income thanks to the higher number of hours worked emphatically improved peace in society and reconciled many workers to the new political regime.

Further growth at the DPAG/DEA hub depended, however, on acquiring new lignite fields. The competition to grab the Central German lignite deposits intensified after the Nazis came to power in light of the swift government focus on rearmament. Both the ASW and DEA wanted to profit from the burgeoning armaments industry by launching new large-scale projects to hydrate lignite or transform it by pyrolysis. Both companies therefore sought to buy up the few still independent lignite works. Walther Randhahn, who, by virtue of his doctorate and his long-standing function as Head of Senior Mining Directorate [Oberbergdirektion] at Altenburg, had an extensive knowledge of who owned what and what cross-ownership existed in

---

5 Niederschrift über die Verhandlungen des Aufsichtsrats der DEA am 4.3.1935, 2, WD-CA, D-PA-0120.

Fig. 27 Dora and Helene open-cast mines, 1934

the Central German lignite fields, played an important role in this regard.[6]

The navy supply contract on the table for signature foresaw a large volume of heating oil being delivered to the military, and DEA would only be able to fulfil the contract if it expanded its Central German lignite base. The corporation therefore sought to buy additional coal mines in the Borna and Meuselwitz fields. Negotiations were initiated to this end in early 1934 with Gewerkschaft Viktoria in Lobstädt, south of Leipzig. Agreement was swiftly reached with the company, which belonged to the Flick corporation, owner of the Maximilian colliery, and in May 1934 DEA acquired the lion's share

6 Walther Randhahn, *Der Wettbewerb der deutschen Braunkohleindustrie gegen die Einfuhr der böhmischen Kohle*, PhD thesis Jena 1908.

of the mining rights.[7] The coal fields owned by Gewerkschaft Viktoria were located opposite the DEA plants in Borna.[8]

Moreover, DEA also managed to round out the coal fields it held by entering into swap agreements with ASW and Niederlausitzer Kohlenwerke, which belonged to the Petschek Group at Aussig.[9] DEA relinquished its Saxonia field, and ASW traded a lignite field in the Breitingen district that formed an enclave in the DEA fields. Another swap involved the Rötingen lignite field close to Regis, acquired from the Niederlausitzer Kohlenwerke. As a result, DEA had a conglomerate of fields that contained 643 million tonnes of lignite, of which 580 million tonnes could be extracted from open-cast mines.[10]

Talks with representatives of Prehlitzer Braunkohlenwerke AG were slightly more complicated. Its lignite field was located about 10 km west of the DEA works in Thuringia, and the company's main shareholders wanted to sell, as they saw no opportunity to expand operations. The sales talks were led by Deputy Supervisory Board Chairman Max Zell and Managing Director Otto Winter, whereby both men dragged their feet.[11] Negotiations ran for two years without making any real progress – until there was a breakthrough in mid-1936.[12]

---

7 Cf. Geschäftsbericht der Deutschen Erdöl-Aktiengesellschaft in Berlin über das 36. Geschäftsjahr 1934, Berlin 1935, 6; DEA-Vorstandssitzung vom 4.5.1934, WD-CA, D-PA-24; Niederschrift über die Verhandlungen des Aufsichtsrats der DEA vom 4.5.1934, 3f., WD-CA, D-PA-0120.

8 Cf. Betriebsverhältnisse und Übernahme durch die Deutsche Erdöl Aktiengesellschaft 1934–35, Bergarchiv Freiberg, 40051, Bergamt Leipzig, No. 566.

9 Niederschrift über die Verhandlungen des Aufsichtsrats der DEA vom 1.10.1935, WD-CA, D-PA-0120.

10 Aktenvermerk betr. DEA-Quartalsbericht vom 5.10.1935, HADB, P 1675, sheet 76.

11 DEA-Vorstandssitzung vom 11.1.1934, 23.1.1934 und 5.4.1934, WD-CA, D-PA-24.

12 DEA-Vorstandsitzung vom 18.3.1936 und 12.6.1936, WD-CA, D-PA-29; Geschäftsbericht der Deutschen Erdöl-Aktiengesellschaft in Berlin über das 39. Geschäftsjahr 1937, Berlin 1938; Krau, *Kohle, Öl und Krieg*, 63.

According to a report in Frankfurter Zeitung, the single largest slice of shares in Prehlitzer Braunkohlen AG was family-owned.[13] In July 1936, a one-for-one share swap was agreed between the main shareholders and DEA, although Prehlitzer Braunkohlen AG had disbursed a higher dividend the prior year than had DEA.[14] The business press commented that the corporation's dwindling liquidity as a result of the forthcoming mandatory participation in BRABAG of about half a million Reichsmark was the main reason why the Prehlitz management had agreed to sell the company to DEA and the related loss of its independence.[15] The merger with DEA meant that its mandatory inclusion in BRABAG was void, as DEA was already a member of the latter.[16] The managing director of Prehlitzer Braunkohlen AG, Otto Winter, was to receive a different position with DEA, but declined the offer. Supervisory Board Chairman Curt Steckner,[17] until 1930 co-owner of the Bankhaus Reinhold Steckner and from 1924 to 1933 President of the Chamber of Commerce and Industry in Halle, forfeited his function but, like all the other Super-

---

13 Frankfurter Zeitung vom 7.8.1936.

14 Frankfurter Zeitung vom 26.11.1936.

15 *Zum Aktienumtausch Prehlitz-Deutsche Erdöl-AG*, in: Deutsche Bergwerkszeitung vom 5.6.1936.

16 Geschäftsbericht der Prehlitzer-Braunkohlen-Aktiengesellschaft für 1935.

17 Bernd G. Ulbrich, *Geschichte der Industrie- und Handelskammer Halle-Dessau 1844–2019*, Halle 2019, 123; Czarnikow had been a councillor of justice in Halle since 1892 and had taken part in the First World War with the rank of major; see also Wolfgang Tittelbach-Helmrich, *Arnstadts jüdische Bürger*, Arnstadt 1995, 34.

visory Board members, received compensation from DEA.[18] Thanks to the acquisitions, DEA raised its direct and indirect stake in the Central German lignite syndicate to over 18 percent (DEA: 14.5; Viktoria 2.04; Prehlitz 1.64 percent) and improved the profitability of its lignite operations.[19]

In 1936, the thus far independent subsidiaries Magdeburger Bergwerks AG, Berlin, Gewerkschaft Viktoria in Lobstädt, Braunkohlengewerkschaft Breunsdorf, Breunsdorf, and Prehlitzer Braunkohlen AG, Meuselwitz, were taken over by the parent company. As a result, all hard coal and lignite mining operations were henceforth managed centrally by the DEA head office.

DEA expanded its access to coal with a bitumen content by acquiring additional fields south of Regis in the Herzogin Adelheid colliery and the Ramsdorf colliery east of Regis. However, the company's senior executives and the management on site were clearly aware that, in the long run, it would only be possible to cover the costs of the plant upgrading and the commitments made by emphatically raising the volume of lignite mined. To that end, DEA needed to acquire extensive coal fields to ensure it had coal reserves that would suffice for decades. The modernization and concomitant new economies of scale were used as an argument to prompt other own-

---

18 The members of the supervisory board of Prehlitzer Braunkohlen-AG were: Chairman Dr. Curt Steckner, banker and honorary president of IHK-Halle (Chamber of Commerce and Industry Halle); Vice-Chairman: Dr. Ing. Max Zell, managing director of Ostelbisches Braunkohlensyndikat (East Elbian lignite syndicate); Prof. Dr. Paul Duden, chairman of the Verein Deutscher Chemiker (association of German chemists); horticultural engineer August Stapel, Jena; bank director B. Spiegel, Nuremberg, judicial councillor Hans Czarnikow, Halle. Ingrid Krau claims in her book *Kohle, Öl und Krieg* on page 63 that Steckner was a Jewish banker who was later murdered in Auschwitz. This is false. Steckner had been a director of Dresdner Bank in Halle since the takeover of Bankhaus Steckner by Dresdner Bank in 1930 and remained so until his death in 1937. Cf. Landesarchiv Sachsen-Anhalt [hereafter: LASA], dept. Merseburg, I 546, No. 41, Korrespondenzen.

19 Niederschrift über die Verhandlungen des Aufsichtsrats der DEA vom 24.9.1936, 3, WD-CA, D-PA-0120.

ers to part company with coal mining rights. For that reason, on 18 February 1935 DEA contacted Aktiengesellschaft Sächsischer Werke (ASW), which was owned by the Saxon State Government, and sought to acquire the 1,100-hectare Heuersdorf-Käferhain coal field, which bordered on the Regis fields, and which would have boosted the DEA coal reserves by about a third to 635 million tonnes. At that point in time, ASW was only willing to enter into a limited swap transaction of the Breitlinger Westfeld for the Grubenfeld Saxonia, which would have spelled a net increase for DEA of only some 12 million tonnes.[20]

The intensive discussions that had already taken place between the Reich Navy and DEA hinged on the former's wish that DEA increase its delivery volumes of lignite-based heating oil by a significant multiple; from DEA's viewpoint this necessitated not just it being allocated construction materials and workers but also, and above all, expanding the coal fields at its disposal. Given the greater urgency of owning access rights to lignite in the vicinity of Mineralölwerke Rositz, in 1936 DEA again approached the ASW Management Board.[21] The project caused unrest at German Labor-Front [Deutsche Arbeitsfront], who started negotiating with DEA Management Board member Randhahn on the issue of the possible transfer of workers to other operations. Since handing over the Heuersdorf-Käferhain coal field would also have affected the industrial interests of Saxony, Saxony's Nazi Party Gauleiter Martin Mutschmann and the Saxon State Minister of Economic Affairs Georg Lenk, likewise a long-standing Nazi and Chairman of the ASW Supervisory Board, announced they intended to inspect the

20 DEA, Vorstand, Vermerk betr. Erwerb des Kohlenfeldes Heuersdorf-Käferhain von ASW, Dresden vom 28.4.1938, 2, BArch Berlin, R 3101, No. 18274, sheet 64.

21 DEA-Vorstandssitzung vom 16.1.1936, 3, WD-CA, D-PA-29.

work. Locking into additional coal reserves through new fields thus entailed clear potential political conflict.[22]

Yet the volume of heating oil the military wished to order kept on growing, and the company therefore had to decide in terms of its fuel policy whether it would concentrate on tar production or would continue to rely on its existing value added, including tar processing. In early August 1936, the DEA Management Board reached the decision that it should continue its "overall policy" and not "let tar processing take a backseat as our [...] very own programme".[23] In early March 1937, it filed the formal application to acquire the ASW's Heuersdorf-Käferhain coal field.[24] The talks hit an obstacle, as the ASW was obliged first to offer the coal fields in question to the Petschek Group, which held pre-emptive purchase rights on the basis of a clause in an old contract,[25] although the importance of this contractual obligation waned the more the Central German lignite industry was restructured.

Thereupon, on behalf of the DEA Management Board, in mid-July 1937 Walther Randhahn submitted a corresponding request to ASW, in which he emphasized the urgency of the matter in military terms and in view of its "technical necessity".[26] For in June 1937 at a meeting with DPAG Director Hans Gröber, the navy had demanded that he issue a declaration stating that the DEA and/or DPAG, with its processing plant, would be able to supply 200,000 tonnes of heating oil within a year. If this were not to happen, the navy intended to instead rely on the I.G. Farben process. In other words, the navy happily banged the thumbscrews on its old partner, and the DEA senior executives had no choice – given the techni-

---

22 DEA-Vorstandssitzung am 18.3.1936, 2, ibid.; DEA-Vorstandssitzung am 2.3.1937, 3, ibid.

23 DEA-Vorstandssitzung am 4.6.1936, 3, ibid.

24 DEA-Vorstandssitzung am 10.3.1937, ibid.

25 DEA-Vorstandssitzung am 23.4.1937, 2f., ibid.; DEA-Vorstandssitzung am 2.12.1937, 1, ibid.

26 DEA-Vorstandssitzung am 7.7.1937, ibid.

cal maturity of the company's plants and the fact that they intended to operate them 24/7 – but to declare that they would be able to deliver. For only in this way could DEA prevent the "navy drifting off in favour of hard coal" and/or I.G. Farben seizing a monopoly on heating oil production.[27] Since the navy, for its part, depended on the DEA supply chain, Gröber wanted his naval contacts to "exert pressure" on ASW to sell the necessary coal fields to DEA.[28] In September 1937, the talks suggested that overall there were good prospects of DEA getting its way, although in the opinion of Randhahn the purchase price was likely to be "quite considerable", given the good quality of the coal.[29] DEA tabled a maximum offer of 20 million Reichsmark in November 1937.[30]

The outcome of the protracted negotiations was a contract for the purchase of the coal field in question, ready for signature and with an agreed price of 26.5 million Reichsmark. A total of 18 million Reichsmark had to change hands in 1938, with the remainder being paid in annual tranches. In this context, the DEA applied to the Reich Economics Ministry for approval of a 40-million-Reichsmark bond with a 20-year tenor in order to raise financing for the short-term costs in the market.[31] DEA estimated the financing requirement for the Rositz hub up to the end of 1941 at a minimum of 113 million Reichsmark. The Reich Economics Ministry approved the bond in principle, but insisted it be subject to a 25 million Reichsmark cap.[32]

---

27 DEA-Vorstandssitzung am 1.6.1937, 1f., ibid.

28 DEA-Vorstandssitzung am 7.7.1937, ibid.

29 DEA-Vorstandssitzung am 29.9.1937, 1, ibid.

30 DEA-Vorstandssitzung am 26.11.1937, ibid.

31 DEA, Vorstand 4, an Reichs- und Preußischer Wirtschaftsminister, MR Dr. Paul Josten vom 27.12.1937, BArch Berlin, R 3101, No. 18274, sheet 45.

32 Reichs- und Preußischer Wirtschaftsminister, MR Dr. Paul Josten, an DEA vom 2.2.1938, BArch Berlin, R 3101, No. 18274, sheet 60; Niederschrift über die Verhandlungen des Aufsichtsrats der DEA am 17.5.1938, 4, WD-CA, D-PA-0120.

The acquisition of large coal fields around Rositz was, in the opinion of DEA Management Board Chairman Richard F. Ullner, the precondition for "the corporation's entire development".[33] For this reason, the unexpected refusal by the ASW Supervisory Board Chairman, State of Saxony Economics Minister Georg Lenk, to green-light the release of the coal field to DEA cut to the quick. Lenk argued his corner by citing not only economic reasons but also the objection made by Nazi Party Gauleiter Mutschmann that, in the persons of Georg Solmssen, Ernst Springer, and Paul von Schwabach, there were still "non-Aryans" on the DEA Supervisory Board. The corporation thereupon hastily severed its ties to the three long-standing supervisory board members in May 1938.

The specialist department at the Reich Economics Ministry suspected that this refusal actually masked "fundamental considerations" on the meaningful use of the lignite deposits for producing oil.[34] For the ASW was, like DEA, a shareholder in BRABAG, which from 1936 onwards derived petroleum from lignite using a high-pressure hydration process at its facility in Böhlen, south of Leipzig.[35] At any rate, the Reich Economics Ministry was not aware whether the agreements the Four-Year Plan Authority and the Reich Office for Economic Expansion had reached with the State of Saxony on the use of the lignite mined there played a role. The fact that Mutschmann and Lenk instrumentalized state anti-Semitism to

---

33 Richard F. Ullner an Karl Kimmich vom 5.5.1938, HADB, P 1659, sheet 74.

34 Reichswirtschaftsministerium, Hauptabteilung I, MinÖl 7 (1007/38g) an Hauptabteilungsleiter I vom 20.10.1938, 1, BArch Berlin, R 3101, No. 30109, sheet 29.

35 On Brabag-Böhlen see for example Rainer Karlsch, *Die Aktiengesellschaft Sächsische Werke (ASW) und das Hydrierwerk der Braunkohle-Benzin AG (Brabag) in Böhlen*, in: Konstantin Hermann (Ed.), Führerschule, Thingplatz, "Judenhaus". Orte und Gebäude der nationalsozialistischen Diktatur in Sachsen, Dresden 2014, 190–193; see also Martin Baumert, *Autarkiepolitik in der Braunkohleindustrie. Ein diachroner Systemvergleich anhand des Braunkohleindustriekomplexes Böhlen-Espenhain 1933 bis 1965*, Berlin 2022, 87ff.

achieve their economic interests was consistent with the political line taken by the authorities.

Since the DEA Management Board had already floated the 25-million Reichsmark bond in March 1938, as it had safely assumed the ASW Supervisory Board would agree to the deal and had ordered mining equipment on a large scale,[36] it now threatened to bring claims for damages and demanded that the Reich Economics Ministry bring its influence to bear on the Saxon state government with a view to the navy's interests in heating oil deliveries.[37] DEA submitted a longer memo on the "acquisition of the Heuersdorf-Käferhain coalfield from ASW, Dresden" to make it clear that both the annual production of the south block of coal fields in Rositz (1937: 4.8 million tonnes) and its coal reserves needed to be boosted significantly in order to cover the navy's requirements. After all, the total volume of coal needed after turnkey of the eight pyrolysis lines in the Regis II pyrolysis plant was estimated to rise to ten million tonnes, a figure that could not be covered by the existing coalfields.[38] DEA Director Gröber rigorously championed the company's position at a meeting at the end of May 1938 at the Reich Economics Ministry.[39]

Although, in May 1938, the Office of the Commander-in-Chief of the navy had reached out through the Armed Forces Supreme Command to get the Reich Economics Ministry to push

---

36 Geschäftsbericht der Deutschen Erdöl-Aktiengesellschaft in Berlin über das 39. Geschäftsjahr 1937, Berlin 1938, 6.

37 Reichs- und Preußischer Wirtschaftsminister, Hauptabteilung I, MinÖl 7 (3473/38), Vermerk Kohlenfelderverkauf ASW an DEA vom 6.5.1938, BArch Berlin, R 3101, No. 18274, sheet 62.

38 DEA, Vorstand, Vermerk betr. Erwerb des Kohlenfeldes Heuersdorf-Käferhain von ASW, Dresden vom 28.4.1938, 7 and 9, ibid., 69 and 71.

39 Reichswirtschaftsministerium, Hauptabteilung I, MinÖl (3740/38), Vermerk über Besprechung mit der DEA am 25.5.1938 vom 28.5.1938, ibid., 78f.

the agreement through, the matter still hung in the balance.[40] The DEA Supervisory Board acknowledged in October 1938 that the purchase of the coal fields was "still not definitively decided".[41] Within the company, the plan was to demand in October 1938 that Reich Minister Walther Funk take a decision on whether pressure could thus be exerted on the State of Saxony's Minister of Economics in this regard to retrospectively approve the contract as negotiated.[42] Mining Director Randhahn likewise felt he would be able to persuade Reich Economics Minister Funk to back DEA, and in a letter of 28 November 1938 he requested "a short personal meeting" with Funk.[43]

Yet the whole affair ground to a halt. Mutschmann even exploited an accident involving an explosion at the Regis II pyrolysis plant in April 1939 to continue to agitate against the sale of the coal fields. He rejected the transfer of the coal fields DEA had applied for with the words that the idea was to "grab them underhand" from the State of Saxony behind his back.[44] State of Saxony Minster of Economics Lenk also called on DEA to abandon its efforts to be awarded the coal fields. "If necessary, Herr Mu[tschmann] will approach the Führer directly."[45]

---

40 Oberkommando der Wehrmacht, Wehr- und Wirtschaftsamt, Ernst Becht, an Reichs- und Preußisches Wirtschaftsministerium, Hauptabteilung I vom 25.5.1938, BArch Berlin, R 3101, No. 30109, sheet 31; Oberbefehlshaber der Kriegsmarine, Hermann von Fischel, an Reichsstelle für Wirtschaftsausbau vom 4.5.1938, BArch Berlin, R 3101, No. 30109, sheet 32f.

41 Niederschrift über die Verhandlungen des Aufsichtsrats der DEA am 11.10.1938, 3, WD-CA, D-PA-0120.

42 Reichswirtschaftsministerium, Hauptabteilung I, MinÖl 7 (1007/38g) an Hauptabteilungsleiter I vom 20.10.1938, 2, BArch Berlin, R 3101, No. 30109, sheet 30.

43 DEA, Walther Randhahn, an Reichswirtschaftsminister Walther Funk vom 26.11.1938, ibid., 16f.

44 Walther Randhahn, Aktennotiz betr. Explosion Schwelwerk II/Regis vom 20.4.1939, 5, StA Leipzig, 20684, DEA-Mineralölwerke Rositz, No. 48.

45 Ibid., 11.

By that time, the Reich Economics Ministry had assessed the matter by evaluating the legal issues and had tabled a compromise: ASW should assign a field north of the DEA field in Regis (the deposits there were put at 100-150 million tonnes of coal) and would in exchange receive DEA's field in Bernsdorf, which held 40 million tonnes.[46] The DEA had originally assumed its reserves would grow by some 450 to 500 million tonnes in lignite deposits, but now the volume up for debate was only a fraction. The Saxon state corporation continued to hesitate and complained to Krauch about the chief DEA negotiators. ASW evidently wanted to enter the lignite pyrolysis market itself but did not possess the requisite know-how. ASW therefore demanded that it be familiarized with a new process for selectively hydrogenating phenol, something DEA rejected, referring ASW to the tried-and-true Edeleanu process.[47]

Krauch's reservations as regards DEA remained. He insisted that before the issue of the coal fields could be decided, the corporation immediately commence planning a second major pyrolysis plant. DEA refused, as there was no resource base for such a move. Things changed when, at the end of June 1939, there were talks between the navy and the Flick corporation's management. On behalf of the navy, Flick brokered a deal between DEA and ASW, and Schirner thereupon declared he was willing to find a "friendly settlement".[48] As a result, the lignite-field swap between ASW and DEA came about after all. On the other hand, this meant DEA was no longer able to participate in the "aryanization" of the Ignaz Petschek Group member companies in Central Germany.

---

46 Niederschrift über die Verhandlungen des Aufsichtsrats der Deutschen Erdöl-Aktiengesellschaft vom 28.6.1939, WD-CA, 3000–81.

47 Ullner/Randhahn an Krauch vom 29.6.1939, WD-CA, D-RW-46.

48 Schirner, Notiz betr. Marinevertrag, ibid.

After investment of 1.8 million Reichsmark in lignite in 1936 alone,[49] the total output of the DEA lignite plants grew between 1936 and 1938 from 7.7 to 10 million tonnes, while briquette production rose during the same period from 2.8 to 3.3 million tonnes. Any further increase in output required an expansion in the mining rail network and in power-plant and boiler capacities.[50] Higher sales and a larger workforce as well as the elimination of idle shifts were, in the opinion of the DEA Management Board, the outcome of an "upturn in the company".[51] However, the fluctuating water and tar content caused irritation between the lignite and pyrolysis factories with regard to the quality of the briquettes supplied. Gröber sought to minimize the potential for conflict by introducing a new invoicing system that reflected the interests of both the processing plants and the special outlays the lignite companies incurred producing suitable briquettes.[52]

Lignite plants: total output (in 1,000 tonnes), 1933–1938[53]

Year	Raw coal	Briquettes
1933	5,118	1,864
1934	5,796	2,151
1935	6,429	2,368
1936	7,768	2,826
1937	9,370	3,233
1938	10,022	3,312

Given the lack of workers, a trend that became ever more pronounced, at the end of March 1939 DEA applied to employ up

49 Niederschrift über die Verhandlungen des Aufsichtsrats der DEA am 4.3.1936, 5, WD-CA, D-PA-0120.

50 Geschäftsbericht der Deutschen Erdöl-Aktiengesellschaft in Berlin über das 39. Geschäftsjahr 1937, Berlin 1938, 2.

51 Ibid., 5.

52 DEA-Vorstandssitzung vom 18.3.1937, 1, WD-CA, D-PA-29.

53 Calculated according to: DEA-Geschäftsberichte 1933–1938.

to 20 women in the briquette factories in Rositz and Herzogin Adelheid to help load the briquettes, something that was approved by the State of Thuringia Ministry of Economics on 25 April 1939, with an exemption permit for women aged 30-40 to work in two shifts of eight hours each until 31 December 1939.[54] DEA successfully applied each year for the short-term approval to be extended.

Presaging the further bottlenecks to come in construction materials during the war-time economy, turnkey of the expansion to the refinery and pyrolysis works started in 1938 was already delayed by first-half 1939. The coal-dust explosion on 11 April 1939 at the Regis II pyrolysis plant left 21 dead (19 DPAG staff and two employees of Frankfurt plant assembly company Lurgi)[55] and caused further delays to the project, as the Regis II plant had to be shut down temporarily. The ring briquette facility, which was affected most by the explosion, had to be re-planned at the instruction of the authorities.

The deaths caused by the accident were exaggerated by the Nazi regime and DEA itself and presented as quasi-military martyrdom that the men had gladly performed in order to implement the Third Reich's strategy of gaining energy independence. The memorial service on 15 April 1939, attended by Saxony's Gauleiter and Reichsstatthalter Martin Mutschmann as well as DAF boss Robert Ley, followed the example of quasi-military honouring of the dead and self-presentation of the NSDAP elite set by the service at Wintershall.[56] This contrasted sharply with the severe accusation that Mutschmann loudly voiced on 12 April 1939 while inspecting the

54 Deutsche Erdöl-AG, Zweigniederlassung Borna an Thüringisches Wirtschaftsministerium vom 27.3.1939, Bergarchiv Freiberg, 40051, No. 1106; Thüringisches Wirtschaftsministerium an Thüringisches Bergamt vom 25.4.1939, ibid.

55 DPAG, Mineralölwerke Rositz, Halbjahresbericht für das erste Halbjahr 1939 vom 30.9.1939, 12, StA Leipzig, 20684, DEA-Mineralölwerke Rositz, No. 5.

56 Manfred Grieger, *In-company social welfare politics and forced labour. The two sides to the Nazi "Betriebsgemeinschaft" (Works community) at Wintershall*, in: id. et al. (Eds.), Expansion at all costs? Studies on the Wintershall AG between crisis and war, 1929–1945, Frankfurt/Main 2020, 160–225, here 186f.

works HQ and the company. Mutschmann had somewhat overhastily concluded that cleaning work performed using an electric hammer drill had caused the accident, whereupon the manager of the pyrolysis plant, Walther Rademacher, and a master craftsman were both arrested.

Franz Landwehr, an authorized signatory in Rositz, rejected this accusation as the DPAG manager suspected two men employed to grease the bearings in the bucket conveyor of having been smoking. Operations management even talked of an "act of sabotage", as at the end of 1938 a man had been caught deliberately starting a fire.[57] In his memorial speech Mutschmann insisted on suggesting the company had "exploited" the workers, who were the most "precious asset" of the operations, and said the "Nazi government leaders" would be conducting an intensive investigation.[58] At the end of the day, Mutschmann hardly had any evidence backing up his claims. The extensive investigation by the public prosecutors was unable to identify a clear cause and did not find the site managers culpable of negligent behaviour.

Firmly in the style of the autocratic representative of the "Führer" in Saxony, Gauleiter Mutschmann swept the objections raised by the ops management from the table as "playing games". He accused the company of "having seized hold of all the oil contracts by paying knockdown prices" but then having no cash left over for the "social facilities" the Nazis considered a must for a large factory. An ops manager had explained to him, so he said, that "the other factories may build housing for workers, we're building pyrolysis plants". During his last visit to the plant in 1936, he claimed, there hadn't even been pithead showers. Franz Landwehr thereupon explained that on taking over an abandoned glass factory you first needed to clear everything out in order to make space for such facil-

---

57 Walther Randhahn, Aktennotiz betr. Explosion Schwelwerk II/Regis vom 20.4.1939, 3, StA Leipzig, 20684, DEA-Mineralölwerke Rositz, No. 48.

58 Ibid., 4.

ities, but Mutschmann ignored this and also refused to acknowledge the necessity resulting from the Four-Year Plan of first installing "production plant" and "then the administrative sections".[59]

Mutschmann simply categorized this as part of the "exploitation" he had attacked, which, he said, "might have been usual in liberal times" but which "he would today not tolerate in any shape or form". He was so incensed that he announced that the DEA Management Board – Richard F. Ullner and Walther Randhahn were both present – would likewise be "ditched".[60] Randhahn pointed out that after 1933 the duty of every company had first and foremost been to "provide employment" by expanding operations. "In the course of the battle for jobs" and in close consultation with Nazi Party district head Munde, the corporation had hired more than 700 people from the immediate vicinity, as a result of which initially no additional lodgings had been necessary. Only when bringing in workers from outside had the corporation started building housing, and that was after 1936. Randhahn also rejected the accusation that Mineralölwerke Rositz had squeezed out rivals by charging the navy only "knockdown prices", citing a fact mentioned by Robert Ley, namely that the production price of the heating oil made using DEA's proprietary process was almost half that for the same products made using the hydration method.

Mutschmann's attack did not even receive full backing among his own ranks, as the DAF District Superintendent went on the record as saying that the Rositz DPAG managers were "good guys" and pointed out that no cases against the company were in the courts. By contrast, the DAF functionary claimed that the DEA, which was in charge of the lignite mines, was "antisocial", as it only offered about a quarter of its married staff works flats.[61] Robert Ley, Head of DAF and Nazi Party Reichsleiter, tried to calm things by

59 Ibid., 6.
60 Ibid.
61 Ibid., 8.

Fig. 28 Construction of the DEA housing estate (1938)

encouraging that "we shouldn't take all the agitation on the part of Mu.[tschmann] too tragically". The latter, he said, "was somewhat feisty and feels responsible to the Führer, after all."[62]

Head of Operations Franz Landwehr agreed with the Nazi Party district heads of Altenburg and Borna that the support fund set up to assist the descendants of the deceased should answer to a jointly appointed board of trustees. After all, more than 80,000 Reichsmark had been made available, as the "Führer" and Reich Propaganda Minister Goebbels had each donated 20,000 Reichsmark from the "Opfer der Arbeit" (Victims of Labour) fund. Furthermore, the DPAG covered the funeral costs, travel expenses, and the memorial service costs, added to which the company also covered the wage costs on the day and travel costs of those who had been injured and whom the DAF had invited – who were meanwhile in the sanatorium for miners in Hartenstein in the Erzgebirge hills. In

62 Ibid., 10.

this way, both the Nazi Party and the DAF used the occasion to pretend to be the champion of workers' welfare.[63]

Rositz – the heavy heating oil production plant

On 23 November 1933, the DEA Management Board resolved the incorporation of Mineralölwerke Rositz into DPAG,[64] and in early 1934 the annual general meetings of DPAG and DEA approved the restructuring of the oil business.[65] The oil business in Rositz developed favourably in the first-half of 1934 thanks to the improvement of the German economy, something the DEA directors attributed to the Nazi government.[66] The directors felt that there was an opportunity to boost output at Rositz by processing local raw materials, and this would necessitate hiring new staff. Even if the expected trend "has not yet become clearly visible", the expansion in armaments would soon have a beneficial effect, the executives opined.[67]

In fact, the nascent Nazi policies to make the country energy-independent led to the Rositz hub fulfilling the "Reich government's wishes" and in the second half of 1934 initiating "projects to expand and add buildings" in order to boost capacity with

---

63 Deutsche Petroleum-AG, Mineralölwerke Rositz, Halbjahresbericht für das erste Halbjahr 1939 vom 30.9.1939, 12, StA Leipzig, 20684, DEA-Mineralölwerke Rositz, No. 5; Deutsche Petroleum-AG, Geschäftsbericht über das Geschäftsjahr 1938, Berlin 1939, 2f.

64 DEA-Vorstandssitzung am 23.11.1933, 1, WD-CA, D-PA-24; cf. also Teerverarbeitungswerk Rositz 1917 bis 1990, et passim, WD-CA, 14-2-3078.

65 Deutsche Petroleum-AG, Geschäftsbericht der Deutschen Petroleum-AG über das Geschäftsjahr 1934, Berlin 1935, 3.

66 Deutsche Petroleum-AG, Mineralölwerke Rositz, Halbjahresbericht für das erste Halbjahr 1934 vom 17.8.1934, 1, StA Leipzig, 20684, DEA-Mineralölwerke Rositz, No. 5.

67 Ibid., 2.

Fig. 29 Aerial photo of DEA's Rositz plant (1934)

the objective of doubling fuel production output.[68] To this end, a second separation plant would be installed along with the requisite equipment for refining and distilling fuels. The plan also included expanding the main distillation and redistillation units, and a tank farm was built, along with a greywater cooling system and a pitch cooling and loading plant. In 1934, output and unit sales both grew appreciably, and the increased demand led to inventories of heating oil and paraffin being reduced. Fuel unit sales surged in particular as a result of "increasing motorization", although some vehicle pools were switched over to diesel engines, which led to the loss of some key accounts as Mineralölwerken Rositz initially had no diesel production capacities. These went turnkey in the second half of

68 Deutsche Petroleum-AG, Mineralölwerke Rositz, Jahresbericht 1934 vom 9.5.1935, 1 and 5, StA Leipzig, 20684, DEA-Mineralölwerke Rositz, No. 5; see on this also DEA-Vorstandssitzung vom 27.6.1934, 2, WD-CA, D-PA-24; DEA-Vorstandssitzung vom 18.7.1934, 2, ibid.

the year, and Mineralölwerke Rositz was thus able to lock into the trend. However, the corporation was concerned by the negative price developments, something triggered, amongst other things, by rivals charging dumping prices.

In 1935, the new refinery units went into operation. Alongside construction of a washing plant to produce lighter oils in the processing of asphalt, a new round of extensions was built in order to up tar processing capacity from 6,000 to 10,000 tonnes. Furthermore, in the course of preparations for war, a first air-raid shelter was built in Rositz. The supply contract concluded with the navy on 14 August 1935 envisaged an annual delivery of 78,000 tonnes of heating oil.[69] Since the Regis pyrolysis plant had been expanded to include a second production line, and a new process was able to carbonize specially pressed briquettes, the Rositz refinery could supply the required quantities, as it was now able to process 120,000 tonnes per annum.[70] Until the navy contract was done and dusted, however, there was no secured demand to meet the higher output, and the company consequently once again faced the risk of larger inventory stockpiles. Indeed, paraffin had to be warehoused in Leipzig and Halle, as storage capacities on site in Rositz did not suffice.[71]

Thanks to the Reich Drilling Programme and DEA'S own surface drilling in Heide and in Gifhorn, total crude oil produced rose to an estimated 130,000 tonnes per annum, but in early 1936 only 100,000 tonnes could be processed in the company's own refineries: 60,000 tonnes in Wilhelmsburg and 40,000 tonnes in Rositz. DPAG Management Board member Gröber therefore proposed to his fellow board members on 28 January 1936 that an additional cracker be installed at Rositz in order to boost the monthly crude-oil processing capacity to 7,000 tonnes. Since the investment required

69 Notiz betr. Investierungen für Marine vom 12.1.1939, 1, WD-CA, D-RW-127.

70 Deutsche Petroleum-AG, Mineralölwerke Rositz, Jahresbericht 1935 vom 19.5.1936, 4f., StA Leipzig, DEA-Mineralölwerke Rositz, No. 5.

71 Ibid., 12.

of roughly one million Reichsmark and the construction lead time of only five months were relatively low compared to the revenues, the Management Board approved the plan on 28 January 1936.[72] The proposal submitted by navy official Friedrich Fetzer, namely that potentially one million tonnes of "Iraq oil" could be refined for the navy each year, was taken up by Gröber to the extent that he consented to construction of a plant with an annual capacity of 200,000 tons, as long as the navy prefinanced the investment required. The figure would be paid back, as it would be netted against the price for the volumes delivered.[73]

The Four-Year Plan announced in 1936 was designed to support the rearmaments drive by intensifying efforts to render the economy independent of foreign supplies. The DEA Management Board discussed it on 29 October 1936,[74] concluding that the programme for economic independence confirmed the validity of the corporation's "expansion of our plants starting in 1934".[75] In February 1936 pyrolysis plant II had gone turnkey, and the very next month saw completion of the expansion of the refinery, upping its capacity to 14,500 tonnes a month. In the course of 1936 output was further boosted, with a greater volume of heating oil, diesel, paraffin and petroleum produced.[76] In September 1936, the negotiations with the navy on the latter procuring larger volumes of heating oil had still not been signed, but DEA agreed "in principle" to supply an annual volume of 40,000 tonnes more than originally planned.[77] To

---

72 DEA-Vorstandssitzung am 28.1.1936, 1f., WD-CA, D-PA-29.

73 Ibid., 2.

74 DEA-Vorstandssitzung am 29.10.1936, 1, WD-CA, D-PA-29.

75 Deutsche Petroleum-AG, Mineralölwerke Rositz, Jahresbericht 1936 vom 5.5.1937, 1, StA Leipzig, DEA-Mineralölwerke Rositz, No. 5; Deutsche Petroleum-AG, Geschäftsbericht der Deutschen Petroleum-AG über das Geschäftsjahr 1936, Berlin 1937, 4.

76 DEA-Vorstandssitzung am 4.2.1936, 1, WD-CA, D-PA-29; DEA-Vorstandssitzung am 18.2.1936, 1, ibid.

77 DEA-Vorstandssitzung am 24.9.1936, 1f., ibid.

Fig. 30 Mineralölwerke Rositz plant and machinery

this end, Gröber had an "overall programme for Rositz" drawn up, which included the installation of four new presses and three pyrolysis plants as well as conversion work in Fichtenhainichen at a total cost of six million Reichsmark through year-end 1936. The plan was thus to expand the Fichtenhainichen pyrolysis plant and significantly expand the Regis II capacity in order to have sufficient tar supplies at hand. A selection facility was to be introduced at the refinery in order to improve product, and a creosol facility was also erected that could turn out new products.

Designed to handle throughput of 220,000 tonnes of tar and 30,000 tons of crude oil and crude oil residues, the Rositz refinery processed the raw material using the DEA splitting method: This meant yields could be calibrated as required, for fuels in the range of 38 and 55 percent, for heating oil 25 to 44 percent, and for coke 8-9 percent. The greater flexibility in responding to market demand and quality went hand in hand with a loss of 10-11 percent, however.

An order note from the Raw Materials and Foreign Currency Staff Unit [Rohstoff- und Devisenstab] in February 1937 ensured the facility clear growth prospects.[78] However, in March 1937 the Supervisory Board also pointed to a negative trend, since the continuous rises in the deliveries demanded under the Four-Year Plans meant DEA would "no longer be able to define the limits to further developments itself".[79] Irrespective of the immense investment sums required, in March 1937 the DEA Supervisory Board had to approve a further 6.5 million Reichsmark for Mineralölwerke Rositz. Nevertheless, DEA Supervisory Board Chairman Karl Kimmich was convinced that for DEA "focussing more strongly on gaining oil from lignite and on oil processing was the right policy".[80] He expressly mentioned the "expansion of our coal base" as a complementary objective.

Gröber informed his fellow board members on 8-9 April 1937 in "broad strokes" about the navy supply contract that was ready for signing.[81] In the negotiations with the navy on the quantities to be supplied, he sought to make certain that tar production and processing would gradually be raised to about 50,000 tonnes, with the plan being to build new plants sequentially, the next one starting each time a new one went into operation. He wanted to avoid inflexible large-scale facilities with a generation and processing capacity of more than 100,000 tonnes.[82] Gröber remained in line with the strategy DEA Chair Richard F. Ullner had outlined as early as March 1935, which was based on the "poor experiences had with the navy" directly after the First World War, when the latter "immediately cancelled all sup-

78 DEA-Vorstandssitzung am 11.2.1937, 3, ibid.

79 Niederschrift über die Verhandlungen des Aufsichtsrats der DEA am 22.3.1937, 6, WD-CA, D-PA-0120.

80 Niederschrift über die Verhandlungen des Aufsichtsrats der DEA am 6.12.1937, 8, ibid.

81 DEA-Vorstandssitzung am 8./9.4.1937, 1, WD-CA, D-PA-29.

82 DEA-Vorstandssitzung am 16.4.1937, 1, WD-CA, D-PA-29.

ply contracts".[83] He estimated the total financing requirement to be 55 to 60 million Reichsmark. Gröber had in mind turnkey of a new plant every two years so that the company would be able to supply the volumes required within the space of 5-6 years.[84]

The fact that the entire activities of the Rositz hub were geared to meeting the navy's supply needs did not automatically mean the company closed ranks with the Nazi regime. For example, on 23 April 1937 the DEA Management Board refused to make a donation to the Hitler Youth Home in Rositz, voting instead for a "smaller donation to the Hitler Youth" in Fulda. The Management Board was evidently still keenly aware of the bitter conflicts with the Nazi Party in Saxony.[85]

The heating oil contract was finally signed by DPAG and the Commander-in-Chief of the navy on 13 December 1937 and 20 January 1938. In it, the DPAG committed to commence part deliveries to the navy of an annual 125-150,000 tonnes of lignite-based heating oil and lignite-based diesel, at the latest by 1 April 1939. The total delivery volume was fixed at 1.5 million tonnes with a price set at 130 Reichsmark per tonne ex works. The contract was expressly designated as "part of an overall delivery contract for 6 million tonnes of oil". The figure thus remained within the parameters of the contractual contents negotiated but definitely required the upfront expansion of the Rositz facility with a pyrolysis plant and a refinery.

The expanded navy programme called for investments of 23.3 million Reichsmark for tar operations with the expansion of the Regis II pyrolysis plant and the erection of a desulphurization facility. DEA estimated it would cost 9.5 million Reichsmark to increase the refinery's processing capacity to 250,000 tonnes p.a. and to build a phenol factory, while the "measures to secure coal supplies", meaning procurement of heavy machinery to commence open-cast

83 Richard F. Ullner an Georg Solmssen vom 7.3.1935, 2, WD-CA, D-PA-69.

84 DEA-Vorstandssitzung am 23.4.1937, 1, WD-CA, D-PA-29.

85 Ibid., 2.

mining at further sites, the expansion of the briquette factories, and energy supplies would cost a further 18.3 million Reichsmark. Expanding the lignite base by acquiring new coal fields was not factored into this sum. The navy deal thus entailed total investments of 51 million Reichsmark.[86]

Walther Randhahn believed that the large supply volumes arising from the navy contract definitely spelled financing and structural problems for DEA. He therefore advocated a cap on plant expansion at Rositz to a third pyrolysis plant and on increasing the refinery capacity to 250,000 tonnes. Randhahn wanted to erect a refinery with an annual capacity of 300,000 tonnes and the relevant pyrolysis plants as an independent entity in order to spread the risk, or to build it and operate it together with ASW. His concerns were subordinate to signing the deal, as this offered DEA extensive options for growth and sales.[87] At Randhahn's insistence, the contract was to include a withdrawal option for the event of technical difficulties, something Gröber also backed. To replace extruded briquettes, in 1936 a Lurgi pilot plant had been installed to produce ring briquettes, which enabled better pyrolysis. The output in 1937 was still less than one tenth of the throughput of 824,000 tonnes of briquettes the pyrolysis plants required.[88] To shore up the trusting relationship with the navy, the DEA Management Board agreed that, despite the necessarily great uncertainties over maximum delivery volumes in the second phase, in the talks Gröber should express DEA's willingness to prepare of its own accord to boost output before the navy exercised its option.[89] In this context, DEA then acquired the pyrolysis plants it had until then only leased.[90]

---

86 DEA, Notiz betr. Investierungen für Marine vom 12.1.1939, 1f., WD-CA, D-RW-127.

87 DEA-Vorstandssitzung am 6.10.1937, 3 and 5f., WD-CA, D-PA-29.

88 Deutsche Petroleum-AG, Mineralölwerke Rositz, Jahresbericht 1937, 2, StA Leipzig, DEA-Mineralölwerke Rositz, No. 5.

89 DEA-Vorstandssitzung am 22.11.1937, 1, WD-CA, D-PA-29.

90 Deutsche Petroleum-AG, Geschäftsbericht der Deutschen Petroleum-AG über das Geschäftsjahr 1938, Berlin 1939, 1.

In January 1939, the navy took the position that the agreed price of 130 Reichsmark per tonne presumed the acquisition of corresponding coal reserves and the expansion of Mineralölwerk Rositz for the "so-called 6-million-tonne programme".[91] DEA, by contrast, wanted a premium on the price, given the high investments. No agreement was expected immediately, as both sides blamed the other for the situation, but work laying the operational foundations was to go ahead all the same.

After all, the Rositz hub was in the middle of a comprehensive expansion phase. The defence-related tasks involved, above all, in the contract with the navy made it all the more urgent that the company complete the expansion work for the refinery, although the group experienced ever greater difficulties recruiting staff. All in all, in the pre-war period Mineralölwerke Rositz clearly performed well: the volume of processing and finished products trebled, with heating oil production even up by a factor of four.

Mineralölwerke Rositz output (in tonnes), 1933–1938[92]

Year	Processing	Finished product	Heating oil	Workforce
1933	59,319	51,198	24,557	634
1934	68,149	57,044	25,855	715
1935	117,001	105,495	51,882	1,274*/893
1936	158,434	148,202	74,266	1,618
1937	165,566	149,825	60,639	1,813
1938	192,165	168,478	100,000	2,323
H1 1939	97,167**	89,715***	48,263****	2,623*****

** incl. the Regis II pyrolysis plant** +2 % on H2 1938 *** +0.6 % on H2 1938*
***** -1.6 % on H2 1938 ***** +12.9 % on 31 Dec. 1938*

91 DEA, Notiz betr. Marinevertrag vom 24.1.1939, 1, WD-CA, D-RW-127.

92 Calculated according to: Jahresberichte der Mineralölwerke Rositz 1933–1939, StA Leipzig, Mineralölwerke Rositz, No. 5.

VI. DEA'S PARTICIPATION IN THE "ARYANIZATION" CAMPAIGN

(Rainer Karlsch)

"Aryanization"

Immediately after the Nazis came to power, the regime started stripping German Jews of their civil rights and terrorizing them in order to induce them to leave the country. In pursuit of this goal, among other things the Nazis organized a nationwide boycott of Jewish businesses on 1 April 1933. This hit both department stores and smaller stores very hard. Jewish civil servants, lawyers, doctors, and artists were all prohibited from exercising their professions or were required to present "proof of Aryan descent", which was tantamount to forbidding them to work. In 1935, the government decreed that no further public contracts be awarded to Jewish companies. Anyone in public employment and members of the Nazi Party were forbidden to buy anything from Jews.

The Nazis termed this policy of gradually squeezing Jews out of business life and the related expropriation or seizure of their assets "aryanization". The process included not only transferring ownership of a factory or store from a Jewish person to a non-Jewish one, but also the loss of a large part of that person's private property, too. Historian Ingo Loose rightly highlights the fact that the term "aryanization" (and it is still frequently used in historical research), is itself ideologically incriminated and, indeed, imprecise, as it excludes the victims' perspective.[1] In the absence of a more precise definition, in the following we shall still use the term "aryanization", albeit subject to the above reservations.

In the period from 1933 to 1937, there was no legal basis for "aryanization". The persons forced to sell assets could still decide for themselves whether they wished to conclude a sales contract. The conditions of the sale were likewise still largely a matter for negotiation, without the authorities exerting any influence. Nevertheless, at this time Jews had already been placed in a coercive situation.[2] Subjected to the pressure of boycotts, of being barred from work, of innumerable bureaucratic forms of harassment, discriminative laws and decrees, not to mention acts of violence, an ever growing number of Jews found themselves coerced into selling their workshops, factories, and stores.[3] They often had to sell below value in order to be able to live off the proceeds or emigrate. Furthermore, if they did emigrate then they had to part company with a considerable portion of the sales proceeds under the terms of the Reich Emigration Tax and new foreign currency regulations. In autumn 1938, of what had been around 100,000 commercial operations owned by Jews, only about 40,000 remained in the hands of their rightful owners.[4]

Violence against Jews escalated immediately after the "Accession" of Austria in March 1938 and in the context of the Reich-wide

---

1 Cf. Ingo Loose, *Die Juden in der Wirtschaft Schlesiens von der Reichsgründung 1871 bis zur Schoah*, in: Werner Brämer et al. (Eds.), Jüdisches Leben zwischen Ost und West Neue Beiträge zur jüdischen Geschichte in Schlesien, 156–217.

2 Cf. ibid.

3 Cf. a.o.: Helmut Genschel, *Die Verdrängung der Juden aus der Wirtschaft im Dritten Reich*, Göttingen 1966; Avraham Barkai, *Vom Boykott zur "Entjudung". Der wirtschaftliche Existenzkampf der Juden im Dritten Reich 1933–1943*, Frankfurt/Main 1988; Irmtrud Wojak/ Peter Hayes (Eds.), *"Arisierung" im Nationalsozialismus: Volksgemeinschaft, Raub und Gedächtnis*. Frankfurt/Main 2000; Götz Aly, *Hitlers Volksstaat. Raub, Rassenkrieg und nationaler Sozialismus*, Frankfurt/Main 2005.

4 Cf. Konrad Kwiet, *Nach dem Pogrom. Stufen der Ausgrenzung*, in: Wolfgang Benz (Ed.), Die Juden in Deutschland 1933–1945, München 1988, 547.

pogroms in November 1938. Jews were robbed, taken into "protective detention", and transported to concentration camps. In order to gain their freedom, even if only temporarily, they were forced to hand over their assets. Three days after the Night of Broken Glass of 9 November 1938, the Third Reich enacted the "Decree to Exclude Jews from German Business Life" and thus introduced a state-controlled coercive process of "aryanization". On 3 December 1938, a further directive was issued, the "Decree on the Deployment of Jewish Property". Under its terms any remaining commercial enterprises owned by Jews were either dissolved or transferred to new "Aryan" owners.

The outcome of the transfer of ownership of Jewish assets depended greatly on the character of the respective buyer. There were unscrupulous profiteers who exploited the coercive situation in which the sellers found themselves and with the assistance of state agencies pushed through bargain-basement prices. There were also the silent beneficiaries who were content to book the profits of aryanization that derived from the lower valuation of the assets in question. In a few cases, there were benevolent buyers who paid an appropriate price or more in an effort to make life easier for the sellers given the latter's precarious situation.

The greatest beneficiaries of aryanization included corporations such as I.G. Farbenindustrie AG and Friedrich Flick AG, as well as banks, amongst them Dresdner Bank and Deutsche Bank, not to mention department stores such as Hertie. By contrast, DEA only crops up in a few instances in the long list of those who profited from aryanization. This is not because DEA acted with less resolution grabbing assets by exploiting the situation of Jewish companies who found themselves in distress, and has more to do with the fact that its rivals were more tenacious when it came to the Petschek corporation coal mines subject to "aryanization". Less well-known today are the instances where Jewish owners of small coal dealerships were forced to sell. Moreover, individual DEA directors also took part in "aryanization" for personal reasons.

Buying up coal dealerships

As the largest coal producer in the country, DEA had several subsidiaries and affiliates that were active in the coal-trading business. The most important subsidiary was Brikett- und Kohlenhandel AG, Leipzig ("Briko").[5] Briko supplied a total of 14 coaling stations and in the 1930s booked annual sales of around 35 million Reichsmark.[6] Other DEA subsidiaries operating in the coal and fuel trading business were: Stöck & Fischer GmbH (with hubs in Mainz and Mannheim); Adolph Hartloff GmbH, Ruhrort, near Duisburg; Mitteldeutsche Kohlenhandel- und Reedereigesellschaft Kuhlen & Co., Essen; and Gottfried Kleinschmidt GmbH, Frankfurt/Main. There was fierce competition among both coal wholesalers and coal retailers, above all in the larger cities.

After the reintegration of Saarland into the Reich in 1935, numerous companies closed shop and sold up. An agreement concluded between the League of Nations and the German Reich on 5 December 1934 offered Jews in the Saar region the opportunity to emigrate legally, with their property protected for a period of one year following the anticipated reintegration.[7] Many thereupon put their businesses up for sale. The beneficiaries of such sales included DEA group member and coal dealership Stöck & Fischer GmbH, Mainz. In February 1935, it acquired the business shares in Weil & Cie. in Saarbrücken.[8]

After Austria's "accession" to the German Reich, Briko benefited there from the "aryanization" which was tantamount to plundering. As early as 23 April 1938, Briko received approval from the

---

5 Cf. Geschäftsbericht 1938, WD-CA, D-GB, 4.

6 Cf. Personalakte Lothar Ritter, WD-CA.

7 Cf. https://sgsaar.de/unsere-gemeinde/geschichte/ [last retrieved on 24.1.2024].

8 Cf. Verkauf der Geschäftsanteile der Weil & Cie. GmbH an Stöck & Fischer GmbH, 16.2.1935, WD-CA, D-RW-00587; Restitutionsklage von Jean Weil, Saarbrücken gegen Kaufmann Berthold Schönbucher wegen Hausgrundstück mit Lagerplatz, Landesarchiv Saarbrücken, Y 8/48.

Reich Commissioner for Austria, State Secretary Wilhelm Keppler, to enter into negotiations to acquire the Dr Bernhard Fischer coal dealership in Vienna.[9] In fact, the term 'negotiations' did not apply at all as sole owner Fischer was simply forced to sell as quickly as possible. Lothar Ritter, a member of the Briko board, met him – and Fischer put ink to paper that same day.

Ritter did not seek to book as great a profit from aryanization as possible for DEA but instead paid an acceptable price and intended to retain the entire staff, some of whom were Jewish. Keppler thereupon intervened. He did not permit the sale at the terms agreed between Ritter and Fischer, and instead made it subject to new conditions. In line with his instructions, the purchase contract was amended on 26 April. Fischer was forced to fire the Jewish staff members, and the authorities withheld part of the purchase price. Briko then became owner of Fischer's coal dealership with effect from 29 April 1938.[10]

The powers of the Property Transactions Office in Vienna, established at the Ministry of Economics and Labour in March 1938 specifically to approve and monitor aryanizations, were vested in it by a decree enacted on 29 March 1939 requiring buyers of Jewish companies to retroactively pay an 'offset surcharge' to government. This payment was due on all transfers of ownership that took place between 13 March and 27 April 1938, or if in the case of later acquisitions the purchase was not based on an expert audit opinion.[11] The Property Transactions Office thus demanded that Briko, too, credit the purchase price of 76,033.55 Reichsmark to the blocked account for "Revenue for De-Jewing". Of the figure, 2,635 Reichsmark was

---

9 Cf. DEA an Reichsstatthalter in Wien, 6.5.1941, WD-CA, D-RW-00566.

10 Cf. Gedächtnisprotoll, 23.4.1939, Hans Heer, Geschäftsführer Fa. Stöck & Fischer GmbH, Kohlengroßhandlung und Reederei, Mannheim (Zeuge), WD-CA, D-RW-00569.

11 Cf. Memo, conc.: Verordnung der österreichischen Landesregierung über Ausgleichszahlungen bei bereits durchgeführten Arisierungsfällen, 12.5.1939, WD-CA, D-RW-63.

meant to be forwarded to the German Labour Front DAF organization "Schönheit der Arbeit" and 34,591 Reichsmark to be paid as a "De-Jewing Levy" to the Ministry.[12] The DEA complained to the Property Transactions Office as in its opinion the decree did not apply in its case. Furthermore, the DEA had not paid too little for the loss-making company, but too much.[13] Prior to emigration, Bernhard Fischer had been forced to pay the "Reich Emigration Tax" and other costs, too. The authorities had only in part managed to secure these compulsory charges. Briko as Fischer's legal successor refused to cover these payment obligations.[14] DEA complained to the Reich 'Industry' Group about how the Property Transactions Office in Vienna was behaving and felt the case needed to be rectified as a matter of precedence.[15] The Reich Group recommended to DEA that it get the Reich Economics Ministry to intervene.[16] The dispute between the Property Transactions Office and DEA dragged on until May 1941 and ended with the "De-Jewing charge" being withdrawn.[17]

A Board member as a "beneficiary of aryanization"

DEA Board member Hans Gröber profited from Jews being squeezed out of German business life in several ways. He was one of the best paid industrial managers. This did not prevent him from increasingly mixing his tasks as a Board member with his own private deals in order to enrich himself by grabbing the property of Jewish businessmen. At the end of 1938, the DEA Supervisory

---

12 Cf. Briko Leipzig an DEA-Vorstandsabt. Berlin-Schöneberg, 1.11.1939, ibid.
13 Cf. Briko Leipzig an DEA-Vorstandsabt. Berlin-Schöneberg, 1.12.1939, ibid.
14 Cf. Briko, Leipzig an DEA-Vorstandsabt. Berlin-Schöneberg, 29.11.1939, ibid.
15 Cf. DEA an Reichsgruppe Industrie, 13.11.1939, ibid.
16 Cf. Reichsgruppe Industrie an DEA, 7.12.1939, ibid.
17 Cf. DEA an Kohlenhof GmbH, 29.5.1941, ibid.

Board had had enough of Gröber's double dealing and prematurely terminated his contract with the group on "amicable terms".

At the end of 1933 Gröber had been made an ordinary member of the DEA Management Board and had become CEO of DPAG. Three of the four DPAG Management Board members had Jewish ancestors and had therefore been forced to withdraw from the DEA subsidiary. This was also the time when the massive expansion in DPAG/DEA heating oil production for the Navy started, a fact that shored up Gröber's position. He was also buttressed by the fact that Dresdner Bank was wooing him into an appointment to its Advisory Council.[18] Solmssen refused to approve such an appointment in light of the fact that Deutsche Bank was DEA's main shareholder. By way of an alternative, he offered Gröber inclusion on the supervisory boards of various affiliated companies, instead. Moreover, Gröber received an additional honorarium of 30,000 Reichsmark for his "*special services to DPAG in the 1934 business year*".[19] This probably referred to Gröber's efforts to push through a new contract with the Navy and the supervisory board had an interest in keeping Gröber on board any way.

Thanks to his increased earnings, Gröber was in a position to look round for a more prestigious home in Berlin. His eye fell on a veritable manor house with gardens in Berlin's Grunewald district, at Bismarckallee 44, designed by renowned architects Breslauer und Salinger. The property belonged to Jewish businessman Alfred Siegel, who wanted to sell, but not at the price Gröber offered.[20] The two therefore concluded a several-year rental contract whereby Gröber, evidently without informing Siegel, had pre-emptive purchase rights entered in his name in the Land Registry. This fact alone

---

18 Cf. Notiz Solmssen, 21.5.1935, HADB, P 1686, Personalia Hans Gröber, no page numbers given.

19 Cf. ibid.

20 Cf. Kimmich an von Burgsdorff, 16.6.1937, HADB, P 1686, Personalia Hans Gröber, no page numbers given.

says a lot about how the authorities and private individuals connived in order to exclude Jews from the "body of the people". Siegel found himself in increasingly dire straits and the property was put up for foreclosure in mid-1937. Gröber agreed with the DEA Management Board that the company would participate in the foreclosure proceedings. The members must have been very sure of getting the nod, as several days before the foreclosure auction commenced, the DEA Management Board and Gröber concluded a contract on the use of the building.[21] DEA acquired the land and rented it to its management board member in order to buy his loyalty.

Gröber complained to the DEA Supervisory Board that Siegel had attempted immediately after the foreclosure auction to sell off some items of furniture. He halted disbursement of the mortgage payment and filed for an injunction for Siegel's arrest to prevent any further sales of furniture.[22] He failed to get the injunction approved, and indeed even the DEA Legal department did not share his opinion on all points.[23] Irrespective of this, DEA had acquired a valuable property and rented it out to its CEO on favourable terms.

As of spring 1933 Gröber was evidently involved as a commercial limited partner in the "aryanization" of Jewish department stores. His brother-in-law Georg Karg played a key role here, who had since 1915 been married to Käthe Schröder, the sister of Gröber's wife Charlotte.[24] Georg Karg and Hans Gröber were linked by various business interests. It was Karg who presumably initiated Gröber's participation in the department stores. He was the retail expert while Gröber played the part of financier; when it came to taking up bank guarantees, Gröber's position as DEA CEO played

21 Cf. Abkommen zwischen der DEA und Direktor Hans Gröber, 11.6.1937, WD-CA, D-RW-00271.

22 Cf. note Gröber, 22.6.1937 and note, Zwangsversteigerung, 10.8.1937, HADB, P 1686, Personalia Hans Gröber, no page numbers given.

23 Cf. note, 1.9.1937, ibid.

24 Cf. Vertrag zwischen der DEA und Hans Gröber, 26.10.1938, WD-CA, D-RW-00271.

an important part. Karg could look back on a successful career as a talented procurement manager at A. Jandorf & Co. and, after that company had been bought out by Warenhauskonzern Hermann Tietz in 1929, had climbed up the ladder to the rank of general authorized signatory.[25] Karg was no anti-Semite as otherwise neither the Jandorf nor the Tietz families would have accepted his inclusion in their inner management circles.[26] Karg stayed out of politics and did not join a party. During the Great Depression, Hermann Tietz OHG found itself in difficulties, a position the creditor banks exploited after the Nazis came to power with the assistance of the Reich Economics Ministry, gradually stripping the Jewish partners of their powers and then their property. In July 1933, the creditor banks founded Hertie Kaufhaus-Beteiligungs-GmbH (in short: Hertie GmbH) and appointed Karg as managing director as he was the sole non-Jew who was an authorized signatory at Tietz.

The Jewish partners were forced to sell their shares to Hertie GmbH well below value. Karg was not, however, the driving force behind the Tietz family being squeezed out of their company and its subsequent "aryanization".[27]

Karg started using his new position as managing director of Hertie to acquire department stores owned by Jews as his personal property. The first such transaction took place in spring 1933: the department store owned by Samuel Mendel in the small town of Ortelsburg in East Prussia (today's Szczytno, north of Warsaw). Mendel had linked his department store to the joint procurement office at the Tietz corporation. Given the anti-Semitic terrorization of Jews in the Nazi-bastion of Ortelsburg, in the spring of 1933 he gave up, sold his company to Karg, and emigrated with his wife to

---

25 Cf. Johannes Bähr/Ingo Köhler, *Verfolgt, "arisiert", wiedergutgemacht? Wie aus dem Warenhauskonzern Hermann Tietz Hertie wurde*, München 2023, 33 and 118ff.

26 Cf. ibid., 119.

27 Cf. ibid., 120.

Palestine.[28] Karg did not finance the purchase himself but succeeded in persuading his brother-in-law Hans Gröber to act as sole limited partner. Later, Karg then involved his older brother Walter Karg and Hans Gröber and other additional "business friends" as backers, among them Arnold von Borsig, a scion of the famous Berlin business family, and Dr Walter Bauer, who until 1938 was a senior executive in the Petschek corporation.

DEA Supervisory Board Chair Solmssen only learned of Gröber's involvement in "aryanizations" through the grapevine, without being able to react in any way to the rumours as his own position was under threat. Shortly after Kimmich assumed the chair of the DEA Supervisory Board, in summer 1936, he was compelled to address Gröber's business deals. Kimmich invited the latter to a personal meeting to clarify matters.[29] Gröber played down his financial commitment, although he did put it at as much as 350,000 Reichsmark. All the important questions, he said, were handled by his brother-in-law Georg Karg. Gröber said he did not intend to increase his financial stake further.

As a member of the Deutsche Bank Management Board, Kimmich had a prime overview of "aryanizations".[30] He clearly knew all about Karg. Kimmich disapproved of Gröber's activities not for moral reasons, but because he was worried that Gröber might neglect his duties as a DEA Board member. He held further talks with Gröber, during which the latter again assured that he was not going to increase his private stake in department stores.[31]

However, Gröber did not keep his promise. He did not hesitate when an opportunity arose for him to make new purchases.

---

28 Cf. ibid., 122f.

29 Cf. Aktenvermerk Kimmich, 5.8.1936, HADB, P 1686, Personalia Hans Gröber, no page numbers given.

30 Cf. Harold James, *Deutsche Bank*, 348f.

31 Cf. Aktenvermerk Kimmich, 30.10.1936, Aktennotiz Kimmich, 28.4.1937, HADB, P 1686, Personalia Hans Gröber, no page numbers given.

What particularly caught the eye was the interest he acquired in a department store in Liegnitz (today: Legnica, southwest Poland). The store had been founded in 1900 by Jewish businessman Ludwig Haurwitz as one of the largest of its kind in the city, where the population had since increased by some 30% to reach about 78,000 inhabitants.[32] The three-story building was designed in the Art Deco style and boasted no less than 19 large show windows.

Evidently pressurized to do so, Haurwitz sold his company to Paul Reetz, who was fronting for Hans Gröber as the financier.[33] Kimmich noted down after a discussion with Gröber that the Liegnitz department store was in far better economic shape than assumed and estimated its net asset value at around 300,000 Reichsmark.[34] Kimmich requested in spring 1937 that Gröber inform him what additional participations in department stores he had acquired. Gröber thereupon revealed that together with Karg he owned a 90-percent interest in department stores in Ortelsburg and Bad Freienwalde as well as in Osterode/East Prussia (today: Ostróda, southwest Poland), Stolp (today: Slupsk, North Poland) and Liegnitz alone. Gröber emphasized that "*all the department stores are doing well. In all cases, the profit margin is good, exceeding the rents and sale commissions.*"[35] Gröber sought in this way to justify his high financial commitment as he had taken out bank guarantees. At that point in time, it was still unclear whether Gröber and Karg intended to keep the department stores or to sell them on.

Kimmich rejected the idea of Deutsche Bank taking over the Liegnitz department store. He felt that in the event of a bank guar-

---

32 Cf. Magistrates Liegnitz, Goldberg, Schönau (Eds.), *Liegnitz, Goldberg: das schöne Katzbachtal*, Berlin 1925, 125; Tamara Włodarczyk, *Aus der Geschichte der Juden in der Region Liegnitz,* Warschau 2016, 51f.

33 Ludwig Haurwitz and his family moved to Berlin. The family was deported to the Riga ghetto in 1942 and murdered there. (Ibid., 52).

34 Cf. Aktennotiz Kimmich, 28.4.1937, HADB, P 1686, Personalia Hans Gröber, no page numbers given.

35 Ibid.

antee there would be a conflict of interests. He was not swayed in this regard by Gröber's argument that the stores' accounts had hitherto been held with Dresdner Bank and it was only because of him, Gröber, that the store was being offered to Deutsche Bank.

Kimmich insisted that by the end of 1937 Gröber needed to have shed the guarantees he had taken up. He recorded: "*In normal times, such guarantees would be an impossible burden. Gröber must scale back his exposure to Liegnitz because it rests on his position with DEA.*"[36] Gröber assured that he would do just that. Possibly it was in order to reel Gröber in and ensure his loyalty to DEA that Kimmich agreed to the afore-mentioned purchase of the villa in Grunewald for DEA, and it being rented out to Gröber.

However, for Gröber the deals with Jewish department store owners who found themselves on the brink of disaster were clearly just that bit too tempting. He wanted on behalf of himself, his brother-in-law, and managers with whom he was friends to exploit the situation into which those concerned had been forced. In this way and at little risk, he wanted to swiftly increase his personal wealth by purchasing department stores and textile businesses at prices well below their value.

The business status of the five department stores in which Gröber held a stake was as follows in autumn 1937: stocks worth 2 million Reichsmark compared with bank and commercial debts of about 0.5 million Reichsmark, leaving a surplus of 1.5 million Reichsmark.[37] Kimmich threatened to inform the entire Supervisory Board of Gröber's dealings. Gröber gave in but asked for approval for one further takeover. He said he wanted to "*avoid missing out on the favourable opportunity*".[38] Kimmich refused, whereupon Gröber replied that he would then ensure a friend of his got the deal.

---

36 Ibid.

37 Cf. Aktenvermerk Kimmich, 23.10.1937, ibid.

38 Ibid.

In the meantime, Kimmich learned of new participations that Gröber and his business associates had made in "aryanizations" through the Deutsche Bank branch in Breslau (today: Wroclaw, Poland).[39] The transaction involved the sale of the Jewish textile business owned by Fedor Karpe in Gleiwitz (today: Gliwice, south Poland). Karpe had sold his business to Arnold von Borsig, whose office was located in the DEA office building in Schöneberg in Berlin.[40] DEA Board member Haussmann had acted as advisor to von Borsig.[41] The bankers felt von Borsig was simply a front and wondered who was actually behind the deal. They could find no direct link to Gröber. However, when shortly thereafter further instances of "aryanizations" in Gleiwitz were reported it became clear there was a network of "Berlin business friends" behind things.

The "business friends" had acquired an interest in three Gleiwitz companies: Getex Gleiwitzer Textilspezialhaus GmbH, Rebenstorf & Co. GmbH; and Textilkaufhauses Rudolf Brandt & Co. GmbH. The new managing directors of these companies were all minor businessmen with no notable assets of their own. They were all friends and were all three funded by Berlin-based financiers "*all of whom have close links to DEA and/or work for the latter*". In the case of the "aryanization" of the textile store of M. Leschziner to Rudolf Brandt, a white-collar staff member with no capital of his own, the purchase price of 600,000 Reichsmark had been paid or rather guaranteed by Walter Bauer. The Deutsche Bank Gleiwitz branch described Bauer as a "*senior executive with DEA in Berlin*".[42]

This veracity of this statement is questionable. Bauer was until 1938 managing director of Thüringische Kohlen- und Brikett-

---

39 Cf. Filiale Deutsche Bank Breslau an Filiale Berlin 4.5.1937, ibid.

40 Cf. ibid.

41 Whether Hausmann, who as a Jew on the DEA board was himself under pressure, was in any way involved in the "aryanization" in Gliwice is not clear from the documents.

42 Memo Deutsche Bank, Filiale Gleiwitz: M. Leschziner Textilkaufhaus, Gleiwitz, 13.4.1938, HADB, P 1686, Personalia Hans Gröber, no page numbers given.

verkaufsgesellschaft in the Petschek group and thereafter worked as a self-employed businessman.[43] He possibly had an office in the DEA building in Schöneberg or business links to Hans Gröber. There is proof of Bauer having been involved in several cases of the "aryanization" of textiles companies. He kept the Nazis at arm's length as a former member of the Deutsche Demokratische Partei (DDP) and then, from 1930 to 1933 of Deutsche Staatspartei (DStP). In 1942, Bauer joined the "Freiburg Circle" supporting Friedrich Bonhoeffer and following the failed 20 July 1944 assassination attempt on Hitler only just escaped execution by firing squad.[44]

The Deutsche Bank staff in Gleiwitz were suspicious of the "aryanizations" as they said they had established that all the financiers, and in particular Gröber, tended to favour their rival, Dresdner Bank.[45] They forwarded the information to Kimmich, who was anything but happy to read it. He was increasingly of the opinion that Gröber was playing a double game and on top of that pushing clients in the direction of the rivals at Dresdner Bank. He was not able to use the information from Gleiwitz directly, however, as it derived from off-the-record conversations with one of the managing directors of an aryanized company.

In his function as Chairman of the DEA Supervisory Board, Kimmich had an opportunity to intervene when in the early summer of 1938 he once again received news of Gröber taking personal advantage of Jews' difficulties. In early May, the company S. Heilbronn in Gleiwitz had been purchased by a "Herr Rebenstorf", who had been active as a staff member in various department stores, most recently in Kaufhaus des Westens in Berlin, which belonged

---

43 Cf. Michael Wischnath, *Bauer, Walter Albert. Biografie*, in: Bernd Ottnad (Ed.), Baden-Württembergische Biografien, Vol. 2, Stuttgart 1999, 16–19; cf. also Sophia Mott, *Der dritte Mann*, in: Liebermann-Villa am Wannsee, 30.6.2023, https://liebermann-villa.de/blog/der-dritte-mann/.

44 Cf. ibid [last retrieved on 4.4.2024].

45 Cf. memo, Deutsche Bank, Filiale Gleiwitz: M. Leschziner Textilkaufhaus, Gleiwitz, 28.4.1938, HADB, P 1686, Personalia Hans Gröber, no page numbers given.

to the Hertie Group. Gröber was again entered as one of the limited partners.[46] Since the department stores "aryanized" in Gleiwitz were together worth several hundred thousand Reichsmark, members of Deutsche Bank tended to assume that while Gröber had provided his name as guarantor it was actually the DEA corporation itself that must be behind the deals. Kimmich categorically denied this: Gröber, he said, was not acting on behalf of DEA, the corporation was in no way implicated, and was also not morally responsible in any way for the liability risk as regards the textile corporations in question.[47]

Kimmich's patience had come to an end. He demanded that Gröber provide a detailed account of his personal assets and at the end of June the two sat down at the table again.[48] Gröber conceded that he had not kept his promise to stay away from further "aryanizations". Gröber stated that he had shouldered bank guarantees of around 250,000 Reichsmark. Thanks to the "*superlative state of the companies in question for him* (Gröber – the authors) *there was no longer any risk.*"[49] Kimmich suggested Gröber should resign from DEA, but incensed, Gröber refused.

Thereupon Kimmich had Gröber again submit a detailed account of his private assets, informed the members of the DEA Supervisory Board of the fact, and commissioned a legal opinion on the rights and duties of a management board member. The opinion was unequivocal: According to the German Commercial Code and the Corporations Act of 1927, management board members of a joint stock corporation were not permitted to engage in a retail trade.[50]

---

46 Cf. memo, Deutsche Bank, Direktion Zweigstelle Hindenburg, an Zentrale Deutsche Bank, Vertraulich, betr.: Direktor Hans Gröber, 3.5.1938, ibid.

47 Kimmich an Direktion der Zweigstelle Hindenburg, Vertraulich, betr.: Direktor Hans Gröber, 14.5.1938, ibid.

48 Vermerk Kimmich, 1.7.1938, ibid.

49 Ibid.

50 Cf. Revision Deutsche Bank an Kimmich, 12.10.1938, ibid.

Participations held by Hans Gröber in aryanized department stores, as at June 1938[51]

Kaufhaus Karg KG, Ortelsburg (East Prussia)
Hans Gröber KG, Osterode (East Prussia)
Walter Pachur KG, Stolp (Pommerania)
Reetz & Gröber KG, Schönebeck (Elbe)
Paul Reetz KG, Freienwalde (Oder)
Paul Reetz KG, Liegnitz (Lower Silesia)
Rebenstorf & Co. KG, Gleiwitz (Upper Silesia)

The assets list for the seven department stores as at 1 January 1938 showed a net profit of around 523,000 Reichsmark. Gröber was sole limited partner in five of the companies, in Osterode he was initially also the personally liable partner. Only in Reetz & Gröber KG in Schönebeck did his brother-in-law Karg hold a 50-percent stake and in Pachur KG in Stolp Walter Pachur was, like Gröber, 50-percent owner. In other words, Georg Karg had meanwhile assigned his entire stake in the Ortelsburg department store to Hans Gröber, possibly in connection with the 1937 acquisition of 51-percent of the Hertie shares, for which Karg needed capital.[52] With two exceptions, the department stores relied on Hertie for central procurement. Karg managed it all.

Irrespective of the investigations the supervisory board were conducting into his business affairs, in the early summer of 1938 Gröber also got involved in the "aryanization" of Munich corporation Böhm & Wagner GmbH. However, in this case he was acting not as a private individual but in his function as a member of the DPAG Management Board. Brothers Wilhelm and Gustav Böhm were both businessmen. Their father Jakob Böhm had established a profitable trading business. Wilhelm Böhm took over at the helm

51 Cf. Beteiligung des Herr G. an Kaufhäusern, 16.8.1938, ibid.

52 I would like to thank Johannes Bähr for the hint.

and together with his brother-in-law Sali Cohen continued to move it forward. Gustav Böhm worked as an attorney-at-law. A company entered under his name was specialized in trading cooking oil. In 1930, Wilhelm Böhm and Sali Cohen acquired the oldest Bavarian petroleum company and with it the company's "Aryan" managing director Johann B. Wagner. The firm operated henceforth as Böhm & Wagner GmbH and emerged as the leading independent fuel trader in southern Bavaria. The company's profit margins from the petrol and diesel business were approx. 13 percent in the years 1930 to 1937.[53] Joint owners were Wilhelm Böhm, Sali Cohen, and Johann B. Wagner. Moreover, the three business partners also owned a general partnership (OHG) that traded in lubricants, turpentine oil, and cleaning wool.

As conditions for Jews in the German Reich became ever more intolerable, the Cohens had only one aim: to leave the country as quickly as possible. Word soon spread among the Munich business community that they wished to sell their shares in the company. Gröber caught wind of this through coal trader Ehrenberg, who had discussed the matter with the Cohens in May 1938. According to Ehrenberg, Sali Cohen saw only two possible routes: "*either to liquidate the business as quickly as possible and to emigrate with what remains to him from the cash revenue, at present about 11 %, or, should he not succeed, to go on working until the presumably bitter end*".[54]

There were several interested parties looking to buy up petroleum dealers Böhm & Wagner GmbH, including the Stinnes Group.[55] Herbert Pschorr, owner of the renowned Munich brewery and other companies, was likewise interested in taking over the business but was unable to pay the expected purchase price of 150,000 Reichsmark in cash as he was constrained by restrictions on an

---

53 Cf. Bericht vom 25.5.1938, Betr.: Arisierung, WD-CA, D-RW-00582.

54 Bericht vom 16.5.1938, ibid.

55 Cf. Bericht vom 20.5.1938, Betr.: Arisierung, ibid.

inheritance. Wagner rejected any purchase price financing based on a bank loan.

Once DEA/DPAG had been informed by Ehrenberg about the dilemma Böhm faced, Dresdner Bank offered its help with the "aryanization". It sent a detailed dossier to Hans Gröber,[56] which was further evidence of his superb contacts to the Dresdner Bank. All further negotiations were then conducted by DEA CEO Ullner and the company lawyer Hugo Griebel.

As news trickled through that "non-Aryan" sales representatives would be forbidden from making business trips as of the autumn of 1938, DPAG pushed for a fast takeover as it feared that its rivals would otherwise grab the prized goods.[57] In mid-August, an agreement was reached in principle and on 3 September 1938 a contract signed to buy the companies of Wilhelm Böhm, Sali Cohen, and Johann B. Wagner. The sole condition that Böhm made was that managing director Wagner be retained by the new owners. Böhm & Wagner GmbH and OHG Jacob Böhm were purchased by DPAG for a total of 160,000 Reichsmark. Owners Wilhelm Böhm and Sali Cohen withdrew from the company. Their place was taken by DEA which henceforth held 80 percent of the capital stock of Böhm & Wagner GmbH.[58] The third owner and managing director Johann B. Wagner thus had 20 percent.

However, the deal now needed to be approved by the Upper Bavaria Aryanization Office. Given the interests of influential Bavarian competitors and other rivals, DPAG director Gröber was not certain how things would pan out. In a letter to the Aryanization Office he emphasized DPAG's intentions: "*Since both companies meet the conditions required to qualify to be awarded ongoing Armed Forces contracts, a massive boost can be expected once the companies have been entrusted*

---

56 Cf. Dresdner Bank an Gröber 27.7.1938, ibid.

57 Cf. Betr.: Übernahmeverhandlungen der Firma Böhm & Wagner, München, ibid.

58 Cf. Urkundenrolle No. 392, Notar Dr. Hans Wöstendiek, Berlin 3.9.1938, ibid.

to Aryan hands." DPAG only wanted to pay for the assets: "*The Jews who were the previous owners will receive nothing for the goodwill.*"[59]

On 15 September, Gröber sought the approval of local Nazi party politician and City of Munich Special Commissioner for Economic Affairs Christian Weber for the purchase contract and its swift certification by the Chamber of Commerce.[60] Gröber backed up the request that same day with a personal letter to "*My Dear Hermann*" SS Standartenführer Hermann Fegelein, Commander of the SS Main Riding School in Munich.[61] Fegelein was by then subordinate only to Reichsführer SS, Heinrich Himmler. The hope was he would appeal to his mentor Christian Weber for the latter to rubber-stamp the aryanization through DPAG. Evidently, this was needed as Weber held a key position on the Munich City Council. He had been one of Hitler's closest companions since 1920, one of the few with whom the Fuehrer was on first-name terms, and in 1933 emerged as the single most important local politician in Munich.[62] He had been a member of the SS since 1932, and in 1937 was made SS Brigadeführer.[63] Weber was also the founder of the SS Main Riding School in Munich and of the German Hunting Museum. He succeeded in laying hands on millions by abusing his powers and by corruption.

Weber and Fegelein were united in their passion for riding and hunting. Gröber leveraged off this and must have known Fegelein well, if not have been friends with him. In bears stating here that at Gröber's suggestion DEA had at the end of 1936 donated 10,000

---

59 Gröber und Griebel an Regierung von Oberbayern, Arisierungsabteilung, 6.9.1938, WD-CA, D-RW-00533.

60 Cf. Gröber an Weber, 15.9.1939, ibid.

61 Cf. Gröber an Hermann Fegelein, SS-Hauptreiterschule, 15.9.1938, ibid.

62 Cf. Thomas von Berg, *Korruption und Bereicherung. Politische Biografie des Münchener NSDAP-Vorsitzenden Christian Weber (1883–1945)*, Munich 2003, 43–48.

63 Cf. ibid., 45.

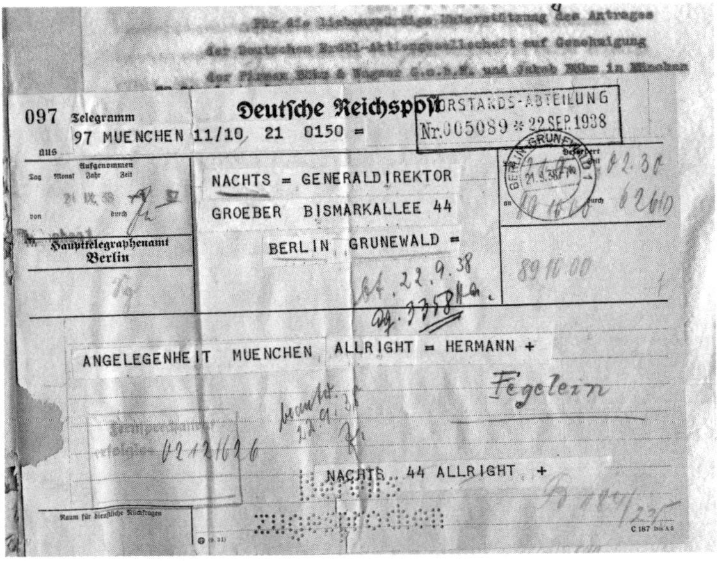
097 Telegramm
97 MUENCHEN 11/10 21 0150 =
aus
Deutsche Reichspost
VORSTANDS-ABTEILUNG
Nr. 005089 * 22 SEP 1938
Aufgenommen
Tag Monat Jahr Zeit
von durch
Haupttelegraphenamt
Berlin
NACHTS = GENERALDIREKTOR
GROEBER BISMARKALLEE 44
BERLIN GRUNEWALD =
Befördert
Zeit
an durch
ANGELEGENHEIT MUENCHEN ALLRIGHT = HERMANN +
Fegelein
NACHTS .. 44 ALLRIGHT +

Fig. 31 Telegramme from Hermann Fegelein
to Hans Gröber's private home

Reichsmark to setting up the Hunting Museum in Munich.[64] Be that as it may, Weber granted Fegelein a meeting, advocated DPAG being supported, whereupon Weber instructed the Chamber of Commerce to authorize the "aryanization".[65] The following night, Fegelein telegraphed Gröber: "*Munich Matter. All good. Hermann.*"[66]

The case of the "aryanization" of Böhm & Wagner GmbH is a prime example of what went on behind the scenes when it came to 'law and order' in the case of company sales by "non-Aryans": If you had good links to the Nazin power apparatus, your business interests would win the day.

---

64 Cf. Vorstandssitzung, 24.9.1936, WD-CA, D-PA-29.

65 Cf. Weber an Gröber, 20.9.1938, WD-CA, D-RW-00582.

66 telegram Fegelein an Gröber, 21.9.1938, ibid.

For DPAG, buying up Böhm & Wagner GmbH was a highly lucrative deal. The DEA Supervisory Board meeting of 14 March 1939 simply records pithily: "*We exploited the favourable buy-opportunity that arose.*"[67] In July 1941, for fiscal reasons ownership of the company was transferred to Deutsche Viscobil Öl GmbH, a DEA subsidiary.[68]

For the Böhm Brothers, sale of their company did not spell salvation. They found themselves caught up in the deadly vortex of the pogroms. In the night of 9 November 1938 and organized by the Nazi regime acts of violence were perpetrated against Jews throughout the Reich territories. Synagogues, businesses, and homes were stormed and destroyed in the so-called Night of Broken Glass. As of 10 November, at least 30,000 Jews were arrested and taken to concentration camps. Hundreds died in detention or committed suicide. The November pogroms marked the transition from discrimination of the German Jews to their systematic persecution and annihilation.[69]

Wilhelm Böhm, attorney-at-law Gustav Böhm, and Sali Cohen were taken into detention on 10 November 1938 and then moved to the Dachau concentration camp. Gustav Böhm was murdered there two days later.[70]

Dresdner Bank declared in a confidential communication of 12 November 1938 to the DEA Board that it has not yet been able to disburse payment to the sellers owing to Reich Emigration Tax Guarantees having been imposed on it. "*The events of recent days, and to our knowledge both Messrs Böhm and Mr Cohen have been arrested, has prompted us to inform you of the state of the deal, above all the agree-*

---

67 Aufsichtsratssitzung 14.3.1939, WD-CA,14–2-00082.

68 Cf. DEA an Notar Bruno Hülsen, 31.7.1941, WD-CA, D-RW-00582.

69 Cf. Wolfgang Benz, *Gewalt im November 1938. Die "Reichskristallnacht". Initial zum Holocaust*, Berlin 2018.

70 Cf. Biographisches Gedenkbuch der Münchener Juden 1933–1945, https://gedenkbuch.muenchen.de/ [last retrieved on 3.5.2023].

ment reached with Mr Wagner."[71] DEA CEO Ullner responded to this letter by writing to Gestapo Senior Inspector Schermer. He pointed out that Dresdner Bank had already deposited the Reich Emigration Tax with the Inland Revenue Office and would then deduct this from the purchase price. Ullner requested the release of the two "*Jews in Detention, against whom, or so we hear, no particular criminal charges have been brought so that the above matters can be put in order.*"[72] Ullner thus demonstrated a touch of human decency.

In fact, at the end of November 1938 Wilhelm Böhm and Sali Cohen were released from the Dachau concentration camp. Both wrote to DEA to have the monies owed credited to them.[73] DEA thereupon made the payments. Together with his family, in March 1939 Cohen left Munich and emigrated to the United States. Wilhelm Böhm no longer had the energy to leave his native Munich. He had served as an NCO in the First World War, felt himself to be a German patriot, and after the traumatic events of November 1938 and the murder of his brother felt shattered. On 20 November 1941, Wilhelm Böhm was deported to Kowno (Kaunas) and murdered there five days later.[74]

Gröber's intervention to have the Böhms' companies transferred to DPAG/DEA in September 1938 did nothing to change the fact that his position on the Board of DEA was untenable. He had long since forfeited any credibility he might have had with them as he had suggested to the Supervisory Board that the group's good business performance since 1933 was primarily attributable to his work as CEO of DPAG and resulted from the profitable expansion of the heating oil production for the Navy. He omitted to say that

71 Cf. Dresdner Bank an DEA, Direktion, Vertraulich, 21.11.1938, WD-CA, D-RW-00582.

72 Cf. Vorstand DEA (Ullner and ?) an Gestapo Oberinspektor Schermer, 21.11.1938, ibid.

73 Cf. Sali Cohen an DEA, 12.12.1938; Wilhelm Böhm an DEA, 22.12.1938; Sali Cohen an DEA, 9.2.1939; Wilhelm Böhm an DEA, 31.3.1939, ibid.

74 Cf. Biographisches Gedenkbuch der Münchener Juden 1933–1945.

the DPAG had only been able to operate at profit because it was able to procure briquettes at a low price from the DEA lignite plants, prices well below those in the market. Ritter and Randhahn had had enough of Gröber's belittling their contribution as engineers and in mid-October 1938 complained to Kimmich.[75] Randhahn was especially annoyed that Gröber had thwarted a portfolio on the achievements of the DEA lignite operations being forwarded to the supervisory board along with all the figures it also contained. For Kimmich, this was a further sign that action was needed. He could no longer tolerate Gröber's repeated violations of the Commercial Code and the Corporation Act. Other members of the supervisory board also insisted that Gröber be relieved of his duties well before the end of his contract, which ran until September 1940.

Kimmich thereupon started paving the way for Gröber to be ejected from the DEA Management Board. This management change came at an inopportune moment as shortly beforehand Haussmann had been fired, Ullner was about to retire, and the future new CEO Schirner still needed time to find his feet. To this extent, Ullner was in a good position to negotiate yet another extension to his contract and Gröber had good cards for getting a better severance package.[76] In Gröber's case, he looked set to enjoy the proverbial "golden handshake".

At an Extraordinary Supervisory Board meeting, conducted with the DEA board present, on 26 Oktober 1938, Kimmich once again did not beat about the bush.[77] Gröber's ongoing membership of DEA was no longer desired. A severance deal would be agreed with him.[78] Gröber retired from his well-paid job as at 31 December 1938. The annual report merely noted that the CEO had "*left on amicable terms with the Head Office in order to dedicate himself to his own*

---

[75] Cf. Randhahn an Kimmich, 19.10.1938, HADB, P 1688.

[76] Cf. Kimmich Aktenvermerk geheim, 19.11.1938, ibid.

[77] Cf. Aufsichtsratssitzung, 26.10.1938, ibid., P 1663, sheet 59.

[78] Cf. Vertrag zwischen der DEA und Hans Gröber, 26.10.1938, D-RW-00271.

interests."[79] Günther Schlicht was somewhat clearer in his memoirs. He noted there that Gröber's new activities would have been incompatible with his duties as a CEO.[80]

To cover all the emoluments to which he was entitled and all other claims, Gröber was granted 150,000 Reichsmark. The DEA also assigned him the villa grounds in Grunewald, Berlin, free of charge.[81] His annual pension claims ran to 34,000 Reichsmark. He did not make personal use of the villa and grounds in Grunewald but sold them before the end of 1938 to Berlin businessman Werner Brüggemann and moved into a flat at Lützowplatz 7.[82]

After the war, Gröber established a network of medium-sized department stores in West Germany, starting in 1949 by registering a new wholesale company in Wiesbaden Großhandelsgesellschaft mbH (Grohag)[83] and later relocating the domicile of Warengroßhandelsgesellschaft mbH (Wagro) from Berlin to the city on the Rhein.[84] Gröber was confronted on several occasions with having been one of the profiteers of "aryanization", without this having any major consequences for him.[85] To what extent Hans Gröber's new spouse, Lotte Schwarz, was aware of his past we do not know. What we do know is that the couple met in Berlin after the war. Lotte Schwarz was a descendant of the family of Jewish doctor Prof. Julius Baer from Frankfurt/Main.[86]

---

79 Geschäftsbericht der DPAG für 1938, WD-CA. DPAG-Geschäftsberichte, 5.

80 Cf. Günther Schlicht, *Erinnerungen*, 72.

81 Cf. Notiz für den Vorstand, 1.3.1957, D-RW-271.

82 Cf. Gröber an DEA-Vorstand, HADB, P 1686, sheet 1ff.

83 Cf. HR B Wiesbaden, 2163.

84 Cf. *Gnad & Rupprecht*, in: http://zinnfiguren-bleifiguren.com/Firmengeschichten/Gnad_Karl_Fuerth/Gnad_Rupprecht_Fuerth.html#Top
Gnad Rupprecht_Fürth (zinnfiguren-bleifiguren.com) [last retrieved on 21.3.2024].

85 Cf. Peter H. Garfunkel an Dr. Engelmann, Wiedergutmachungsamt von Groß-Berlin, 9.12.1952, Landesarchiv Berlin (LAB), B Rep. 025–02, No. 360/51.

86 Cf. Lotte Baer-Schwarz, in: https://www.geni.com/people/Lotte-Baer-Schwarz/6000000040612286363 [last retrieved on 20.3.2024].

In 1967, Hans Gröber had a "charitable foundation"[87] registered in Liechtenstein. Two years later he had it renamed the "Hans Gröber Stiftung". After his death on 1 February 1983 in Locarno, Switzerland, Lotte Schwarz dedicated herself to being a patron of medicine and the arts. The "Hans Gröber Stiftung was entered in the commercial register in 1984 as a charitable foundation under Liechtenstein law. The Administrative Council of the Roncana Foundation, Hubert Batliner, acted on Hans Gröber's death as his legal executor.[88]

The Petschek Group gets broken up

In the inter-War years, there was a pronounced concentration of lignite mining and processing in Germany in the hands of a few stock corporations. The lignite fields in Central Germany and Saxony were dominated by the corporations belonging to the Petschek brothers from Bohemia, Aktiengesellschaft Sächsische Werke (ASW), and DEA.

Ignaz Petschek had by the end of the 19th century succeeded in gaining a stake in the main mines in the North Bohemian coal fields and dominated the commission business with coal. In Germany, by 1915 brothers Ignatz and Julius Petschek controlled almost 40 percent of the briquette production in the Central German fields and around 44 percent in the fields east of the River Elbe.[89] They had a controlling position in the Central German lignite syndicate

---

87 Cf. letter from Rita Kieber-Beck, Hans-Gröber-Stiftung, to Friederike Steensen, 29.2.2024.

88 Cf. "Wir wollten den Wega-Hagi-Konkurs verhindern", in: FAZ, 3.8.1983.

89 Cf. Walter Hermann, *Das Kapital im mitteldeutschen Braunkohlenbergbau*, PhD thesis Universität Leipzig, 1930, 78f.

and controlled a large part of the coal trade.[90] The Duchy of Anhalt and the Kingdom of Saxony therefore issued "blocking laws" to prevent a monopoly in lignite production. As a result, coal fields that were still privately owned devolved to the state. The Petschek brothers' heirs argued and parted company, so that the heirs conducted their respective business-independently of each, the one based in Prague, the other in Aussig (today: Ústí nad Laben, Czech Republic).

Concentration was especially advanced in the lignite mining area of Meuselwitz-Rositz southwest of Leipzig. There, the Ignaz Petschek Group (Leonhard AG, Phönix AG, Niederlausitzer Kohlenwerke) accounted for 51.5 percent of total lignite mined in 1928, DEA followed with 20.0 percent, and the Julius Petschek Group (Anhaltinische Kohlenwerke) with 13.6 percent.[91] In the 1920s, DEA only succeeded in acquiring a few smaller participations the Petscheks held in Central Germany.

ASW was founded at the end of 1923 by the State of Saxony by merging all lignite and hard coal mines owned by the government along with its electricity works.[92] The government corporation floated dollar bonds, invested strongly in growth, and developed a corresponding large hunger for coal. Its rivals and the various conservative parties criticized ASW for purportedly not being economically viable and for the strain this placed on the Saxon government budget.

After the Nazis came to power, the competition for the few lignite companies not yet owned by the major corporations became

---

90 Cf. Bernhard Gotto, *Adaption und Kooperation: Neue Geschäftspraktiken in Dritten Reich*, in: Johannes Bähr et al., Der Flick-Konzern im Dritten Reich, München 2008, 295–387, here 321.

91 Cf. Hermann, *Das Kapital*, 79.

92 Cf. Erhard Weber, *Der staatseigene Industriekonzern in Sachsen*, Leipzig 1928; Thomas Schmidt, *Der Großtagebau Espenhain. Wir für unsere Kohle. Die AG Sächsische Werke 1923–1947*, in: http://www.tagebau-espenhain.de [last retrieved on 21.3.2024].

even fiercer. Both ASW and DEA wanted to expand their lignite field holdings in order to shore up their expansion projects.

In the summer of 1937, there were rumours that possibly the Julius Petschek Group might be putting up its extensive lignite holdings in Germany for sale. The Prague-based Petschek Group had extensively protected its positions by founding the US-British holding company, the United Continental Corporation (UCC). However, given the ever-worsening anti-Semitic atmosphere in the Third Reich and word that the Nazi government was on the verge of intervening, the owners were prepared to sell of their entire German portfolio. This consisted mainly of Anhaltische Kohlewerken AG (AKW) and Wersche-Weissenfelser Braunkohlen AG (WW).[93]

In several locations, the lignite fields owned by the Julius Petschek Group abutted fields that belonged to ASW or DEA for this reason, in the past there had repeatedly been negotiations over swapping and buying/selling lignite fields. The triangle of Petschek-ASW-DEA negotiated in 1936–7 on the "Fortschritt" colliery. DEA expressed a certain interest in acquiring it, but in the final instance missed out.[94] More important from the viewpoint of the DEA management was, with a view to the pending conclusion of the deal with the Navy, clarification of its relationship with ASW. In order to expand production in Rositz, DEA depended on acquiring a large coal field owned by ASW.

In July 1937, DEA learned from ASW director Heinrich Ehlers that the Julius Petschek Group intended to sell shop. In early December 1937, Gröber and Randhahn informed the other members of the management board of pending "*restructuring in the Julius Petschek corporation*".[95] Prague had proposed they start talks. They responded with reservation. There was no firm basis for concrete negotiations.

---

93 Cf. Gotto, *Adaption und Kooperation*, 324.

94 Cf. Vorstandsprotokoll, 29.9.1937, WD-CA, D-PA-29, part 3.

95 Cf. Vorstandsprotokoll, 7.7.1937, ibid.

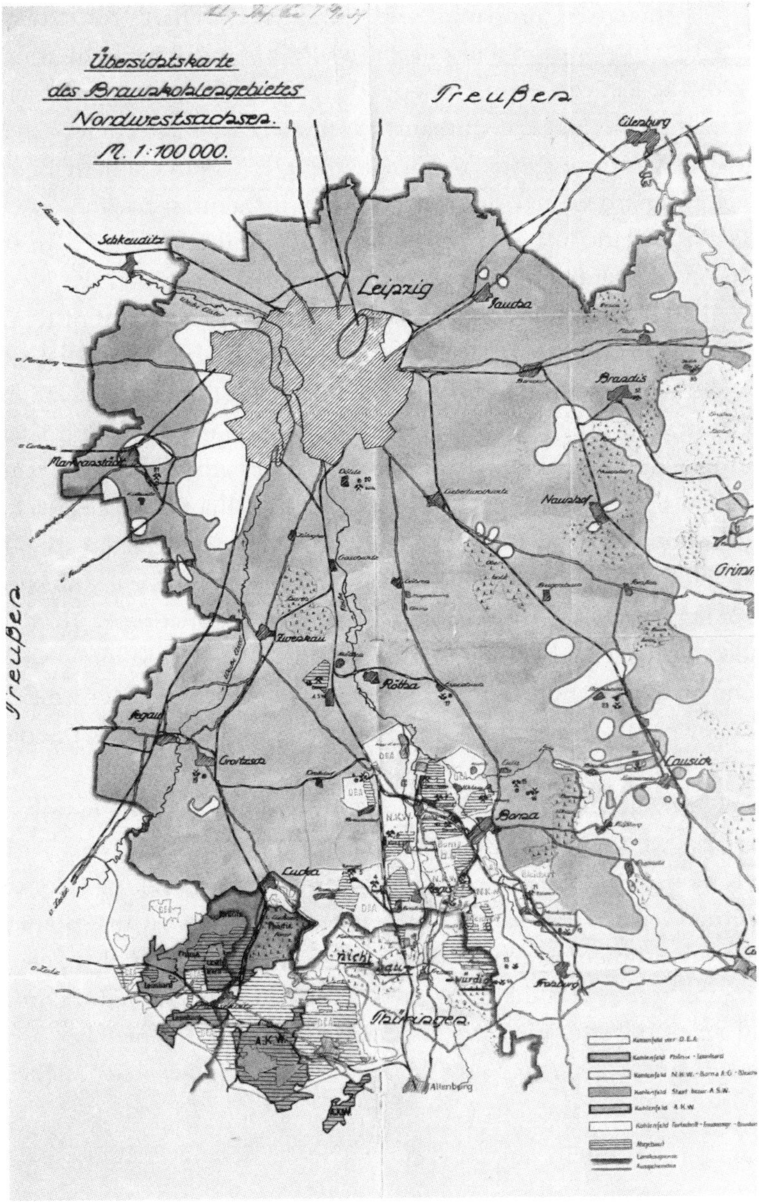

Fig. 32 Demarcation lines between the various lignite fields in northwest Saxony (1938)

There were probably various reasons for DEA's restraint: In 1936, the corporation had purchased Prehlitzer Braunkohlen AG, one of the last remaining independent producers, and hoped with the help of the Naval Command to land a large-scale colliery swap with ASW. Quite apart from that, the DEA Management Board under Richard Ullner did not have any influential backers in the Four-Year Plan Authority or the Reich Economics Ministry. In the field of economic policy, the group had mainly lobbied the Naval Command. What was probably worse from the viewpoint of representatives of the Nazi power apparatus was the fact that DEA was reputed to be controlled by Jewish bankers. Not until May 1938 did DEA shed its long-standing supervisory board members Solmssen, Springer, and Schwabach, and also fired Haussmann from his management board position.[96] This occurred, as Ullner explained to the DEA supervisory board, above all with a view to the acquisition of the coal field that formed the basis for the "*entire future development of the corporation*".[97] At that point in time, the negotiations with ASW had not progressed among other things because the Saxon government-owned corporation has refused to approve the lignite field swap by pointing the figure at the "non-Aryans" on the DEA Supervisory Board.

While the DEA management board was busy focussing on the talks with ASW, VIAG, Wintershall AG and I.G. Farben has as early as the end of 1937 expressed their interest in taking over the Central German companies in the Petschek Group. At this point in time, government agencies were already treating Petschek assets as something they could handle as they liked.[98] They wanted the mineral deposits to go primarily to companies which occupied key positions in the Four-Year Plan. Approval would be granted for those

---

96 Cf. chapter 2.

97 Ullner an Kimmich, 5.5.1938, HADB, P 1659, sheet 74.

98 Cf. Gotto, *Adaption und Kooperation*, 324.

corporations that could best justify their "claim" in terms of its benefit to the nation's economy and the re-armaments effort.

Representatives of the Flick Group were the most skilful in this regard. Friedrich Flick managed at the end of January 1938 to persuade Hermann Göring as Head of the Four-Year Plan Authority to grant him the exclusive mandate for negotiations with the Julius Petschek Group and/or the UCC. Initial talks had failed given insurmountable differences on the purchase price, and the situation for the Petschek Group had deteriorated fast after Austria's "accession" to the Third Reich. The German government issued a series of laws and decrees on "aryanization". The ball was set rolling on 22 April 1938 with a decree that made "camouflaging" a Jewish company from government eyes a crime.[99] Only four days later, the "Decree on Registration of the Jews' Assets" was enacted. It also obliged Jews outside Germany to declare their assets located in Germany.[100] If a Jew held an interest in the business, the sale or lease of a company was declared to be subject to approval by the authorities.

This was the background that in May 1938 informed a new round of talks between representatives of the Flick Group and of UCC. Flick acquired all the Central German interests of the Prague arm of the Petschek family. Flick passed some of the coal fields on to other interested parties and in exchange bagged the foreign currency he needed to bankroll the purchase. He then negotiated with the Aussig-based arm of the Petschek family (the Ignaz Petschek Group). Karl Petschek, son of Ignaz Petschek, who had died in 1934, dug in his heels and refused to sell, pointing out that his father had already sold off the Group's companies in Germany and the remainder was now in the hands of holdings outside that coun-

99 Verordnung gegen die Unterstützung der "Tarnung" eines jüdischen Gewerbebetriebes, 22.4.1938, RGBl., 1938 I, 404.

100 Cf. Verordnung über die Anmeldung des Vermögens der Juden, 26.4.1938, RGBl., 1938 I, 415.

try.[101] The authorities thereupon started turning the screws such as to slowly throttle the Petschek companies in Bohemia. That no longer happened, as after the Wehrmacht entered what was then declared "Sudetenland" (the German-speaking Sudeten territories) in October 1938 it occupied the Petschek Group Head Office in Aussig and in January 1939 the Reich Economics Ministry appointed a fiduciary agent to manage the assets of the Ignaz Petschek Group. German tax inspectors ferreted through the head office in the hopes of uncovering incriminating materials. All things seemed to point to expropriation through nationalization.[102]

In the meantime, Paul Pleiger, General Director of Reichswerke AG in charge of the mining "Hermann Göring" ore mine and iron smelter in Salzgitter and one of the most important armaments managers, had expressly registered his corporation's interest in the Petschek properties. Reichswerke AG lacked mines for hard coal, he argued, and wanted to acquire them in exchange for lignite operations. Flick no longer succeeded in getting his negotiating mandate on behalf of the Four-Year Plane extended. Things seemed to be heading for an open battle over who got the Ignaz Petschek Group assets, a race between all the major coal and steel players and the chemicals corporations, too.

DEA likewise took to the starting blocks and sought to participate in the pending break-up of the Petschek Group. To this end, the management board had an extensive memorandum drawn up in January 1939 on the "*Acquisition of the lignite plants of the Ignaz Petschek Group by Deutsche Erdöl-Aktiengesellschaft, Berlin*".[103] The memorandum was sent on 17 January 1939 to Oscar Gabel at the Mining

[101] Cf. Kim Christian Priemel, *Flick. Eine Konzerngeschichte vom Kaiserreich bis zur Bundesrepublik*, Munich 2013.

[102] Cf. Gotto, *Adaption und Kooperation*, 347f.

[103] Randhahn, Memorandum betreffend Erwerb von Braunkohlewerken des Ignaz-Petschek-Konzerns durch die Deutsche Erdöl-Aktiengesellschaft, Berlin, 16.1.1939, HADB, P 1659, sheet 231–237.

section of the Reich Economics Ministry and to Head of Department Helmuth Wohlthat. The latter was Hermann Göring's Special Commissioner in the Four-Year Plan Authority where he was responsible for the "Petschek aryanization".[104]

The memorandum emphasized the fact that DEA had since as long ago as 1916 sought to curb the influence of "*non-Aryan foreigners*" and in particular the two Petschek groups, in the Central German lignite fields. Moreover, DEA had done the nation a service with its elaborate heating oil production process for the Navy. The Petscheks, so the paper argued, had simply been interested in making the proverbial 'fast buck'. This tack locked into the Nazi hypothesis of a contrast between "productive German capital" and "rapacious Jewish capital". The authors thus went on to conclude: "*In the event of the lignite plants in the Ignaz Petschek Group being farmed out, given what it has achieved in this domain Deutsche Erdöl-A.G. has the greatest claim to consideration of all corporations.*"[105]

Another argument put forward was that the Petschek plants lay in the middle of DEA collieries. "*Incorporating the Petschek plants would form the capstone for a conglomerate of coal fields that would be quite unprecedented on this scale in the German lignite industry, which has undergone such great rationalization over the last two decades.*"[106]

Specifically, DEA wanted to acquire the Petschek shares in Braunkohlenwerke Borna AG, Bleichert'sche Braunkohlenwerke AG, Neukirch-Wyhra, and three power plants attached to Niederlausitzer Kohlenwerke AG. These corporations owned four opencast mines, five briquette factories, and a carbonization plant. The Ignaz Petschek companies were able to draw on coal fields that could be mined at low cost, something that translated into an appreciably higher briquette output per man and shift than in the DEA operations. As regards raw lignite, the Ignaz Petschek companies held a

104 On Wohlthat cf. Gotto, *Adaption und Kooperation*, 336–339.
105 Ibid.
106 Ibid.

higher syndicate quota than did DEA. Their financial status was rated as favourable, and their high profits went towards extraordinarily high amortization.[107]

To what extent the assets targeted derived from covert agreement with the Flick corporation is a matter of conjecture. There is evidence that the Flick executives sought to assert their interests through strategic alliances with other companies, specifically BRABAG, I.G. Farben, VIAG, and DEA. Ullner corresponded with the Flick management on the subject and drew on the arguments presented in the above memorandum.[108] On 15 February 1939, Ullner and Kimmich presented their view on the "Petschek Problem" to the Reich Economics Ministry.[109] Ullner doubled down the next day and in a letter to Ministry Director Gabel once again highlighted the operational and economic arguments in favour of DEA taking over the Petschek companies. Both the state and the Nazi party expressly called for further rationalization in lignite mining and processing, he said. "*However, there can be no doubt that the Petschek Group will in future be excluded from the plants it has operated to date.*"[110] Ullner cunningly stated no purchase price: "*The purchase price the new owners should put up would first be transferred to the Inland Revenue which would for its part then have time to undertake all deductions from the prior owners.*"[111] In other words, the prior owners would only receive a sum well below the net asset value.

While DEA was already busy establishing the economic viability of the Petschek operations Kimmich learned that the payroll at Bornaer Kohlenwerke AG did not welcome the idea of being bought

---

107 Cf. Gutachten betreffend die Braunkohlenwerke des Ignaz-Petschek-Konzerns im Revier Borna, streng vertraulich, HADB, P 1659, 253–263.

108 Cf. Ullner an Steinbrink, 6.2.1939, ibid., sheet 238–240; Gotto, *Adaption und Kooperation*, 348.

109 Cf. Ullner an Gabel, betr.: Ignaz Petschek-Gruppe, 16.2.1939, HADB, P 1659, sheet 242.

110 Ibid.

111 Ibid.

up by DEA.[112] The in-company benefits at the Petschek companies were judged to be better than at DEA. A corresponding submission was sent to DAF.

On 20 March 1939, Randhahn presented a strictly confidential report on the economic viability of the Ignaz Peschek companies to his fellow Management Board members and Supervisory Board Chairman Kimmich.[113] He recommended, if at all possible, acquiring all the companies. Calculating the purchase price was complicated. Randhahn assumed half the book value, or about 47.5 million Reichsmark. A higher purchase price would, he said, "severely stress" the DEA balance sheet.[114]

The DEA management and supervisory boards were strongly resolved to acquire the Ignaz Petschek companies. The purchase price was of secondary importance if it did not hurt too much. Only the potential prospective considerable growth counted. The DEA management board knew that the final decision on breaking up the Petschek assets lay with the Four-Year Plan Authority and banked on an alliance with Flick.[115] However, the strategic coalition with the Flick Group did not prove to be as strong as the DEA executives had hoped. Reichswerke AG was not willing to do a swap deal of hard coal for lignite coal assets at the terms Flick proposed.

Talks between Flick and the others in the alliance, including Braunkohlen- und Brikett-Industrie AG (Bubiag), I.G. Farben, and DEA, all of whom wanted to trade hard coal mines for Reichswerke lignite, were not easy.[116] Moreover, Flick did not inform the DEA executives of his strategic take on swapping coal fields. When, in

---

112 Cf. Aktennotiz für Kimmich, 1.3.1939, ibid., sheet 243f.

113 Cf. Gutachten betreffend die Braunkohlenwerke des Ignaz-Petschek-Konzerns im Revier Borna, streng vertraulich, 20.3.1939, ibid., 253–263.

114 Ibid.

115 Cf. DEA-Aufsichtsratsprotokoll, 14.3.1939, ibid.

116 Cf. Bernhard Gotto, *Adaption und Kooperation. Neue Geschäftspraktiken im Dritten Reich*, in: Johannes Bähr et al., Der Flick-Konzern im Dritten Reich, Munich 2008, 298–378, esp. 351f., *Geschäfte mit dem Staat. Der "Fall Petschek"*.

May 1939 negotiations between Flick and Pleiger gained momentum and Flick was not able to achieve what he wanted, the Flick-DEA alliance became only so much paper.

Unusually for him, Kimmich as DEA Supervisory Board Chair intervened directly in the talks and in mid-May 1939 spoke to Flick in order to push DEA's interests. Flick was not impressed and pointed to Pleiger's demands. Kimmich thereupon threatened that if DEA were excluded it would "*go to the ministries and highlight the fact it had justified industrial interests that were being trashed for capitalist reasons.*"[117] The DEA, he insisted, had to be given the cherished assets. Kimmich's words fell on deaf ears. Unlike in the case of the "aryanization" of the Julius Petschek Group, Flick failed to realize his concept and after sluggish negotiations was forced largely to accept the terms the Reichswerke had set.[118]

The Central German companies in the Ignaz Petschek Group were mainly acquired by Reichswerke AG. In a swap transaction, Flick handed over valuable hard coal mines to Reichswerke and received in exchange less valuable lignite plants.[119] DEA's targets of Braunkohlenwerke Borna AG and Bleichert'sche Braunkohlenwerke AG both went in 1940 from Reichswerke AG to Salzdetfurth AG.[120]

DEA therefore had to find a different path to round out its lignite holdings in order to shore up the expansion programme agreed with the Navy. Here, the contacts to the Flick management proved useful after all. At the end of June 1939, Flick acted as intermediary between the Navy, DEA, and ASW. This will be discussed in detail in the next chapter.

---

117 Kimmich, memo, 19.5.1939, HADB, P 1659, sheet 289. [The first sheet of the memo is missing from the documents. Kimmich presumably sent this letter to Ullner].

118 Cf. Gotto, *Adaption und Kooperation*, 365–378.

119 Cf. James, *Die Deutsche Bank*, 366f.

120 Cf. Thomas Bergner/Almut Zimmermann, Kohlespuren-Tour 2021 — Digitaler Input zu Orten der Kohle, in: https://histsax.hypotheses.org [last retrieved on 24.3.2023].

As regards "aryanization", it bears saying that DPAG/DEA was primarily interested in rounding out its colliery assets in Central Germany. When in 1937–8 "aryanization" of the Julius Petschek Group properties was on the agenda, DEA bided its time and left it to ASW to sound things out. It did so because there were contractual ties between ASW and the Julius Petschek Group. It also had to weigh up the fact that the Julius Petschek owned Anhaltische Kohlenwerke AG (AKW) and Wersche-Weissenfelser Braunkohlen AG (WW) and thus had a stake in Braunkohle-Benzin-AG (BRABAG). DEA had after all resisted joining the mandatory cartel.

When in early 1939 the government instructed that the Ignaz Petschek Group be broken up, the DEA management went into action, driven by CEO Richard Ullner, Supervisory Board Chair Karl Kimmich and Director of DEA's lignite operations Walter Randhahn. Through an alliance with the Flick Group, DEA sought to acquire the Ignaz Petschek assets in Central Germany. This would have offered DEA considerable potential growth, especially as the assets included completely operational coal fields and briquette factories. DEA only missed out because by then it was no longer Flick, but Reichswerke AG who dictated the rules of the game for the "aryanization" of the Petschek assets.

In the case of the "aryanization" of small companies, coal dealerships, and in dealings with owners of independent mines in Austria, and they will be discussed elsewhere, DEA acted no differently than most German corporations.

To a far greater extent than his fellow board members, Hans Gröber acted as an "aryanizer" both within the company and as a private individual. He gradually assumed that role as of the spring of 1933 together with his brother-in-law Georg Karg. They established a small network of financial backers who participated in squeezing Jewish textile companies out of business. Gröber increasingly extended the limits of what was morally acceptable. He acted without scruples and did not shy away from calling for the arrest of businessman Alfred Siegel simply in order to get the latter's furniture at a cheap price.

We can discern moral scruples in the case of DEA CEO Richard Ullner as regards Jewish colleagues on the board and individual Jewish businessmen. Ullner tried to help his fellow Board member Fritz Haussmann emigrate to England and in November 1938 sought to ensure the Böhm brothers were released from the Dachau concentration camp, something that saved neither of their lives, however. Lothar Ritter, Briko CEO, also acted decently in the one known case: He did not exploit the distress of Vienna coal dealer Bernhard Fischer but was instead willing to pay an appropriate price for the latter's businesses.

For all the differences in how DEA Board members and authorized signatories used the scope they had, the fact is that management accepted that Jewish businessmen were considered as not belonging to the "people's community". The DEA memorandum of January 1939 legitimized the attempted grab of assets from the Ignaz Petschek Group by citing racist and economic arguments and in this way followed the logic of the Nazi system. The possible seizure of the assets of others was something they dressed up in operational reasons. The fact that DEA did not acquire the Ignaz Petschek Group's Central German operations occurred solely because of the constellations in the Nazi power apparatus and the strong position of Reichswerke AG, which successfully achieved its objective.

VII. DPAG/DEA IN THE "OSTMARK" – AUSTRIA AFTER ITS INCLUSION IN THE GERMAN REICH

(Rainer Karlsch)

The Vienna Basin as an oil region

The beginnings of the oil industry in Austria date back to the days of the Austro-Hungarian Empire. At that time, oil extraction was in full swing in Galicia, the second most important oil-producing region after Romania back then. Oil production in the region around Boryslav (today in the Ukraine) peaked around 1908. As a result of the war, from 1916 onward the oil from Galicia was no longer accessible to the Axis powers (Austro-Hungary, Germany, Bulgaria), and the resulting ever-greater bottlenecks in petroleum and fuels led the War Ministry to become interested in oil exploration in the Vienna Basin. Among geologists, the region had long since been considered to potentially contain oil fields, so in 1917 the War Ministry commissioned engineer geologist and diviner Friedrich Musil with prospecting for the black gold.[1] He did not

[1] Cf. Doris Rothauer, *Das Tiefbohrunternehmen van Sickle – seine Entwicklung und Tätigkeit im Rahmen der gesamten österreichischen Mineralölindustrie*, PhD thesis, Vienna 1985, 5f.; Stefanie Musil an Dr. Danner, 27.5.1938, Österreichisches Staatsarchiv Vienna [hereafter: ÖStA], Bundesministerium Handel und Verkehr, Abt. Oberste Bergbehörde, 1938, 157.201–158.000.

manage to find anything other than traces, but that was already a beginning.[2]

After the First World War, oil exploration in the Austrian First Republic was left to private investors due to the persistent economic depression. In order to crank up exploratory drilling, in 1921 the government issued the Act on Exploration Permit Allocation and the next year modified the Mining Act by distinguishing oil and gas deposits from landed property, with the exception of gas basins already being tapped.[3] Another stimulus was the Act on Oil Extraction resolved on 17 January 1929. With this, drilling work was given an exemption from tax and levies for several years.

The key aspect behind prospecting for oil was the regulations governing exploration permits.[4] An exploration permit covered a circular area with a diameter of 425 metres, the centre of which was the site of the exploration file number. The owner had to pay an annual charge to the Mining Authority and was obliged to undertake at least one drilled well in the area. If the drilling struck oil, the permit holder could apply to be awarded a mining field or a mining section, in which case the provisional right became actual ownership.

Post-war inflation led to a sell-out of Austrian businesses and favoured the entry of foreign companies and financiers. This was especially true of oil prospecting.[5] Among the most important companies that acquired exploration rights were Steinberg Naphta GmbH, owned by Polish industrialist Thomas Laszcz and operating with French capital, Gewerkschaft Raky-Danubia, run by German deep-drilling entrepreneur Anton Raky, and Erdölproduktions-Ge-

2 Cf. Gerhard Ruthammer, *Öldorado Weinviertel. Zur Geschichte des Erdöls im Weinviertel*, Schlainhut 2011.

3 Cf. Walter M. Iber, *Die sowjetische Mineralölverwaltung in Österreich. Zur Vorgeschichte der OMV 1945–1955*, Innsbruck 2011, 34.

4 Cf. Exposé conc. Tiefbohrunternehmen Richard K. von Sickle, Wien, Freyung I (no date), Chronik James van Sickle, GeoSphere Austria-Archiv Rohstoffe, Vienna, A 18888-R.1.

5 Cf. Rothauer, *Das Tiefbohrunternehmen van Sickle*, 10.

sellschaft mbH (EPG), owned by Viennese banker Albert Brunnenbauer, which relied on capital from Switzerland.

After several small oil finds, in August 1934 EPG made a breakthrough with its "Gösting II" probe. For the first time, a large field was tapped in the Vienna Basin. This success kindled the interest of foreign oil companies, and at the end of 1934 American company Socony Vacuum Oil together with a subsidiary of Royal Dutch Shell founded Rohöl-Gewinnungs-AG (RAG). Gewerkschaft Austrogasco, which was controlled by US financiers, acquired countless exploration permits. Within a very short period of time, RAG and Austrogasco managed to grab almost half of all the exploration permits for the Vienna Basin.[6]

In 1937, oil production in Austria was still a very modest 33,000 tonnes, but the proof was there of oil fields offering commercial quantities.[7] In early summer 1937, the Upper Mining Authority attached to the Federal Ministry of Trade and Transportation in Vienna reported a mood similar to a gold rush and anticipated there would be fierce competition among the drilling companies.[8] Their activities were braked, however, by bottlenecks for pumping pipes and drilling equipment that primarily had to be imported and were subject to foreign currency regulations.

Although German companies had also tried to get involved in oil prospecting in Austria, in 1937 their share of the exploration rights was less than five percent.[9] The key local player was the construction company owned by Georg Rumpel, Rumpel AG, Vienna. Since 1927 it had been controlled by the Mannesmann Group, and

---

6 Cf. *Verteilung der Freischürfe in Österreich Ende 1937*, in: Hans Seidel, Österreichs Wirtschaft und Wirtschaftspolitik nach dem Zeiten Weltkrieg, Vienna 2005, 422.

7 Cf. M. Iber, *Die sowjetische Mineralölverwaltung in Österreich*, 36.

8 Cf. BMHuV, 12.5.1937 ÖStA, Bundesministerium Handel und Verkehr, Oberste Bergbehörde, 1937, 163.701.

9 Cf. *Verteilung der Freischürfe in Österreich Ende 1937*, 422.

it was active in deep drilling and likewise in plant engineering.[10] Within the German Reich, the growing interest among foreign companies in prospecting for oil in Austria was clearly noticed, and private individuals interested in speculating with exploration permits tried to get a foot in the door and were supported in their efforts by Reich authorities and the German mission in Vienna.

After Austria's incorporation into the Third Reich with its so-called "Accession" in March 1938, the Austrian oil industry went into overdrive. The "*Programme for Strengthening Austria*" announced by Hermann Göring as early as 26 March 1938 emphasized the importance of oil production.[11] Already on 1 April 1938, a representative of the Upper Mining Authority of the German Reich presented a draft bill on the use of mining rights to the members of the Austrian Association for Oil and Gas Production.[12] The bill was not enacted, however, and the matter was instead solved more skilfully. The Mining Act in place since 1854 remained in force, but the exploration and extraction of bitumen now came under the Bitumen Bill enacted on 31 August 1938.[13] In this way, prospecting for and producing oil, gas, and bitumen, etc. was the sole privilege of the state. The exploration permits that existed at the time the law came into force would expire at the latest on 31 July 1940 if no petition for the issue of a mining section had been filed beforehand. Every oil company that wished to operate in Austria after the "Anschluss" (Accession), as of when the territory was officially called the "Ostmark", thus had only 23 months to strike oil in the areas covered by its exploration permits. Even in normal times, it would have been impossible given the low number of drilling rigs to prospect a larger

10 Cf. Austria-Forum, Bilfinger VAM Anlagentechnik GmbH, austria-forum.org/Unternehmen/Bilfinger_VAM_Anlagentechnik_GmbH [last retrieved on 26.4.2023].

11 Cf. Iber, *Die sowjetische Mineralölverwaltung*, 38.

12 Cf. Exposé conc. Tiefbohrunternehmen Richard K. von Sickle, Wien, Freyung I (no date), Chronik James van Sickle, GeoSphere Austria-Archiv Rohstoffe, Vienna, A 18888-R.1

13 Cf. Gesetzblatt für das Land Österreich, year 1938, 31.8.1938, 1719f.

area of exploration permits in less than two years and develop the field to the point where it could be classified as a mining section. The time pressure left companies two options: either to boost their exploration activities and commit a lot of capital or to sell their exploration permits, which was what the Nazi regime were aiming for. The Bitumen Act was intended to enable the expropriation of foreign companies.

Speculation on exploration permits

Until the "Anschluss", DPAG/DEA was not active in any way in oil prospecting in Austria, but the pace of events accelerated dramatically as of 13 March 1938 with the declaration in Vienna of the law sanctioning it. The very next day, the board of DPAG was summoned to a meeting at the Reich Economics Ministry, where the managers were encouraged *"in no uncertain terms"* to acquire Austrian contractual rights from Berlin businessman Karl Eugen Schmid.[14] Working on his own behalf but also as trustee for a consortium of German financiers, Schmid had concluded contracts with several holders of exploration permits for them to assign their permits to him.[15] The DPAG/DEA managers were surprised, as they did not know Schmid and about his activities in Austria.

The driving force behind the ministry's insistence was the fact that payments had to be made within a very short space of time, as otherwise Schmid would forfeit his mining rights, and the Reich Economics Ministry feared that in such an event the rights might land up in foreign hands. DPAG thereupon negotiated with repre-

---

14 Cf. Sachdarstellung: Erdölgerechtsname in Österreich, 28.7.1938, WD-CA, D-RW-00473.

15 Cf. note conc.: Sachdarstellung über den Erwerb von Freischürfen in der Ostmark, 4.4.1941, WD-CA, 14-2/3136.

sentatives of Schmid, among them Friedrich Kadgien and Horst von Petersdorff.

The DPAG/DEA documentation at no point mentions what role these men played in the Nazi power apparatus. Little is known about Schmid, but he is said, as a retired Prussian major, to have been a confidante of Major General Fritz Löb, Director of the Office for German Raw Materials and Production Materials in the Four-Year Plan Authority, and therefore also to have been in close contact with SS-Oberführer Wilhelm Keppler, who was Reich Commissioner in Austria and General Expert for German Raw Materials and Production Materials at the Four-Year Plan Authority until July 1938.[16] We can assume from the sequence of events that Schmid was acting with the knowledge of said authority and the Reich Economics Ministry. It would seem logical that Schmid was either a member of the SS or that the "Black Order" at least had his back. This is underscored by the fact that SS-Sturmbannführer Dr Bruno Lettow from the Gestapo Command HQ in Vienna was appointed his "curator" in July 1938.[17]

Another relevant fact points to this being an SS operation. Schmid's legal counsel was Friedrich Kadgien, who from 1934 onwards was active as the judicial assessor attached to the Reich Economics Ministry. Kadgien had been a Nazi Party member as early as 1932 and joined the SS in 1935. In August 1938, he moved to the authority for the Four-Year Plan and was Special Commissioner for Foreign Currency and Precious Metals. Among other things, he

---

16 Cf. memo: Crackanlage für in Österreich gefördertes Erdöl, 27.3.1938, Bundesministerium Handel und Verkehr, Abt. Oberste Bergbehörde, 1938, 158.001.

17 Dr. Schindler an Regierungsrat Dr. von Lettow, Gestapo, Wien, Gegenstand "Terrol", Rechtsansprüche K.E. Schmid und van Sickle, 4.7.1938, ÖStA, Bundesministerium Handel und Verkehr, Oberste Bergbehörde, 1937, 157081. For further information on the Gestapo Command HQ in Vienna see: Franz Weisz, *Die personelle Zusammensetzung der Gestapo Wien 1938 – 1945*, Vienna 2019. For information on Dr. Bruno Lettow: Michael Wildt, *Generation des Unbedingten. Das Führungskorps des Reichssicherheitshauptamtes*, Hamburg 2002, 335 and 355.

coordinated the sale of stolen shares and securities through Swiss banks and was considered to be Göring's right-hand man.[18]

Horst von Petersdorff was the scion of a wealthy family of officers and had himself seen combat in the First World War, setting up a Freikorps in 1918–9 that bore his name. He purchased a piece of land on the Obersalzberg, where his next-door neighbour was publicist and "Party poet" Dietrich Eckart, a source of various ideas for Adolf Hitler. It was through Eckart that he met Hitler at an early date.[19] From 1922 onwards, Petersdorff earned a living as a businessman. He joined the Nazi Party in 1922 and the Storm Troopers (SA) a year later, rose through the ranks to become an SA leader, but lost his position in mid-1931. He thereupon quit the Nazi Party and the Storm Troopers and lived in Austria for a while. He himself said he worked there on behalf of Österreichisch-Alpine Montangesellschaft, which was majority-owned by Germany's Vereinigte Stahlwerke AG, and busied himself with acquiring oil concessions in the region around Zistersdorf, northeast of Vienna.[20] In 1936, Petersdorff succeeded in rejoining the Nazi Party.[21]

Kadgien and Petersdorff represented the interests of several German financial backers – among others, renowned expert in international law Professor Viktor Bruns of Berlin University and Erich Koch, Gau Head for East Prussia. In the period from March 1937 to January 1938, as the crises relating to the Sudeten territories and Austria's independence were coming to a head, Schmid concluded contracts with seven individual partners on purchasing a total of 1,512 sets of exploration rights and had made down-payments on these.[22]

---

18 Cf. Ralf Banken, *Edelmetallmangel und Großraumwirtschaft*, Berlin 2009, 257 and 727.

19 Cf. Aktenvermerk, Zeugenschrifttum, 28.5.1957, ZS-1473-1, Archiv des Institut für Zeitgschichte Munich [hereafter: IfZ].

20 Cf. ibid.

21 Cf. Horst von Petersdorff, BArch Berlin, NS 5-VI/17695.

22 Cf. DEA, memo, 24.3.1938, WD-CA, 14-2/3136.

The search for oil was a bit of a lottery. For a small stake, you could get rich if the exploration rights covered an area where oil was struck. In that case, the gross percentage yield on the sales of the crude oil (as a rule 1–7 percent) went to the financial backers – but this was the case only rarely. Most exploration rights turned up nothing, which spelled the complete loss of the capital committed. The financiers therefore tried to spread their risk by acquiring as many exploration rights as possible.

At the end of March 1938, further payments became due on the rights Schmid had acquired, if the option rights were not to be forfeited. Schmid had himself gambled and had spent some of the monies entrusted to him for other purposes. And not all the contracts he had drawn up were legally watertight, something that would lead to years of litigation. Although the legal position was thus anything but clear, on 17 March 1938, DPAG stepped into Schmid's shoes in most of the contracts.[23] DPAG wired 50,000 Austrian schillings to "Terrol", a company closely associated with Schmid, and a further 51,000 schillings to the British drilling outfit Terrol had hired, van Sickle. With immediate effect, DPAG entered into the contractual arrangement with van Sickle and Terrol.

A few weeks later, DPAG also acquired exploration rights from Viennese lawyer Max Weiss and from Viennese businessman Emmerich Back. Both were Jews and evidently had to sell their rights under duress and below value.[24]

---

23 Cf. Notary Hans Wöstndieck, No. 106 Urkundenrolle 1938, 17.3.1938, WD-CA, D-RW-00473; Note: Sachdarstellung über den Erwerb der Freischürfe in der Ostmark, 4.4.1941, WD-CA, 14-2-3136.

24 Cf. DEA, conc.: Erwerb von Freischürfen in Österreich vor dem 31.7.1940, Oktober 1947, WD-CA, DEA "Österreich-Ordner".

DPAG was no longer able to enter into the contract with Rumpel AG, as the deadline had lapsed.[25] In mid-May 1938 a syndicate agreement was reached with Mannesmann, as the parent company of Rumpel AG, Wintershall AG, and DPAG.[26]

Independent of the contract with Schmid, DPAG also acquired exploration rights from Privy Councillor Oskar Pöller, engineer Hugo Keller, and Gewerkschaft Zillingsdorf. In these three instances, it was again "Aryanized" property that was at stake. Real estate businessman Oskar Pöller, who had lived in Berlin until 1933, received the symbolic figure of 500 Reichsmark for his 142 exploration rights. He was murdered in Auschwitz in 1942.[27] Hugo Keller, a Czechoslovak citizen, sold DPAG 1,788 exploration rights in Upper Austria that the firm intended to drill along with other German companies.[28] We can assume that DPAG exploited the seller's desperate straits, as indicated by the low purchase price. In the wake of the Bitumen Act coming into force, Keller's exploration rights went on offer to Erdölwerke Ostmark.[29]

It was only reluctantly that on 23 March 1938 DPAG acquired the fixed assts of Terrol Erdölförderungsgesellschaft mbH, Vienna. The company, not founded until January 1938, was the successor company to Musil & Co. Steinberg-Rohöl-Gesellschaft

---

25 Cf. DPAG an Ministerium für Wirtschaft und Arbeit, Vienna, 24.6.1939, WD-CA, D-RW-00489. In a questionnaire filled out for the NGOC in 1947, the DEA board stated on record that the Austrian businessman Dr. Emmerich Back was "probably a half-Jew". He was paid around RM 51,000 for his mining rights. (cf. WD-CA, DEA "Österreich-Ordner").

26 Cf. note: Sachdarstellung über den Erwerb der Freischürfe in der Ostmark, 4.4.1941, WD-CA, 14-2, 3136.

27 Cf. Mineralölwerke Wietze an Notar Dr. Hans Graskopf, 15.10.38, WD-CA, D-RW-00489; On the biography of Oskar Pöller (1883–1942) cf. Beschluss der Kommission für Provenienzforschung, Vienna 30.11.2012.

28 Cf. contract DPAG Ing. Hugo Keller, Vienna (22. März 1938), Große/Schlicht, WD-CA, D-RW-00473.

29 Cf. note: Sachdarstellung über den Erwerb der Freischürfe in der Ostmark, 4.4.1941, WD-CA, 14-2, 3136.

mbH.[30] The buy-out proved to be a flop, as Schmid was not legally entitled to dispose of Terrol. It later turned out that he had been deceived by the managing director of Terrol, Senior Engineer Jean Lohma. The controversy between the two men ended in a punch-up in the Terrol office.

The existing partners in Terrol, Mr and Mrs Musil, did not want to give everything up to DPAG without a fight. They stated that they were "*the only Nazi oil company in Austria that operated without foreign capital*",[31] and said that during the "*Republican system*" in Austria the company "faced major difficulties from all sides." Moreover, all the senior managers at Terrol were well-known Nazis. Schmid, with whom the Musils had come into contact in 1937 via the German mission and "*Party circles*", deceived both his German backers and Terrol, they claimed. And it was, furthermore, DPAG that was benefiting from the situation and seeking to "steamroller" Terrol, with its lesser capital resources.[32] If Terrol were to fail, "*then the only Nazi company will be expunged, while all the others working with oil companies that rely on financing related to Jews and foreign capital will then continue to play a decisive role.*"[33]

Stefanie Musil, a member of the Nazi Party from 1922 and leader of the Gau Women's section, wrote in May 1938 to the Upper Mining Authority in Vienna to present her view of things and solicit support for Terrol.[34] She did indeed receive support from the Gau

30 Cf. BMHuV, Dr. Kern, Hinterlegung: K.E. Schmid: Bohrtätigkeit der in Gründung begriffenen "Terrol" Erdölförderungsgesellschaft mbH, Vienna, Besprechung am 20.1.1938, ÖStA, Bundesministerium Handel und Verkehr, Oberste Bergbehörde, 1938, 157.691.

31 Hans Jost Waldschmidt an den Reichsbeauftragten für Österreich, Staatssekretär Keppler, 6.4.1938, ÖStA, Bundesministerium Handel und Verkehr, Oberste Bergbehörde, 1937, 157081.

32 Ibid.

33 Ibid.

34 Stefanie Musil an Dr. Danner, 27.5.1938, ÖStA, Bundesministerium Handel und Verkehr, Oberste Bergbehörde, 1938, 157.201–158.000.

directors in this regard.[35] As a last gasp, Terrol even mooted the idea of a possible contract with DPAG/DEA,[36] but all the firms they approached turned them down, and the Upper Mining Authority was itself sceptical of Terrol – especially since Friedrich Musil, as a diviner and speculator, did not have a particularly good reputation.[37]

The Reich Economics Ministry insisted that the contractual basis be clarified swiftly and appointed Bruno Lettow, from the Gestapo Command HQ Vienna, as "curator" for Schmid, "*to clear up the issue relating to 'Terrol'.*"[38] An investigation was opened into the managers of Terrol and into Schmid, and it emerged that Schmid was "*pledged up to the hilt*".[39] The financial backers were so fed up, they thereupon decided to withdraw from the project completely. DPAG suspected that Schmid had deceived his backers or had acted out of some "*diseased state of mind*".[40] Gau Director Erich Koch exploited his own network in order to bid farewell to the project, doing so through the intervention of Karl Grosse in early 1939. He thus sold his mining rights to International Tiefbohrgesellschaft AG (ITAG) for 225,000 Reichsmark.[41]

When DPAG struck oil in exploration areas to which van Sickle had held the rights, Schmid demanded settlement of the gross payment yield, something DPAG refused given the prior history. DEA (which merged with DPAG as of April 1940) reached an out-of-court settlement with the group headed by Professor Bruns (to

---

35 Cf. NSDAP, Gau Wien, Wirtschaftsamt an BMHuV, Dr. Danner, 24.7.1938, ibid.

36 Cf. Terrol an Dr. Danner, 27.7.193, ibid.

37 Cf. Memo Dr. Schindler, 29.7.1938, ibid.

38 Dr. Schindler an Regierungsrat Dr. von Lettow, Gestapo, Wien, Gegenstand "Terrol", Rechtsansprüche K.E. Schmid und van Sickle, 4.7.1938, ÖStA, Bundesministerium Handel und Verkehr, Oberste Bergbehörde, 1937, 157081.

39 Cf. memo, 25.8.1939, WD-CA, D-RW-270.

40 Cf. Sachdarstellung: Erdölgerechtsname in Österreich, 28.7.1938, WD-CA, D-RW-00473.

41 Cf. DPAG an Wirtschaftsbeauftragten der Provinz Ostpreußen, 14.1.1939, D-RW-270.

which von Petersdorff and Kadgien belonged), and the group was awarded a participation in the revenue from the annual crude production of 0.5 – 1 percent.[42] In October 1942, the group agreed that the interest thus being paid would be awarded in equal halves only to von Petersdorff and Kadgien. DEA thereupon made both of them an offer in January 1943 to buy out their claims with a one-time payment of 400,000 Reichsmark each.[43] Kadgien accepted; von Petersdorff did not.

DPAG/DEA acquired not only part of the exploration rights held by Schmid, but also additional mining rights in Austria; in autumn 1938 it held a total of 2,116 exploration rights.[44] Of particular significance was DPAG's entering into the contract concluded between Canadian-British businessman Richard Keith van Sickle and Schmid on 9 November 1937. DPAG acquired 20 exploration rights, for which it paid 226,000 Reichsmark.[45]

After many years preparing the ground, Richard Keith van Sickle[46] had in July 1935 acquired from Friedrich Musil 48 exploration rights close to Neusiedl an der Zaya in Weinviertel north of Vienna and founded "Britol Oil Aktiengesellschaft".[47] His sites were in two sections: one to the south with 20 exploration areas, the other in the north with 28. Fatally, his deep drill "van Sickle 1", where the rig started work on 15 August 1937, was a failure. The small com-

---

42 Cf. note: Sachdarstellung über den Erwerb der Freischürfe in der Ostmark, 4.4.1941, WD-CA, 14-2, 3136.

43 Cf. DEA an Bundesministerium der Finanzen, 4.7.1956, WD-CA, D-RW-270.

44 Cf. Supervisory Boardssitzung 11.10.1938, WD-CA, 3000-67.

45 Cf. note: Sachdarstellung über den Erwerb der Freischürfe in der Ostmark, 4.4.1941, WD-CA, 14-2, 3136.

46 On the biography of van Sickle Cf. Benjamin Steininger; *Die Sammlung Rohstoff Geschichte – ein Findbuch*, Vienna 2016.

47 Cf. Exposé concerning Tiefbohrunternehmen Richard K. von Sickle, Wien, Freyung I (no date), Chronik James van Sickle, GeoSphere Austria-Archiv Rohstoffe, Vienna, A 18888-R.1; Van Sickle an Ministerialrat Dr. Danner, Handelsministerium, 20.6.1938: Tätigkeitsbericht des Tiefbohrunternehmens van Sickle, ÖStA Bundesministerium Handel und Verkehr, Oberste Bergbehörde, 1937, 157.000-157.200.

pany faced bankruptcy, as his British financial backers were not prepared to up the ante given the uncertain political situation in Austria. In order to be able to continue work, in January 1938 van Sickle concluded a drilling contract with Terrol and through the intermediation of that company sold his 20 northern sites to Karl Eugen Schmid for 350,000 Austrian schillings.[48] The contract was signed on 9 November 1937,[49] although after the war a representative of van Sickle claimed Schmid had squeezed him into the contract by making political threats.[50] The rights were first to be assigned after payment of the entire purchase price. Schmid made a down-payment of 10,000 schillings but was unable to put up any more cash. On 17 March 1938 he transferred his contract with van Sickle to DPAG. The Berlin group paid the outstanding sums and on 29 March 1938 officially replaced Schmid in the contract with van Sickle.[51]

Karl Grosse conducted all the key negotiations in Austria, in part with the support of Hugo Griebel and Günther Schlicht. Grosse acted here as the representative of the seemingly all-powerful German Reich and let the men on the other side of the table know this.[52] He tried to procure the remaining 28 exploration rights from van Sickle, or at least make sure the sites were prospected jointly.[53] Van Sickle rejected the idea and was only prepared to handle drilling under contract to DPAG in the north section – "St. Ulrich 1"

48 Cf. Hermann Fritsche: Schlussbericht über Verwaltungstätigkeit, 1.3.1946, GeoSphere Austria-Archiv Rohstoffe, Vienna, A 18888-R.5.

49 Cf. Chronik James van Sickle, GeoSphere Austria-Archiv Rohstoffe, Vienna, A 18888-R.1.

50 Cf. exposé conc.: Tiefbohrunternehmen Richard K. von Sickle.

51 Cf. Sachdarstellung, 19.2.1940, WD-CA, D-RW-00483; exposé conc.: Tiefbohrunternehmen Richard K. von Sickle.

52 Keith van Sickle's memoirs and letters show that he only met Grosse with reluctance and only agreed to meetings if it could not be avoided. (Chronik James van Sickle, GeoSphere Austria-Archiv Rohstoffe, Vienna, A 18888-R.1). Große, on the other hand, described his relationship with van Sickle as friendly in December 1945 (cf. Große, *Mein Leben*, 40).

53 Notiz Große, 1.4.1938, WD-CA, D-RW-00489.

and "St. Ulrich 2". Wintershall AG was also interested in van Sickle's rights and made him an offer, which he turned down as unacceptable.[54]

In order to be able to do the contract drilling for DPAG, van Sickle needed a trade licence. In his application to the Upper Mining Authority he cited, among others, DEA Director Grosse and Wintershall's Director Zentgraf as references. As regards his political outlook, he cited Oberstaffelführer Hagen, Adjutant to the NSKK National Socialist Motor Corp "Ostmark" Motorized Group, and Sturmbannführer Eilers of the Economics section of the Sicherheitsdienst (SD) Reichsführer SS in Vienna.[55] For van Sickle, saving his company was the top priority.

"Reich drill site St. Ullrich no. 1"

On 25 September 1938, the first "Reich drilling" commissioned by DEA in the Ostmark was inaugurated in Neusiedl to great festivities. Vienna's "Bohrtechniker-Zeitung" newspaper reported: *"The pace of work in the Ostmark is progressing at the customary fast Nazi tempo."*[56] The "St. Ullrich no. 1" rig struck oil at a drill site that had been defined by DPAG together with Alfred Bentz. Once the German and the Austrian hymns had been sung, Reichsstatthalter Arthur Seyss-Inquart as Austrian Governor of the Ostmark, DEA Director Karl Grosse, and Operations Manager Hermann Fritsche of the van Sickle deep-drilling company (who doubled up as District Group Head of the Nazi Party in Palterndorf) spoke to the employees. The latter all wore the uniforms of the National Socialist Motor

---

54 Cf. Van Sickle an Große, 15.7.1938, WD-CA, D-RW-00473.

55 Cf. Van Sickle an Gewerbeabteilung des Handelsministeriums, 10.6.1938, ÖStA, Bundesministerium Handel und Verkehr, Oberste Bergbehörde, 1937, 157.000-157.200.

56 Bohrtechniker-Zeitung, Wien 10 (1938), 152f.

Fig. 33 Celebrating the inauguration of the St. Ullrich probe, attended by Reichsstatthalter Arthur Seyß-Inquart on 25 September 1938

Corp (NSKK). Keith van Sickle, who was himself not present, had encouraged his Austrian operations manager to join the NSKK.[57]

Van Sickle was definitely now a sympathizer with the Nazis, as his biography shows.[58] However, given the intensifying political tensions in Europe, with Hitler threatening to attack the Republic of Czechoslovakia and escalating the crisis in the Sudeten territories, he was fighting tenaciously to preserve his company and entered into compromises he probably personally felt were intolerable.

The Neusiedl-St. Ulrich oil field was to prove the most productive in Central Europe, and DEA had bagged it without really having to do anything itself. British Army major and geologist Albert Everard Gunther, member of North German Oil Control (NGOC), an organ of the British Military Government's economic administration structure, commented, looking back on the German oil industry during the war, as followed: "*Within the period of only four years it [the St. Ulrich oil field] propelled Deutsche Erdöl A.G., a newcomer in the Vienna Basin, to the top of the oil producers. This contribution to the German war machine was of inestimable importance.*"[59]

While the German corporation profited from the commencement of oil production, van Sickle's firm was in dire need of cash, as he wanted to be able to continue drilling work at all costs. Van Sickle transformed the "Britol Oil AG" into a one-man business as "Tiefbohrunternehmen Richard K. van Sickle" and concluded a loan agreement with DPAG.

DPAG exploited the dilemma the British businessman found himself in, and the loan agreement signed on 7 February 1939 was about as one-sided as they come.[60] Under normal circumstances,

---

57 Cf. Hermann Fritsche, *Schlussbericht über Verwaltungstätigkeit*, 1.3.1946, GeoSphere Austria-Archiv Rohstoffe, Vienna, A 18888-R.5.

58 Cf. Benjamin Steininger, *Die Sammlung Rohstoff Geschichte – ein Findbuch*, Vienna 2016.

59 Albert E. Gunther, *The German war for Crude Oil in Europe 1934–1945*, in: The Petroleum Times, 3.1.1948, 22–26.

60 Cf. Vertrag van Sickle-DPAG, 7.2.1939, WD-CA, D-RW-00483.

Fig. 34 Oil production near Neusiedl an der Zaya, Austria (1939)

such a contract would have been declared unethical (*"monstrously beyond the pale"*).[61] The deep-drilling company received a loan of 400,000 Reichsmark but had to pledge all its exploration rights and plant and machinery as well as sell the entire oil production from all drills that struck black gold to DPAG at 15 percent below the respective market price.[62] DPAG/DEA booked profits of around 11 million Reichsmark from the deal.[63]

The deep-drilling company had to shoulder a further commitment on the pledge on the area covered by the exploration rights, namely eight percent of the revenue, something that it had to assume

---

61 Cf. Wietze an Dipl. Ing. Teuter (DPAG, Verwaltungsstelle Ostmark), 10.12.1938, WD-CA, D-RW-00489.

62 Cf. Chronik James van Sickle, GeoSphere Austria-Archiv Rohstoffe, Vienna, A 18888-R.1.

63 Cf. Hermann Fritsche, *Schlussbericht über Verwaltungstätigkeit, 1.3.1946*, GeoSphere Austria-Archiv Rohstoffe, Vienna, A 18888-R.5.

if the rights were sold. This meant the former creditors were able to participate in the revenue from oil production.

At the DEA Supervisory Board meeting in March 1939, Richard Ullner reported with great satisfaction on the agreement: "*This agreement has the purpose of transferring to us the presumed production from the oil fields he owns, which overlap with ours in geological terms and can therefore be considered very promising because, for all our great efforts to acquire the same over the last year or so, we have not managed to get them.*"[64] He felt the financial deal was at no risk to DEA and offered the prospect of huge profits.

Unlike DEA, van Sickle was in a very difficult position. His company was under SD observation and almost entirely dependent on DEA.[65] When, in spring/summer 1939, his drilling at "van Sickle 2 and 3" hit oil, DPAG/DEA suspended the lien that had been prepared on his plant and machinery but soon wanted to encumber his oil field.[66] Van Sickle tried in vain to get the contractual terms improved, and when the political situation dramatically deteriorated at the end of August 1939, the English consul recommended that he leave Austria immediately.[67] Van Sickle issued his operations manager Hermann Fritsche with full powers of attorney and headed for Britain.

When the terms of the Bitumen Act came into effect from 31 July 1940 onwards – according to which all exploration rights reverted to the state if, until then, they had not led to a mining field being awarded – Fritsche, for his part, tried to prompt DEA to grant better contractual terms. Paying for the oil deliveries from van Sickle at well below market price, or so he argued, could lead to DEA being

64 Supervisory Boardssitzung 14.3.1939, WD-CA, 3000-82.
65 Cf. Mineralölwerke Wietze, Verwaltungsstelle Ostmark an Große. 4.4.1939, confidential, ibid.
66 Cf. ibid.
67 Cf. Fritsche an DPAG, 27.8.1939, WD-CA, D-RW-00489.

accused of "*war profiteering*".[68] Grosse rejected this suggestion most indignantly and drew it to Fritsche's attention that DEA had "*made considerable sums available to a company completely bereft of financing*" and that Fritsche worked for an "*enemy foreigner*".[69] Fritsche's lawyers spoke of "*usurious interest*". Grosse and Schirner countered that an oil company from time to time needs a "bull's eye" to cover its high costs and other wells that contained no oil.[70] They stuck to this opinion later on and made certain not to mention that far earlier, namely in autumn 1938 after the success of the rig at "St. Ulrich 1", there was a high probability that oil would be struck in the area where van Sickle was drilling wells on his own behalf only a few hundred metres away.

Fritsche then tried to on-board the Nazi Gau Director of the Lower Danube as an ally.[71] Yet he had no success with this move, intended to show that he was protecting Austrian interests, especially as by this time van Sickle only employed Austrians. DEA had sought the support of the Reich Commissioner for the Treatment of Enemy Assets,[72] saying that a company belonging to an "*enemy foreigner*" should not be supported.

The immense significance of DEA'S swiftly expanding oil production in Austria can be gauged from a comparison with the other corporations active on the ground. Its share was even higher than the table shows, as DEA also had access to all the oil van Sickle produced.

---

68 Fritsche an Große, 13.10.1939, WD-CA, D-RW-00483.

69 Große an van Sickle, 26.10.1939, WD-CA, ibid.

70 Memo, 1.3.1940 (Schirner, Ritter, Große), ibid.

71 Cf. Fritsche, Schlussbericht über Verwaltungstätigkeit, 1.3.1946, GeoSphere Austria-Archiv Rohstoffe, Vienna, A 18888-R.5.

72 Cf. memo, 8.7.1940: Gespräch Schirner mit Dr. Ernst, Reichkommissar für die Behandlung feindlichen Vermögens, WD-CA, D-RW-00483.

Oil production in Austria 1939–44 in tonnes [73]

	1939	1940	1941	1942	1943	1944
DEA	152,600	323,700	316,000	407,000	534,000	673,000
RAG			265,000	320,000	320,000	281,000
EPG			150,000	160,000	140,000	123,000
Vacuum	95,000	180,000	125,000	115,000	110,000	89,000
Preussag	100,000	180,000	117,000	62,000	55,000	56,000
Elwerath	170,000	170,000	160,000	163,000	215,000	260,000
Wintershall	108,000	130,000	140,000	140,000	150,000	140,000
Van Sickle	24,400	85,500	144,000	144,000	120,000	100,000
Others	185,000	350,800	143,000	169,000	168,700	211,000
Total	835,000	1,420,000	1,560,000	1,680,000	1,880,000	1,990,000

Purchase of the "Nova" refinery in Schwechat, northwest of Vienna

After DPAG/DEA had struck oil in Neusiedl in autumn 1938, it needed to decide which refinery it would use to process the crude oil. Transporting the latter to the "Old Reich", to Rositz, Wilhelmsburg, or Heide, was not commercially viable given the high freight costs.

The political situation played into DEA's hands in this regard. After the ink was put to the Munich Agreement on 30 September 1938 by Hitler, Mussolini, Chamberlain, and Daladier, the Republic of Czechoslovakia forfeited its borderlands that were inhabited mainly by German speakers. Under pressure from the Germans, on 14 March 1939 the First Slovak Republic was declared, and on 18 March it concluded a "protection agreement" with the German Reich,[74] effectively making it a client state. On 15 March

73 Compiled according to: Jahresberichte der DEA-Erdölbetriebe, lfd. WD-CA, 41112.

74 Cf. Herder-Institut, *Protektorat Böhmen und Mähren. Chronologie*, www.herder-institut.de/digitale-angebote/dokumente-und-materialien/themenmodule/modul/20/seite/67.html [last retrieved on 6.5.2023].

Bohemia and Moravia were occupied by German forces, and the next day Hitler declared the foundation of the Protectorate of Bohemia and Moravia, an unprecedented legal entity under international law. Given this fundamental upheaval, foreign companies abandoned their subsidiaries and participations in Bohemia and Moravia and in the Slovak Republic.

The Romanian company Creditul Minier, which owned the "Nova" refinery in Schwechat outside Vienna and the "Apollo" refinery in Pressburg/Bratislava in Slovakia, wanted to sell both facilities and was on the look-out for buyers.[75] The majority of the Creditul shares were held by a French group headed by Baron d'Allemagne,[76] and the sale talks therefore took place in Paris. It is worth noting that DEA had already started showing an interest in the Nova a few weeks before the Republic of Czechoslovakia was broken up, with Ullner stating at the DEA Supervisory Board meeting of 14 March 1939 in this regard: "*In our search for a way of processing [close to the oil fields], we have come across an existing refinery that first went into operation only in March last year and belongs to a French group that for political reasons wishes to withdraw from the 'Ostmark'.*"[77]

In 1936, "Nova Oel- und Brennstoffgesellschaft AG" had started construction of a new refinery in Schwechat. It went turnkey in early January 1938 and replaced the older petrol refinery in Drösing (Lower Austria) that had been built forty years earlier.[78] The refinery was to be supplied with pre-mixed Romanian oil types by barge up the Danube. As early as spring 1937, the directors of the Nova had developed the idea of possibly erecting a cracker to produce petroleum. Such deliberations were prompted by the oil pro-

75 Gerhard A. Stadler, *Das industrielle Erbe Niederösterreichs. Geschichte-Technik-Architektur*, Vienna 2006, 139–142.

76 Cf. Hinterlegung: Verwaltungsratssitzung "Nova" vom 21.2.1939, ÖStA, Ministerium für Wirtschaft und Arbeit, OB, 653–654, 1939–1940.

77 Supervisory Boardssitzung 14.3.1939, WD-CA, 3000-82.

78 Cf. "Nova" an Bundesministerium der Finanzen, Wien, 3.7.1937, ÖStA, Bundesministerium Handel und Verkehr, Oberste Bergbehörde, 1937, 163.701.

duction just starting up in the Weinviertel north of Vienna. Austrian crude oil was primarily suitable for producing lubricants and heating oil, so a cracker was needed in order to derive larger quantities of petroleum from it. The issue of the day was whether it was at all probable that local oil production would justify building a cracker that required an input of 100,000 tonnes per annum if its capacity was to be duly utilized. Nevertheless, the Nova management was interested in building one: "*Domestic crude oil output and thus the installation of a cracker will, at a time of political unrest in Europe, secure part of the supplies of the fuel necessary for the armed forces and transportation companies, etc.*"[79] To realize this plan, pursued in "*the higher interests of state*", Nova wanted the Austrian government to provide collateral and all manner of help – tax exemptions, protection against foreign competition, default guarantees, no mandatory spirit additives. The Upper Mining Authority attached to the Austrian Federal Ministry of Trade and Transport in Vienna showed a clear interest, but first wanted to discuss construction of the cracker plant with all five refineries based in Austria.[80]

Given the escalation of the political conflict in Central Europe as the Third Reich made ever more strident demands of the Republics of Czechoslovakia and Austria, the French owners of the Nova and of the Apollo refinery in Pressburg (Bratislava) sought to sell out as quickly as possible. The ministries in Vienna pondered making the acquisition, especially as all refineries in Austria had foreign owners,[81] and an engineer closely familiar with the oil industry stated that the construction of crackers was the "crux" for the entire Austrian oil business, which is why it definitely needed to be the

79 Cf. ibid.

80 Cf. "Nova" an Bundesministerium für Handel und Verkehr, Sektionsrat Klemens Danner, 1.10.1937, conc.: Crackanlage, ibid.

81 Cf. Einlegung, 5.3.1938, conc.: Verwaltungsratssitzung der Nova am 25.2.38, Bundesministerium Handel und Verkehr, Abt. Oberste Bergbehörde, 1938, 158.001.

property of the Austrian state.[82] The idea was abandoned, however, after the "Anschluss", and all the Jewish members of the Advisory Council of Nova were swiftly relieved of their duties.[83] For a short time, Terrol mooted that it could act as the developer, which was quite preposterous given its uncertain financial status.

In the meantime, both DPAG and I.G. Farben had entered the discussion, both players of a quite different calibre. I.G. Farben wanted to acquire the Apollo refinery in Slovakia. As it was connected in terms of the production technology to the Nova, it was necessary for I.G. Farben and DEA to coordinate their approach. The French owners intended to sell the two refineries as one, so DPAG left it to I.G. Farben to lead the negotiations, especially as issues of foreign currency also needed to be clarified.

Ministry Councillor Clemens Danner of the Upper Mining Authority attached to the Austrian Federal Ministry of Economics and Labour in Vienna, also State Commissioner for the Nova, arranged a site inspection for Karl Grosse. Afterwards, DPAG/DEA initiated talks with the French owners.[84] The staff at the Nova were very agitated when they caught wind of the German corporation's interest in taking it over. To prevent social hardship among the payroll in the event of a "*hostile takeover*", the staff called for the DAF or the Nazi Party itself to acquire a stake in the plant.[85]

Negotiations with the French owners dragged on until the late summer of 1939 when DPAG/DEA finally acquired roughly 87 percent of the shares in Nova Oel- und Brennstoffgesellschaft AG, Vienna, for a price of 3.6 million Reichsmark.[86] Karl Schirner was appointed new Chair of the Supervisory Board, with Richard

---

82 Cf. memo: Crackanlage für in Österreich gefördertes Erdöl, 27.3.1938, ibid.

83 Cf. Einlegung, 12.5.1938, conc.: Verwaltungsratssitzung der Nova am 6.5.1938, ibid.

84 Cf. Min. Rat. Dr. Danner an General a.D. Bührmann, Wien, 6.1.1939, conc.: Errichtung einer Raffinerie in der Ostmark, ÖStA, Ministerium für Wirtschaft und Arbeit, OB, 653–654, 1939–1940.

85 Cf. Hinterlegung: Verwaltungsratssitzung "Nova" vom 21.2.1939, ÖStA, ibid.

86 Cf. Supervisory Boardssitzung 19.1.1940, WD-CA, 3000-80.

Ullner as his deputy, and the equity capital was set at 1.6 million Reichsmark.[87] After the takeover, the Nova was switched over to processing Austrian crude oil. DPAG/DEA implemented the now two-year-old plan to build a cracker plant at a cost of about 4.8 million Reichsmark.[88]

Despite the high price tag, the purchase of the Nova was a good deal for DPAG/DEA in several respects. DEA acquired not only the most modern refinery in Austria, but from now on could start processing the crude oil from the Ostmark locally.

Thanks to the swift expansion in oil production and the acquisition of the Nova, DEA now had the potential for significant growth in its oil activities. The DEA management board therefore decided it was time to realize a long-standing plan and merged DPAG and DEA in spring 1940. Thus, oil production and processing at DEA, having taken a backseat there for some two decades, was now firmly on the front burner.

After completion of the Olex sales in early 1933, it had seemed obvious to merge DPAG and DEA. Under Chairman Ullner, the DEA board had considered the matter primarily in accounting terms. The DPAG had booked liquidity at the time of about 18 million Reichsmark. DEA skimmed off part of the sum by selling the Rositz tar refinery to DPAG and leasing the latter its carbonization plants. All the corporation's oil activities were pooled in DPAG in order to place all the risk involved on the subsidiary. Ullner added: "*We were also of the opinion that the state would not hit the smaller DPAG as hard as it might the larger DEA, be it analogously to the state's approach for BRABAG or fiscally speaking.*"[89] After the beginning of the war, all these arguments for keeping DPAG independent became obsolete. Above all, tax reasons now favoured DPAG ceasing to be an independent entity.

---

87 Cf. ibid.

88 Cf. ibid.

89 Supervisory Boardssitzung 19.1.1940, WD-CA, 3000-80.

The fusion of DPAG (Berlin), Nova Öl- und Brennstoffgesellschaft AG (Vienna), and DEA (Berlin) was then completed as of 1 April 1940.[90] The four DPAG Management Board members were given limited DEA employment contracts with improved emoluments. After the merger, the administration of the oil operations was relocated from Wietze to Berlin, which henceforth controlled all operations relating to oil production.

Structure of the DEA oil operations as of 1 April 1940[91]
Branches:

1. DEA, HQ for oil operations, Berlin Schöneberg, (Directors: Karl Grosse, Erich Greiser, Günther Schlicht)
   – Erdölwerke Wietze, Wietze Kr. Celle
   – Erdölwerke Ostmark in Vienna I at Graben 29
   – Erdölwerke Holstein in Heide
   – Kalksandsteinfabrik Heide in Heide
2. DEA, Erdölwerke Wilhelmsburg, (Director: Eugen Bauer)
3. DEA, Erdölwerke "Nova", Schwechat near Vienna, (Directors: Eduard Hoffmann, Heinrich Schram)
4. DEA, Mineralölwerke Rositz (Directors: Hans Hase, Hans Collischonn, Robert Hanke, Franz Landwehr)
5. DEA, HQ for lignite operations Borna

In mid-1942, new management was appointed at Erdölwerke "Nova". It was henceforth headed by Erich Greiser as Commercial Director. In 1944, Fritz Staiger was appointed new Technical Director, likewise a German from inside the Reich.[92]

---

90 Cf. Handelsregisterauszug, WD-CA, 3000-860.

91 Cf. Verschmelzung DPAG, Berlin, "Nova" Öl und Brennstoff AG, Wien mit Deutsche Erdöl AG, ibid.

92 Cf. Erich Greiser, Zeugnis für Fritz Staiger, 16.3.1947, WD-CA, D-RW-96.

Dispute over the Niederdonau Erdöl GmbH booty

As of autumn 1938, the oil producers in Austria were included in the Four-Year Plan and, after the war started, in the labour programmes stipulated by the Expert Group Oil, meaning their scope was limited. The primary objective was to control production as far as possible.

The Bitumen Act, with its short deadlines, arose not least at the urging of the German oil companies that were calling for the legal systems to be aligned in order to enable them to take over larger parts of the oil-development zones in the Ostmark. In order to protect the interests of Austrian entrepreneurs who owned exploration rights, the Vienna Upper Mining Authority called for the deadline for forfeiting mining rights to be extended until after the end of the war. However, the Reich Economics Ministry, as the agency now responsible for awarding concessions, was not prepared to accept any extension of mining rights beyond 31 July 1940. At the same time, almost no new concessions were awarded as most oil-development areas were in the zones under independent operators, above all those held by RAG, van Sickle, and Explora. "*The battle over the oil-development zones held by these firms now commenced.*"[93]

After the Netherlands was occupied in June 1940, the 50-percent stake that Royal Dutch Shell held in RAG came under German administration.[94] Further-reaching plans for the complete nationalization of RAG failed, as part of the company was owned by Americans. As regards van Sickle GmbH, which was owned by the British, the Upper Mining Authority in Vienna accurately asserted that DEA ipso facto owned van Sickle's mining rights.

Several smaller Austrian companies founded the Donauländische Erdölförderungs-Gesellschaft mbH with the objective of bag-

---

93 Ministerium für Wirtschaft und Arbeit: Erdölreviere der Ostmark, 17.5.1941, ÖStA, Oberbergamt für die Ostmark, Vienna, Sign. 38, 1941, 30021.

94 Cf. Rothauer, *Das Tiefbohrunternehmen van Sickle*, 29.

ging concessions. They cited the purported pioneering achievements of a female diviner around Neusiedler See and pointed to political support from the office of Rudolf Hess as "Deputy Fuhrer" as well as the Nazi Gau Director Niederdonau.[95] Even more ambitious was an attempt by the company which amounted to a concessioning of the entire zone in which van Sickle was active. The reasoning was: "*This is a zone of business interest of the Gau Lower Danube …*".[96] The Donauländische Erdölförderungs-Gesellschaft mbH was acting under instruction from Gau Head Hugo Jury,[97] but the Reich Economics Ministry nipped the Gau's nascent particularist interests in the bud. The contract between DEA and van Sickle was left intact, and Donauländische Erdölförderungs-Gesellschaft mbH subsequently dissolved itself in November 1940.[98] Nevertheless, the players led by Hugo Jury did not abandon their plans to participate in oil production.

The Department of Mining at the Reich Economics Ministry pursued the idea of founding a new petroleum company in the Ostmark. Its original plan was to entrust to the latter operational management in the entire Vienna Basin, to which end the company would be assigned all RAG's forfeited exploration rights and those of all other companies to the extent that they were accessed from or adjacent to the RAG area.[99] The intention was to conclude a lease agreement with the deep-drilling company van Sickle, which

95 Cf. Donauländische Erdölförderungs-Gesellschaft mbH an Oberbergamt Wien, 30.7.1940: Ansuchen um Verleihung einer Erdölkonzession, ÖStA, Oberbergamt für die Ostmark, Vienna, Sign. 38, 1941, 30021.

96 Ibid.

97 Cf. Stefan Eminger et al., *Nationalsozialismus in Niederösterreich. Opfer. Täter. Gegner*, Innsbruck 2021, 73f.

98 Cf. Donauländische Erdölförderungs-Gesellschaft mbH an Oberbergamt Wien, 17.1.1941 Ansuchen um Verleihung einer Erdölkonzession, ÖStA, Oberbergamt für die Ostmark, Vienna, Sign. 38, 1941, 30021.

99 Cf. Wintershall AG an Reichswirtschaftsminister, Streng vertraulich, 20.12.1940, WD-CA, D-RW-118.

lost 21 exploration rights and held onto a remaining seven with a view to uniform processing of the entire zone north of the Danube. DEA oil wells would also be incorporated into the new company. The Reich Economics Ministry plan envisaged DEA holding 26 percent, RAG 25 percent, Elwerath and Preussag 16 percent each, Wintershall 12 percent, and I.G. Farben 5 percent of the shares. The name suggested for the new company was, "*for reasons strongly tinged with local politics*", Erdöl AG Niederdonau.[100] At the insistence of the Gau Head, the entire RAG administration, staffed almost entirely by Austrians, would be taken on.

To discuss their plan, in December 1940 the Department of Mining at the Reich Economics Ministry invited the four German oil corporations to talks,[101] with I.G. Farben also invited. For DEA, the proposal of transferring van Sickle's operational wells to a new company under a lease agreement was quite unacceptable, as it would have meant DEA having to dissolve its lucrative contract with van Sickle. Wilhelm Zentgraf, Wintershall AG Director, was also against the plan, as he saw his company disadvantaged by the number of shares it would receive in the new company. Karl Grosse went to the Reich Economics Ministry a second time on 2 January 1941 in order to present DEA's reservations as regards the Ministry's plan.[102] He was not prepared to tolerate the February 1939 contract between DPAG/DEA and van Sickle essentially being annulled, although neither the Upper Mining Authority in Vienna nor the Reich Economics Ministry were completely convinced of its legality. He spoke in this context of the "*DEA being expropriated by the Reich without recompense*".[103] Various Vienna agencies were likewise anything but

---

100 Ibid.

101 Cf. Aktennotiz über die Besprechung in der Bergbauabteilung des Reichswirtschaftsministeriums am 6. Dezember 1940, WD-CA, D-RW-118.

102 Cf. memo: Gründung der Niederdonau Gesellschaft, Rohöllieferungsvertrag van Sickle, 4.1.1941, ibid.

103 Ibid.

pleased by the Reich Economics Ministry's plans, as these were considered at the end of the day to spell preferential treatment of companies from the Reich.[104]

The pushback from all sides caused the Reich Economics Ministry to hesitate, and the decision to found Niederdonau Erdöl GmbH was postponed. The original Reich Economics Ministry plan was then shelved in April 1941, meaning before the Third Reich was at war with America. RAG retained its mining sections but was excluded from any new concessions. Thus, any new Niederdonau Erdöl GmbH would have lacked what it required most: productive oil fields.

At the end of 1941, the Reich Economics Ministry put a new plan forward. Now the idea was to allocate the new company an extensive zone under concession, but one that included no active oil wells (mining sections already awarded). However, since the zone also included the promising van Sickle area (albeit excluding its mining sections), it was expected to soon be producing crude.[105] This idea would mainly spell losses for DEA because, apart from a 50 percent stake Wintershall AG held in EPG, the other syndicate members hardly had any share in oil production in the Ostmark at that point.

The plan was for the four German oil corporations to each get a 20-percent stake, I.G. Farben five percent, and an "*Ostmark group*" consisting of Austrian non-oil companies the remaining 15 percent. DEA was appointed by the other companies to lead the negotiations with the Reich Economics Ministry. The German companies agreed that the slice of equity to go to the "Ostmark group" needed to be reduced, and the group was also to be excluded from crude supplies. United operational management by Niederdonau

104 Cf. Ministerium für Wirtschaft und Arbeit: Erdölreviere der Ostmark, 17.5.1941, ÖStA, Oberbergamt für die Ostmark, Vienna, Sign. 38, 1941, 30021.

105 Cf. DEA, Verwaltung der Erdölbetriebe an Wintershall, Elwerath und Preussag, 1.11.1941, ibid.

Erdöl GmbH using RAG staff and setting up a large HQ was also rejected by the four corporations, who wanted instead to have their own local staff run operations.

In early January 1942, representatives of the four German oil corporations met in Berlin to discuss the proposal for the articles of incorporation of the Niederdonau Erdöl GmbH. Preussag demanded it chair the Supervisory Board, something DEA rejected, citing its heavy investment in oil production and processing in the Lower Danube region, its higher oil production quotas, and the fact that it ran the Nova refinery in Schwechat.[106] DEA laid claim to leading the syndicate and chairing the Supervisory Board, to which Wintershall AG and Preussag eventually agreed.[107] The entire crude pumped by Niederdonau Erdöl GmbH was to be supplied to the four German corporations, and the equity capital on foundation was put at 1 million Reichsmark, with the new company not intended to turn a profit. The intentions of the four German corporations were clear: The new corporation was essentially to function like a syndicate lead-managed by DEA. The four German oil corporations considered Niederdonau Erdöl GmbH as not much more than an object for amortization. For companies in Austria after the Anschluss, it hardly made sense to invest in it.[108]

On 10 July 1942, Reich Minister for Armaments and Munition Albert Speer, Karl Krauch of GemChem, and Fritz Pleiger as Director of Reichswerke AG toured the oil fields in Zisterdorf.[109] Speer demanded that output be boosted, making it clear he suspected that the corporations involved in producing oil "*withheld*" a part of the stock "*for purely capitalist interests*". In order to ratchet up

---

[106] Cf. Memo, 8.1.1942 as well as Schirner an Zentgraf, 14.1.1942, WD-CA, D-RW-118.

[107] Cf. Zentgraf an Schirner, 20.1.1942, Schirner an Zentgraf, 23.1.1942, ibid.

[108] Cf. Oberbergamt für die Ostmark, Bohrinspektor Thon: Statuten der Niederdonau Erdölgesellschaft mbH, 11.3.1942, Oberbergamt für die Ostmark, Vienna, Sign. 38, 1942, 70.304.

[109] Cf. Gunther, *The German war for Crude Oil*, 22–26.

the pressure on them, he appointed Hugo Jury as Gau Director and Reichsstatthalter of the Lower Danube, "*Commissioner in charge of increasing production in the Zistersdorf oil fields*".[110] Representatives of the Upper Mining Authority pointed out that the increase in production being demanded would only be possible with excess tapping of the wells. Jury responded by saying that this was the price to be paid, as after the war there would be enough oil for all.

The Gau head also made use of his appointment as commissioner in charge of boosting output in order to try and persuade the Reich Economics Ministry that greater consideration should be paid to Austrian interests. The Ostmark was thereupon guaranteed the granting of a 19-percent participation in Niederdonau Erdöl GmbH.[111] The Gau Head had requested that the syndicate members all have equal rights in the company, but the Department of Mining at the Reich Economics Ministry turned this down, since the DEA was able to block the Gau Director's approach through its good links to the Ministry.[112] Likewise, the "Ostmark group" was also not accorded its own concession area.

Given these restrictions, the group refused to participate in Niederdonau GmbH. Since the smaller Austrian companies were no longer interested in getting on board, the Gau directorship tried to at least get a large Austrian-based corporation involved, and thus the path was clear for I.G. Farben to increase its stake. The powerful chemicals corporation had already acquired Donau-Chemie AG, Moosbierbaum (Pischelsdorf), and the Apollo refinery in Bratislava (Republic of Slovakia) in 1938–9. Furthermore, its Ammoniakwerke Merseburg GmbH subsidiary had bought the mining rights of Amer-

---

110 Cf. Bergrat Dr. Bartosch: Sitzung bei Gauleiter Dr. Jury 28.7.1942, WD-CA, D-RW-478.

111 Cf. Aktenvermerk über die Besprechung beim Gauleiter und Reichsstatthalter Dr. Jury am 29.6.1942, ibid.

112 Cf. Schirner/Ritter an Kimmich 20.3.1943, HADB, P 1660, sheet 90ff.

ican Austro Gasco in May 1942,[113] and the corporation had concluded contracts with other firms with participations in oil production in Austria. This led to the following capital structure: DEA, Gewerkschaft Elwerath, Wintershall, and Preussag held 21.375 percent each, and the two I.G. Farben subsidiaries jointly held 14.5 percent of the shares in Niederdonau Erdöl GmbH.[114]

Hardly had the dispute with the Gau directorship been settled than a conflict arose among the German syndicate members. The background to this was the shift in a demarcation line between the areas to which DEA held the exploration rights and those of van Sickle. When DEA made a major find at its "St. Ulrich 28" well in mid-1941, in the section of the area covered by the exploration rights it had bagged from van Sickle that lay furthest west, it secretly applied to the Reich Economics Ministry for a concession, which was granted, and thus sidestepped the other companies involved in founding Niederdonau Erdöl GmbH.[115] The well in question should actually have come under the aegis of the new joint company. This triggered an argument that got increasingly personal. The one corner was held by Schirner, with Wilhelm Zentgraf of Wintershall AG in the other. Even the intervention of heavyweights August Rosterg (Wintershall), Heinrich Bütefisch (I.G. Farben), and Director Heinrich Wisselmann (Preussag) in January 1943 failed to patch things up.[116] Skilful tactician Kimmich tried to nudge Schirner into giving a little ground in order to avoid "*an unnecessary edge*" arising in the relationship to the other German oil producers, but the DEA Chairman stuck to his guns.[117] A meeting of the two combatants at the

---

113 Cf. Memo from the Leuna-Werke from 16.11.1942, Bayer-Archiv Leverkusen, 012, No. 019, no page numbers given.

114 Cf. Landgericht Berlin, 8.12.1943, D-RW-00482; Durchschrift eines Schreibens der Donau Öl GmbH an die IG Farbenindustrie AG, Stickstoffkalkulation, vom 28.1.1943, in: BASF-Archiv, IG M 20, No. 1, no page numbers given.

115 Cf. Urteil des Landgerichts Berlin, 23.2.1945, WD-CA, D-RW-478.

116 Cf. DEA betr.: Niederdonau, 17.2.1943, HADB, P 1660.

117 Cf. Aktenvermerk Kimmich über ein Telefonat mit Schirner, 1.3.1943, ibid.

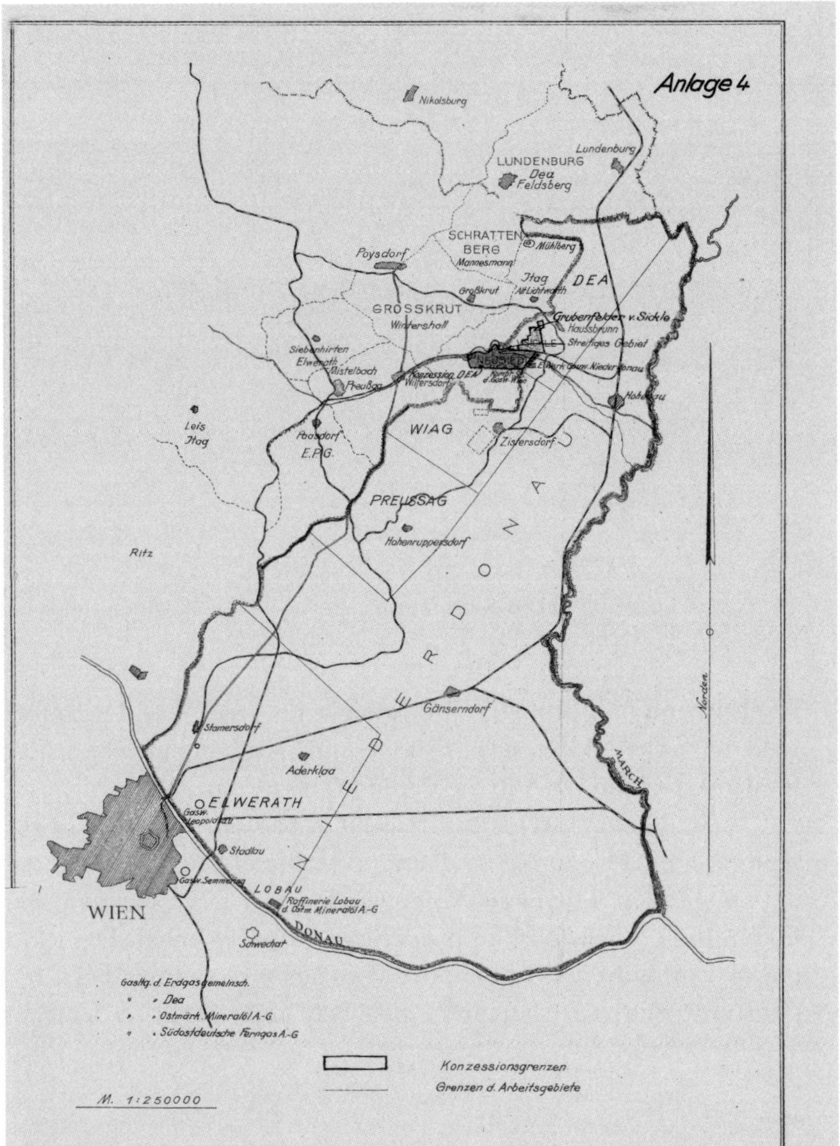

Fig. 35 Areas in which the members of the Niederdonau Erdöl GmbH consortium had interests (1942)

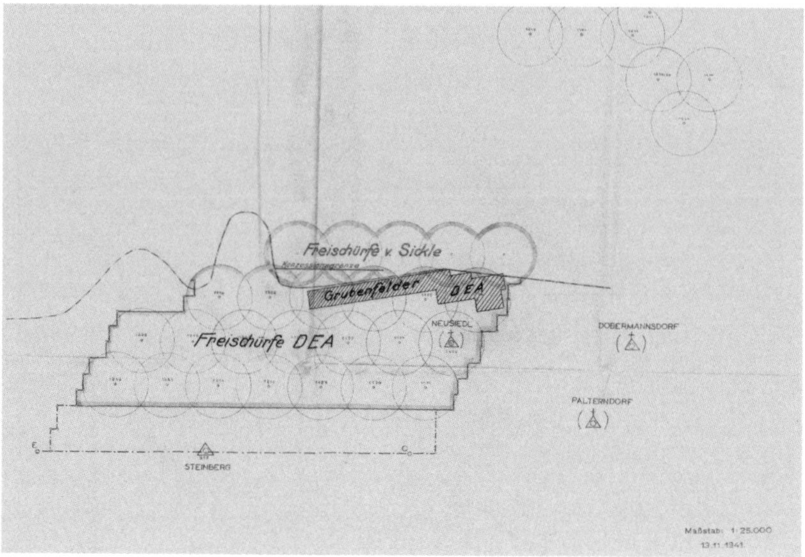

Fig. 36 Location of the exploration permits in the St. Ulrich field

Reich Economics Ministry also brought no peace.[118] In December 1943, the other Niederdonau Erdöl GmbH syndicate members filed for damages from DEA in the Berlin District Court.[119]

Wintershall AG stated that DEA had taken control of the strip of land close to Neusiedl and in so doing had violated existing obligations. The plaintiffs demanded that DEA pay damages of 5 million Reichsmark to Niederdonau Erdöl GmbH. DEA lost the case initially, and in October 1944 again recommended a settlement.[120] Schirner thereupon gave way and sought to "*take the*

118 Cf. Schirner/Ritter an Kimmich, 5.5.1943, HADB, P 1660.

119 Cf. Klage der Firmen Gewerkschaft Elwerath, Preussag, Wintershall AG gegen die DEA, Nebenintervention der Ammoniakwerke Merseburg GmbH und der Donauchemie AG, wegen Schadensersatz, 8. Dezember 1943, WD-CA, D-RW-482.

120 Cf. Aktenvermerk Kimmich, 12.10.1944, HADB, P 1660.

sting" out of the relationship to the other syndicate members.[121] He failed. The case remained before the district court, where the lawyers for both sides were kept busy until 1945, with the affair assuming bizarre proportions. In February 1945, DEA lost its appeal and was sentenced to payment of damages.[122]

The short length of time in which Niederdonau GmbH was active was not much more than a minor episode, but it says a lot about how DEA operated during the war. In 1942 the entire oil output of Niederdonau Erdöl GmbH stemmed from DEA wells in the Hauskirchen area.[123] Not until 1943 did Wintershall AG start making any noteworthy contribution, which came from its Maustrenk fields. By contrast, the volume produced by Gewerkschaft Elwerath and Preussag was insignificant. Niederdonau GmbH did not succeed in the brief period in which it existed in anything like fulfilling the expectations the Reich Economics Ministry had of it. The company made barely any new prospecting finds, and its oil output thus remained well behind that of the other companies active in the Vienna Basin.[124]

Dachs II: an underground refinery in Ebensee, outside Salzburg

In the course of the Allied offensive against "oil targets", it became clear that it was impossible to protect the German armaments industry's large plants against Allied bombing raids. The military leadership and industry were forced to start responding to the changed

121 Cf. Schirner an Wisselmann, conc.: Prozess Niederdonau, 14.10.1944, ibid.

122 Cf. Urteil des Landgerichts Berlin, 23.2.1945, WD-CA, D-RW-478.

123 Cf. Die Erdölproduktion der Niederdonau GmbH ab August 1942, WD-CA, 14-2-3128.

124 Cf. Erdölförderung der verschiedenen Erdölfirmen im Gau Niederdonau 1942–1944, WD-CA, 14-2-3136.

conditions by opting for massive relocation programmes.[125] As of the end of June 1944, the staff led by Carl Krauch was busy devising a programme to build underground plants to produce aircraft fuel and gasoline and also to produce at small plants. The idea was to use caves, gorges, and mines as protection.[126] Essentially, the Secure Petroleum Plan of 1 August 1944 envisaged building 40 substitute distilleries (Project Furnace), relying on existing boilers as distillery systems (Project Rust), building 15 oil shale plants in Württemberg (Project Desert), erecting three bomb-proof lubricant plants (Project Badger), and installing a larger aircraft fuel factory (Project Cuckoo) and two crackers (Projects Pigeon and Titmouse).[127] The Reich Office for Soil Exploration identified the best sites for possible relocations.[128] Given the increasing shortfall in materials and transportation difficulties, the Secure Petroleum Plan was reduced in November 1944 to 12 key projects.[129]

The most important project that the Reich Economics Ministry commissioned DEA to operate in August 1944 was the one code-named "Dachs II" ("Badger II") in Ebensee.[130] The name itself showed that the plant was to be like a set and thus underground – in fact a refinery to produce fuels and lubricants. The annual processing capacity was supposed to be about 300,000 tonnes of crude.[131]

Originally the plan was to erect a system of underground galleries near Ebensee – eight galleries ten metres high and wide

---

125 Cf. Dietrich Eichholtz, *Geschichte der deutschen Kriegswirtschaft*, Vol. 3, Berlin 1996, 24ff.

126 Cf. NI-8845, 67–69.

127 Cf. Entwurf vom 25. Juli 1944 (Krauch), BArch Berlin, R3/1906.

128 Cf. Frank Baranowski, *Rüstungsprojekte in der Region Nordhausen, Worbis und Heiligenstadt während der NS-Zeit*, Duderstadt 1998, 24.

129 Complied according to: Rohstoffamt, Bauplan der Ausweichanlagen, 11. November 1944, BArch Berlin, R3/1906.

130 Cf. CIOS No. XXVIII-57, DEA, Erdölwerke "Nova" Dachs II Plant, Ebensee.

131 Cf. Fritz Staiger: Die Raffinerie Ebensee, Dachs II, Ebensee 1.4.1946, WD-CA, D-RW-96.

with a length of up to 300 metres and smaller tunnels with half the diameter, their combined total length being 4,550 metres, in order to accommodate the Peenemünde rocket development plant,[132] which had largely been destroyed by a British air raid on the island of Usedom in the Baltic Sea on 18 August 1943 along with the testing facility for series production. In the summer of 1944 the relocation plans were changed, however. Now the tunnel system in Ebensee was subdivided into separate sections. Instead of the development plant, the plan was now to relocate and re-erect production facilities for the A 9 long-distance missiles and for tank components. Moreover, a refinery capable of turning out 300,000 tonnes of crude was to be built there.

A total of about 27,000 slave labourers were deployed to build the tunnels in Ebensee, most of them prisoners from the Ebensee sub-camp of the Mauthausen concentration camp. Working and living conditions there were even worse than in other concentration camps, and by the time the camp was liberated by the US Army on 6 May 1945, over 8,200 inmates had died in Ebensee.[133]

The plans for the underground refinery were drawn up by Rhenania-Ossag, with the idea being for eight "furnaces" and a skimming plant to produce petrol and diesel. After the fuels had been extracted, some 52 percent of the crude oil processed remained as a residue that constituted heating oil. The latter could then be processed by vacuum distillation and refined by sulphuric acid and selective refining, as well as through dewaxing to obtain lubricants. The plan also envisaged producing paraffin.[134] From October 1944 onwards, DEA was commissioned to operate the plant, and for its

---

132 Cf. Florian Freund, *Das Konzentrationslager Ebensee – Raketenrüstung im SS-Arbeitslager "Zement"*, Innsbruck 2006; Florian Freund, *Konzentrationslager Ebensee. Ein Außenlager des KZ-Mauthausen*, Vienna 2015.

133 Cf. Florian Freund, *Die Toten von Ebensee. Analyse und Dokumentation der im KZ Ebensee umgekommenen Häftlinge 1943 – 1945*, Vienna 2010.

134 Cf. Bericht über die Erdölraffinerie in Ebensee (Deutsches Reich), 1.12.1945, WD-CA, D-RW-96.

part assigned the task to its Vienna Nova subsidiary. The latter's directors, Erich Greiser and Fritz Staiger, now also assumed management of the refinery in Ebensee. When the Red Army arrived at Vienna's doorstep they withdrew to Ebensee.

Construction work and assembly of the "furnaces" was undertaken by German specialists and by inmates from the concentration camp. Other slave labourers built roads or water pipes for the refinery as well as an oil trap to prevent the refinery polluting the lake.[135] Given increasing bottlenecks in materials, only the fuel production lines were erected, whereas the lubricant refinery was not installed. The skimming plant was "simply a war-time facility",[136] with an estimated service life of only 3–4 years.

Operations commenced on 6 February 1945.[137] By the end of the war, around 15,400 t of crude had been processed, but the underground refinery had high operational costs, and safety was impossible given the cramped space. A US Combined Intelligence Objectives Sub-Committee report, one of the many written appraising the status of industrial plant and equipment in Germany, summarized in June 1945: "*For the relatively small amount of motor fuel that it is capable of producing the amount of investment required to put it underground would be considered absurd in any peacetime economy.*"[138] Nevertheless, after the war the DEA executives and Austrian regional politicians advocated not immediately writing off the equipment and materials but rather, at least in the interim, continuing operation of the completely intact refinery.

---

135 Cf. Florian Freund, *Arbeitslager Zement. Das Konzentrationslager Ebensee und die Raketenrüstung*, Vienna 1989, 98 and 268.

136 Bericht über die Erdölraffinerie in Ebensee (Deutsches Reich), 1.12.1945, WD-CA, D-RW-96.

137 Cf. Fritz Staiger: Die Raffinerie Ebensee, Dachs II, Ebensee 1.4.1946, ibid.

138 CIOS No. XXVIII-57, DEA, Erdölwerke "Nova" Dachs II Plant, Ebensee, 4f.

VIII. THE OIL-PRODUCING FACILITIES DURING THE SECOND WORLD WAR

(Manfred Grieger)

Mineralölwerke Rositz

The expansion of the refinery and the pyrolosis plants in Rositz scheduled for completion in 1938 was behind schedule. Moreover, progress was delayed by the coal-dust explosion on 11 April 1939 in the Regis II pyrolosis plant, which led to the temporary shutdown of Regis II and thus set the entire project back. The authorities decreed that the heavily damaged ring briquette factory had to be rebuilt.

The transportation ban imposed by the Nazi regime once the Second World War began, which granted military transport by road and rail absolute priority over civilian goods haulage, was to the immediate detriment of work processes at the Rositz hub. Since the monthly output of 1,200 tonnes of coke for electrodes could not be moved by rail to the customer (Siemens Planiawerk in Berlin's Lichtenberg district) and there was not much storage space on site in Rositz, the transportation ban meant "incisive restrictions on operations".[1] This also undermined the plant's ability to meet its fuel, heating oil, and paraffin production targets, so the Reich Coal Board

---

1 DPAG, Vorstand 41/Z, an Reichsstelle für Kohle vom 13.10.1939, 1, BArch Berlin, R 10-VII, No. 34, sheet 21.

was asked to champion the provision of at least two rail waggons a day. The transportation ban was lifted on 24 October 1939 after the Office of the Reich Commissioner for Coal had drawn the attention of the Reich Minister of Transportation to the "importance for the war effort of producing coke for electrodes".[2]

After the beginning of the war, at the "insistence of the navy" the company compiled a detailed heating oil programme for its Rositz site that set fixed monthly output volumes. In early 1940 the Supreme Naval Command (Oberkommando der Kriegsmarine (OKM) had the impression that, owing to the skimming plant in Heide, completion of the Rositz plant was "no longer being pushed with the necessary emphasis". Proxy member of the DEA Management Board Hans Hase therefore sought to calm things on the occasion of a visit by Lt. Commander Wolfgang Boecker in Rositz.[3] Hase explained the shortfall in volumes delivered in January and February 1940, firstly referring to the cold snap that had prevented sufficient steam being produced for full operations. Secondly, he suggested that "transportation conditions and the lack of transportation capacity allocated to us" had impaired performance. The overall plan had been to increase the existing processing volumes from 90,000 tonnes p.a. of tar products to 220,000 tonnes in order to be able to turn out almost three times the original volume of heating oil, meaning 145,000 rather than 50,000 tonnes.[4] However, the navy's requirement did not rise to the level initially expected, after it turned its back on its original intention of using a thicker heating oil for the cruisers, battleships, and the aircraft carrier under construction "for

---

2 Reichsbeauftragte für Kohle an DPAG vom 16.10.1939, BArch Berlin, R 10-VII, No. 34, sheet 23; Deutsche Reichsbahn, Eisenbahnabteilungen des Reichsverkehrsministeriums (10 Vusg) an Reichsstelle für Kohle vom 23.11.1939, ibid., 26.

3 Dr. Hans Hase, Programm für die Besichtigung der mitteldeutschen Werke durch Herrn Dr. Boecker von der Kriegsmarine vom 6.3.1940, 2, StA Leipzig, DEA-Mineralölwerke Rositz, No. 33.

4 Heizölgewinnung aus Braunkohle beschrieben an Hand des Verfahrens der Deutschen Petroleum-AG n.d., 1941, 3, StA Leipzig, DEA-Mineralölwerke Rositz, No. 33.

the duration of the war", as "conversion of existing ships" did not prove possible.[5]

Nevertheless, at the end of August 1940 the Reich Office for Petroleum (Reichsstelle für Mineralöl) instructed DEA to gear processing of existing tar volumes "at any rate to producing the maximum volume of diesel possible".[6] From September 1940 onwards, full operation of the Regis II pyrolosis plants ensured the requisite substitution of oil from the well with oil from tar products. The Rositz refinery increased output of finished products between January and September 1940 alone by no less than 19.5 percent to 166,736 tonnes.[7] Almost all the heating oil and diesel fuel went to the navy.

Despite existing bottlenecks in raw materials and the chronic lack of skilled labour in a workforce reduced by conscription, by spring 1940 the ring briquette plant was back operating at the planned output level.[8] However, as a result of operational interruptions in the Regis I pyrolosis plants and in Rositz, the drastic shortfall in tar output was compensated for in volume terms with procurement of oil until pyrolosis plant II was back up and running by August 1939, but the offset was not economically viable.[9] Moreover, the refinery, which had just been ramped up for tar processing, now had to switch back to also processing oil.

Arbeitsgemeinschaft für Erdölgewinnung, the Working Party for Oil Production, took the return to processing oil as an

---

5 Oberkommando der Kriegsmarine (A IV No. 1450 conf.), Vizeadmiral Werner Grassmann, an Oberkommando der Wehrmacht, Wehrwirtschaftsstab, Generalleutnant Georg Thomas vom 10.6.1940, 2, BArch Freiburg, RW 19, No. 3015, sheet 58.

6 Der Reichsbeauftragte für Mineralöl (IIMin.Öl 4104/40), Strommenger, an Deutsche Erdöl-AG, Dr. Schirner vom 27.8.1940, ibid., 119.

7 Niederschrift über die Verhandlungen des Aufsichtsrats der DEA am 25.10.1940, 4, WD-CA, D-PA-0120.

8 Deutsche Petroleum-AG, Mineralölwerke Rositz, Jahresbericht für das Jahr 1939 vom 20.4.1940, 8, StA Leipzig, DEA-Mineralölwerke Rositz, No. 5.

9 Deutsche Petroleum-AG, Mineralölwerke Rositz, Halbjahresbericht für das erste Halbjahr 1939 vom 30.9.1939, ibid., 1f.

Fig. 37 The Regis I pyrolysis plant

occasion to criticize DPAG/DEA for persistent delivery difficulties. It said that providing heating oil that was in part produced from oil instead of from coal broke the terms of the contract.[10] This, in turn, led to a sharp response from Karl Schirner, who accused the navy of simply ignoring the severe consequences of the accident in the Regis plant. DEA, according to Schirner, had actually "done more than was envisaged in the contract".[11] In purely commercial terms, the crude oil could have been processed into other products. The navy command eventually gave ground in the dispute with its most important supplier of heating oil and made barges available to at least facilitate haulage of the final product.

---

10 Arbeitsgemeinschaft für Erdölgewinnung an DEA, 2.4.1940, WD-CA, D-RW-533.

11 Note: Besprechung beim OKM, 10.4.1940, ibid.

Owing to the urgency of producing heating oil and diesel, from October 1939 onwards the Labour Office provided additional construction workers. As a result, the planned crushed coal drying and ring press plant and the southern ring briquette conveyor belt bridge, as well as the tar purification plant, the gas desulphurization unit, and the two pyrolosis lines, were ready to operate in April 1940. In June 1940, when the last two of the ten pyrolosis lines went turnkey, the expansion of the pyrolosis plant was completed. Compared with the same period the prior year, in the first nine months of 1940 tar output as good as doubled, from 76,936 to 140,246 tonnes.[12] By the end of the year, the volume of briquettes inputted rose to 1,134 million tonnes, with which a total of 189,000 tonnes of tar could be produced in 1940 as against 110,500 tonnes the prior year.[13]

In order to emphasize its loyalty to the regime and allay the reservations shown it, the site managers presented DAF Gau Superintendent (Gau-Obmann) Fritz Triebel in May 1940 with a lengthy list of welfare provisions made to support the "factory community", ranging from company trips, assistance for people wanting to attend Nazi Party events, reduced prices for canteen meals, loudspeaker systems, in-company sports, the hiring of a company medical doctor, and there were even exemplary air-raid protection facilities. The DAF works group (Werkschar), termed a "political task force", was regarded along with the marching band deployed for "parades and appeals" in the company as an expression of political loyalty.[14]

However, from early 1940 onwards there were great difficulties in recruiting the workforce required to operate Regis II, and the ops managers sent a request to the OKM in March 1940 ask-

---

12 Niederschrift über die Verhandlungen des Aufsichtsrats der DEA am 25.10.1940, 4, WD-CA, D-PA-0120.

13 DEA, Mineralölwerke Rositz, Leistungen der Braunkohlen-Schwelbetriebe 1933–1940, WD-CA, 134-2-3179.

14 Hans Hase, Unterlagen betr. Triebel-Besuch am 21.5.1940, 1f., StA Leipzig, DEA-Mineralölwerke Rositz, No. 33.

ing for support in the allocation of conscripted labour.[15] The navy's ever greater requirement for oil and fuels put the pressure on Mineralölwerke to deliver the volumes ordered on time. Since the Regis I pyrolosis plant and its equipment was in part still 1917 technology, at the end of January 1941 the Reich Office for Economic Construction approved its modernization and expansion, with the objective of boosting output by 8,000 tonnes p.a. and thus achieving peak capacity of 155,000 tonnes p.a. of carbonized tar.[16]

In Rositz, from 1941 onwards supplementary facilities in the pyrolosis plants and the refinery were meant to enable production of a further 800 tonnes of fuel and 1,200 tonnes of heating oil. These volumes did not signify any real expansion in production given the refinery's processing capacity of 240,000 tonnes of tar a year; however, the simplifications in production technology they enabled guaranteed the full target capacity could be reached.[17] For these measures, the DEA Supervisory Board approved investments of just short of 5.1 million Reichsmark. In the course of 1941, Mineralölwerke Rositz boosted tar and coke output, as the Regis II pyrolosis plant ran the whole year without interruption and technical modernization meant even the old pyrolosis plants increased their output. Of the DEA 1942 new-build programme covering total investments of 22.7 million Reichsmark, almost half, or 10.7 million Reichsmark, was destined for the group's lignite operations, in particular for the procurement of heavy equipment for open-cast mining, and more than 3.1 million Reichsmark for Mineralölwerke Rositz.

Tar output from the pyrolosis plants grew in 1942 by 7.8 percent, and the volume of finished products by no less than 25 per-

---

15 Dr. Hans Hase, Programm für die Besichtigung der mitteldeutschen Werke durch Herrn Dr. Boecker von der Kriegsmarine vom 6.3.1940, 3, ibid.

16 Reichsstelle für Wirtschaftsausbau, Baureiferklärung vom 29.1.1941, 1, BArch Berlin, R 3101, No. 18229, sheet 96 and 114.

17 Niederschrift über die Verhandlungen des Aufsichtsrats der DEA am 23.10.1940, 11, WD-CA, D-PA-0120.

cent. The Rositz refinery in October 1942 scored new records in producing heating oil and diesel, with the volume of tar processed up almost a quarter. However, the refinery throughput exceeded the tar volumes produced in-company or procured, so when inventory stocks were exhausted, there was a real threat from 1 December 1942 that the refinery's production would have to be throttled back.[18]

The DEA executives complained that despite the exceptionally satisfactory development of the Rositz hub, the contracts with the OKM had not provided the expected "safety and stability" for the construction and expansion programme.[19] Parts of DEA's lignite production also went as deliveries to the BRABAG hydration plant near Zeitz. By mid-1943, in the context of capacity expansion coordinated by the Reich Association for Coal (Reichsvereinigung Kohle), the briquette factory in Regis-Breitlingen and the briquette factory at the Dora-Helene Colliery raised their output by just under ten percent to a daily figure of 2,221 tonnes each.[20] In the first half of 1943, tar production thus climbed by slightly more than ten percent to 123,000 tonnes and coke roll-out by as much as 18 percent to 393,600 tonnes. Refined products reached 138,900 tonnes.[21] The coke for electrodes that arose as a by-product of the pyrolosis plants' operations mainly went to Siemens Planiawerke AG for coal products. However, in mid-June 1943, the Reich Coal Board (Reichsstelle für Kohle) instructed Mineralölwerke Rositz "for war-related reasons" to redirect 160 tonnes of coke for electrodes from its July out-

18 Niederschrift über die Verhandlungen des Aufsichtsrats der DEA am 4.11.1942, 5, ibid.

19 Niederschrift über die Verhandlungen des Aufsichtsrats der DEA am 24.3.1943, 3, ibid.

20 Generalbevollmächtigte für Sonderfragen der chemischen Erzeugung, Baureiferklärungen vom 26.1.1942, BArch Berlin, R 3101, No. 18275, sheet 48ff. and 55ff.

21 DEA, Bericht des Vorstands über das 1 Halbjahr 1943 vom 30.7.1943, 3, WD-CA, D-PA-65.

put to Italy and deliver only the remainder to Siemens-Planiawerke.[22] A further 160 tonnes of petroleum coke was meant to be sent to Italy in October and November 1943.[23]

As larger investment projects that had already been approved were waiting for implementation, the new approvals for Mineralölwerke Rositz for the 1944 cycle were trimmed to 2.1 million Reichsmark, while a further 3.3 million Reichsmark was to be committed to the lignite operations.[24] As for many companies active in the war effort, output at Mineralölwerke Rositz had peaked by 1944. Tar production actually fell in the first nine months of 1944 on the prior-year period by 6.2 percent to 173,800 tonnes, while refined products sagged by 16.5 percent, dropping to 172,100 tonnes.[25] For the year as a whole, tar throughput at Mineralölwerke Rositz was down almost a third in 1944 at 210,000 tonnes.

Until 1943, the Rositz complex was spared direct bombing raids, with the exception of a few dips in production owing to the sirens sounding and operations being briefly halted. In the summer of 1944, the Allies launched an aerial offensive against the German oil industry, and the destruction in Rositz led to the main lignite operations office (DEA-Hauptverwaltung der Braunkohlenbetriebe) being relocated from Borna to the castle in Altenburg, where it started work on 29 June 1944.[26] Moreover, the bombing raid on 16 August 1944, when in the early afternoon about 700 bombs were

---

22 Reichsstelle für Kohle, Plitz, an DEA-Mineralölwerke Rositz vom 19.6.1943, BArch Berlin, R 10-VIII, No. 34, sheet 72.

23 Reichsstelle für Kohle an DEA-Mineralölwerke Rositz vom 21.9.1943, ibid., 77; Reichsstelle für Kohle, Heimburg, an DEA-Mineralölwerke Rositz vom 22.10.1943, ibid., 81.

24 Niederschrift über die Verhandlungen des Aufsichtsrats der DEA am 14.4.1944, 7, WD-CA, D-PA-0120.

25 DEA, Bericht des Vorstands über die Zeit vom 1. Januar bis 30. September 1944 vom 2.11.1944, 1, WD-CA, D-PA-65.

26 DEA, Mineralölwerke Rositz, Robert Hanke/Wilhelm Frey an den Beauftragten IX des GB Chemie, Ernst Müller vom 30.6.1944, StA Leipzig, DEA-Mineralölwerke Rositz, No. 38.

dropped on the Rositz works and 200 on the surrounding area, led to substantial destruction of buildings, pipelines, and the tank farms. The fires that broke out consumed 45,000 tonnes of tar as well as semi-finished and finished products. The tar distillation plant was more or less destroyed and the refinery severely damaged, seven lives were lost and many injured.[27] Erdölwerke Rositz operations were suspended for several weeks.

Just how fraught conditions were in Germany generally and at Rositz complex can be seen from the blanket ban on vacations issued on 20 August 1944 and announced on company noticeboards with reference to the "current situation".[28] At the intervention of Edmund Geilenberg, the General Commissioner for Immediate Measures (Generalkommissar für die Sofortmaßnahmen) attached to the Reich Minister for Armaments and War Production, the Organisation Todt (OT) Kyffhäuser Task Force was brought on board to handle the repair work, and it proceeded to set up a construction management office on site in consultation with the OT Senior Construction Management (Oberbauleitung) in Jena. One idea voiced was to bring in inmates from the Buchenwald concentration camp as labour "whose deployment [...] may, under certain conditions, prove mandatory", and this was discussed by the DEA construction managers and the OT Senior Construction Manage-

27 DEA, Kriegstagebuch, Eintragung vom 16.8.1944, WD-CA, D-PA-64; DEA-Mineralölwerke Rositz, Werk Rositz (100/135), betr. Bericht über den Luftangriff am 16.8.1944 auf die Mineralölwerke Rositz vom 25.9.1944, 1, StA Leipzig, DEA-Mineralölwerke Rositz, No. 51; see also DEA, Bericht des Vorstands über die Zeit vom 1. Januar bis 30. September 1944 vom 2.11.1944, 2f., WD-CA, D-PA-65.

28 Mineralölwerke Rositz, Franz Landwehr/Hans Georg Kayser, Aushang vom 19. August 1944, StA Leipzig, DEA-Mineralölwerke Rositz, No. 49; Seidel, *Ruhrbergbau*, 467.

Fig. 38 Bombing damage in Rositz (1944)

ment on 29 August 1944,[29] although concentration camp inmates were not eventually deployed in Rositz.

In rapid succession, Allied bombers continued to conduct raids, bombing in unpredictable sequences the briquette factories, open-cast mines, pyrolosis plants, and refinery belonging to DEA. During the bombing attack of 7 October 1944 the plant was hardly

29 Bauleitung Werk Rositz, Noack/OT-Oberbauleitung Jena, Festlegung der organisatorischen Fragen des OT-Einsatzes in Rositz bei Altenburg vom 29.8.1944, StA Leipzig, DEA-Mineralölwerke Rositz, No. 52.

hit, but two foreign workers were killed outside the grounds.[30] On 30 November 1944, a raid targeted the Prehlitz and Beuna briquette factories.[31] A later raid flown on the evening of 14 February 1945 set the southeastern section of the refinery on fire, and although the petroleum plant hardly sustained any damage, the upstream refinery section was destroyed and refinery operations went down. The nearby housing for the German staff was heavily hit, and a total of 180 "bombed-out workers" had to be temporarily vacationed so that they could sort out their affairs.[32]

The raid on 2 March 1945 was classified as a "heavy attack", with 400 bombs hitting the works and destroying the coal boiler house. There was no prospect of getting the refinery going again at full capacity quickly, given the damage to the coal conveyor plant and the rail tracks, the generators, the distillation lines, and the fuel units.[33] The company estimated the repair costs were in the region of nine million Reichsmark, with a sum of 3.25 million Reichsmark having already been required between 16 August 1944 and 14 February 1945. This did not factor in the costs of the massive deployment of Organisation Todt.[34] It seemed obvious that the advance

30 Mineralölwerke Rositz, Werkluftschutzleiter, betr. Bericht über den Luftangriff am 7.10.1944 vom 10.10.1944, StA Leipzig, DEA-Mineralölwerke Rositz, No. 51.

31 Fernschreiben DEA Borna an DEA-Vorstands vom 1.12.1944, WD-CA, D-PA-64.

32 DEA, Kriegstagebuch, Eintragung vom 14.2.1945 und 16.2.1945, ibid.; Erster Bericht über den zweiten Angriff auf Rositz am 14. Februar 1945 um 21 Uhr vom 15.2.1945, 1, ibid.; Zweiter Bericht über den zweiten Angriff auf Rositz am 14. Februar 1945 um 21 Uhr vom 17.2.1945, 1, ibid.; Sagan, *Ostthüringen*, 98ff.

33 DEA-Mineralölwerke Rositz, Werk Rositz, Gruppe IV/14/DÖ, betr. Fliegerangriff am 2.3.1945 vom 5.3.1945, StA Leipzig, DEA-Mineralölwerke Rositz, No. 51; Wesentliches aus den Berichten über den Fliegerangriff am 2.3.1945 11:05–11:10, ibid.; Einsatzbeauftragter Landwehr an Arbeitsstab Geilenberg, Major Stolz vom 5.3.1945, 1, WD-CA, D-PA-46.

34 Mineralölwerke Rositz, Direktion 2/67, Hans Hase/Erwin von Diezelski, Aktenvermerk betr. Finanzierung des Wiederaufbaus in Rositz vom 25.3.1945, StA Leipzig, DEA-Mineralölwerke Rositz, No. 52.

payments made by the state war indemnification fund (Kriegsschadenerstattung) would not suffice.

Nevertheless, on 19 March 1945 DEA Rositz concluded a contract with OT Senior Construction Management East Thuringia as if the damage could be repaired after all, appointing OT "to handle all the clearing and repair work necessary to ensure the war-driven reconstruction of the plant within the framework of the Geilenberg Programme".[35] This was delusion, if only because the transport routes were all down.[36] As at other DEA sites, the operations management sought to the very end to at least get rudimentary production back up and running, even though the war was evidently lost.

Stagnating crude oil production in Wietze

The oil production plant outside Wietze formed the traditional core of DEA's oil operations. Crude oil was produced in oil wells and through mining of oil sands, meaning that in Wietze there were two sets of very different working and production conditions. While crude oil output in 1923 ran at a total of 34,000 tonnes, crude oil from wells slowly dwindled as of 1924. By contrast, the production from mining led to considerable increases in the volume of oil.

After 1933, the economy picked up, which translated into far brighter prospects for the oil industry. Crude oil production by Deutsche Petroleum-AG (DPAG) edged up in the course of that and

---

35 Vertrag zwischen dem Deutschen Reich vertreten durch die Organisation Todt, Oberbauleitung Ostthüringen in Jena und DEA-Mineralölwerke Rositz vom 19.3.1945, 1, ibid.

36 DEA-Verwaltung der Braunkohlenbetriebe, Lampe, an DEA, Abteilung II vom 20.3.1945, WD-CA, D-PA-46.

Fig. 39 Mining oil sands in Wietze

the following year, and the increased number of wells drilled somewhat south of Wietze kindled hopes of high-yield deposits.[37]

New finds near Gifhorn painted a favourable outlook, as the DPAG "first struck oil in commercial quantities there".[38] The expanded DPAG activities led to new hirings, and the total payroll grew to 2,167 staff members with the integration of Mineralölwerke Rositz. In Wietze, the workforce increased in the space of only one year by 186 blue and white-collar staff and by 64 at Rositz.[39] Payroll increases continued, and in 1935 the staff expanded by almost one fifth.[40]

DPAG payroll, 1934-8

	Blue and white-collar staff	New hires	Percentage increase
1934	2,167	250	+ 11.5 %
1935	2,576	409	+ 18.8 %
1936	3,542	966	+ 37.5 %
1937	3,877	335	+ 9.4 %
1938	4,661	784	+ 20.2 %

The end of short-time and idle shifts strengthened the staff's loyalty to both the company and the regime. The company linked the expansion in workforce to implementation of key aspects of the Nazi policy on companies, with DPAG heeding the principles of the DAF campaign for "Schönheit der Arbeit" ("the beauty of labour") when erecting new buildings and paying attention to include social spaces, such as canteens and common rooms, and sanitary facilities such

37 Deutsche Petroleum-AG, Geschäftsbericht der Deutschen Petroleum-AG über das Geschäftsjahr 1934, Berlin 1935, 3.

38 Niederschrift über die Verhandlungen des Aufsichtsrats der DEA am 1.10.1935, 9, WD-CA, D-PA-0120.

39 Deutsche Petroleum-AG, Geschäftsbericht der Deutschen Petroleum-AG über das Geschäftsjahr 1934, Berlin 1935, 4.

40 Deutsche Petroleum-AG, Geschäftsbericht der Deutschen Petroleum-AG über das Geschäftsjahr 1935, Berlin 1936, 4.

Fig. 40 Politicization of operations: Pithead building in Wietze with various swastika flags, 1938

as washrooms and shower-rooms. DPAG continued its tradition of granting employees loans to build their own homes in order to "promote the workforce's local roots", meaning ensure their loyalty. The company also nurtured a "spirit of comradeship" with "comrades' evenings, Christmas parties, grants for "Kraft durch Freude"

Fig. 41 The "Comrades' Building" as part of the DAF "Beauty of Work" programme

("strength through joy", KdF) trips, etc."[41] Moreover, the company appreciably expanded the other voluntary support it offered.

DPAG felt it important to place these social welfare services in the context of a longer company tradition, as no fewer than 789 members of staff had been with the company for over ten years, and 184 for as much as over 20 years.[42] The 1937 annual report underlines the support provided for efforts by the DAF office for "KdF" by "granting special holiday quotas, monies, and providing sports opportunities".[43] One indicator of the increasing penetration of the

41 Deutsche Petroleum-AG, Geschäftsbericht der Deutschen Petroleum-AG über das Geschäftsjahr 1936, Berlin 1937, 6.

42 Ibid.

43 Deutsche Petroleum-AG, Geschäftsbericht der Deutschen Petroleum-AG über das Geschäftsjahr 1937, Berlin 1938, 6.

Fig. 42 Staff parade at the colliery coop (1938)

DPAG companies by the Nazis was the implementation of DAF works units to "train" the workforce in the Nazi outlook.

In 1936, the Wietze hub was allocated 700,000 Reichsmark for investments, and for the very next year the DEA Supervisory Board approved no less than 2.3 million Reichsmark,[44] which led

44 Niederschrift über die Verhandlungen des Aufsichtsrats der DEA am 4.3.1936, 5, WD-CA, D-PA-0120; Niederschrift über die Verhandlungen des Aufsichtsrats der DEA am 6.12.1936, 6f., ibid.; DPAG-Vermerk vom 2.3.1937, 1, WD-CA, D-PA-29.

to a significant improvement in metres drilled. Oil production fell slightly in 1937, then the expected increases associated with the greater drilling activity materialized the following year. The importance of Wietze receded after the "Anschluss" of Austria and the development of the oil fields there.

From 1938 onward, DPAG felt the effects of the general shortage of workers in a German economy typified by the rearmament effort, and the company strengthened its efforts accordingly to expand training. In Wietze, a workshop for apprentices was opened in 1939,[45] and a growing number of staff took part in the "Reich Vocational Contests" (Reichsberufswettkampf).[46]

Mineralölwerke Wietze, which, under Director Günther Schlicht, controlled both the traditional hub in Wietze and the operations in Heide in Holstein as well as the wells in the "Ostmark", boosted its oil production in 1939 by 41 percent to 150,000 tonnes p.a. Above all, the new "finds" in Heide and in the former Republic of Austria drove this outstanding achievement.[47] The senior executives started to focus noticeably more on the oil fields in the "Ostmark" and expanding the "Nova" refinery outside Vienna, while in the "Old Reich" the majority of DPAG investments were dedicated to the expansion of the Heide hub.[48] Wietze's importance waned appreciably after 1938 such that, in the first nine months of

---

45 Deutsche Petroleum-AG, Geschäftsbericht der Deutschen Petroleum-AG über das Geschäftsjahr 1937, Berlin 1938, 6.

46 Alexander Stiller, *Die ideologische Instrumentalisierung des Wettkampfes im Nationalsozialismus zur Erziehung der männlichen Jugend. Selbstinszenierungen und Praktiken des Regimes zwischen 1933 und 1945*, Hamburg 2017, 58ff., https://openhsu.ub.hsu-hh.de/server/api/core/bitstreams/554fa3c3-8a3a-4281-a5be-9d8a6b1f61cb/content [last retrieved on 1.6.2024].

47 Niederschrift über die Verhandlungen des Aufsichtsrats der DEA am 19.1.1940, 7, WD-CA, D-PA-0120.

48 Niederschrift über die Verhandlungen des Aufsichtsrats der DEA am 25.10.1940, 11, ibid.

1944, only a minor portion of DEA's total oil production of 488,700 tonnes stemmed from oil sands.

Wietze oil mining, oil production 1933-45 (in tonnes)[49]

1933	29,922
1934	30,504
1935	29,785
1936	29,792
1937	30,243
1938	31,241
1939	30,936
1940	29,315
1941	28,310
1942	28,501
1943	28,083
1944	25,485
1945	15,198

Oil production and heavy heating oil manufacture using oil shale at the DEA Heide hub

Things were very different when it came to the development of the oil production and oil processing facilities, as operations at the Heide site show. The importance of the oil deposits at Hemmingstedt outside Heide grew in the course of the Nazis' expansionist oil policies and the rearmament of the Reich Navy. Alongside the wells already drilled, attention started to focus on the oil shale deposits (where exploration had been ongoing since 1920 and the fields were at one point depleted) as the intention was to expand heavy heating oil pro-

---

49 Rolf Wolter, *Werdegang des ehemaligen Erdölbergwerkes Wietze in der Gemeinde Wietze, Landkreis Celle*, Wietze 2001, 69.

duction. The Naval High Command pressed for the exploitation of the oil shale deposits in Heide not least because of the short distance between there and the naval harbours. Moreover, the DPAG had know-how in drilling shafts for oil wells and therefore seemed particularly well suited to the task. However, precisely because of its experiences in the past, the company viewed the project sceptically. In July 1934, only two men were handling maintenance of the plant and equipment that had in the early 1920s formed Holsteinische Erdölwerke GmbH and its then payroll of close to 500 persons.[50] In order to obtain "oil shale fresh from the mines" for trial purposes, the first step was to pump out the water that had accumulated in the level at the bottom of the shaft and ran up to a depth of 30 meters, to which end Holsteinische Erdölwerke GmbH, a DPAG subsidiary, on 5 August 1934 filed an "operational plan for sloughing the oil shale mine near Hemmingstedt" to the Celle Mining Office (Bergrevier Celle). The plan envisaged that after approx. three months, 30,000 cubic meters of water would have been removed and the level base of the mine would be accessible again.[51] Sloughing commenced on 19 September 1934 and was completed by the end of the year, enabling the company to reactivate the oil shale mine, which initially employed on average 16 staff members. Exploration boreholes were drilled starting in November/December 1934 with the intention of further prospecting the oil shale deposits.[52] After all, the oil shale reserves looked set, after deducting the losses for the sloughing and

---

50 Holsteinische Erdölwerke GmbH an Bergrevierbeamten Celle vom 10.7.1934, NLA, Hann. 190 Celle, Acc. 2003/204, No. 488; cf. also Hinrich Dürkop, *Die Erdölwerke bei Heide in Dithmarschen 1856-2006*, Hamburg 2007; Chronologische Entwicklung der Erdöl-Schachtbauinteressen der DEA n.d. [around 1947], WD-CA, 3000-752.

51 Holsteinische Erdölwerke GmbH, Günther Schlicht, Betriebsplan für das Sümpfen des Ölkreidebergwerks bei Hemmingstedt vom 5.8.1934, NLA, Hann. 190 Celle, Acc. 2003/204, No. 488.

52 Holsteinische Erdölwerke GmbH, Jahresbericht für 1933 und 1934 vom 20.10.1934, ibid.; Holsteinische Erdölwerke GmbH an Bergrevier Celle vom 12.2.1935, 1f., ibid.

de-oiling, to be sufficient to allow up to 1.5 million tonnes of oil to be produced.

The Reich Navy wanted fast action tapping the oil-shale deposits. The results gained in handling such deposits in Estonia had been carefully examined and the Navy had signed an agreement with the Estonians for the delivery of heating oil as early as 1935.[53] Against this background, the first investment round in the DPAG programme for 1935 also included developing the Heide site by commencing mining of the shale and trial oil extraction in a pyrolysis plant modelled on that in Estonia. The supervisory board approved one million Reichsmark for the project.[54] In October 1935, DEA put the expansion of the Heide facilities on the backburner for the time being "with a view to tight liquidity" as it did the other expansion measures.[55] Oil shale mining therefore remained idle in the summer of 1936.[56]

In April 1935, DPAG had filed an application for a mining concession in anticipation of the positive outcome of exploratory shafts,[57] and on 13 September 1935, the second exploratory borehole "Holstein 2" struck black gold at a depth of 400 metres. Further drilling showed there to be larger deposits above all on the western flank of the Heide salt dome, where in January 1937 a second oil field was discovered under the village of Lieth at a depth of 900 metres. The rigs busy at the oil fields made further progress.[58] The scheduled

---

53 Rasch, *Zur Mineralölpolitik der Kriegsmarine*, 71–101.

54 Niederschrift über die Verhandlungen des Aufsichtsrats der DEA am 4.3.1935, 5, WD-CA, D-PA-0120.

55 Niederschrift über die Verhandlungen des Aufsichtsrats der DEA am 1.10.1935, ibid.

56 Holsteinische Erdölwerke GmbH an Bergrevier Celle vom 8.2.1936, NLA, Hann. 190 Celle, Acc. 2003/204, No. 488.

57 DPAG an Preußisches Oberbergamt Clausthal-Zellerfeld vom 12.4.1935, ibid.; DPAG an Reichswirtschaftsministerium vom 11.4.1935, ibid.

58 Niederschrift über die Verhandlungen des Aufsichtsrats der DEA am 24.9.1936, 5, WD-CA, D-PA-0120; Vermerk Erdölwerke Heide und ihre Beziehung zur Kriegsmarine vom 27.7.1945, 1f., WD-CA, 14-3_3019; Deutsche Petroleum-AG, Geschäftsbericht über das Jahr 1938, Berlin 1939, 4.

Fig. 43 Oil rigs in Heide (1937)

drilling delivered the expected increase in oil production here, too. The "Holstein 36" rig tapped a further field in Rickelshof in 1939. On this basis, oil production surged.

In March 1937, the Office for German Raw Materials and Production Materials' attention fell on the Heide plant. Specifically, together with Paul Pleiger, who sailing in the wake of the Nazi regime had emerged Director of Reichswerke AG für Erzbau und Eisenhütten "Hermann Göring", former Hitler confidante Wilhelm Keppler approached DEA. After a meeting at which the two stated their express interest in the oil shale deposits being mined, the DEA Management Board resolved in early March 1937 to take the time to show both men the plant in Heide in order to convince them that extracting the material by drilling rigs was the "more expedient" approach.[59]

Parallel to this and given the constantly rising quantity of heating oil the Navy required, DPAG did not completely abandon the idea of producing oil from oil shale alongside the drilling operations, which were churning out about 25,000 tonnes of oil in 1938. Although Gröber and Schlicht remained sceptical, they were not able to completely duck the pressure being exerted by the Navy High Command that the company explore all paths to boost heating oil production. DPAG chose as the preferred production process "distillation of batch feeds" as per the tunnel pyrolysis method developed by Estnische Steinöl AG in 1929, and applied for a licence to use the method.[60] Negotiations with the Navy gave rise to the idea of starting out by producing 10,000 tonnes in Heide and depending on the technical know-how gained and the financial results, to later boost volumes to 40,000 tonnes or more.[61] The project was expressly sup-

---

59 DEA-Vorstandssitzung am 2.3.1937, 3, WD-CA, D-PA-29.

60 DPAG an Reichswirtschaftsminister, Hauptabteilung II Min. Oel 3 vom 19.6.1939, 3 BArch, R 3101, No. 18229, sheet 11.

61 DEA-Vorstandssitzung am 16.4.1937, 1, WD-CA, D-PA-29; DEA-Vorstandssitzung am 12.8.1937, 4, ibid.

ported by Walther Randhahn and Hans Gröber.[62] A sum of 1.5 million Reichsmark was made available for trial operations.[63]

Initially, DEA commissioned installation of a pilot plant to "test the real economic significance of Heide" for 350.000 Reichsmark.[64] DPAG intended to expand the oil production plant over the course of four years in two phases. In November 1937, the DEA Management Board estimated the investment cost for the first phase to be 2.7 million Reichsmark.[65] At year-end 1937, DPAG informed the Upper Mining Office [Oberbergamt] in Clausthal-Zellerfeld that it "was starting our oil-shale mining facility" and outlined the work stapes planned for 1938. Alongside setting up a new shaft running from the existing level at 80 metres underground to a new level 150 metres down a small pyrolysis pilot plant would go into operation. In 1939, daily output was scheduled to reach between 400 and 500 tonnes, and once the entire plant was built, output would be treble that.[66] The mining pilot plant initially had about 20 staffers but had only gone active in order "to avoid the state authorities forcing us to throw more resources at the project".[67]

However, on 4 April 1938, part of the new shaft collapsed under the pressure of the rock and the level bulged upwards, pointing to the difficulties such a mine would involve.[68] By contrast, the pilot plant ran satisfactorily in technical terms and the yield was on

---

62 DEA-Vorstandssitzung am 26.5.1937, 2, ibid.

63 DEA-Vorstandssitzung am 21.7.1937, ibid.

64 DEA-Vorstandssitzung am 2.11.1937, 2, ibid.; Niederschrift über die Verhandlungen des Aufsichtsrats der DEA am 6.12.1937, 7, WD-CA, D-PA-0120.

65 DEA-Vorstandssitzung am 2.11.1937, 1f., WD-CA, D-PA-29.

66 DPAG an Oberbergamt Clausthal-Zellerfeld vom 20.12.1937, NLA, Hann. 190 Celle, Acc. 2003/204, No. 488.

67 Niederschrift über die Verhandlungen des Aufsichtsrats der DEA am 11.10.1938, WD-CA, D-PA-0120.

68 DPAG an Bergrevier Celle vom 9.4.1938, NLA, Hann. 190 Celle, Acc. 2003/204, No. 488; Betriebsführer Czerwonski, Bericht vom 7.4.1938, ibid.; Oberbergamt Clausthal-Zellerfeld an Landesplanungsgemeinschaft Schleswig-Holstein vom 22.6.1938, ibid.

par with expectations. DEA was dependent on the goodwill of the Four-Year Plan Authority and in light of the special interests that Hermann Goering himself showed in the oil-shale undertaking, found itself in corner. The investment of ten million Reichsmark promised a return of only six percent, which DEA Management Board member Ullner considered not to be very attractive.[69] The Supervisory Board sought to hedge the risk by insisting the Navy sign a bulk heating oil purchase agreement of 50,000 tonnes p.a. at a fixed price.[70]

There was agreement from the very outset that the heating oil generated from oil shale would be forwarded in its entirety to the Navy, with talks on a supply contract between DEA and the Reich Navy still ongoing. At the end of January 1939, the Navy made its signature to the contract dependent on a laboratory examination of the oil produced there and practical tests at sea. To this end, initially ten kilogrammes were to be made available to the Navy lab and 100-200 tonnes for the on-board trials. Even if no agreement was reached on the price for the test volumes, DEA Management Board member Ullner indicated the sample for the lab would be sent at short notice. For the trials at sea, the relevant oil "first needs to be collected".[71] The relevant tests revealed that the oil produced from oil shale "was most probably suitable for practical Navy operations".[72]

Since the investment was dedicated to supplying a resource to a government client, on 19 June 1939 DPAG filed with the Reich Economics Ministry for financing through a Reich loan of seven million Reichsmark, given the intrinsic risks that the "initial plant [...] has to be structured as a lost financial commitment" in the event

69 Niederschrift über die Verhandlungen des Aufsichtsrats der DEA am 14.3.1939, WD-CA, D-PA-0120.

70 Niederschrift über die Verhandlungen des Aufsichtsrats der DEA am 28.6.1939, 3f., ibid.

71 DEA, Notiz betr. Marinevertrag vom 24.1.1939, 1, WD-CA, D-RW-127.

72 Oberkommando der Kriegsmarine (6894 BB II) an DPAG vom 19.4.1939, NLA, Hann. 190 Celle, Acc. 2003/204, No. 488.

of "permanent operation of the plant" not materializing.[73] The Celle Mining Office expressly supported the application because of the significance of the project for the national defence, the economy, mining technology and the mining business.[74] Although new boreholes drilled gave grounds for hope, at the end of June 1939 the DEA Supervisory Board made any decision to build a new refinery contingent on the further outcome of prospecting and a firm estimate of the volume of oil that could be produced. Given the overarching importance of the oil-shale project in Heide, for its September meeting the Supervisory Board undertook a site inspection.

The lack of a refinery made processing ever more cost intensive given the clear increase in crude oil produced. The crude had to be transferred by tank wagons or tankers to the Wilhelmsburg refinery or to Rositz. In terms of economic viability, it made sense to build a refinery which in the opinion of Günther Schlicht as a skimming plant with a processing capacity of 100,000 tonnes p.a. Part of the extensive project hinged on the idea of, if necessary, erecting a twin and thus boosting capacity to 200,000 tonnes p.a.

Shortly before the outbreak of war, after preparatory talks with Carl Krauch, DPAG submitted a summary of the proposal for the expansion of the oil-shale production plant to the Reich Office for Economic Expansion [Reichsstelle für Wirtschaftsausbau]. The DPAG Management Board made it clear that oil shale mining operations would work in synchrony with the planned skimming plant attached to the oil drilling unit; in the context of the heating oil programme for the Navy it would thus when fully installed generate at least 50,000 tonnes a year. Together with the skimming plant that

73 DPAG an Reichswirtschaftsminister, Hauptabteilung II Min. Oel 3 vom 19.6.1939, 7, BArch Berlin, R 3101, No. 18229, sheet 15; Niederschrift über die Verhandlungen des Aufsichtsrats der DEA am 28.6.1939, 3f., WD-CA, D-PA-0120; Exposé betreffend Ausbau der Ölkreideanlage in Heide/Holstein vom 31.8.1939, WD-CA, 14-2_3019; DPAG an Erster Bergrat Sauerbrey vom 10.10.1939, NLA, Hann. 190 Celle, Acc. 2003/204, No. 488.

74 Bergrevier Celle an Oberbergamt Clausthal-Zellerfeld vom 12.10.1939, 5, ibid.

Fig. 44 In-company social welfare policies and Nazi indoctrination: Interior view of the "Comrades' Building" (1938)

would then be in operation, DPAG assumed the Heide facility would supply 100,000 – 120,000 tonnes of heating oil a year. DPAG emphasized that unlike drilling operations which customarily entailed fluctuations in output, oil-shale production over the next 20 or more years would be constant. DPAG estimated the total oil volumes that could be obtained to run at 1.2 to 1.5 million tonnes but believed it would be able to supply up to four million tonnes from oil-shale processing in Heide.[75]

[75] DPAG, Vorstand, an Reichsstelle für Wirtschaftsausbau vom 24.8.1939, 1ff., ibid.

Fig. 45 Oil-shale mine in Heide (1938)

A total of 350 workers were required to build and assemble the plant. The oil-shale shafts and heating oil production led to the core payroll in Heide rising from 270 to more than 600, including 10 women and 500 unskilled workers. DPAG estimated the annual coal requirement at 15,000 tonnes of coke and 7,500 tonnes of fine coal to be provided by the Graf Bismarck Colliery. The total investment requirement was estimated at 9.5 million Reichsmark. Since the erection of the industrial plant and the mining operations meant new workers arriving and all the corresponding infrastructure, the project impacted the town of Heide and the state planning bureau

[Landesplanungsgemeinschaft] recommended compiling a masterplan for the local economy.[76]

Immediately after the beginning of the war, the DEA Management Board resolved on 2 September 1939, to "put the oil-shale project on hold for the time being given the political situation". Instead, the emphasis was to be on "pressing ahead" with installation of the skimming plant in order to process the oil produced by the wells.[77] By contrast, the Reich Office for Economic Expansion declared the expansion of the oil-shale shaft plant outside Heide in Holstein to be "ready for construction" at a total output of 50,000 tonnes p.a.[78] DEA Director Günther Schlicht, who supervised the construction planning and realization at Hemmingstedt near Heide, spoke in January 1940 of investments totalling 11 million Reichsmark. A few months later, DEA already put the costs of the expansion at 14 million Reichsmark.[79] Initially the 20-month delivery lead-time for the Lurgi tunnel kilns were the reason for the total construction time of 24 months, meaning construction would first start at the end of 1940. According to Schlicht, a distillation plant for 145,000 tonnes p.a. of crude needed to be built first. A total of 500 workers were on site, but a further 120 were required and the company was "at present not able to find them".[80] The specialist department of Reich Economics Ministry agreed to send across the paper-

---

76 Notiz betr. Besprechung über Wirtschaftsplanung der Stadt Heide am 2. Februar 1939 vom 11.2.1939, ibid.

77 DEA-Vorstand, Aktennotiz betr. Ölkreide-Anlage Heide und Heizöllieferungen an die Marine vom 2.9.1939, WD-CA, 14-2_3019.

78 Reichsstelle für Wirtschaftsausbau, Vermerk vom 4.9.1939, 1, BArch Berlin, R 3101, No. 18229, sheet 1.

79 Reichswirtschaftsminister, MR Dr. Römer, Aktenvermerk über Besprechung am 16.1.1940 betr. Ausbau Ölkreideschachtanlage Heide vom 18.1.1940, 2, ibid., 33RS; Reichswirtschaftsminister, ORR Dr. Römer, Aktenvermerk über Besprechung am 2.4.1940 betr. Ausbau Ölkreideschachtanlage Heide vom 8.4.1940, 1, ibid., 35.

80 Ibid.

work qualifying for a loan from Deutsche Industriebank and to push the Navy to sign a long-term supply contract.[81]

A meeting scheduled with the Navy High Command on 21 May 1940 revealed surprisingly that the Navy was "at present not interested" in concluding a supply contract for heating oil owing to severe difficulties with materials and personnel and instead wanted all available energy to be devoted to the installations under construction. Since heating oil supplies to the Navy remained an "important task" not only "in times of war, but also afterwards", the Navy High Command declared that it remained "highly interested" in the oil shale deposits. The statement also pointed out that the Reich Office for Economic Expansion had still not reached a positive decision although Hermann Goering was also interested in the heating oil derived from oil shale. On behalf of DEA, Günther Schlicht, the Board member responsible for oil operations, sought to guide those at the negotiating table to come up with a binding contract to be prepared for the event that "one day a decision be taken to immediately realize the project.[82]

For his part, the President of the Reich Office for Economic Expansion, Carl Krauch, initially desisted from taking a decision "in light of the current situation" but recommended putting "the formal conditions in place for the possible beginning of construction".[83] Altpeter, who was responsible for oil issues at the Reich Office for Economic Expansion, informed Günther Schlicht on 19 August 1940 that the Navy High Command wanted the oil-shale construction

81 Vertragsentwurf zwischen dem Deutschen Reich, Reichswirtschaftsminister und der DPAG betr. Darlehnsvertrag o.D., ibid., 37ff.; Reichswirtschaftsminister, MR Dr. Römer/RR Wasel, an Oberkommando der Kriegsmarine, Fregattenkapitän Großmann vom 25.4.1940, ibid., 39.

82 Günther Schlicht, Notiz betr. Verhandlung mit dem OKW über Liefervertag von Ölkreide-Heizöl vom 21.5.1940, 1f., ibid., 42f.; OKM an Reichswirtschaftsministerium, MR Dr. Römer von 29.5.1940, ibid., 45.

83 Reichsamt für Wirtschaftsausbau, Dr. Altpeter, Nachschrift vom 21.5.1940, ibid, 45RS.

project to be realized as part of the current construction programme. The Reich Economics Ministry was definitely willing in the event of a supply contract being concluded to issue a Reich guarantee for disaster damage.[84] The agreement between DEA and the Navy High Command took time as the Navy had entered unilateral changes to the proposed contract sent by DEA on 19 August 1940, such as lowering the preliminary invoicing price by ten to 150 Reichsmark and the loan from six to 4.8 million Reichsmark, as the Navy loan was supposed to only cover 80 percent of the investment costs. Following consultation between the various Reich offices, new negotiations with DEA were therefore necessary.[85] DEA wanted to further limit its financial risk and on 5 December 1940 in a discussion with the relevant ministerial director [Ministerialdirektor] Arthur Nasse at the Reich Finance Ministry [Reichsfinanzministerium] expressly pointed out that DEA would not "tackle" construction of the oil-shale plant from a "purely profit-oriented vantage point". Moreover, actual delivery of heating oil to the Navy was not to be expected for at least two years, meaning "presumably after the end of the current war".[86] Since the Reich Office for Economic Expansion upheld its interest in the expansion project, on 7 May 1941 DEA put the ink to a corresponding contract with the Reich, which reduced the corporation's risk.[87]

In 1940, the oil production facilities in Heide made a not insubstantial contribution to DEA's profits, in comparison to the

---

84 Reichsamt für Wirtschaftsausbau, Dr. Altpeter, Vermerk betr. Ölkreide Heide Telefonanruf bei Dir. Schlicht am 17.8.1940 vom 19.8.1940, ibid., 48.

85 OKM, Dr. Boecker, an Reichswirtschaftsministerium, MR Dr. Römer vom 15.10.1940, ibid., sheet 57; Vom OKM geänderter Entwurf des Lieferungsvertrags von Ölkreideheizöl o.D. [October 1940], ibid., 58ff.; DEA an OKM betr. Vertragsentwurf Lieferung von Ölkreideheizöl o.D. [19.8.1940], ibid., 68f.

86 Notiz betr. Ölkreideanlage vom 3.12.1940, 2, WD-CA, CA, 14-2_3078.

87 DEA, Albert Ritter/Günther Schlicht an Oberkommando der Kriegsmarine Kapitän Großmann vom 21.5.1943, 1, ibid.

prior year.[88] Parallel to this, some of the rigs struck oil, as a result of which DEA expected oil output to continue to rise. To that end, the plan was to install a second distillation plant operating according to the skimming method in order not only to produce prime motor spirit and distillation residues but also diesel, and double turnout to 200,000 tonnes p.a., of which 30,000 tonnes would be prime motor spirit, 40,000 tonnes petroleum and gasoil and naval diesel oil. At that point, it had not yet been conclusively decided whether the annual volume of 125,000 tonnes of distillation residue that accumulated would be processed in the Pölitz hydration plant or locally using a viscosity cracker to produce naval heating oil or inputted into a full cracker plant to produce petroleum and diesel. Since the expansion plant was a carbon copy of the existing skimming plant, the new facility was expected to go into operation in April 1941. To transport the product away, the plan was to build a pipeline to the Kaiser Wilhelm Canal or to the Navy docks at Büsum that were then being built, thus ensuring the Navy's requirements could be safely met.[89] The investment costs of 735,000 Reichsmark for the pipeline were to be financed by DEA. The skimming plant designated to produce heating oil for the Navy went turnkey on schedule.[90] However, ever greater difficulties in "recruiting staff" were experienced at the site.[91]

---

88 Niederschrift über die Verhandlungen des Aufsichtsrats der DEA am 25.10.1940, 5 and 8, WD-CA, D-PA-0120.

89 Reichsamt für Wirtschaftsausbau, Baureiferklärung vom 9.10.1940, 1 and 4, BArch Berlin, R 3101, No. 18229, sheet 109 and 112.

90 Niederschrift über die Verhandlungen des Aufsichtsrats der DEA am 25.10.1940, 5, WD-CA, D-PA-0120.

91 Niederschrift über die Verhandlungen des Aufsichtsrats der DEA am 2.4.1941, 7, ibid.

Crude oil production in Heide 1936–1945 (in tonnes)[92]

Year	Output
1936	7,700
1937	4,700
1938	25,500
1939	77,100
1940	231,400
1941	206,700
1942	141,300
1943	115,800
1944	125,800
1945	90,800

On 15 November 1940, the Reich Economics Ministry approved the doubling of oil output capacity to 200,000 tonnes p.a. The Reich Office for Economic Expansion took charge of the construction project.[93] Two weeks previously, DEA received the requisite "declaration of construction readiness" [Baureiferklärung] from the Reich Office for Economic Expansion, and was thus authorized to install a plant to produce propellant and gasoline, with a capacity of 7,100 tonnes p.a. of propellant and 3,400 tonnes p.a. of gasoline from the natural gas accruing as associated gas in line with the greater volume of oil pumped. The declaration of construction readiness also covered a planned petroleum stabilization unit for 34,000 tonnes of petroleum a year. The plan envisaged being able by November 1941 to produce an additional 10,000 tonnes a year of fuel at a cost (to be borne by DEA) of 950,000 Reichsmark and with comparatively low material inputs; half of the volume would, so the executives expected, be ready for delivery within six months. Owing to the direct impact this would have on fuel provisioning, the Reich

92 Compiled according to WD-CA, D-RW-158 (statistics).

93 Reichsamt für Wirtschaftsausbau, Carl Krauch, an DEA, Verwaltung der Erdölbetriebe vom 5.11.1940, 1, BArch Berlin, R 3101, No. 18275, sheet 35.

Office classified the project as "of especial importance to matters of state".[94] The second skimming plant went turnkey in August 1941.[95]

In June 1940, it first became clear that the site's location close to the German Bight meant it could be targeted by the Royal Air Force bombers. In June 1940, the air raid sirens sounded no less than 16 times, which spelled 830 man-hours lost and reduced the distance drilled by 181.40 metres. In September 1940, the sirens signalled the alarm 31 times, resulting in the loss of 1,539 man-hours, and in October 1940 the situation initially peaked with the sirens sounding 41 times, operations were discontinued for two months as they required adequate lighting for the night-time shift but that would have flown in the face of the black-out regulations. By the end of 1940, a total of 7,338 man-hours had been lost, which reduced the total distance drilled by more than 4.6 kilometres. In 1941, the total of man-hours and drilled metres lost dipped again.[96]

The decrease in oil production in the Heide field gradually made itself felt, and the DEA Board was prompted to consider the "future prospects" of oil production in the "Old Reich" as a whole. There was a consensus that in future the exploratory drilling which had been scaled back owing to the war, needed to be ramped back up, to which end allocations in the order of three million Reichsmark needed to be made to the reserves. In the interim, the corporation's leaders attached most hope to expanding oil-shale mining and processing; the lion's share of the total investments scheduled for 1941 of 11 million Reichsmark would be committed to this task, and the management board applied to the supervisory board for approval of

---

94 Reichsamt für Wirtschaftsausbau, Baureiferklärung vom 5.11.1940, 1 and 5, BArch, R 3101, No. 18229, sheet 96 and 100.

95 Niederschrift über die Verhandlungen des Aufsichtsrats der DEA am 23.10.1941, 2, WD-CA, D-PA-0120.

96 DEA, Verwaltung der Erdölbetriebe, Betriebseinwirkungen durch Fliegeralarme Heide vom 28.11.1941, WD-CA, D-RW-129.

Fig. 46 Oil-shale processing at DEA's plant in Heide (1939)

additional funding.[97] After all, the increasing depletion of the Heide oil field had become clear to all from the not inconsiderable decrease in oil production. The fact that no new extensive oil deposits had been tapped was something that on 1 April 1942 DEA Management Board member termed "overexploitation".[98] Shortly thereafter, a rig struck a larger oil deposit near Meldorf that was felt to contain commercial quantities. Although Karl Schirner did not want to be overhasty in overestimating the yield, the deposits found there seemed to him to be "further proof" that oil production in Holstein offered

97 Niederschrift über die Verhandlungen des Aufsichtsrats der DEA am 23.10.1941, 3 and 11, WD-CA, D-PA-0120.

98 Niederschrift über die Verhandlungen des Aufsichtsrats der DEA am 1.4.1942, 9, ibid.

"further opportunities".[99] In the autumn of 1942 the corporation was forced to concede that output was continuing to drop in Heide.[100] For that reason, throughput at the skimming plant also fell almost 30 percent.

Oil-shale mining, which had for some time been considered a welcome alternative, was likewise slow in picking up steam. The shafts for Pit I had been sunk to a depth of 159.5 metres and a new level cut 40 metres down. In Pit II, the freezing method was used to sink shafts down to the oil-shale seams, which began 40 metres down, and the shafts then extended "by hand operations" down to 90 metres. At the two levels at 80 and at 140 metres respectively, a connecting tunnel was envisaged through to Pit I. In addition, a tubular elevator shaft was built at the western edge of the mining zone, about 1.2 kilometres from the pits, in order to have a rescue tunnel and an additional ventilation shaft at hand. This was required if only because the mine was not uncomplicated and had seen outbreaks of gas, for example.

A mining disaster made the "little researched risks of oil-shale mining" apparent.[101] At Pit I, when a shaft was sunk down to 165 metres, on 5 August 1941 there was a firedamp explosion, and five miners were killed by the sole suddenly bulging upward.[102] This marked a clear repetition of a mining accident that had occurred on 26 June 1924 and which had led to the deaths of two miners. The fatalities in 1924 had not only led to the mining director and the operations manager both being sentenced in the courts but also to

99 Niederschrift über die Verhandlungen des Aufsichtsrats der DEA am 28.4.1942, 3, ibid.

100 Niederschrift über die Verhandlungen des Aufsichtsrats der DEA am 4.11.1942, 5, ibid.

101 Niederschrift über die Verhandlungen des Aufsichtsrats der DEA am 23.10.1941, 2, ibid.

102 Dürkop, *Erdölwerke*, 60f.

the discontinuation of oil-shale mining.[103] Since oil-shale production played a prominent role for DEA in meeting its supply obligations to the Navy, the management of the oil operations ignored the now evident dangers to the miners. Given the expected high yields, and these formed the bedrock of the agreements reached with the Navy, mining continued.[104]

Production was originally scheduled for spring 1943 but was delayed considerably. DEA cited difficulties in procuring materials and personnel as well as several new organizational changes to iron allocations. In May 1943, the DEA Management Board targeted September/October 1943 as the possible date for initial operational turnkey, but made this dependent on the immediate assignment of the contingent of miners it had requested.[105] Internally, the Supervisory Board had already been informed in autumn 1942 that there would be delays in manufacturing the pyrolysis plant of at least one year, putting start back to the end of 1943.[106] DEA placated the Navy by indicating that it would mine 1,000 tonnes of oil shale a day, which would enable the production of as much as 37,000 tonnes p.a. of oil from pyrolytic conversion. The large-scale pyrolysis pilot run had to be discontinued after six months as there had been deflagrations and fires. After some process modifications, Tunnel Pyrolysis Plant I went back into operation at the end of February 1944. Yet, even together with Pyrolysis Plant II, which went live at the end of March 1944, the oil yield was below expectations.[107]

---

103 Schöffengericht Itzehoe, Urteil gegen Otto Lohse u.a. vom 13.4.1926, NLA, Hann. 190 Celle, Acc. 2003/204, No. 1553; Dürkop, *Erdölwerke*, 41f.

104 Niederschrift über die Verhandlungen des Aufsichtsrats der DEA am 23.10.1941, 3, WD-CA, D-PA-0120.

105 DEA, Albert Ritter/Günther Schlicht an Oberkommando der Kriegsmarine Kapitän Großmann vom 21.5.1943, 1, WD-CA, CA, 14-2_3078.

106 Niederschrift über die Verhandlungen des Aufsichtsrats der DEA am 4.11.1942, 6, WD-CA, D-PA-0120.

107 Dürkop, *Erdölwerke*, 73ff.

The insufficient number of skilled face-workers for the mines was a second problem and meant that daily output of oil shale remained lodged at 400 instead of 1,000 tonnes. In May 1943, 86 carters were on site, but for all the efforts in the prior 18 months over half the face-workers, apprentice face-workers and conveyor operators required were still lacking, a total of 107 skilled workers. In line with an internal DEA reposting scheme, 30 miners were meant to relocate from the Graf Bismarck Colliery over to the oil shale mines, and the Wehrmacht wanted to release 44 miners who had been conscripted, amongst them 17 from the Graf Bismarck Colliery, "in the framework of the oil-field campaign" to work in Heide. Under certain conditions, the DEA Pechelbronn also planned to transfer 15 to 20 miners to the north.[108] From 1943 onwards, the order of the day was to conduct mining with ever greater intensity. By the end of June 1944, the workforce in the mining operations had risen to about 800, of which 38 were "Eastern workers" and 193 POWs. Drilling operations had a workforce of 1,134 persons, of which 56 were "Eastern workers" and 224 POWs, meaning staffing levels were a third higher.[109]

In addition to the construction delays, for all the technical mining studies undertaken it was uncertain how the mine would behave once operational. Moreover, in particular the problems down under the ground made expansion work considerably more expensive. Alone the air-raid protection measures taken given the increasing number of overflights and bombing raids also contributed to the expansion costs estimated in 1941 at 7.5 million Reichsmark had risen to at least 10.88 million Reichsmark.[110]

---

108 DEA, Albert Ritter/Günther Schlicht an Oberkommando der Kriegsmarine Kapitän Großmann vom 21.5.1943, 2, WD-CA, CA, 14-2_3078.

109 Dürkop, *Erdölwerke*, 77.

110 DEA, Albert Ritter/Günther Schlicht an Oberkommando der Kriegsmarine Kapitän Großmann vom 21.5.1943, 4, WD-CA, CA, 14-2_3078.

The expansion of the oil-shale plant, the pace of which was upped at the Navy's insistence, consumed far more financial resources than assumed, whereupon at DEA's request in mid-1943 the Reich Navy raised the scale of the loan it granted.[111] Once mining operations and the pyrolysis plant had transpired to be a large technical pilot project that would not be able to reach economic viability, DEA and the Navy agreed to run the mining operations from 1 June 1943 onwards "at cost to the Navy" and the same status applied to the pyrolysis plant as of 1 December 1943. In August 1944, the Navy High Command agreed to assume the costs of the actual trial operations initially through to the end of 1944.[112] DEA first booked a sum of 5.4 million Reichsmark as "reimbursement of operating costs" and in mid-September 1944 the DEA head office reported receipt of a payment of a further 1.5 million Reichsmark for the expenses associated with trial operations.[113] The DEA Management Board expected further reimbursement payments in the course of the year meaning that there was a realistic prospect of recouping all the costs of the project from the Navy.[114]

In the course of the Allies bombing campaign waged against the German oil industry, the Heide site increasingly became a target of attacks from the air. On 18 July 1944, about 200 bombs set fire to large parts of the refinery. One hit a dormitory hut and killed 25 men, amongst them 19 Frenchmen.[115] In August 1944, the US Air Force flew raids in short waves causing considerable damage of more than 13 million Reichsmark.[116] One month later the US

---

111 DEA, Bericht des Vorstands über die Zeit vom 1. Januar 1943 bis 30. September 1943 vom 1.11.1943, 4f., WD-CA, D-PA-65.

112 Oberkommando der Kriegsmarine (Skl/Adm.Qu.III B II b B.No. 8303/44), Kapitän Großmann, an DEA vom 8.8.1944, WD-CA, 14-2_3019.

113 DEA, Karl Schirner, Lagebericht vom 16.9.1944, 1, WD-CA, D-PA-65.

114 DEA, Bericht des Vorstands über die Zeit vom 1. Januar bis 30. September 1944 vom 2.11.1944, 4, ibid.

115 Dürkop, *Erdölwerke*, 78f.

116 DEA, Kriegstagebuch, Eintragung vom 6.8.1944, WD-CA, D-PA-64.

Air Force again bombed the Heide facility and damaged the tank farm and the pump house. The local management team led by Max Breder estimated the damage to the fixed assets in Heide caused by the next heavy bombing raid on 30 September 1944 at 8.7 million Reichsmark, of which 2.2 million Reichsmark was attributable to the oil-shale project. The agency attached to the state government in Schleswig responsible for compensation for war damages evaluated the destruction caused by the bombing during a site visit on 30 January 1945.[117] Such was the scale of the damage that the plant could only be rendered operational by makeshift repairs.

Eight further waves of heavy bombing were truly destructive and yet it was not until early May 1945 that operations in Heide came to a complete standstill. The oil-shale project launched on the basis of the loan from the Navy and guarantees from the Reich never got beyond the stage of a large-scale pilot plant and proved to be a typically unprofitable undertaking in the context of the government's wish for energy independence. The fact that DEA had managed to minimize the financial risk could not in the end disguise the fact that the project was a complete failure. Things were very different as regards the oil wells drilled and the two skimming plants, realized without government subsidies. Oil production in Holstein was admittedly first and foremost the outcome of the Navy's greater strategic fuel requirement. After the war, oil production and the refineries were swiftly back in action and the oil pumped from the local wells was soon being distilled. By switching over to machinery imported from Wilhelmsburg, in 1951 Heide was already churning out 150,000 tonnes of oil a year and became one of DEA's most important plants in Germany.[118]

---

117 DEA, Erdölwerke Heide an DEA, Verwaltung der Erdölbetriebe vom 2.2.1945, 1f., WD-CA, D-RW-129.

118 Fritz Staiger, *Wiederaufbau und Ausbau deutscher Mineralölwerke. Die DEA-Raffinerie Heide*, in: Erdöl und Kohle 6 (1953), 17–21, esp. 17.

The Wilhelmsburg lubricants refinery

DEA's refinery operations were firmly established at an early date, with five plants set up during the First World War. In 1923, they processed no less than 83,000 tonnes, and planned conversion work and plant expansion at the Wilhelmsburg refinery outside Hamburg were intended to boost annual output to 150,000 tonnes.[119] Under the aegis of DPAG, meanwhile, the refinery's profitability remained a tough proposition. While the volume processed was raised slightly in 1933, unit sales of finished products suffered from the enduring price war with foreign competitors, and the low prices the latter offered resulted in unit sales dropping 15 percent on the year.[120]

In the mid-1930s, the Wilhelmsburg refinery's processing capacity was 60,000 tonnes, but the DPAG board believed the plant was "outdated" in terms of buildings and technology.[121] DPAG Management Board member Hans Gröber proposed the steam boilers be replaced and a deparaffination plant be installed at a cost of about one million Reichsmark, to be financed from the expected 1.5 million Reichsmark in surplus profits to be garnered. However, the DEA Management Board initially approved using plant from the Central German lignite works in Wilhelmsburg to keep the capex lower, even if the operating expenses were therefore to rise compared to new plant.[122] Once capacity utilization in Wilhelmsburg improved, the DEA board changed tack in mid-1936 and approved additional investments.

In early 1937, the Office for German Raw and Raw Materials [Amt für deutsche Roh- und Werkstoffe] instructed DEA to increase

---

119 Geschäfts-Bericht der Deutschen Erdöl-Aktiengesellschaft zu Berlin über das 25. Geschäftsjahr 1923, Berlin 1924, 2. Following the expansion of the Wilhelmsburg refinery, DEA shut down its refineries in Grabow and Rheinau in 1924.

120 Geschäftsbericht der Deutschen Erdöl-Aktiengesellschaft in Berlin über das 35. Geschäftsjahr 1933, Berlin 1934, 2 and 5.

121 DEA-Vorstandssitzung, 18.2.1936, 1, WD-CA, D-PA-29.

122 Ibid., 2.

Fig. 47 Construction of a new deparaffination plant in Wilhelmsburg

the capacity of the Wilhelmsburg refinery to produce lubricants to at least 5,000 tonnes p.a. by 1 April 1938.[123] The additional buildings required to achieve this target meant the capex of 3.2 million Reichsmark in November 1936 had risen to five million Reichsmark by May 1937.[124] In June 1937, DPAG then planned to increase oil processing in the Wilhelmsburg facility from about 60,000 tonnes p.a. by a third to 80,000 tonnes p.a. and to further enhance the quality of the products. To this end, additional distillation, deparaffination, and refining units were erected on the grounds (16 hectares in size) along with the requisite auxiliary systems.[125] The contract concluded with the navy at the end of 1937 made it necessary to expand the Wilhelmsburg refinery further in order to ease the strain on the sister facility in Rositz when it came to processing oil and "free it up" to produce heating oil from lignite tar.[126] DEA estimated the costs for the expansion meanwhile to have reached 4.4 million Reichsmark.[127]

In 1939, Wilhelmsburg scored a new record refinery throughput of 90,000 tonnes of crude. However, capacities did not suffice to process all the crude from Heide.[128] The new-build programme initiated to raise capacity further included expansion of the boiler-house

123 Amt für deutsche Roh- und Wertstoffe an DEA vom 21.1.1937, 1, BArch Berlin, R 3101, No. 18274, sheet 14.

124 Niederschrift über die Verhandlungen des Aufsichtsrats der DEA am 20.11.1936, 11, WD-CA, D-PA-0120; DPAG-Vermerk vom 2.3.1937, 1, WD-CA, D-PA-29; DEA an Amt für deutsche Roh- und Wertstoffe vom 30.5.1937, 1, BArch Berlin, R 3101, No. 18274, sheet 22.

125 Landesplanungsgemeinschaft Hamburg, Schuhmacher, an Reichsstelle für Raumordnung vom 2.6.1937, BArch Berlin, R 113, No. 1355. The Reich Office for Spatial Planning [Reichsstelle für Raumordnung] erroneously assumed that a new hydrogenation plant would be built.

126 DEA, Notiz betr. Investierungen für Marine vom 12.1.1939, 2, WD-CA, D-RW-129.

127 Deutsche Petroleum-AG, Geschäftsbericht der Deutschen Petroleum-AG über das Geschäftsjahr 1938, Berlin 1939, 4.

128 Niederschrift über die Verhandlungen des Aufsichtsrats der DEA am 19.1.1940, 7, WD-CA, D-PA-0120.

and the deparaffination facilities, a new destillation, and the procurement of tank waggons.[129]

Given its location on the Elbe River outside Hamburg, on 8-9 May 1941 the Wilhelmsburg refinery suffered from British bombing raids at a relatively early date, with the dispatch plant and an interim tank farm destroyed. Between 700 and 800 tonnes of lube leaked.[130] Owing to the importance of the facility to the war effort, on 4 September 1941 the Reich Economics Minister approved the rebuilding of the units. Since the General Plenipotentiary for Special Questions of Chemicals Production [Generalbevollmächtigter für Sonderfragen der chemischen Erzeugung], Carl Krauch, considered the restoration of the refinery's full capacity to be "an important matter of state" for reasons of "national defence", he assumed responsibility for realization of the repairs, costed at 1.3 million Reichsmark, which meant DPAG could expect preferential allocations of materials and labour and thus "a speedier restoration".[131]

The expanded deparaffination went into operation in early autumn 1941, and a new crude-oil pipeline was also ready to go turnkey. Given the great danger of bombing raids, splinter shields and camouflage buildings were also almost complete in October 1941.[132] By October 1942, the refinery had boosted throughput and production by 14 percent.[133] The spaciously dimensioned deparaffination plant proved to be "superb" in permanent operation and could also

---

129 Niederschrift über die Verhandlungen des Aufsichtsrats der DEA am 25.10.1940, 5, ibid.

130 DEA, Kriegstagebuch, Eintragung vom 9.5.1941, WD-CA, D-PA-64.

131 Der Generalbevollmächtigte für Sonderfragen der chemischen Erzeugung, Prof. Carl Krauch, an DEA-Erdölwerke Wilhelmsburg vom 20.9.1941, 1, BArch Berlin, R 3101, No. 18274, sheet 120; Niederschrift über die Verhandlungen des Aufsichtsrats der DEA am 25.10.1940, 5, WD-CA, D-PA-0120.

132 Niederschrift über die Verhandlungen des Aufsichtsrats der DEA am 23.10.1941, 2f. and 6, WD-CA, D-PA-0120.

133 Niederschrift über die Verhandlungen des Aufsichtsrats der DEA am 4.11.1942, 6, ibid.

be used for job processing of other companies' oil. Moreover, the crude oil distillation went turnkey while the dispatch plant was close to completion.[134]

The "Operation Gomorrah" carpet-bombing by the Allies from 21-25 July 1943 caused a terrible firestorm in the city but missed the Wilhelmsburg refinery south of the Elbe River.[135] Passive air-raid protection steps were taken all the more intensively at the premises, with underground shelters for the workers and splinter and fire protection measures in the tank farms. On 20 June 1944, an attack on the refinery in Wilhelmsburg completely destroyed the tubular furnaces, the refining plant and the deparaffination system as well as the tank farm in large parts.[136] In the early afternoon of 6 August 1944, bombs set fire to large parts of the plant, in particular the tank pit, the diffusion plant, and the diffusion distillation equipment.[137] On the morning of New Year's Eve 1944, another wave of bombing took place, severely damaging the remaining unscathed parts of the refinery and destroying about 40 percent of the storerooms and the admin block. The continuous water-bath distillation plant was set on fire and the refinery closed down for at least four weeks, and when it reopened it could not emulate its earlier output.[138]

As was the case at the Rositz hub, in the context of the restoration programme for the oil refineries organized by the "Geilenberg staff unit", the Wilhelmsburg refinery additionally made use of foreign slave labour for clearing the rubble. Between June 1944 and March 1945, these groups also included inmates from the Work Education Camp [Arbeitserziehungslager] that the Gestapo in Hamburg

---

134 Ibid.

135 DEA, Bericht des Vorstands über das 1. Halbjahr 1943 vom 30.7.1943, 1, WD-CA, D-PA-65.

136 DEA, Kriegstagebuch, Eintragung vom 20.6.1944, WD-CA, D-PA-64.

137 DEA, Kriegstagebuch, Eintragung vom 6.8.1944, ibid.

138 DEA, Kriegstagebuch, Eintragung vom 31.12.1944, ibid.; DEA an DEA-Zechen Graf Bismarck und Königsgrube, Max Grotowsky vom 2.1.1945, ibid.

had set up at Wilhelmsburg in April 1943.[139] The Gestapo prisoners confined there, usually for up to 56 days by way of punishment, disciplining, and abuse, were ruthlessly forced to work. Working conditions for the slave labourers at the DEA refinery in Wilhelmsburg were undoubtedly no different. The death of AEL prisoner Bruno Ziebell, probably during an accident in the plant shortly before Christmas 1943, clearly speaks for itself.

Decline of the company and its output in the closing days of the Third Reich

On 26 February 1945, bombs severely damaged the DEA head office in Berlin. Since bombing raids were as good as continuous, and therefore the communication wires were frequently down and the long-distance roads and rail tracks often impassable, managing the group and guiding the actions of the decentralized business divisions from Berlin was as good as impossible. After management of the oil operations was transferred to Wietze in consultation with Reich Armaments Ministers Albert Speer and the Head of the Raw Materials Office [Rohstoffamt], Hans Kehrl, in early April 1945, the remaining executives also headed there, with the exception of Albert Ritter who stayed in Berlin.[140]

Irrespective of the Allies' superiority in the air, which made it almost impossible to bring in materials or for the staff to get to work, the mines stayed in operation. In the first quarter of 1945, production in the hard coal mines ran at 295,000 tonnes of coal and 25,000 tonnes of coke, or less than a third of the same period in

---

139 Martin Reiter, *Das Arbeitserziehungslager Wilhelmsburg. Aktuelle Forschungen zu einem kaum bekannten NS-Lager,* in: Christine Eckel et al. (Eds.), Stigmatisierung – Marginalisierung – Verfolgung, Berlin 2015, 184–202, here 193f.

140 DEA-Vorstand, Karl Schirner/Günther Schlicht, Bericht des Vorstandes über die Zeit vom 1. Januar bis 30. September 1945 vom 24.10.1945, 2, WD-CA, D-PA-70.

1944. Shift productivity also dropped "dramatically",[141] and higher prime costs and severely reduced revenues squeezed the mining operations into the red. The lignite operations likewise saw production fall, albeit to 2.251 million tonnes in the first quarter of 1945 and thus not as sharply as it did for their hard coal counterparts. Briquette production decreased accordingly to 674,000 tonnes. Mineralölwerke Rositz had to limit output owing to a lack of transportation capacity. Moreover, US bombers again hit the refinery, where operations had been restored in sometimes makeshift fashion, hard on 15 February 1945, and until the end of the war heating oil and fuel production were halted.

Crude oil production in Wietze and near Heide ran at 48,200 tonnes and was thus only slightly more than half the output in the "Ostmark". Production at the facilities in Heide outperformed that outside Hanover. Oil chalk resources in Heide ceased to be used in March 1945 following heavy bombing and the destruction of the pyrolosis plants. In the first quarter of 1945, the oil processing plants only rolled out 24,100 tonnes of product, and in March 1945 bombing attacks put a complete stop to the Wilhelmsburg refinery.

At the latest in early February 1945, the group head office had almost no contact with its various sites as the telegraph network had collapsed.[142] Couriers could only reach their destination with great delay owing to roads being destroyed or the risk of strafing. In early March 1945, transportation routes were more or less all down, for example with the bombing of the Wanne-Eickel main railway station on 4 March 1945 and attacks on the canal network. This meant that in the first week of March 1945 the DEA mines were only able to dispatch 13,983 tonnes of coal, while production remained fairly constant at 23,642 tonnes.[143] The following week, dispatch sagged

[141] Ibid.

[142] DEA, Kriegstagebuch, Eintragung vom 5.2.1945, WD-CA, D-PA-64.

[143] DEA-Zechen Graf Bismarck und Königsgrube, Wilhelm Friedrich/Max Fröhlich, Wochenbericht (26.2.-4.3.1945) vom 7.3.1945, 1, ibid.

further and was a mere 4,945 tonnes, less than eight percent of the order volume.[144] As a result of the March 1945 conscriptions to the "Volkssturm" brigades and a dire lack of wood, the mine managers expected with "a fair degree of certainty" that at least one mine would have to close, selecting colliery VII as it was most "sensitive to war".[145]

The hard coal mines in Gelsenkirchen and Eickel looked likely to become the first inside the so-called "Old Reich" [Alt-Reich] to be occupied by Allied troops. In this context, the collieries agreed to be "patrons" for the erection of tank traps at important road intersections. At the same time, even "key personal" [Schlüsselkräfte] were conscripted to attend short training courses at the Volkssturm,[146] the last military reserve of largely untrained men aged 16 to 60 – although the emergency staff was expressly meant to be protected.[147] In the early hours of 28 March 1945, a "Party Office" informed the mine directors that the advance US Army tanks were approaching. POW Labour Group 205 R sounded alarm level 1 for the Soviet POWs and began to have them moved off site for fear of attempted uprisings.[148]

The Wehrmacht armed the works security force, among other things, with two machine guns, and the operational managers were told that the POWs would no longer appear for work. Mining Assessor [Bergassessor] Werner arranged for the POWs to be transported off along with other foreign civilian workers. At a meeting between the DAF district office and Nazi Party district head Otto

---

144 Ibid.

145 DEA-Zechen Graf Bismarck und Königsgrube, Wilhelm Friedrich/Max Fröhlich, Wochenbericht (12.3.-18.3.1945) vom 21.3.1945, 1, ibid.

146 David K. Yelton, *Hitler's Volkssturm. The Nazi Militia and the fall of Germany, 1944–1945*, Lawrence 2002, 105ff.

147 DEA-Zechen Graf Bismarck und Königsgrube, Wilhelm Friedrich/Max Fröhlich, Wochenbericht (5.-11.3.1945) vom 13.3.1945, 1, WD-CA, D-PA-64.

148 Kellner, Lagebericht der DEA-Zechen Graf Bismarck und Königsgrube vom 30.3.1945, 1, ibid.

Plagemann on the morning of 29 March 1945, the conclusion was that the "civilian foreigners" should be "marched" northwards to the Weser-Ems Gau and/or to the Reich Railway HQ [Reichsbahndirektion] in Münster.[149] In the early morning of 29 March 1945, the security guards from the POW Battalion D based in Recklinghausen marched the POWs placed under their command off eastwards.

DEA wanted to negotiate with the DAF Gau management, which had been moved to Haltern-Annaberg in the north, as regards transportation of other groups of forced labourers away from the mines, and a company representative arrived there on the afternoon of 29 March 1945 but found no managers around. Since DAF Gau Superintendent [Gauobmann] Ferdinand Schürmann was likewise not to be found at the police bunker HQ in Recklinghausen, Nazi Party Gau head Alfred Meyer told the DEA official to go to the police HQ in Recklinghausen. The latter promised to provide escorts for the transportation of the foreign civilian workers, but in the final instance none were forthcoming. The train with 20 goods waggons that had been approved thanks to the good business relationship with the Reich Railway Authority and which were to be used to transport 1,200 foreigners eastwards likewise did not materialize. The civilian foreigners were thereupon forced on 29 March 1945 at 6 p.m. to march off in the direction of the Osnabrück Labour Office. The corporation evidently found it important to remove the various different categories of foreign slave labourers from its premises and not to be associated by the Allies with the exploitation of foreign citizens.

During this time, demolition squads from the Luftschutzpolizei working at the instruction of the Reich Defence Commissioner [Reichsverteidigungskommissar] and Nazi Party Gau head Alfred Meyer spent the evening of 28 March 1945 preparing the destruction of collieries III and VII. In particular, the boilers

149 Ibid.

and the turbines were targeted for destruction. The order, signed in person by the Reich Defence Commissioner, was sent to the head of Gelsenkirchen operations, Mining Assessor Max Fröhlich, on 28 March 1945. He said the decision to destroy the plant was directly the "responsibility of the leader of the company". In agreement with DEA Management Board member Max Grotowsky, who was still on the ground in Gelsenkirchen, Fröhlich directed that the demolition squad from the Luftschutzpolizei should quit the site and abandon other measures to "paralyze" coal production. He thus had the compressors' tilting-pad bearings dismantled and sent them to Wietze. The Nazi Party district head threatened him on the morning of 29 March 1945 with summary court martial should he disobey the demolition order, so Fröhlich instructed the Wehrmacht demolition squad, which had arrived at 2 p.m., to destroy the 2,500-kilowatt generator and the power-station condenser at colliery II. That night, the more senior DEA managers left the site in the fire engine for Wietze.[150]

The DEA head office, which the management board had left in time and was already severely damaged by bombing, was hit by "a number of heavy explosive grenades" when, on 25 April 1945, the Red Army surrounded Berlin and moved into the city centre.[151] In the late evening, a large Russian unit seized the building and took control. After three days, most of the soldiers left again, and cigarettes thrown away carelessly or incoming incendiary or explosive bombs caused several fires in the period up to 2 May 1945. There was also some plundering. The subsequent attempt to get the Soviet military administration to put protective measures in place failed, with the janitor receiving a reply stating that the "Russ. military does

150 Kellner, Lagebericht der DEA-Zechen Graf Bismarck und Königsgrube, 30.3.1945, 3, WD-CA, D-PA-46.

151 DEA-Hausverwaltung an Ausweichstelle der DEA, Direktor Ritter betr. Bericht über die Entwicklung der Kämpfe um den Rathausblock; Verlauf u. Abschluss vom 4.5.1945, 1, WD-CA, D-PA-46.

not plunder and the mil.[iltary] adm.[inistration] is not responsible for acts by civilians".[152] In the late night of 3 May 1945, the Germans present at the DEA house were able to "sleep for the first time peacefully" in ten days. At eight in the morning, the building's staff started cleaning the street outside. "Cleaning the offices" was still "to be undertaken by the employees, who will hopefully arrive soon".[153]

At all the DEA sites, the arrival of Allied troops spelled the end of Nazi rule and at least for a short time the complete discontinuation of operations. Fearful silence prevailed, as the future of the conglomerate in what would be a new era was far from clear.

152 Ibid., 3.

153 Ibid.

IX. THE OIL DEPOSITS GRAB IN THE CONQUERED TERRITORIES

(Rainer Karlsch)

The Südostkonsortium and tackling Britain's Olex

The stake in the consortium for Southeast Europe

On 5 November 1937, Hitler secretly addressed the four most senior military commanders and the Reich Foreign Minister von Ribbentrop. He told them that force should be used against Austria and Czechoslovakia to assert German demands,[1] and the German High Command was instructed to be ready for a war soon. German business was likewise getting ready to mobilize. The Military Supply & Economics Unit at the High Command (OKW) and the Four-Year Plan Authority calculated the volume of petroleum needed to wage war,[2] and this led the General Commissioner for Special Issues of Chemical Production, Carl Krauch, to affirm in April 1939 that *"our economic region in Greater Germany is too small to completely cover the petroleum volume we need for a wartime economy."*[3] At this point in time, Austria and the Sudeten territories were already occupied and preparations to attack

1 Cf. Wilhelm Deist et al., *Das Deutsche Reich und der Zweite Weltkrieg*, Vol. 1: *Ursachen und Voraussetzungen der deutschen Kriegspolitik*, Stuttgart 1979, 522.

2 Cf. Eichholtz, *Deutsche Ölpolitik*, 287.

3 As cited in: ibid.

Poland were in full swing. The Military Supply & Economics Unit had therefore devised a strategy of forming a Southeast and Central European economic area led by Germany, with a key role to be played by Romanian oil deposits. In a treatise by the Reich Office for Economic Construction of July-August 1939, plans were fleshed out for creating a large European economic area with 20 European countries inside it.

To what extent the German oil companies were involved in these plans to "survive blockades" and prepare for war is unclear. There can be no doubt, however, that the dramatic political developments were being followed very closely by most corporate executives. After the occupation of Austria in March and after the Sudeten territories had been carved out of Czechoslovakia in October 1938, shifts in who controlled what in Southeast Europe were on the cards. The German oil majors wanted to be ready, and at the end of December 1938 they agreed to form a consortium to explore for oil in the Danube region.[4]

Gewerkschaft Elwerath had the most experience in prospecting for oil in southeastern Europe from the days of drilling pioneer Anton Raky. Elwerath was also the company that prompted the founding of the Southeast European consortium. The occasion for the first meeting was a concession deal that Wilhelm Keppler, State Secretary in the German Foreign Office and Director of the Reich Office for Georesearch, had negotiated in early December 1938 with the Carpatho-Ukrainian State Government. It was approved by the corporate representatives present, namely Schunck for Elwerath, Grosse, Schlicht, and Kraiss for DPAG/DEA, Zentgraf and Hoffmann for Wintershall, and Franke for Preussag.

The Allies had assigned the territory of Carpatho-Ukraine to the Republic of Czechoslovakia after the collapse of the Aus-

---

4 Cf. note: Besprechung über Konsortialarbeit im Donauraum, 29.12.1938, WD-CA, D-BBW-1.

tro-Hungarian Empire,[5] but the autonomy the government in Prague had promised existed only on paper. With Slovakia proclaiming its independence in the wake of the early October 1938 Sudeten Crisis and the concomitant destruction of the Republic of Czechoslovakia, an autonomous government formed on 11 October 1938 in Carpatho-Ukraine.[6]

Gesellschaft für praktische Lagerstättenforschung GmbH, Berlin, and the four oil majors concluded a deal which laid the basis for developing oil in Carpatho-Ukraine for "*German circles*".[7] The idea was to exploit two smaller oil deposits near the village of Luh and Yasinia since DPAG/DEA's chief geologist Alfred Kraiss[8] had studied the terrain and developed an exploration and development strategy. The concession areas on offer were not really promising in economic terms and, as the company executives quickly realized, it was political motives that counted, which is why they put in claims for Reich grants.

The contract between Gesellschaft für praktische Lagerstättenforschung and the Carpatho-Ukraine state government was never important, since Hungary did not recognize the new state and proceeded to occupy it and annex it in March 1939. Irrespective of this, the four German oil companies continued to discuss their collaboration in developing oil deposits in Central and Southeast Europe, and in March 1939 they founded a consortium,[9] with each corporation

5 Cf. Christian Ganzer, *Die Karpato-Ukraine 1938/39. Spielball im internationalen Interessenkonflikt am Vorabend des Zweiten Weltkriegs*, Hamburg 2001.

6 After the Second World War, most of Carpatho-Ukraine had to be ceded by the Czechoslovak Republic to the Soviet Union.

7 Cf. transcript draft contract, 7.12.1938, WD-CA, D-BBW-1.

8 Alfred Kraiss (1885–1979): Studied geology in Munich, Kiel and Berlin, doctorate, from 1911 employee of the Prussian Geological Survey in Berlin. In 1912 he was the first German geologist to join the DEA on a full-time basis. From 1918 DEA chief geologist. Habilitation in 1931, lectures in petroleum geology at the Technical Universities of Berlin and Hanover. 1938 associate professor, 1952 retirement.

9 Cf. memo, Stand der Angelegenheit betr. Zusammenarbeit DPAG, Elwerath, Preussag, Wintershall am 17.3.1939, ibid.

holding an equal stake in it. DPAG/DEA was appointed the lead for the Protectorate of Bohemia and Moravia as well as Slovakia, while Wintershall was in charge of Hungary operations, Elwerath for Yugoslavia, and Preussag for Romania.[10] The consortium members thereupon set about trying to gain an idea of geological conditions in the countries in question and identified the concessions that interested them.[11] Negotiations were then started with the relevant governments on concluding concession agreements.

On 10 June 1939, the Slovakian government and DPAG signed a contract on "searching for and exploiting bitumen", although it excluded the oil region of Egbell (Gbely), where oil had been in production since 1914. In 1937, Gbely together with the Göding field in Moravia was pumping about 18,000 t, and in November 1939 the contract was then expanded to include the promising oil deposits in Gbely, too.[12]

DPAG/DEA acted on behalf of the consortium, which received exclusive rights to prospect for oil, natural gas, and bitumen in the region in question. In the case of oil being produced, a crude oil levy of 12 to 22 percent of the volume produced was payable to the Slovakian government, to be delivered to the state refinery in Dubova. The approx. 600 Slovak blue and white-collar workers employed in the Gbely oil field were all taken on by DPAG.[13] The Gbely oil field made only a marginal contribution to the German war effort, and all in all, the consortium remained of only subordinate importance to DEA. By far the most important oil deposits in Europe were to be found in Romania.[14]

---

10 Cf. Albert E. Gunther, *Der deutsche Krieg um Erdöl in Europa 1934–1945*, Kapitel XI – Auslandsunternehmungen.

11 Cf. note, 8.9.1939, WD-CA, D-RW-533.

12 Cf. contract between the slovak state and the DPAG, 13.11.1939, WD-CA, D-RW-533.

13 Cf. Jahresberichte der Erdölbetriebe, WD-CA, 4112–1274/1275.

14 Cf. Eichholtz, *Deutsche Ölpolitik*, 281–361.

The DEA and Olex joint venture

By 1931, DPAG/DEA had sold all the shares in its well-versed distribution organization, Olex GmbH, to APOC. Even after the sale, however, Olex contributed to handling the sales of its petroleum products. The Olex HQ was located in the "DEA Building" at Martin Luther Strasse 61-66 in Berlin's Schöneberg district, so executives in both corporations had only to take the stairs to continue their negotiations. People knew one another and appreciated the proximity.

When the Nazis took power, British state-owned Olex was plunged into crisis, as Berlin Nazi functionaries viewed it as a "Jewish corporation".[15] At the instruction of the British parent company, in May 1933 it thereupon fired almost all the Jewish staff, more than 30 men and women in total. The Nazi Party then confirmed that Olex was an "Aryan company",[16] so Olex was able to "smoothly" continue its business inside the Third Reich and until just before the outbreak of war procured crude oil from its parent company.[17]

Benzolverband (the Benzene Association), meanwhile, was increasingly interested in exercising a greater influence on the Olex Supervisory Board. Ullner, who chaired the Olex Supervisory Board, tried to avert the association and interest it in something else. He was helped here by the "aryanization" in Austria, which also impacted on the Czechoslovak economy, and in March 1938 he turned to Kimmich and suggested that after "aryanization", Fanto AG should go to the Benzolverband.[18] Fanto AG was a corporation established in roughly 1878 by Viennese family Fanto and had grown to be one of the largest oil corporations in the Austro-Hungarian Empire.[19] After

---

15 Cf. Karlsch/Stokes, *Faktor Öl*, 161f.

16 Cf. Protokoll der Aufsichtsratssitzung vom 9.5.1933, WD-CA, D-RW-278.

17 Cf. Olex-Aufsichtsratssitzung, 7.12.1939, WD-CA, 14-2-3083.

18 Cf. Kimmich an Hermann J. Abs, Kimmich, 21.3.1938, HADB, P 1659, sheet 65.

19 Cf. *Fanto Benzin Aktiengesellschaft*, in: Wikipedia, https://de.wikipedia.org/wiki/Fanto_Benzin_Aktiengesellschaft [last retrieved on 20.06.2024].

the end of the First World War, Fanto AG had increasingly relocated its activities to the Republic of Czechoslovakia, where its main plant was based in Pardubice, some 100 kilometres east of Prague.

Kimmich took up Ullner's suggestion and requested that his CEO Hermann J. Abs turn to "its fraynds" at Fanto AG and make certain that they only sold to Benzolverband. This is what then happened a few weeks later.

With the beginning of the war, Olex was cut off from APOC in London, which made it harder for the company to procure petroleum. All that it could still do was offer more German petroleum products instead and try and establish strong links to DEA. In December 1939, Olex and DEA concluded an interest-pooling agreement,[20] and the British company thus placed itself under the protective wing of DEA, hoping this would enable it to better ward off the tentacles of the German state. DEA benefited economically from the deal.

Richard F. Ullner played a decisive part in the interest-pooling agreement coming about. In 1940, he withdrew from the function of chair of the DEA Management Board and moved to the Supervisory Board, but remained Chair of the Olex Supervisory Board at the same time. His intention was to tie Olex as closely as possible to DEA but to preserve the distribution company's operational independence, since the experienced banker saw no point in completely burning the bridges to the British state corporation. Georg Gubisch, a Nazi, was made Olex Managing Director.

Just how far-sighted the interest-pooling agreement was first emerged in spring 1940. The Reich Office for Petroleum and the Reich Economics Ministry exerted pressure to ensure Olex, as a British company, was excluded from importing Romanian oil. Ullner and Gubisch protested against the step,[21] and the Reich Office

---

20 Cf. Interessengemeinschaftsvertrag zwischen der DEA and der Olex GmbH, 30.12.1939, WD-CA, D-RW-47.

21 Cf. Olex-Aufsichtsratssitzung, 3.4.1940, WD-CA, 14-2-3083.

responded that the top of the Olex hierarchy ended at British Prime Minster Churchill.[22] The other subsidiaries of major foreign parent companies, namely Rhenania and DPAG, were rated more favourably, especially as DPAG participated in establishing a hydrogenation plant in Pöhlitz.

Olex also had a tough time of things at the Reich Economics Ministry. Ernst R. Fischer, Head of the Oil section at the ministry, intimated that among German oil industry circles there was much criticism of the continued existence of Olex, as DEA was not able to completely utilize Olex's distribution capacities on its own. Fischer would have liked to see Olex sold to Rheinische AG für Braunkohlenbergbau, Cologne (Rheinbraun),[23] since after the end of the war, he said, the company would be taken over anyway.

Ullner regarded these proposals as unacceptable. He played for time and tried to keep rivals at arm's length from Olex for as long as possible. After the "Decree on the Treatment of Enemy Assets" came into force on 15 January 1940, attorney-at-law Hans Wöstendiek was appointed administrator of Olex in August 1940.[24] He had already worked for a long time with DEA and had a good relationship with Ullner.

In summer 1940, Olex lost its status as a partner among equals in the German lubricants cartel at the instruction of the Reich Office for Petroleum,[25] and its cartel quota went to DEA. From 1934 onwards, DEA and Olex had formed a quota partnership, with Olex benefitting from DEA's "partner prices". When Olex lost its quota,

---

22 Cf. Notiz betr.: Unterredung mit Reichsstelle für Mineralöl am 13.3.40, WD-CA, D-RW-52.

23 Notiz: Besuch bei Dr. Fischer (RMW), 23.9.1940, ibid.

24 Cf. Abschrift: Bestallung für einen Verwalter, 14.8.1940, D-RW-586; cf. Stephan H. Lindner, *Das Reichskommissariat für die Behandlung feindlichen Vermögens im Zweiten Weltkrieg. Eine Studie zur Verwaltungs-, Rechts- and Wirtschaftsgeschichte des nationalsozialistischen Deutschlands*, Stuttgart 1991, 71ff.

25 Cf. DEA: Aktennotiz, 27.7.1940, D-RW-280.

however, DEA terminated the lubricants contract and introduced new pricing models.[26]

DEA's competitors continued to try and gain access to the "enemy assets". In the summer of 1941, the Reich Economics Ministry indicated to the Benzolverband, as the leading fuels manufacturer in the German Reich, that it would be able to acquire Olex. The Reich Commissioner for the Treatment of Enemy Assets decreed that in a first step a representative of the Benzolverband must be included in an Olex advisory council that he instructed be established.[27] Olex and both Ullner and Wöstendiek opposed the plan.[28] While they succeeded in blocking a sale, they could not prevent the director of the benzene association, Oskar Ruperti, being mandatorily included on the advisory council.[29] Subsequently, there was repeatedly tension on the advisory council between Benzolverband and DEA. In the final instance, Benzolverband was prevented from taking over Olex primarily by the fact that the war was increasingly going against the Third Reich. As a result, through to the end of the war Olex remained tied to DEA. Without the long-standing interaction between the main players at DEA and Olex, this would have been impossible.

The German managing director of Olex, Georg Gubisch, gave a blazing speech on New Year's Eve 1944, urging the employees – who were all listening – to hold out. At this point, about 900 Olex staff members had been called up for active duty in the Wehrmacht. Gubisch praised their heroic courage, did not wish to tolerate any vacillation, and felt there were no grounds for viewing Olex's future pessimistically.[30] Ullner did not comment on Gubisch's speech.

26 Cf. DEA an Olex, 30.6.1942, ibid.
27 Cf. Reichskommissar für die Behandlung feindlicher Vermögen an Ullner, 9.6.1941, D-RW-586.
28 Cf. Wöstendiek an Ullner, 30.1.1943, ibid.
29 Cf. Olex-Beiratsratssitzung, 5.11.1942, WD-CA, 14-2-3083.
30 Cf. Gubisch an Ullner, 4.1.1945, WD-CA, D-RW-52.

Administration of Pechelbronner Erdölwerke

The chequered nature of Franco-German history from the 18th to the 20th centuries is perfectly reflected in the small oil fields near Pechelbronn in Alsace. The commercial exploitation of the oil deposits there commenced in 1735, and from 1759 onwards it was successfully expanded over four generations by the Le Bel family. The family company improved production by digging shafts to mine oil sands and seepage oil. Later, oil was also obtained by drilling wells and pumping.[31] After the 1870–1 war with France, the German Reich seized Alsace, and in 1899 the Le Bel family sold its company to Pechelbronner Ölbergwerke, a firm owned by prosperous Alsatian entrepreneurs. They, in turn, sold the company along with others to Deutsche Tiefbohr AG (DTAG), the predecessor of DEA, in 1906.[32] DTAG had at that time already acquired two other oil firms in Alsace: Gewerkschafft Gute Hoffnung in Durrenbach and Elsässische Petroleum Gesellschaft in Biblisheim. DTAG merged these new acquisitions to form "Vereinigte Pechelbronner Ölbergwerke AG". Oil production was considerably boosted with DTAG at the helm, the number of oil shafts sunk increased, and the pumping stations were connected by pipelines to the refineries in Biblisheim, Durrenbach, Soultz, and Merkwiller.

After the end of the First World War, Alsace-Lorraine reverted to France. Vereinigte Pechelbronner Ölbergwerke AG was promptly sequestered and nationalized, and the French government subsequently leased the company to *Société Alsacienne d'Etudes*

---

31 For the history of the Pechelbronner Erdölwerke cf. esp. the dissertation of René Walther, *Pechelbronn*. In contrast to the printed version, the unprinted longer version of the dissertation also contains a number of tables and footnotes. Chapter X of the unprinted version is therefore quoted below. I would like to thank Friederike Steensen for sending me the unprinted version.

32 Cf. Geheim: Karl Große: Bericht betr. die früheren Vereinigten Pechelbronner Ölbergwerke AG, Berlin-Schöneberg 28.6.1940, WD-CA, D-RW-387. The 25-page report, including extensive annexes, can also be found in the file WD-CA, 14-2-4400 (Treuhandverwaltung Pechelbronn).

Fig. 48 Oil operations in Pechelbronn (around 1920)

Minières (SAEM) in 1921. Crude oil production, in part from wells and in part from a network of shafts running some 300 kilometres, was increased as of that point in time, with SAEM ramping output up from approx. 51,000 t to an average of 70,000 t a year. Crude oil processing was handled by the modern refinery in Merkwiller-Pechelbronn, which churned out a slightly higher figure of more than 100,000 t per year from 1930.[33]

In August 1922, DEA filed for compensation from the Reich Compensation Office to cover the loss of its Pechelbronn operations. After a seven-year tussle, the RCO granted the company a payment totalling 5.7 million Reichsmark,[34] on top of which there were 828,000 Reichsmark as compensation for the loss of Allgemeine Bohrgesellschaft.

---

33 Cf. ibid.

34 Cf. Aktennotiz: Pechelbronn – Entschädigungsverfahren, 2.7.1940, ibid.

After the Second World War began, the oil deposits in Alsace came back into focus. The OKW set up Economic Troop Units that were meant to follow in the van of the combat troops in order to gain an overview of existing resources in the occupied territories.[35] As it became clear that the French Armed Forces were fast crumbling, in mid-May 1940 Karl Grosse approached the Head of the Oil Group in the Raw Materials section of the OKW's Military Supply & Economics Unit, Naval Captain Gottfried Griebel. (In 1940 Grosse, together with Erich Greiser and Günther Schlicht, headed DEA's oil operations management, which had been relocated from Wietze to Schöneberg in Berlin in April 1940.) Grosse insisted that if Pechelbronn were occupied, it should be DEA alone that managed all the oil operations there and that all other companies be excluded from participation.[36] He stated that the necessary personnel for the takeover would consist of men who had worked in Pechelbronn prior to 1918. Griebel agreed.

In the wake of the meeting, a DEA commando unit was set up under Grosse,[37] who was appointed commissioner accordingly by the OKW and the Reich Economics Ministry. Moreover, Dr Brandte (refinery operations), pit inspector Heinrich Tegtmeier (shaft operations), Klaus Wolf (drilling operations) and other staff members familiar with Pechelbronn operations were onboarded.[38] German units broke through the Maginot Line near Lembach on 19 June 1940, and on 21 June the DEA commando unit headed through the narrow breach and reached Pechelbronn. There were great risks attached to such a boots-on-the-ground approach, as the DEA men were not in uniform and could, had they been captured, have been

---

[35] Cf. Gottfried Griebel, *Deutsche Mineralölprobleme,* manuscript Bad Münder 1950.

[36] Cf. DEA-Vorstand: Notiz über den Besuch bei Fregattenkapitän Griebel am 17.5.1940, Vertraulich, WD-CA, D-RW-387.

[37] Cf. Gunther, *Der deutsche Krieg um Erdöl*, Chapter XII.

[38] Cf. Geheim: Karl Große: Bericht betr. die früheren Vereinigten Pechelbronner Ölbergwerke AG, Berlin-Schöneberg 28.6.1940, WD-CA, D-RW-387.

Fig. 49 Mine in Pechelbronn destroyed by French army engineers (1940)

sentenced as spies.[39] Yet given the pending French capitulation, Grosse and his men seem to have been fairly sure of themselves.

Why, or so asks French historian René Walther, did Grosse take such a huge risk? He explains the haste to occupy the oil plants with reference to the militarization of the German business world and the wish to take revenge for 1918.[40] As already mentioned above, shortly after joining DEA, Grosse had been instructed by General Director Noellenburg in 1915 to expand the oil shafts in Pechelbronn. He evidently took great satisfaction from his triumphant return to Pechelbronn, and with his commando unit he gained the reputation of being an energetic and fearless daredevil. His unit was also meant to prevent any of the plants being destroyed, but French

---

39 Cf. Griebel, *Deutsche Mineralölprobleme*.

40 Cf. Walther, *Pechelbronn*, Chapter X, 13.

army engineers had set fire to the tank farm and part of the refinery shortly before beating a retreat, with a vacuum unit destroyed in the process and part of the oil shafts blown up.[41] That said, damage to the oil fields was minimal, as the detonations had been conducted on the fly and hence poorly executed. Only two days after the occupation, Grosse was tasked with securing the oil factories with military means.[42]

In the countries occupied by German troops, the predominant policy was to rely on trustee management of the conquered assets, and only in a few cases was ownership of the assets transferred.[43] Not until after the end of the war were ownership issues finally regulated, and it went without question that the German companies acting as trustees were meant to have first dibs. The situation in Alsace was different, though, given its chequered history, and issues of ownership were left unresolved for some time.

After the French capitulation, various German companies applied to the OKW to be permitted to strip the assets of industrial plants. On 16 August 1940, the General Commissioner for Special Issue in the Chemicals Industry, Carl Krauch, therefore sent the OKW a list of French refineries that he wished to use in the German Reich.[44] Prof. Ernst Terres, Managing Director of Edeleanu-Gesellschaft, a wholly owned DEA subsidiary, must have caught wind of this, as he filed a similar request to OKW three days later, asking

---

41 Cf. W. Geistert an Rudolf Dittrich, 22.1.1971, WD-CA, 3000-518; Gunther, *Der deutsche Krieg um Erdöl*.

42 Cf. Bericht des Beauftragten des OKW and des Reichswirtschaftsministeriums zur Wiederinbetriebnahme der früheren Vereinigten Pechelbronner Ölbergwerke, BArch Freiburg, Rüstungsinspektion V, Stuttgart, RW 20-5/41.

43 Cf. Dietrich Eichholtz, *Geschichte der deutschen Kriegswirtschaft, 1939–1945*, Vol. 1: 1939–1941, Berlin 1969, 195f.

44 Cf. Krauch an OKW, 16.8.1940, BArch Freiburg, Rüstungsinspektion V, Stuttgart, RW 20-5/41.

whether DEA might take down the French refinery plant and transport it to the German Reich.[45] None of these plans were realized.

In early November 1940, DEA applied to Armaments Inspectorate Stuttgart for confiscation of two French rotary drill sets that they wanted moved to Pechelbronn in order to increase access to the deposits there,[46] and the application was duly approved. Later on, DEA again sought to gain access to French plant and equipment, hence in March 1941 Schlicht filed for allocation of well-preserved parts of a cracker plant and pumps from the discontinued Dunkirk refinery. In April 1941, the Reich Economics Ministry approved heating oil pumps from the Port Jerome refinery being taken over by the DEA plant in Rositz.[47]

By that point, Pechelbronner Erdölwerke had been completely integrated into the DEA Group, and the executive positions had been filled with DEA managers and operational structures aligned to those inside the Reich.[48] The new director was Karl Grosse's son-in-law Klaus Wolf, whose father had been a senior executive in Pechelbronn before 1918.[49] Wolf had good links to his French predecessor and was described by the French staff as a man who kept his distance from the Nazis.[50] After he was posted to Karpathen Öl AG in the autumn of 1942, his place was taken by Paul Krau.[51] Less than ten DEA employees from the "Old Reich" were active in the Pechelbronner Erdölwerke head office,[52] and most of

---

45 Cf. note, telefonische Anfrage Prof. Terres ans OKW, 19.8.1940, ibid.

46 Cf. Rüstungs-Inspektion Wehrkreis V, Stuttgart an OKW, 7.11.1940, ibid.

47 Cf. Aktenvermerk 28.3.1941, betr.: Antrag Schlicht; Einverständniserklärung RWM 24.4.1941, ibid.

48 Cf. Walther, *Pechelbronn*, chapter X, 25–28.

49 Cf. ibid.

50 Cf. ibid., 25. Indirect confirmation of this assessment can be found in his personnel file. (Dipl. Ing. Klaus Wolf, 18.7.1904, Ludwigshafen WD-CA, PA Wietze). Accordingly, Wolf had to be transferred within the company in 1937 due to a conflict with the DAF.

51 Cf. ibid., 26; Krau, *Kohle, Öl und Krieg*, 93.

52 Cf. Gunther, *Der deutsche Krieg um Erdöl*, Chapter XII, 9.

the salaried staff were French. The Nazi Party organizations now started to gain a foothold in Alsace with both Deutsche Arbeitsfront (DAF) and "Opferring Elsass" ("Alsace Circle of Sacrifice", the preliminary stage before full Nazi Party membership) going into action in autumn 1940.[53]

The French production programmes were simply continued, and the parts of the refinery French troops had damaged were fully back in working order by spring 1941. After six months of the occupation, oil processing was almost back at the pre-war level, and despite members of the Alsatian population being conscripted into the Wehrmacht and the Reich Labour Service (RAD), the payroll as good as held steady. From 1943 onwards, POWs and slave labour were deployed, accounting for four percent of the total staff in 1943 and seven percent in 1944 and therefore well below the figures for the other DEA sites.[54]

Payroll at Erdölwerke Pechelbronn – from 1940 to 1944[55]

Year	**Blue-collar workers**	**White-collar staff**	**Total**	**of which:** foreigners	POWs
1940	1,274	215	1,489		
1941	1,953	316	2,269		
1942	2,043	341	2,384	12	0
1943	2,004	362	2,366	15	85
1944	2,011	328	2,339	99	71

The top management at DEA played through the pros and cons of repurchasing Pechelbronner Erdölwerke. In the event of a buyback, the sum would have to be netted against the compensation

53 Cf. Lothar Kettenacker, *Nationalsozialistische Volkstumspolitik im* Elsass, Stuttgart 1973, 207ff.

54 Cf. Walther, *Pechelbronn*, Chapter X, 31.

55 Compiled according to: *ibid.*

payment.[56] DEA Chairman Schirner rejected a repurchase in wartime.[57]

Prior to the war, as part of his appeasement policy Hitler had declared he would forgo reincorporating Alsace-Lorraine into the German Reich.[58] The issue was not included in the ceasefire negotiations, and Hitler transferred civil administration of Alsace to the Reichsstatthalter of Baden, Robert Wagner.[59] Alsace and Lorraine were not formally treated as part of the German Reich, but in practice Wagner did everything to "re-Germanize" Alsace and integrate it into the German war economy, hence what followed was a covert annexation. The line of the border was moved westwards to follow that of the border in 1871. Alsace was then attached to Gau Baden and the Gau Upper Rhine was formed, with Lorraine attached to Gau Saar-Palatinate and the Gau Westmark created.

There were unresolved legal issues, as SAEM insisted that Pechelbronner Erdölwerke was not Alsatian property but owned by the French state and therefore protested against its sequestration. Nevertheless, the civil administration urged DEA in December 1940 to conclude a lease agreement, and the leading German oil geologist, Alfred Bentz, was asked to offer an expert opinion on the draft of the agreement. His evaluation stated that the technically difficult production of oil in the Pechelbronner field would only be possible at the level of about 50,000 t of oil for a maximum of a further eight years.[60] Bentz gave a subdued rating accordingly for its economic viability and proposed a low lease rate of 2.5 percent of the annual

---

56 There is no evidence that the Foreign Office objected to the repurchase, as Thomas Sandkühler assumes in Thomas Sandkühler, *"Endlösung" in Galizien. Der Judenmord in Ostpolen und die Rettungsinitiative von Berthold Beitz 1941–1944*, Bonn 1966, 294.

57 Cf. excerpt from a file note by Schirner, 7.5.1943, WD-CA, D-RW-387.

58 Cf. Kettenacker, *Nationalsozialistische Volkstumspolitik*, 32–44.

59 Cf. ibid., 59–75.

60 Cf. DEA an den Chef der Zivilverwaltung im Elsass, 8.4.1941, WD-CA, D-RW-387.

gross crude oil output.[61] His report reinforced Schirner's scepticism as regarded concluding a lease or purchase deal.

In autumn 1941, it was still unclear how the negotiations between the German Ceasefire Commission and the French ceasefire delegation for economic affairs would pan out for the liquidation of French corporations in Alsace-Lorraine. The civil administration expected the "*swift liquidation of assets held by enemies of the people and the Reich*" and sought a "*definitive purge of ownership*".[62] DEA was therefore asked to file a purchase offer, and the pending negotiations on a lease contract were discontinued.

Robert Wagner, as head of the civil administration, was increasingly dissatisfied with the sluggishness of the negotiations conducted by the Ceasefire Commission, and in December 1941 he took matters into his own hands. He issued a decree on the utilization of confiscated French assets and disposed at will of the assets of Alsatians who had been expatriated and French government assets.[63] The civil administration now wanted to sell Pechelbronner Erdölwerke to DEA for a good price, so Rheinische-Treuhandgesellschaft, Mannheim, was instructed to pave the way for the sale.

DEA tabled an offer in the summer of 1942, but the two sides were still a long way apart.[64] The DEA negotiating team was led by Karl Grosse with the support of DEA lawyer Hugo Griebel and Klaus Wolf. The director of the civil administration's economics unit, Günther Bung, insisted in September 1942 that DEA issue a binding commitment to the sale,[65] but Grosse played for time and refused a takeover, citing the lack of a fundamental valuation. DEA wanted to commit its cash to more lucrative oil fields in other occu-

61 Cf. Alfred Bentz an den Chef der Zivilverwaltung im Elsass, Straßburg, betr.: Pachtvertrag der DEA Treuhandverwaltung Pechelbronn, Schreiben vom 17.12.1940, 4.4.1941, ibid.

62 Cf. Aktenvermerk Bung, 19.9.1941, ibid.

63 Cf. Kettenacker, *Nationalsozialistische Volkstumspolitik*, 159.

64 Cf. Aktenvermerk, Übernahme von Pechelbronn, 23.9.1942, WD-CA, D-RW-387.

65 Cf. Aktennotiz, 21.9.1941, ibid.

pied countries, depending on how the war went, and eventually the two sides agreed that trusteeship would be extended until the end of 1942. Talks on the purchase price continued, with both sides agreeing that "*there was no German interest in giving the French unnecessarily high liquidation proceeds*".[66]

Not until May 1943 did the civil administration and DEA agree on the mainstays of the contract.[67] Schirner had first stated his reticence once again about approving a purchase, since he was in no doubt that, in purely business terms, DEA would not benefit at all from a takeover. The DEA Supervisory Board Chair Kimmich was of a similar opinion, and he put on record that DEA would acquire Pechelbronner Werke for 6.75 million Reichsmark, commenting: "*It's not a good deal, particularly given that the oil reserves there are fast drying up.*"[68] The group, he said, was not able to withstand the pressure from the civil administration any longer. Nevertheless, the purchase negotiations came to nothing, particularly since the Foreign Office had reservations.[69]

Given the course of the war, DEA concentrated its efforts on sites that promised the highest oil output in the short term: Neusiedl in the "Ostmark" and Heide in Holstein. In Pechelbronn, the fields were being rapidly depleted, on top of which, in 1943 rotary drilling systems were removed from Pechelbronn and transported to Slovakia.[70] As a result, the number of exploratory wells drilled in Pechelbronn slumped.

On 3 August 1944, the US Air Force bombed the Merkwiller refinery.[71] Part of the plant was destroyed, leading to a sharp drop in production, but repairs of the skimming plant were nevertheless

---

66 note, Pachtvertrag Pechelbronn, 23.9.1941, ibid.

67 Cf. Verhandlungen mit dem CdZ über den Erwerb von Pechelbronn vom 11.5.1943, ibid.

68 Cf. Notiz Kimmich, 14.5.1943, HADB, P 1660, sheet 134.

69 Cf. Aufsichtsratssitzung vom 14.4.1944; Walther, *Pechelbronn*, chapter X, 19.

70 Cf. Walther, *Pechelbronn*, chapter X, 39.

71 Cf. ibid., 45–51.

successful – at least until it was destroyed during the German retreat on 10 December 1944. The US Army nevertheless had to pull back from parts of Alsace and thus Pechelbronn during the last German offensive on the Western Front, codenamed "Nordwind", from 31 December 1944 to 25 January 1945.

Works manager Paul Krau arrived back in Pechelbronn on 30 January 1945 and issued instructions for immediate repairs to be made.[72] Engineers and materials were taken from other DEA sites in order to help with the refinery rebuild, and despite the lack of materials and labour, oil production and refining resumed in February 1945. The strategy of perseverance didn't work, and by the time German troops withdrew from Pechelbronn on 17 March 1945 only a few tons of oil had been produced.[73]

Oil production in Alsace was of limited importance for the war effort. In the occupation years, DEA at least managed to hold output steady, with Pechelbronn contributing about 10 percent of DEA's total oil production during the war.[74]

Oil production in Pechelbronn 1938–44 (in tonnes)[75]

Year	Crude oil from wells	Crude oil mined	Total
1938	41,601	29,900	71,807
1939	39,371	30,187	69,559
1940	31,736	19,491	51,000
1941	34,585	23,520	59,108
1942	39,095	25,903	65,998
1943	43,195	24,122	67,317
1944			58,724

72 Cf. Krau an Schlicht, 16.2.1945, WD-CA, D-RW-387; Krau, *Kohle, Öl und Krieg*, 112.
73 Cf. Walther, *Pechelbronn*, chapter X, 68.
74 Cf. ibid., 24.
75 Compiled according to: Gunther, *Der deutsche Krieg um Erdöl*, chapter XI, 5.

Karpathen Öl AG

The Beskid companies

The oil deposits in Galicia did not play a special role in the thinking of either the Reich agencies or DEA after the Germans invaded Poland. The complicated ownership structures in the Polish oil industry and their meagre productivity meant restraint seemed in order. About 40 percent of the capital was in French hands, 30 percent owned by the Polish state, and just short of 30 percent belonged to Polish private individuals, with small stakes held by Belgian and American companies or entrepreneurs.[76]

The Galician oil deposits ran along the northern edge of the Carpathian Mountains for 350 km and were about 60 km wide, amounting to some 20,000 km2. About half the oil was produced in the Boryslav region, and one quarter each in East and West Galicia.[77] The Polish oil industry's prime capital was its superbly skilled employees, a fact grudgingly accepted even by the German oil industry experts, who felt they were superior to the Poles.[78]

After the Polish Army capitulated, at the end of September 1939 the country was occupied for the fourth time in its tormented history. West Poland went to the German Reich, the East to the Soviet Union. Between the annexed Polish territories, all that remained was the General Government (GG) as Polish territory. While it belonged to the Reich in the broader sense, it was an "ancillary country" with sovereignty in terms of customs tariffs and its own currency. The GG came directly under Hitler, meaning it

---

76 Cf. Schreiben von Klaus Dietel (Abwickler) an das Landgericht Lüneburg in der Armenrechtssache Siebzehner gegen Karpathen Öl AG i.L. vom 22.1.1965, Archiv der BEB Hannover, L-165, "Karpathen Öl AG".

77 Cf. Oil Fields Investigation, Part VIII/2, Oil and Gas Fields of Poland. Development and Exploitation up to 1943 (unpublished).

78 Bericht über die Lage im ostgalizischen Ölgebiet 1941 vom 12. Juli 1941, BArch Berlin, R 52, I/8.

was not subject to control by the specialist Reich ministries. As of 26 October 1939, the GG civil administration was headed by Hans Frank,[79] whom Hitler entrusted with executing a "devil's task". The GG was to "purge" the old and new Reich territories of all "Jews, Polacks, and scum"; hence it was here that the Nazi genocide commenced and reached its ghastly climax.[80]

What was supposed to happen with the economy in vanquished Poland was a matter of some controversy. While Göring's line was initially to completely rob the country of its industrial base, others in the Berlin ministries were more interested in maintaining specific elements of industry that had potential.[81] Both approaches shared an emphasis on ruthlessly exploiting Polish raw material and labour resources, but in early December 1939 the tables turned more in favour of maintaining the industrial corporations, with the Director of the Economics Main Section at the GG, Walter Emmerich, championing the idea of an economy run on a "colonial scale".[82]

Relations between Berlin and Cracow, the seat of the GG government, were tense from the outset[83] with various conflicts, not least over the approach adopted for the oil industry. On 14 December 1939, Cavalry Captain of the Reserves Erich Will, previously Director of Pits at Gewerkschaft Elwerath, was made Acting Head

---

79 Cf. Müller's comments on the role of Frank in: Bernhard R. Kroener et al. (Eds.), *Das Deutsche Reich und der Zweite Weltkrieg. Organisation und Mobilisierung des deutschen Machtbereichs – Teilband 2: Kriegsverwaltung, Wirtschaft und personelle Ressourcen 1942 bis 1944/45*, Stuttgart 1999.

80 Cf. Gerhard Eisenblätter, *Grandlinien der Politik des Reiches gegenüber dem Generalgouvernement 1939–1945*, PhD thesis Frankfurt/M. 1969; Mechthild Rössler/Sabine Schleiermacher (Eds.), *Der "Generalplan Ost". Hauptlinien der nationalsozialistischen Planungs- and Vernichtungspolitik*, Berlin 1993.

81 Cf. Czeslaw Madajczyk, *Die Okkupationspolitik Nazideutschlands in Polen 1939–1945*, Cologne 1988.

82 Vortrag des Leiters der HA-Wirtschaft, Dr. Emmerich, vom 6.6.1942 an der Verwaltungsakademie Krakau über die gewerbliche Wirtschaft im GG, BArch Berlin, RG/52/I.

83 Cf. Eisenblätter, *Grundlinien*.

of Oil Operations in the GG.[84] In addition to trustee administration, the GG government wanted to exercise direct influence on the restructuring of the Polish oil industry, to which end Will was deployed as "Special Commissioner for the GG Oil Industry" from mid-1940. When he was reposted in autumn 1941 to the Caucasus project, when the Wehrmacht attempted not only to get as far as Moscow, but also to seize the Caucasus, he was succeeded by Walther Birnbaum, legal officer at Mansfeld AG.

Parallel to the activities by the GG, the OKW and the Reich Economics Ministry insisted the previous oil entrepreneurs in West Galicia be removed from operational functions and these be transferred to a consortium of German oil companies. The consortium thereupon founded the "Beskid Companies" on 20 October 1939.

The following corporations had a stake of 50,000 Reichsmark each in Beskiden Erdöl-Gewinnungsgesellschaft mbH, Berlin: DEA, Gewerkschaft Elwerath, Preussag, Schachtbau und Tiefbohrgesellschaft mbH (merged into Kohle-Öl Union von Busse K.G.), and Wintershall AG. The following had a stake in Beskiden Erdöl-Verarbeitungsgesellschaft mbH, Berlin: Gewerkschaft Neue Erdöl Raffinerie (Nerag) (of 100,000 Reichsmark), as well as DPAG, Deutsche Gasolin AG, and Wintershall AG with 50,000 Reichsmark each.

Wintershall AG had the lead slightly with regard to posting executives of the Beskid companies, as it held multiple participations, alongside the parent company, and its subsidiary held Nerag

---

84 Dr. Erich Will, a brother-in-law of Hugo Stinnes, was the mine manager of the Elwerath trade union from 1926 to 1942. In the fall of 1941 he was transferred to the Mineral Oil Command (K)aukasus, where he headed the Mineral Oil Technical Brigade. He was killed in a plane crash on August 9, 1942. (cf. Bericht über die deutsche Ölexpedition in den Kaukasus, Archiv der Bundesanstalt für Bodenforschung, No. 58277; Helmut Fahrion, *Die Gewerkschaft Elwerath. Chronik eines Erdölunternehmens 1866–1969*, Hanover 1987.)

shares.[85] The first managing directors deployed at "Gewinnungsgesellschaft" were Hans Schönemann (commercial director) and Mining Assessor Wilhelm Fabian (technical director), both Wintershall AG executives. Meanwhile, "Verarbeitungsgesellschaft" was managed by refinery experts Hermann Petri (Benzolverband) and Kurt Glöckner (Malopolska).[86]

There was also a supra-ordinated management level, however. Hugo Griebel, a member of DEA Chairman Karl Schirner's staff, was in charge of coordinating all activities in the Beskid companies, and he also constantly updated Karl Grosse in his functions as DEA Management Board member, head of the Oil Extraction Expert Group, and Chair of the Supervisory Board of the Beskid companies. Grosse also had supervisory authority in the Beskid companies owing to the instructions of Reich Economics Ministry – over and above his normal statutory powers.[87] Given these executive positions, DEA was in the driving seat at the Beskid companies.

Despite the ongoing rivalry between Wintershall AG and DEA, the composition of the management at both Beskid companies was initially of lesser importance. Both corporations felt that the oil industry in Galicia was not a big play and instead thirsted for the far greater oil deposits in the Caucasus.

Since even before the war, the German oil majors faced a shortage of skilled staff, so seconding employees to companies outside Germany was a permanent problem. DEA tried to have as many staff as possible classified by the Wehrmacht conscription offices as

---

85 Cf. Kasper, *Die Ausplünderung polnischer und sowjetischer Erdöllagerstätten im Gebiet der Vorkarpaten durch den deutschen Imperialismus im Zweiten Weltkrieg*, in: Jahrbuch für Wirtschaftsgeschichte 4 (1978), 41–64, here 48.

86 Cf. Geschäftsbericht 1942/43, 20.1.1944 (Ablage Petri), WD-CA, D-43-13-19. The Malopolska Group was a group of French oil, industrial and trading companies in Poland. (cf. *Jahrbuch der polnischen Industrie and des Handels,* Warschau 1938, No. 1223).

87 Cf. Abschrift des Gesellschaftsvertrages für die Beskiden "Vera" GmbH, 20.10.1939, WD-CA, D-43-13-20.

"exempted posts" in order to keep its core staff in place. At the same time, though, there were some engineers who sought new career opportunities through positions outside the main DEA sites.

Among the first DEA executives who moved to sign on with the Beskid companies directly after their foundation was engineer Alfred Rautenkranz, a scion of the famous family of deep-drilling pioneer Hermann Rautenkranz, who had worked from October 1935 to September 1938 as head of operations in Nienhagen and Gifhorn.[88] As a young engineer, Alfred Rautenkranz had worked from 1890 to 1897 in Gorlice, southeast of Cracow, and from 1 December 1939 to August 1944 he acted as technical director of the Western Group at the Beskid companies and as Director of the Operational Inspectorate Gorlice of Karpathen Öl AG.[89] Gustav Rautenkranz was another engineer who was sent East. He worked for Kontinentale Öl AG, and in October 1942 was moved to Karpathen Öl AG in order to take part in oil exploration in the region around Romny, now in Northeast Ukraine.[90]

Others did not head for Galicia voluntarily but were posted there as part of the war effort. Among them was another engineer, Klaus Wolf,[91] who was operations manager at two fairly unprofitable oil companies in Baden and Bavaria in the 1930s. In both locations, little oil was produced at great cost. In early 1937, Wolf found himself in conflict with the DAF, as the latter did not accept him firing a worker, and this may have been one of the reasons why he was posted as manager to the oil operations in Gifhorn in September 1937. Having served as a soldier in the Poland campaign, he had been declared "indispensable/exempted" and from the summer of 1940 to 1942 was ops manager in Pechelbronn. Whether his father-in-law, none other than Grosse, played a role in this posting

88 Cf. Personalakte Alfred Rautenkranz, WD-CA, PA.

89 Cf. ibid.

90 Cf. Programm der Besprechung am 23.10.1942, WD-CA, D-43-13-11.

91 Cf. Personalakte Dipl. Ing. Klaus Wolf, WD-CA, PA Wietze.

is not clear from the documents. In autumn 1942 Wolf was reposted to Karpathen Öl AG, where he became head of the Operational Inspectorate Krosno in southeast Poland.[92] It was a move up the career ladder for him, and he continued upward, becoming director and member of the Management Board of Karpathen Öl AG. Karl Grosse repeatedly and successfully obtained the support of those on high for the "indispensable/exempted" status of his son-in-law.

Karpathen Öl AG

One week before the attack on the Soviet Union, the GG government discussed incorporating the East Galicia oil companies into the Beskid companies. Erich Will had drawn up a secret report on this,[93] and he did not neglect to say that the companies' payrolls were too large and called for the firing of all Jewish staff members.[94] After the conquest of East Galicia, the Beskid companies immediately had personnel lists drawn up, which stated the profession, address, nationality, and knowledge of German for each person. In July 1941, the staff of the petroleum trust included 44 Poles, 20 Jews, 15 Ukrainians, and three Russians. Jews were entered in the lists with a red cross next to their name.[95]

Göring instructed that the East Galicia oil fields be assigned to the Beskid companies and Kontinentale Öl AG pay the tab. Frank, by contrast, tried to exert his authority over these oil companies, but had to succumb to the pressure from the Berlin authorities and accept the foundation of a new company, with Kontinentale Öl AG set to hold half the equity.[96]

---

92 Cf. Sandkühler, *"Endlösung" in Galizien*, 293; Große, *Mein Leben*, 60.

93 Cf. Der Sonderbevollmächtigte für die Erdölwirtschaft im GG, Dr. Erich Will, Geheim: Lagebericht, 17.6.1941, BArch Berlin, R 52 VI/14.

94 Ibid.

95 Cf. Liste der Angestellten des Petroleumtrusts, 2/3.7.1941, WD-CA, D-43-13-12.

96 Cf. Görings Erlass vom 20.8.1941 "Mineralölwirtschaft in Ostgalizien", in: Russisches Staatliches Militärarchiv Moscow [hereafter: RGVA], 1458-40-38.

Liste No. I vom 2/7.

Liste der Angestellten des Petroleumtrustes

Name	Nation.	Wohnung	Art der Beschäftigung	Spricht deutsch?
Piórko Pinchus	Jude	Sniadeckich 14	Ingenieur	ja
Tokarsewska Eugenie	Polin	Maczynskiego 35	Stenotypistin	ja
Monee Marja	"	Listopada 45	Buchhalt.Stenotyp.	ja
Wezyk Henryk	Pole	Traugutta 7a	Tankstellen	nein
Sereda Helena	Ukrain.	Marienplatz 8	Stenop.Zeichnerin	nein
Rostiak Gregor	Ukrainer	Pelczynska 22	Autoführer Mechan.	ja
Kamiński Karol	Pole	Gipsowa 38a	" "	ja
Andrianowa Lydie	Russe	Marienplatz 8	Ingenieur von der Raffinerie	nein
Zang Dora	Jüdin	Holowki 11	Bibliothek.u.Sten.	ja
Kätz Albert	Jude	Chrzanowskiej 10	Ingenieur Elektr.	ja
Fränkel Eleonore	Jüdin	Boguslawskiego 12	Kassiererin	ja
Klaus Christine	Polin	Zródlana 46	Hausversorgerin	nein
Lozinska Irene	Polin	Zyblikiewicza 43	Buchhaltung	ja
B[illegible]lwan Karl.	Ukrainer	Glowinskiego 17	Normenabteilung	schwach
[illegible]ki Leon	Pole	Teresy 32	Lichtbilderabteilg.	nein
[illegible]a Boleslaus	"	Lyzwiarska 18	Techn.Aufseher der Raffinerie	ja
Halikowska Sophie	Polin	Zyrzyńska 8	Stenotypistin	ja
Tyka Joseph	Pole	Zimna Woda 335	Buchhaltung	Schwach
Dreyer Gustav	"	Zeromskiego 13 a	Administrat.	ja
Orschulik Johanna	Polin	Wyspianskiego 14a	Buchhaltung	ja
Piroń Wladyslaw	Pole	Franciszkanska 2	"	schwach
Schiff Josue	Jude	Zamojskiego 8	Maschinen Ingenieur	ja
Skalniski Taddeus	Pole	Tarnowskiego 66	Elektro Ingenieur	ja
Melman Heinrich	Jude	Paderewskiego 6	Ingenieur Technologe	ja
Choróbska Marja	Polin	Nabielaka 53 b	Stenotypistin	ja
Wozniak Stanislaus	Pole	Zielona 5	Zeichner	nein
Tkaczow Johann	Ukrain.	Chodkiewicza 9	Chemiker Technologe	nein
Nalepa Johann	"	Mireckiego 4	Schlosser Mechanik.	schwach
Gonczarowa Marja	"	Stryjska 3	Stenotypistin	schwach
Bielecki Jan	Pole	Piekarska 16	Arbeiter	nein
Maresch Bronislaw	"	Koszowa 3	Autoführer	ja
Kuz Michael	Ukrain.	Stefczyka 10	Buchhalt.Kontr.	schwach
[illegible]aban Emanuel	Jude	Lazarza 6	Finanzverwaltung	ja
[illegible]kula Nikolaus	Ukrain.	Macana 46	Ingenieur	ja
Kossowski Joseph	Pole	Drohobycz	Chemiker Ingenieur	ja
Werter Markus	Jude	Sykstuska 44	Personalabt.Leiter	ja
Zolubek Katherine	Ukrain.	Halicka 12	Kurier und Köchin	nein
Lewin Jakob	Jude	Rozwadowskiego 34	Technologe	ja
Steuerman Moritz	"	Zofji 4	Ekonomist Buchhalt.	ja
Töpfer Zenon	"	Nabielaka 8	" "	ja
Dr.Wróblewski Józef	Pole	Domsa 12/8	Jurist	ja
Chamaides Bernard	Jude	Kochanowskiego 3	Technologe	ja
Koter Stefan	Pole	Obertyńska 39	Ober Spediteur	ja
Gala Adalbert	"	Zyrzyńska 32	Hausbesorger	nein
Pilpel Franciszka	Jüdin	Stryjska 38	Buchhaltung	ja
Dabroś Michal	Pole	Batorego 3a	Tankstation	schwach
Kurdyna Michal	Ukrain.	Tarnowskiego 24	"	schwach
Górka Bronislaw	Pole	Trześniowskiego 9	Autoführer	ja
Dunca de Sajo Leon	"	Snopkowska 24	Jurist Administr.	ja
Solewski Leopold	"	Torosiewicza 21	Statistik	ja
Hanisch Bronislau	"	Antoniego 11	Tanklager Leiter Stellvertreter	ja
Kuchta Michal	"	Gródecka 24	Spedition	schwach
Szelichowski Eugen	"	Sobieszczyzna 4	"	schwach

Fig. 50 List of the staff of Petroleum trust, 2–3 July 1941

At this point, however, overcoming the German Reich's fuel bottlenecks seemed to depend solely on the pace at which the Red Army was pushed back. Not until the German campaign, planned for only a few weeks, came to a halt outside Moscow, did exploitation of Galicia's oil and gas deposits become more important. This was expressed in the foundation of Karpathen Öl AG on 28 August 1942, into which both "Beskid companies" were incorporated.

The following shareholders had a stake in Karpathen Öl AG, domiciled in Lemberg (today's Lviv, Ukraine) and its share capital of 15 million Reichsmark:

Kontinentale Öl AG	7.50 million Reichsmark
DEA	1.50 million Reichsmark
Gewerkschaft Elwerath	1.50 million Reichsmark
Preußische Bergwerks- und Hütten AG	1.50 million Reichsmark
Wintershall AG	1.50 million Reichsmark
Deutsche Gasolin AG	0.75 million Reichsmark
Kohle Öl Union von Busse KG	0.75 million Reichsmark

Karl Grosse, originally intended as the man to take over the Caucasian oil fields, was appointed CEO. DEA Chairman Günter Schlicht noted that Grosse was to be released by DEA in order to discharge his "*honourable appointment*", and his statement continues: "*In the firm belief in the victory of our weapons, we do not doubt that Herr Grosse will perform a task for life of great importance in Galicia that will last well beyond the war [...].*"[97]

Hermann Malz (Preussag) was nominated as Grosse's deputy, with the Management Board also including Hermann Petri (Benzolverband), Kurt Glöckner (Malopolska), and Mining Assessor Wilhelm Fabian (Wintershall AG). In May 1943, Klaus Wolf (DEA)

97 Schirner, Ritter: Organisationsänderung, 8.7.1942, HADB, P 1655, sheet 4f.

also joined it.[98] The Supervisory Board was made up of: Walter Emmerich as Chair and Financial President Hermann Senkowsky (both of the GG government); Mining Assessor (retd.) Heinrich Wisselmann for Preussag; Director Hans Brochhaus for Gewerkschaft Elwerath; Director Karl Blessing for Kontinentale Öl AG; Ernst Rudolf Fischer for the Reich Economics Ministry; Mining Councillor (retd.) Erich Franke for Preussag; Mining Assessor Albert Ritter for DEA; Mining Director Wilhelm Zentgraf for Wintershall AG; and Ministerial Director Friedrich Kadgien for the Four-Year Plan Authority.[99]

Karpathen Öl AG was to acquire all the Beskid companies' assets and current assets by purchase contract from the Special Commissioner for the Oil Industry at the GG.[100] This did not happen, as the Foreign Office and the Reich Justice Ministry raised objections, since they feared this would impact ongoing negotiations with French companies whom they were wooing to participate in exploiting the oil fields in the Caucasus.[101] Instead, up to spring 1945 negotiations were conducted on a lease agreement.[102]

Until the end of the war, Karpathen Öl AG remained an instrument used by the Third Reich to exploit the Ukrainian and Polish oil deposits. According to Karl Grosse, the company ran a "*management with no brief*" and acted with no legal basis.[103] At the height of its activities at the end of 1943, Karpathen Öl AG had almost 33,000 blue- and white-collar workers, roughly half of whom

98 Tätigkeitsbericht vom 28.6.1945, WD-CA, D-43-13-19.

99 Cf. Schreiben von Dr. Petri an den Oberpräsidenten von Hannover vom 24.7.1946, Betr.: Beteiligungen des Reiches and des Landes Preußen, ibid.

100 Cf. Vermerk zur Vorgeschichte des Pachtverhältnisses zwischen der Karpathen Öl AG und dem Generaltreuhänder, 16. 2.1945, WD-CA, D-43-13-03.

101 Cf. Sandkühler, *"Endlösung"* in Galizien, 297.

102 Cf. "Abwicklung der Karpathen Öl AG", BArch Berlin, R 52 I/2 (Feindvermögen im GG), No. 1, sheet 21.

103 Karl Große: Die galizischen Erdölfelder unter deutscher Verwaltung, 2.8.1945, WD-CA, D-43-13-03.

Fig. 51 Layout of operational units of Karpathen Öl AG
in East Galicia (1942)

were Poles, more than 40 percent Ukrainians, and about eight percent Jews. There were also some French and several hundred Soviet POWs.[104] Less than two percent of the staff were Germans, with a total of 142 of them classed as technical staff, 171 as commercial staff, and 144 as support staff.[105] The operational hierarchies followed the Nazis' racial ideology, so German salaried staff and engineers were at the top. At the second level (ops managers, foremen), the preference was for employing Poles, and right at the bottom of the scale were Jewish slave labourers.

Karpathen Öl AG East Group, payroll as at 1 October 1942[106]

Employees	Number	Share
Germans	288	2.0 %
Poles	6,909	48.7 %
Ukrainians	5,852	40.9 %
Others	1,180	8.4 %
Total	14,229	100.0 %

Poles constituted the main employees in the oil companies in West Galicia, where the number of Ukrainians was well below ten percent. Nevertheless, the latter had been given a special status in West Galicia in the mid-management levels in order to instrumentalize the national differences between them and the Poles. The company security staff, headed by a German, was also made up entirely of Ukrainians.

104 Cf. Große an Dr. Rasch, 8.6.1944, WD-CA, D-43-13-22.

105 Cf. Vorstand and deutsche Gefolgschaft der Karpathen Öl AG im Januar 1944, WD-CA, D-43-13-19.

106 Compiled according to: Belegschaftsmeldungen, WD-CA, D-43-13-10.

Payroll of Karpathen Öl AG West Group as at 1 August 1943[107]

Employees	Number	Share
Germans	101	1.1 %
Poles	8,389	93.1 %
Ukrainians	785	8.7 %
Other	8	0.1 %
Total	9,041	100.0 %

Two events contributed to a clear upgrading of the importance of oil from Galicia for the German armaments industry: the failure of the Caucasus offensive at the end of 1942 and the increase in Allied bombing raids on locations inside the Reich.[108] Karl Grosse announced the new strategy: "*Maximum output is the order of the day. Everyone involved in running the oil business in the GG shall subordinate their interests to this objective.*"[109]

Alongside boosting oil output, Karpathen Öl AG also sought to modernize the ancient refineries in Drohobyc (Ukraine) and Jaslo (Poland) and set up a construction office headed by Herbert Kamptner.[110] Part of the plant required was to be assembled through cannibalizing the Caucasus company.[111] Several members of the Supervisory Board objected to the modernization plans, although Chemicals Commissioner Carl Krauch, by contrast, supported the plans. At the end of May 1943, the Reich Economics Ministry confirmed the programme to expand the refineries, and Krauch himself then approved it on 12 June 1943.[112] In 1944, the investment programme was itself

107 Compiled according to: ibid.

108 Cf. Griebel, *Deutsche Mineralölprobleme*, IX/4.

109 Geschäftsbericht 1942/43, 20.1.1944 (Ablage Petri), WD-CA, D-43-13-19.

110 Cf. Baubüro Raffinerien (Kamptner): Niederschrift, 7.2.1944, WD-CA, D-43-13-13.

111 Cf. Niederschrift über die Aufsichtsratssitzung der Karpathen Öl AG vom 29.5.1943 in Berlin, WD-CA, D-43-13-04.

112 Cf. Ausbau der Verarbeitungskapazitäten bei der Karpathen Öl AG, Celle, 3.4.1947, WD-CA, D-43-13-19.

upped,[113] and by the time of the German retreat in the summer of 1944, large parts of the programme had been realized. Moreover, an exploration programme authorized by the Reich Office for Georesearch commenced, with the plan being to further tap an oil field near Romny, halfway between Kyiv and Kharkiv. Grosse expected structures there to be similar to those in Holstein,[114] but the geological exploration did not come up trumps.[115]

The results of the expansion programmes failed to meet the expectations of the head office of Karpathen Öl AG and the Reich authorities, despite the massive manpower and materials committed. This can presumably be attributed mainly to the fact the project was forced on the company, while the workers were suffering from malnutrition and exerting passive resistance, and operations were also impaired by groups from the Ukrajinska Powstanska Armija = UPA, the Ukraine nationalist partisan organization, and by Soviet-led partisans.

Karpathen Öl AG's contribution to the German war effort remained modest at about 400,000 t p.a. of crude oil as well as fuels of a primarily lower quality.

---

113 Ibid.

114 Cf. Mitteilung Große, 21.3.1942, WD-CA, D-43-13-21.

115 Cf. Ukraine Öl Vertriebs GmbH: Bericht über Aussprache mit Prof. Marly vom wissenschaftlichen geologischen Institut Kiew am 29.11.1941 sowie Dr. Sommermeier an HV Lemberg, 8.7.1943, WD-CA, 43-13-21.

Crude oil production in Galicia – 1939 to 1944[116]

Year	Total	West Galicia	East Galicia
1939	474,660	124,705	349,955
1940	475,320	124,847	350,473
1941	425,140	130,650	294,490
1942	378,331	118,543	259,788
1943	401,162	147,722	253,440
1944	274,174	.	.

Workers suffering from malnutrition

The largest problem for the Beskid companies, and later for Karpathen Öl AG, was the lack of suitable managers, bottlenecks in materials and transportation, and above all the lack of food supplies. The oil companies' workers were going hungry, with many workers suffering from malnutrition and diseases and some so weak they collapsed at work.[117] As early as May 1940, Hermann Petri, as director of the "Vera" refinery, was the first to complain to representatives of the Four-Year Plan Authority and the GG government that his oil workers were not receiving enough food, but his description of the dire straits was rejected.[118]

After the Wehrmacht occupied East Galicia, the lack of food got even worse. A report of 1 August 1942 stated: "*There is a striking contrast between the sharp drop in the output curve and the sharp rise in the number of coffins that the company gifts its loyal members in the event of death. While in the autumn of 1941 two such coffins were issued a month, in autumn/September the figure had risen to four, and in March 1942 as many as 18, with the figure now on average 15 – 20 coffins a*

116 Compiled according to: *Oil Fields Investigation*, Part VIII/2.

117 Cf. Bericht vom 26.6.1943, WD-CA, D-43-13-12.

118 Cf. Bericht über die Reise ins Erdölgebiet vom 17./18.5.1940, BArch Berlin, R 52 VI/13.

month. Something that of course goes hand in hand with malnutrition is that workers fall prey to just about all kinds of diseases." The author of the report concludes: "*And yet the workers ... are especially well-qualified labour material [sic!] that can certainly not be replaced. The entire state of affairs and the public indifference to this all creates the impression that there is no interest in maintaining the abilities of the workers in the oil field to perform. This view must be rebutted most vigorously.*"[119]

The chronic lack of food for the oil-field workers is apparent if one compares the rations for the Galician oil-field workers with those for normal consumers and those performing heavy labour inside the Reich in July 1942.

Food rations in the Reich and in the Galician oil industry (in kg) – July 1942[120]

Consumer	Food volume in kg	Normal consumers = 100
Normal consumers in the Reich	14.4	100
Manual labourers in the Reich	22.6	157
Heavy workers in the Reich	29.4	204
Galician oil-field workers	10.3	72

There were nevertheless those in the German administration in the occupied territories who felt the workers were not being treated with sufficient brutality, although various factors spoke against this being the case when it came to Karpathen Öl AG: 1) Its operating sites were spread across a vast area. 2) There were few Germans in the company, meaning work discipline on the ground was often in the hands of Polish engineers and technicians. 3) There were few oil-field workers to be found, and they couldn't easily be replaced by unskilled workers.

119 Ernährungslage und Abwehrschutz im Erdölgebiet, 1.8.1942, WD-CA, D-43-13-12.
120 Compiled according to: ibid.

Prior to the foundation of Karpathen Öl AG, a GG government meeting attended by Grosse and Malz mentioned the critical status of food for the workers in the East Galicia oil fields as the main obstacle to output. The Kontinentale Öl AG management, to which Grosse was still subordinate at this point, demanded that he set up works kitchens.[121] After consultation with the GG government, Grosse thereupon insisted the workers in the East Galician oil fields be treated the same way as armaments workers. To improve their food provisions, all Operational Inspectorate offices were to set up works kitchens, and Göring approved the measures in his function as the Commissioner for the Four-Year Plan.[122]

Each member of staff was to be given one warm meal a day, and to a growing extent staff family members were also fed in the works kitchens. Moreover, the works kitchens had the real advantage, from the viewpoint of the occupying regime, that food for workers crucial to the war effort could be kept separate from that for the rest of the population, and the black market dampened with the tying of workers to their companies.

Nevertheless, making certain the kitchens received halfway enough produce depended on whether the company was granted the status of an armaments operation. In February 1943, Göring granted Karpathen Öl AG the status of a "military firm", which meant that, as of 15 May 1943, the food rations allocated to it could be increased.[123] Only then did the food situation for the staff and their family members actually improve.[124]

According to a list in December 1943, at Karpathen Öl AG 32,679 blue and white-collar workers and 46,785 family members

---

121 Cf. Kontinentale Öl AG an Generaldirektor Große vom 17.9.1942, Geheim, WD-CA, D-43-13-12.

122 Cf. Göring (i.A. Friedrich Kadgien) an Bentz, 28.9.1942, ibid.

123 Cf. Hautverwaltung der Karpathen Öl AG (Malz/Müller): Rundschreiben No. 148, 14.8.1943, as well as Manuskript der Karpathen Öl AG, Celle, 7.9.1945, ibid.

124 Cf. Malz: Bericht 1943 über die Versorgung der Belegschaft, Lemberg 4.6.1944, WD-CA, D-43-13-4.

– i.e., a total of more than 79,000 persons – were fed through 80 company distribution points.[125] From the summer of 1943, there were almost no further incidents of malnutrition. Karl Grosse remarked: "*Given the war situation, we can say that in this area we have done what was humanly possible. Nutrition for the employees from among foreign peoples at Karpathen Öl is now at least sufficient so that we can demand they work to the full.*"[126]

Alongside distributing food, the company had also started distributing clothes, shoes, fuel, and petroleum.[127] In-company provisions were issued at fixed, low prices, and the system of bonuses paid with such articles was more important to the workers than their wages. Outside the company, the wages were hardly even subsistence wages given inflation and high black-market prices.

The improvement in food provisioning did not change the fact that the German occupiers pursued a regime based on force. Resistance grew among the population, and it was also aimed at Karpathen Öl AG's activities. It reached such a scale that the Carpathians increasingly eluded military control by the Wehrmacht, and Karpathen Öl AG's operations were increasingly impaired by attacks by Ukrainian nationalists. As the partisan units led by Soviet Major General Kovpak and the Red Army moved closer, the latent anti-Polish sentiment among parts of the Ukrainian population turned into a series of acts of open violence.[128] The company management resignedly had to concede: "*The terror has a disastrous effect. It bears considering that a large part of our best skilled staff and almost all senior engineers in our operations were recruited from Poland. They have*

---

125 Cf. ibid.

126 Rede von Karl Große vor dem Aufsichtsrat der Karpathen Öl AG, 20.1.1944, WD-CA, D-43-13-19.

127 Cf. Malz: Bericht 1943 über die Versorgung der Belegschaft, Lemberg 4.6.1944, WD-CA, D-43-13-4.

128 Cf. Tätigkeit der Beskiden Erdöl-Gewinnungs-Gesellschaft mbH, der Beskiden Erdöl-Verarbeitungs-Gesellschaft mbH and der Karpathen Öl Aktiengesellschaft in Polen (Entwurf), 28.6.1945, WD-CA, D-43-13-19.

either been killed, have fled, or are in hiding and refuse to go to the pits without sufficient protection."[129]

As of October 1943, SS-Obersturmbannführer Heinz Jennessen from the SD in Lemberg took charge of works security at Karpathen Öl AG.[130] Under him, the Sicherheitspolizei and the SD responded to the attacks on company property with terror attacks and group executions.[131]

Rebuilding the refineries in vain in 1944, withdrawal and dissolution

As of spring 1944, the Karpathen Öl AG head office prepared to break up and clear the operations in East Galicia.[132] The most modern equipment was removed, loaded onto about 400 freight waggons, and moved west to the sections of Poland still held by the Wehrmacht and at the end of March 1944 the main office in Lemberg was abandoned. The operations in Nadvorna (Ukraine, 21 March 1944) and Kalusz (Ukraine, 30 March 1944) were discontinued under chaotic conditions, marked by mutually contradictory assessments of the situation and orders. While the Armaments Inspectorate in Cracow forbade any discontinuation, company officers on the ground followed their own judgement. In mid-April 1944, the Wehrmacht briefly retook districts round Nadvorna and Kalusz, then on 27 June 1944, 72 US Air Force B-17s bombed the refinery in Drohobych and destroyed parts of it.[133] Grosse estimated that it would take two months to complete repairs and deployed refinery expert Her-

---

129 Bericht über die Einwirkung der Frontannäherung auf die Betriebsanlage Styri vom 16.5.1944, WD-CA, D-43-13-23. also: Der Abwehrbeauftrage an Kommandeur der Sicherheitspolizei and des SD im Distrikt Galicia, betr.: Mordanschlag auf Ing. Zborowsli, 12.5.1944, WD-CA, D-43-13-23.

130 Cf. Sandkühler, *"Endlösung" in Galizien*, 301f.

131 Cf. ibid.

132 Cf. Bericht vom 23.5.1944, WD-CA, D-43-13-19.

133 Cf. Telegramm Große an Fischer, Griebel, Krauch, 27.6.1944, WD-CA, 43-13-1.

bert Kamptner as Commissioner for Reconstruction.[134] Petri advised Grosse that, given the problems with the GG government, he should contact Armaments Minister Albert Speer directly and get the highest priority for the repairs to the refinery, something that would only be possible with their inclusion in the Geilenberg Programme.[135] On 7 July 1944, Grosse received full authority from the Reich Minister for Armaments and War Production to repair the Drohobych East refinery.[136]

Just how urgent the project was can be seen from the meeting the company then had with all GG agencies and representatives of the Wehrmacht on 12 July 1944 in Cracow.[137] Grosse set the pace at the meeting and called for the greatest possible support. He suggested that work time be raised to 12 hours a day, so the Polish workers would need to receive a double meal from the works kitchens. Moreover, Karpathen Öl AG wanted to propose a weekly bonus per person of one litre of schnapps and 100 cigarettes. Representatives of the GG turned this down, saying that "*the Poles are better off than our German workers back in the Reich*".[138] In reality, the Poles were certainly not better off. The food for workers on the construction site was insufficient, even in the opinion of the German managers.[139]

By mid-July 1944, the construction work on expanding the Jaslo refinery was almost 80 percent complete,[140] but due to the military situation Carl Krauch, as General Commissioner for Special

---

134 Cf. Besprechung in Jaslo, 1.7.1944, WD-CA, D-43-13-1. For Kamptner cf. chapter "DEA in der Ostmark".

135 Cf. Telegramm der V-Stelle Jaslo (Dr. Petri) an Generaldirektor Große, 3.7.1944, as well as Aktennotiz 4.7.1944, betr.: Wiederaufbau der Raffinerie Drohobycz-Ost, WD-CA, D-43-13-1.

136 Cf. Vollmacht des Reichsministers für Rüstung and Kriegsproduktion, 7.7.1944, ibid.

137 Aktennotiz über die Sitzung am 12.7.1944, ibid.

138 Ibid.

139 Cf. Raffinerie Drohobycz-Ost, Aktennotiz vom 19.7.1944, ibid.

140 Cf. Notiz für Generaldirektor Große als Unterlage für das Fernschreiben an Prof. Krauch vom 17.7.1944, ibid.

Issues of Chemical Production, had tools downed. The head office of Karpathen Öl AG tried madly to find new tasks for the company, which was essentially doomed. After the evacuation of East Galicia, the corporate managers cited new contracts from Göring and Bentz to prospect for oil in Silesia and Moravia and clutched at the last straws of renewal of operations at the Jaslo refinery and continued operation of other plants. Presumably they were interested less in the corporation per se and solely in maintaining their status as exempt from military service.

In January 1945, Karpathen Öl AG was finally forced to evacuate its offices in Jaslo and thus lost its last base in Galicia. Given the problems in the military theatre, its withdrawal from Galicia was surprisingly orderly. In total, the company managed to load 1,664 rail waggons with plant and operating materials and 272 waggons with oil products and sent them westwards.[141] Part of the plant and equipment that could be moved was taken to the territory within the Reich and to Bohemia and Moravia. The largest part of it landed up in fallback storage in the Province of Brandenburg (Oderberg) east of Berlin, to Lower Saxony (Garssen) and to Hessen (to the Herzog Julius smelter near Goslar). The total value of the materials removed was estimated at 21.8 million Reichsmark.[142] The German staff went to work in the fallback storage facilities for materials and equipment or were conscripted by the Wehrmacht.

The fate of Jewish slave labourers

Few Jews were employed in the West Galician oil industry prior to 1939, but things were very different in East Galicia. Some small oil companies had been owned by Jews until September 1939, but after the Red Army invaded they were expropriated by the Soviets. In the

---

141 Cf. Schreiben der Karpathen Öl an den Generaltreuhänder, 20.2.1945, WD-CA, D-43-13-05.

142 Cf. Bericht zum Umfang der Räumungsaktion, 19.11.1945, ibid.

remaining oil companies and refineries there were many Jewish blue and white-collar workers. After the German occupation in the late summer of 1941, they were all thrown out of their jobs,[143] yet there was no replacing their technical and language skills, so the Beskid companies and/or later Karpathen Öl AG tried to get government agencies to ease the prohibition on employing Jews.[144]

The German occupation entailed a systematic destruction of the basis for life among the Jewish minority in Galicia. Hunger, disease, plundering, abuse, and the loss of their civil rights made their lives hell. The occupation authorities considered Jews to be workers who cost nothing and in early August 1941 introduced compulsory work for all persons aged between 18 and 65, with their deployment coordinated by the labour offices. At the same time, they were subjected to a selective policy of starvation, and as of autumn 1941, the authorities started to expel them from their homes and set up ghettos and slave labour camps.

As of the end of 1941, the Drohobych labour office allowed Jews to work in the oil industry again.[145] At first, only a small number of technicians were taken on, but a little later white-collar staff for the accounts, inventory, and secretariats were allowed, and then workers. In autumn 1942, almost 2,000 Jewish slave labourers were working at Karpathen Öl AG, more than 1,700 of them in Boryslav.[146] Only by working in the oil industry could they hope for a

---

143 Cf. Stellungnahme zu dem Stande des Rechnungswesens der Beskiden Erdöl Verarbeitungsgesellschaft vom 11.1.1943, WD-CA, D-43-13-19.

144 Cf. numerous letters from the head office of Karpathen Öl AG and individual companies in the collection of documents on the criminal proceedings against Hildebrand before the Bremen Regional Court in 1966, Staatsarchiv Bremen [hereafter: StAB], Az 29 ks 1/66, Mappe "Juden-Einsatz" der Karpathen Öl.

145 Cf. Dieter Pohl, *Nationalsozialistische Judenverfolgung in Ostgalizien 1941–1944*, München 1997, 166.

146 Cf. the statistics in Sandkühler, *"Endlösung" in Galizien*, 346.

little, if temporary, protection, By this time almost 2,000 other Jews had been murdered in Drohobych alone.[147]

The mass murder of the Jewish population now turned into systematic genocide.[148] What was happening in Galicia was something that all the German staff at Karpathen Öl AG could experience for themselves every day. DEA directors who only visited Lemberg briefly heard of the deportations and murdering, and DEA Director Günther Schlicht wrote in his memoirs: "*For the first time I saw columns of Jews wearing the Star of David when driving round the Galician oil fields; they were forced to go to work. Now, initially I did not think it was so bad (…) Then rumours started cropping up. Malz, the Beskiden Öl GmbH commercial manager, had to retire after a nervous breakdown. People said he had had an awful experience at a Polish railway station. When he spoke to an SS man about the Jewish transports that were passing through being badly treated, the guy tore a child out of a train and smashed its head on the platform before asking: 'Anything else you want to know?' We no longer heard from Malz, but he died a little while later and we were not therefore able to establish whether this was true, and we didn't want to believe it could be.*"[149]

Schlicht also heard of ghastly occurrences from Erich Will. Will had been expected to take part, together with some of his oil experts, in firing squads executing Jews.[150] Will refused, and a Nazi Party functionary then commented: "*I don't understand you, why don't you want to let your men enjoy themselves?*" Will had been "*very troubled*" by this. Schlicht believed such excesses were "*one-off aberrations*".[151]

[147] Martin Gilbert, *Endlösung. Die Vertreibung und Vernichtung der Juden. Ein Atlas*, Frankfurt/Main 1983, 111.

[148] Cf. Ulrich Herbert, *Eine "Führerentscheidung" zur "Endlösung"?*, in: Neue Züricher Zeitung, 14./15.3.1998.

[149] Schlicht, *Memoiren*, 126f.

[150] Since Will was killed in an airplane crash in May 1942, the events probably took place in 1941 or early 1942 at the Beskid companies.

[151] Schlicht, *Memoiren*, 127.

Senior engineer Erich Höchsmann, head of the "Galizin" refinery outside Drohobych, speaking as a witness in 1953 in the criminal case brought against Friedrich Hildebrand, Head of the Jewish unit at the SS Polizeiführer staff section (SSPF) in Galicia, said: "*I was aware that the extermination of the Galician Jews was an order.*"[152]

On 5 September 1942, the Head of OKW, Wilhelm Keitel, ordered that all Jewish labourers in the GG be dismissed from Wehrmacht and armaments operations and replaced by Poles.[153] Friedrich Katzmann thereupon imposed a general prohibition on having Jews work and declared that the Jewish labour deployment was terminated.[154] The management of Karpathen Öl AG felt its production targets were at risk and appealed to the Economic Armaments Office of OKW and presumably via Carl Krauch to Reichsführer-SS, Heinrich Himmler – and their interventions had some effect. The OKW sent an instruction to the Armaments Command in Lemberg, which informed Katzmann of the OKW's intentions on 15 September 1942 in a secret communication: "*Any disruptive interventions in the oil industry's operations must be avoided. Jewish labourers may only be removed after replacements have been provided.*"[155] Two days later, Adolf Eichmann, head of the "Jewish unit" at the SS Reichssicherheitshauptamt (RSHA) and the man mainly responsible for organizing the Holocaust, relayed this instruction by paraphrase in a communication to Katzmann.[156]

Hitler's opinion was sought on the dispute over the ongoing use of Jewish skilled workers, and he resolved to leave them working in the armaments industry. Himmler was told to make certain the

152 Testimony of witness Erich Höchsmann in the criminal proceedings against Friedrich Hildebrand, 27.4.1953, StAB, 4.89/2-546.

153 Sandkühler, *"Endlösung" in Galizien*, 183.

154 Cf. Pohl, *Judenverfolgung*, 342.

155 Rüstungskommando Lemberg an SSPF Katzmann, 15.9.1942, WD-CA, D-43-13-29.

156 Cf. Sandkühler, *"Endlösung" in Galizien*, 347.

Jewish skilled workers were kept in SS slave labour camps that would then rent the prisoners out to the companies, although Himmler left no doubts as to the goal of annihilating all Jews: "*There, too, one day in line with the Führer's wish, all Jews will disappear.*"[157]

On 6 November 1942, Katzmann then issued detailed guidelines after consultation with the GG Armaments Inspectorate on the deployment of Jewish labourers in the occupation authorities and companies.[158] Jews who worked in an armaments factory would be designated with an R on the uppermost article of clothing; thus only this symbol offered a certain protection against immediate deportation. Katzmann only issued 1,670 "R" patches to Karpathen Öl AG, and fierce arguments ensued thereafter on the awarding of the patches and whether they could be passed on.

For the Karpathen Öl AG operations, between October and December 1942 slave labour camps for more than 2,200 Jews were installed in barracks in Boryslav, in ten houses, and in a villa in Drohobych, and a smaller camp established in Styri.[159] The slave labour camps emerged as the most important place to flee "Judenaktionen", yet "Armaments Jews" still fell victim to arrest. Katzmann had declared that the foremost principle was "*the swiftest extraction of these Jewish workers from the work process*",[160] and demanded that Karpathen Öl AG submit "labour deployment lists" in order to prepare selections. These lists, which decided over life and death, had to be compiled on behalf of Friedrich Hildebrand, the Jewish unit head in Katzmann's staff.

Some of these lists are to be found among the few surviving Karpathen Öl AG documents, stating the names, professions,

157 As cited in: ibid., 348.

158 Cf. Katzmann: Rundschreiben betr.: Jüdische Arbeitskräfte, Geheim, 6.11.1942, IfZ Munich, Fa 506, sheet 192–198.

159 Cf. Pohl, *Judenverfolgung*, 343.

160 Katzmann: Randschreiben betr.: Jüdische Arbeitskräfte, Geheim, 6.11.1942, IfZ Munich, Fa 506, sheet 196.

and deployment points of the Jewish slave labourers.[161] The columns "*indispensable*" or "*dispensable*" and/or "*how many of them can be released*" decided over life or deportation to a death camp and/or immediate execution. All operations managers at Karpathen Öl AG faced awful decisions over which workers were "dispensable".

The head office appealed to the Armaments Command each time another "Judenaktion" was pending: "*We therefore request that with reference to the pending resettlement action for Jews, that the relevant SD and SS units be instructed that our operations not be affected by the action.*"[162] For economic reasons, the company had an interest in continuing to use the Jewish slave labourers. Whether the salaried staff at the head office in Lemberg and the operations managers at the various sites acted primarily with regard to company/business considerations or consciously sought to save people by keeping them at work can only be judged on a case-by-case basis to the extent that this is even possible.

It is with good reason that today the actions of Berthold and Else Beitz are remembered, since they showed great courage in trying to save Jewish slave labourers. Berthold Beitz worked from May 1938 onwards as a commercial staff member at Rhenania-Ossag, a subsidiary of Royal Dutch Shell in Hamburg, and it was there that he met Else, who was later to become his wife. His company applied for him to be registered as "exempt" and posted him to Jaslo to Beskiden-Gesellschaft, hence from July 1941 onwards Beitz was Commercial Director at the Operations Inspectorate in Boryslav. His wife worked as a secretary.[163]

Beitz's position in Boryslav was strengthened by the foundation of Karpathen Öl AG. Several men employed at the head office in Lemberg sought to improve the provisioning of the staff and

161 Cf. e.g.: Gruppenverwaltung Boryslaw: Nachweis der jüdischen Arbeitskräfte zum 1.7.1943, StAB, 4.89/2-601.

162 As cited in: Pohl, *Judenverfolgung*, 347.

163 Cf. Joachim Käppner, *Berthold Beitz. Die Biografie*, Berlin 2010.

demanded that Jewish slave labour continue to be deployed. They included Hermann Malz (previously Preussag) as director of the Lemberg head office, Hermann Petri (previously Benzolverband) as head of the "Vera" refinery and member of the Karpathen Öl AG Management Board, and Konrad Kleinert, Karpathen Öl AG legal officer.

Beitz worked out how to shore up his scope by buttering up Grosse. He remarked after the war: "*Grosse and his men came and inspected the Operations Inspectorate in Boryslav and expected to drive home with a few slabs of bacon, ham, butter, and the like.*"[164] The Boryslav Operations Inspectorate, of which he was head, had the largest number of Jewish slave labourers at work, and Beitz had a "VIP camp" established in order to protect "key persons", office clerks, and doctors. On several occasions, he saved Jews at the railway station from being transported to the death camps.[165] He also had Jews at home whom he claimed were "skilled workers", and the Beitz couple even helped hidden Jewish children. They were in permanent danger of being denounced. What distinguished Beitz from all the other directors was that he rejected the selections based on purely business reasons. He acted out of the depths of his heart and helped Jewish staff irrespective of whether they were skilled workers or not and of their age.

In the summer of 1943, the final phase of the genocide of the Jews began in the Generalgouvernement. Himmler ordered that all ghettos and slave labour camps be dissolved, and the inmates killed ("Aktion Erntefest") – and Karpathen Öl AG was not exempt. Eye-witness Karoline Schnepf was a Jewish slave labourer from the end of 1941 to April 1944 in Drohobych, first working in the refineries and later in the accounts section. She described how the selections took place: "*During those Aktionen, the Jews condemned to the fir-*

---

[164] As cited in Sandkühler, *"Endlösung" in Galizien*, 299.
[165] Cf. ibid., 338ff.

Fig. 52 Crude oil production near Boryslav (around 1920)

ing squads were selected. All Jews who worked in the Nafta refinery stood in the courtyard. There, Krause [Deputy Director, "Refinery Süd" – the authors] personally selected the persons to be shot. [...] Everybody knew that these people would be taken to the forest of Bronica and shot."[166]

As of June 1943, the head office of Karpathen Öl AG tried to get a special exemption for its operations, since the Jews were cheap labour and performed better than all the other employees. At the urgent request of Karpathen Öl AG, Krauch again sought out Himmler and wanted a special exemption.[167] In July 1943, the company also appealed to Oil Commissioner Professor Alfred Bentz, Four-Year Plan Commissioner Hermann Göring, SD Boss Ernst Kaltenbrunner, and the OKW in Berlin.[168] These interventions proved successful, and on 2 August 1943 Himmler order that "indispensable" Jewish skilled labour in the Galician oil industry be allowed to live.[169]

There was nevertheless no uniform policy. The labour offices were supposed to assign Karpathen Öl AG other workers as quickly as possible, with the idea being to release the Jewish skilled labour and hand them over "*to the police for their use elsewhere*".[170] The corporation was forced to report how many of its workers could be replaced. Of the 1,963 Jewish slave labourers working at Karpathen Öl AG, 560, including 118 engineers and technicians, were classified as indispensable. All the others were not to be released but instead to be deployed expanding the Drohobych and Jaslo refineries. Corre-

166 Testimony Karoline Schnepf, Tel Aviv, 4.10.1962, Bundesarchiv Ludwigsburg, B.162, Vol. 5832, 322–324, in: A story of destruction and survival. The Holocaust in the Galician Oi belt, http://remembertogetheracrossborders.eu/deutsch/geschichte/zeitzeugen/ [last retrieved on 12.4.2024].

167 Cf. Witness statements in the criminal proceedings against Friedrich Hildebrand, StAB, 4.89/2-548.

168 Cf. Pohl, *Judenverfolgung*, 360.

169 Cf. Sandkühler, *"Endlösung" in Galizien*, 382.

170 Cf. Arbeitsamt, Distrikt Galicia an Hauptverwaltung Karpathen Öl AG, Lemberg 30.8.1943, IfZ Munich, Fa 506-15.

sponding reports were sent by the Karpathen Öl AG head office to Krauch and Bentz on 21 September 1943.[171]

On 18 October 1943, Krauch reported in a secret communication to Himmler that most of the skilled workers at Karpathen Öl AG were Jews.[172] "*I am aware that Jewish workers are to be removed from the general economy and no longer to be deployed.*"[173] Such a removal was, however, "*preliminarily not to be applied*" as regards the expansion of the Drohobych and Jaslo refineries. Instead, all Jewish slave labourers would remain active on the building sites and be joined by others. Krauch faithfully adopted the arguments provided by the Karpathen Öl AG head office.

While Himmler had not yet decided what to do about Krauch's petition to him, Bentz's office complained on 2 November and 13 December 1943 about reports from Karpathen Öl AG of "*actions combing for Jews and replacing them*".[174] Krauch also demanded on 14 December to be informed about whether German concentration camp inmates were to be deployed to replace Jewish construction workers. Bentz and Krauch took a more restrictive stance on the matter than did the SS leadership, and under such pressure the head office now decided it would release the majority of Jews in order to be able to retain the most important skilled workers. All ops managers now had to draw up lists with the "*dispensable Jewish workers*",[175] but in fact the workforce did not get thinned out by "combing", as no order from Himmler was forthcoming, and in January 1944 Karpathen Öl AG asserted that the use of 606 Jewish

---

171 Cf. Karpathen Öl AG an Beauftragten für die Förderung der Erdölgewinnung, Benz, Geheim 21.1.1944, ibid.

172 Cf. Carl Krauch an Reichsführer SS, Geheime Reichssache, 18.10.1943, IfZ Munich, Fa 506-15, sheet 11f.

173 Ibid.

174 Cf. Sandkühler, *"Endlösung" in Galizien*, 396; telegram, 13.12.1943, "Abzug jüdischer Arbeitskräfte", ITS Archive Bad Arolsen, 1.2.7.8. /82187353.

175 Cf. Sandkühler, *"Endlösung" in Galizien*, 396–405.

workers for new builds at the refinery hubs had already reduced the workforce.[176]

The Karpathen Öl AG head office rejected the deployment of German concentration camp inmates that Krauch had proposed, pointing to the lack of accommodation. Moreover, it expressed reservations about whether "*for reasons of hierarchy, it was possible to deploy German inmates alongside Poles and Ukrainians as well as Jews from camps and POWs of various nationalities*".[177]

Individual rescue acts?

Until September 1942, Karl Grosse was primarily active in Berlin. After taking the helm at Karpathen Öl AG, he usually only made short trips to the head office in Lemberg, to government offices in Cracow, and to the various Operations Inspectorates in the GG. The head office and the inspectorates enjoyed great independence, and to meet their production targets, they insisted on an improvement of the provisions for the workforce and on ongoing deployment of Jewish slave labourers. Grosse accepted their demands and turned to the relevant authorities. In individual cases, he even supported Jewish staff members whom Malz, Beitz, Petri, and Kleinert had classified as indispensable.

This was the case for Sophie Hager, who worked at the head office. She had a doctorate in German Studies and a command of five languages and had been head of the Polish oil industry library in Lemberg since 1933. She kept the job after East Galicia was occupied by Soviet troops at the end of September 1939 and in summer 1941 was taken on by Beskiden-Gesellschaft. Grosse contacted SS

176 Cf. Karpathen Öl AG an Beauftragten für die Förderung der Erdölgewinnung, Bentz, Geheim 21.1.1944, IfZ Munich, Fa 506-15.

177 As cited in: Sandkühler, *"Endlösung" in Galizien*, 398.

Police Chief Katzmann and advocated keeping Sophie Hager on.[178] With the agreement of the latter, the Special Commissioner for the Oil Industry in the Lemberg Office, issued a provisional letter of safe conduct on 30 September 1942. It stated: "*Jewish Hager is henceforth under the special protection of my office and cannot be resettled without my approval.*"[179]

One year later, even this did not help: Sophie Hager was arrested and taken to the Ravensbrück concentration camp. The CEO of Karpathen Öl tried to get her released and, among others, approached the Commandant of the Ravensbrück concentration camp and the SD in Cracow.[180] These interventions and forged attempts to prove she was German all failed.

To pre-empt things, Sophie Hager survived the Nazi terror regime in Ravensbrück and after its liberation worked for the International Red Cross (IRC) in Switzerland. In the summer of 1945, she headed for Celle in Central Germany to repossess the library of the Galician oil industry she had set up in Lemberg, which had been transferred to the Hanover Technical University.[181] In Celle, she encountered Karl Grosse, Hermann Petri, and Konrad Kleinert again.[182] Hager describes Grosse as being "*one of the most noble and generous men*" she knew and also stated that she owed her survival to him, Petri, and Kleinert.[183] In his memoirs, penned in December 1945, Grosse records how important this meeting was for his reputation being restored: "*Suddenly, Mrs Hager appeared at my house in Celle like an angel sent by God, several months after the capitulation. I*

---

178 Cf. Hauptverwaltung Karpathen Öl an SS- and Polizeiführer Galicia, 24.11.1942, StAB, 4.89/2-601, sheet 30.

179 Cf. official photo ID, 30.9.1942, ibid., sheet 32.

180 Cf. No. 19 der Urkundenrolle für das Jahr 1945, verhandelt am 27.7.1945 in Celle von RA Dr. Walter Bennemüller, StAB, Akte Sophie Hager, sheet 10–11.

181 Cf. Karpathen Öl an Prof. Hager, z.Z. Celle 14.8.1945, ibid., sheet 10.

182 Cf. No. 19 der Urkundenrolle für das Jahr 1945, verhandelt am 27.7.1945 in Celle von RA Dr. Walter Bennemüller, sheet 10–11.

183 Ibid., sheet 13.

simply said, since I was now in a situation similar to that which she had been in back in Lemberg, 'God really exists'."[184] The way Grosse more or less places himself on a par with a Holocaust survivor is absurd. After all, since autumn 1942 he had headed a corporation founded solely for the purpose of exploiting the oil resources of occupied Poland and the Ukraine and which had relied on thousands of Polish, Ukrainian, and Jewish slave labourers.

On the other hand, there is documentary proof that, as of early 1944, the head office of Karpathen Öl had attempted to get several Polish geologists who worked in Boryslav released from concentration camps, but the requests sent to the Dachau concentration camp and the Gestapo in Katowice were not successful.[185]

In Jaslo, Karpathen Öl AG was supposed to build its own concentration camp in mid-1944, but the company's construction office objected, saying that it would need 6–7 months to build it and that the materials required were unobtainable.[186] The company therefore felt there were only two paths to mobilizing workers to expand the refineries: Either POWs should be deployed for the purpose, or – and this was what Karl Grosse favoured – workers reposted from the oil extraction operations.

In the meantime, the original plan of relocating all Jewish slave labourers to Jaslo had been changed. Some of them were supposed to be transported instead to the concentration camp in Cracow-Plaszów and from there reassigned to the company. On 10 April 1944 Lemberg/Lviv and Drohobych were bombed, and four days later SS and police units drove the Jewish slave labourers into cattle trucks. The management of the Drohobych refinery sought in

184 Große, *Mein Leben*, 69.

185 Cf. HV Karpathen Öl an Sipo Dachau, 10.1.1944 (signatures illegible); KZ Dachau an HV KÖ, 18.1.1944; Kommandeur der Sipo and des SD an KÖ, Raffinerie Jaslo, 23.3.1944, StAB, 4.89/2-601.

186 Cf. Notiz für Vorstandssitzung, 3.6.1944, betr.: Arbeiterfrage für Jaslo, Karpathen Öl, Sekretariat Generaldirektor, WD-CA, 43-13-29.

vain to at least have 47 engineers and technicians exempted from the deportation. On 14 April, 1,022 Jewish slave labourers of Karpathen-Öl (245 women and 777 men) arrived at the Cracow-Plaszów concentration camp. Twelve of them managed during the evacuation of Cracow to get their names on the list of workers at Oskar Schindler's Deutsche Emailwarenfabrik and survived the war.[187] All the others were transported from Plaszów to the Mauthausen/Gusen concentration camp.

Nevertheless, there were still Jews in the camps in Boryslaw and Drohobych, as well as those who had escaped but returned voluntarily from the woods as they were completely cut off from food and constantly had to fear they would be killed by units of the Organization of Ukrainian Nationalists (OUN) or groups of partisans.[188]

On 1 May 1944, when the Red Army offensive had come to a temporary halt, Karpathen Öl AG, the Higher SS-Polizeiführer (HSSPF), and the Generalgouvernement authorities agreed that "Jewish camps" would be erected at several of the company's sites. In Jaslo, Jewish slave labourers were assigned to expand the refinery and to work in the coal pits, in the car repair shop, in Glinik on construction of the shoe factory, and in the accounting section in Libusza,[189] although the company had to promise that "*it would be ever restrained in demanding staff, in particular women*".[190]

On 17–18 May 1944, Himmler and the director of the SS Economics Administration Head Office (WVHA) Oswald Pohl vis-

---

[187] Cf. Arbeitslager im besetzten Polen - Distrikt Galizien, www.deathcamps.org [last retrieved on 30.4.2024].

[188] Zum Antisemitismus der OUN cf. Franziska Bruder, *"Den ukrainischen Staat erkämpfen oder sterben!" Die Organisation Ukrainischer Nationalisten (OUN) 1928–1948*, Berlin 2007, 217ff.

[189] Cf. Notiz über Judenläger, Glinik, 24.4.1944 also for Dir. Kubelka, Jaslo, 18.5.1944: Auszug aus dem Vorstandsprotokoll vom 12.5.1944, WD-CA, D-43-13-24; note: Barackenaufstellung, Plan vom 6.6.1944 (signature: Petri), WD-CA, D-43-13-25.

[190] Aktenvermerk, betr.: Judenläger, 4.5.44 (Dr. Petri), WD-CA, D-43-13-24.

ited Lemberg for the last time, as Himmler was keen to find out how Jewish slave labourers could be used for the SS projects to exploit solid paraffin and manganese deposits.[191]

At Karpathen Öl AG, the workforce issues had further intensified. The plan to rebuild the refinery in Jaslo was at risk, and it was only for this reason that the company managed to get approval to relocate its Jewish slave labourers from East to West Galicia.[192] A few Jews were still active in the accounts section, and their deportation could be expected at any time, causing Petri to comment: "*If we have to expect the removal of the Jews, we'll find ourselves in a new situation where we will then have to apply for special staff allocations.*"[193]

On the evening of 28 June 1944, Petri telegrammed Grosse about whether the repairs to the Drohobych East refinery could be included in the Geilenberg Programme. He also mentioned the urgent enquiry from the SS in Cracow asking for a date to be set for it to pick up the Jewish inmates, which Petri wanted to simply turn down.[194] Grosse wired Petri only one hour later: "*I ask you to wait in answering the questions as regards the Jews being picked up until I have myself issued a statement on it.*"[195]

Grosse wanted to wait to talk with the new SSPF in Lemberg, SS-Brigadeführer Christoph Diehm, and he did so in early July 1944. No details are known, but we can assume that the focus was on the fate of the remaining Jewish inmates working at Karpathen Öl. On 6 July 1944, Grosse had his thanks conveyed to Diehm for his support.[196] Does this mean that the company had managed to have its wishes heard and was able to continue relocating the Jewish inmate workers to Jaslo? After the end of the war, Grosse describes

---

191 Cf. Sandkühler, *"Endlösung" in Galizien*, 402f.

192 Cf. Programm für Generaldirektor Große für Krakau 15.6.1944, WD-CA, D-43-13-24.

193 Petri: Vermerk für LG, Sehr dringend, betr.: Einsatz nichtdeutscher Buchhaltungskräfte, 6.6.44, WD-CA, D-43-13-24.

194 Cf. Telegramm Dr. Petri (Jaslo) an Große, 28.6.44, 18.50 Uhr, WD-CA, D-43-13-11.

195 Große an Petri 28.6.1944, WD-CA, D-43-13-27.

196 Cf. Große an Becker (KÖ), 6.7.1944, WD-CA, D-43-13-11.

v stelle jaslo fs j 775 28.6.44 18.50h an
hauptverwaltung fuer herrn gd. grosse

1. reg.rat schmidt hat im auftrag von professor buch, als gebietsbeauftragten des gebechem auf anfrage von berlin einen bericht ueber die lage in drohobycz angefordert, der unverzueglich erstellt werden muss, insbesondere auch mit beantwortung der frage, ob der aufbau in drohobycz ost in das geilenbergprogramm einzubeziehen ist. ich habe weitergabe nach lemberg zugesagt und mitgeteilt, dass zur frage der einbeziehung von drohobycz ost in das geilenberg-programm uns baldigst aeussern wuerden und dann einen zustandsbericht ueber drohobycz erteilen wuerden. ihre entscheidung wird durch fs an ostenergie krakau erwartet.
2. der stellvertreter der oberfeldkommandantur, general von hartlieb, general ottlaender, hat sich heut ploetzlich ueber ortskommandantur krosno fuer donnerstag vormittag anmelden lassen. er will "etwas vom erdoel" sehen, wie es heisst. es ist wohl daraus zu schliessen, dass diesem besuch dann keine besondere bedeutung beizumessen ist. nur ruecksprache mit dem ihm begleitenden oberstleutnant wagner, von der oberfeldkomm. tarnow, wird von wichtigkeit sein.
3. es liegt eine dringende anfrage von der ss-krkau wegen nennung des termins der uebernahme der juedischen haeftlinge vor. habe beantwortung bis zu ihrer rueckkehr ausstehen lassen. falls sie morgen nicht kommen koennen, bitte ich mir mitzuteilen, ob die lage so anzusehen ist, dass wir heute schon eine endgueltige absage auf uebernahme der juden erteilen koennen.

v stelle jaslo/sta petri.

Fig. 53 Telegramme from Dr Hermann Petri to Karl Grosse, 28 June 1944, 6:50 p.m.

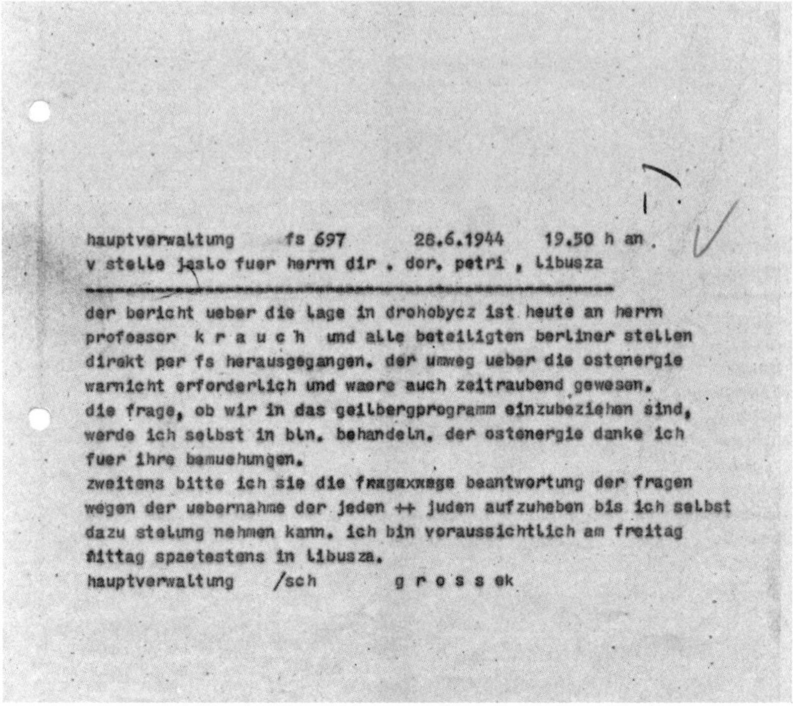

hauptverwaltung fs 697 28.6.1944 19.50 h an
v stelle jaslo fuer herrn dir . dor. petri , libusza

---

der bericht ueber die lage in drohobycz ist heute an herrn
professor k r a u c h und alle beteiligten berliner stellen
direkt per fs herausgegangen. der umweg ueber die ostenergie
warnicht erforderlich und waere auch zeitraubend gewesen.
die frage, ob wir in das geilbergprogramm einzubeziehen sind,
werde ich selbst in bln. behandeln. der ostenergie danke ich
fuer ihre bemuehungen.
zweitens bitte ich sie die fragaxxage beantwortung der fragen
wegen der uebernahme der jeden ++ juden aufzuheben bis ich selbst
dazu stellung nehmen kann. ich bin voraussichtlich am freitag
mittag spaetestens in libusza.
hauptverwaltung /sch g r o s s ek

Fig. 54 Telegramme response from Karl Grosse to Dr Hermann Petri, 28.6.1944, 7:50 p.m.

what happened as follows: "*I succeeded in ensuring the Jews were not taken from us but that we could redeploy them in West Galicia, in Jaslo. That did not then happen because we had to evacuate that territory, too.*"[197]

Given the military situation, preparations for repairing the refinery were discontinued, and the last slave labour camp run by Karpathen Öl AG in Mraznica (near Boryslav) was dissolved on 22 July 1944 as good as overnight. The inmates were transported to Auschwitz, where Jews from Plaszów had also been taken.[198] Some of them were immediately sent to the gas chambers, others moved on to the concentration camps in Mauthausen/Gusen, Gross-Rosen, and Bergen-Belsen. How many of them survived the Nazi terror is not known, but it was probably not more than a few hundred.

As regards the participation of DEA in the Beskid companies and Karpathen Öl AG, we can conclude: The group possessed a precise knowledge of the Polish oil industry thanks to the activities of its subsidiaries in Galicia prior to the First World War. In light of the Polish oil industry's limited oil deposits and low productivity, DEA had little interest in taking over facilities there; rather, the initiative to found German operating companies was driven by the Reich Economics Ministry and OKW. After the failed attempt by the German military to take the oil fields in the Caucasus, from 1943 onward Karpathen Öl AG led by Karl Grosse had far greater importance for the German war effort. Its head office succeeded in securing itself high priority in the allocation of materials, improving food provisions for its workforce, and obtaining a partial special statute allowing it to continue to keep Jewish slave labourers at work. The goals of the Nazi regime – namely to boost the war-time economy and to move ahead with the annihilation of all European Jews – were permanently at cross-purposes.

---

197 Große, *Mein Leben*, 68.

198 Cf. Arbeitslager im besetzten Polen - Distrikt Galizien.

Kontinentale Öl AG

The foundation of Kontinentale Öl AG

After the German victories in 1940, the Four-Year Plan Authority had leading German oil experts Alfred Bentz and Ernst R. Fischer (since the summer of 1939 Head of the Oil Section at the Reich Economics Ministry and previously senior executive and oil expert at I.G. Farben) compile studies on oil supplies for Central Europe.[199] They both came to the conclusion that Europe was unable to cover its own needs and required oil from the Middle East. There were advocates of a Mediterranean-Middle East strategy not only in the Four-Year Plan Authority but also in the OKW, the navy, and the Foreign Office. They assumed England could be beaten and the rich oil fields in the Middle East seized.

As of the summer of 1940, these protagonists attempted to gain a foothold in Iraq. To this end, the Foreign Office instrumentalized Arab "liberation movements" against British colonial rule, and these activities prompted Deutsche Bank to get involved, as it saw an opportunity to regain the oil concessions lost in the First World War. Kurt Weigelt, Deutsche Bank board member, registered these old claims with all Reich agencies and authorities that might come into question and informed DEA Chairman Schirner of the fact, since he wanted to persuade DEA to take a joint approach.[200] Schirner showed his interest in his response, dated 8 August 1940, stating: "*in the event that it [Deutsche Bank – the authors] should in the further course of things be in a position to realize its old rights in Iraq and ensure they can be industrially exploited*", then his company would fundamentally be interested in collaboration.[201] As in the case of the Ecuador Project (1936–8) and the Mexico Project (1938), Schirner

---

[199] Cf. Eichholtz, *Deutsche Ölpolitik*, 401–415.

[200] Cf. Weigelt an Schirner, 3.8.1940, HADB, R 8119 F, P-8369, sheet 28.

[201] Cf. Schirner an Weigelt, 6.8.1940, ibid.

proved to be a cautious tactician. He wanted to make sure DEA was part of the play but waited to see how things developed. He also had in mind that DEA had limited resources in terms of oil experts and drilling rigs. At the same time, it also bears noting that the DEA Management Board was definitely open to participating in the Nazi regime's policy of expansion and war as soon as a realistic opportunity for the company arose.

For a few weeks in April–May 1941, the OKW started to focus on Iraqi oil. An anti-British revolt by Iraqi officers was swiftly supported by German troops dispatched to Mosul and Baghdad,[202] although the small special unit was not able to achieve anything given the military superiority of the British. After only three weeks, the uprising and thus the attempt to seize control of oil fields in the Middle East had come to nothing. DEA staff were not involved in the advance on Mosul.

DEA was also not involved in any way in the plans to found a state-controlled oil company operating world-wide. The initiative for the latter was down to Ernst R. Fischer,[203] and from autumn 1940 onwards, the Four-Year Plan Authority sought to establish an oil company that would form the German opposite number of world market leader Standard Oil.

On 5 October 1940, Göring was informed by Friedrich Kadgien, the man whose services he used to handle foreign-ex-

---

202 Cf. Eichholtz, *Deutsche Ölpolitik*, 410–413.

203 The history of Kontinentale Öl AG is well researched, mainly thanks to the work of Dietrich Eichholtz, Titus Kockel, Harald Wixforth and Anand Toprani. Cf. Eichholtz, *Deutsche Ölpolitik*, 387–400; Titus Kockel, *Eine Quelle zur Vor- and Gründungsgeschichte der Kontinentale Öl AG aus dem Jahr 1940*, in: Jahrbuch für Wirtschaftsgeschichte 1 (2003), 175ff.; Harald Wixforth, *Die Ausbeutung von Ressourcen im Zeichen der Kriegswirtschaft: die Kontinentale Öl AG*, in: Johannes Bähr (Ed.), Die Dresdner Bank in der Wirtschaft des Dritten Reiches, München 2006, 360–370; Anand Toprani, *Germany's Answer to Standard Oil: The Continental Oil Company and Nazi Grand Strategy, 1940–1942*, in: Journal of Strategic Studies 6–7 (2014), 949–973. For the current state of research Karsten Linne, *Die Gründung der Kontinentale Öl AG*, manuscript Hamburg 2023.

change deals, as with the acquisition of the oil concessions in Austria, that Deutsche Bank saw an opportunity to acquire a major slice of the shares held in France in Belgian oil company "Concordia" for between 20 and 25 million Reichsmark.[204] On top of this, there were the shares still owned by the French in "Columbia", so the Four-Year Plan Authority thereupon formally commissioned the Director of Deutsche Bank, Hermann J. Abs, with buying the shares and thus to be invoiced for it. The idea was for the Franco-Belgian shares to form the launchpad for a "*realignment of international oil interests*".[205]

The Four-Year Plan Authority had an easier time of penetrating the Romanian oil industry, as it had confiscated the gold reserves in Holland and Belgium. It had already set up a special fund for the repurchase of international bonds and stocks, and the gold reserves thus plundered were assigned to it. Kadgien noted: "*The debt relief action is essentially not to be financed from the basic foreign-exchange fund but instead from the monies supplied by the occupied territories.*"[206] The Four-Year Plan Authority and the Reichsbank were able to push ahead with the "debt relief action" and also had sufficient money left in the kitty for the state share in the forthcoming Kontinentale Öl AG.

The private oil companies were not pleased that they had to participate in the foundation of a new government-dominated oil company, but their specialist know-how was indispensable. The decisive meeting with representatives of the big banks and the oil-industry "Big Four" took place on 18 March 1941.[207] The actual foundation of Kontinentale Öl AG (Konti Öl) took place a good week later, on 27 March 1941 in Berlin.

---

204 Cf. Aktennotiz (Kadgien): Dem Herrn Reichsmarschall vorzulegen, 5.10.1940, RGVA Moscow, 700-1-29, sheet 172.

205 Cf. note, Geheime Reichssache, 17.10.1940, ibid., sheet 230f.

206 Vierjahresplan, Referat Kadgien, Geheime Reichssache, betr.: Entschuldungsaktion, 15.10. 1940, RGVA Moscow, 700-1-29, sheet 232.

207 Cf. Eichholtz, *Geschichte der deutschen Kriegswirtschaft,* Vol. 1, 233ff.

Konti Öl was destined to represent German oil interests outside the country, acquire participations, and take all the necessary measures to "*promote*" German oil supplies "*through active involvement outside the country.*"[208] Of the capital stock of 80 million Reichsmark, the Reich itself held registered shares with multiple voting rights valued at 30 million Reichsmark through the purpose-founded Borussia GmbH. The oil industry, represented by I.G. Farben, DEA, Preussag, Wintershall AG, and Gewerkschaft Elwerath, subscribed to registered shares valued at 3 million Reichsmark each. Bearer shares for 2 million Reichsmark each went to BRABAG and Preussag as trustees for the fuel interests of the hard coal corporations, while the remaining 1 million Reichsmark was to be handled by a bank as fiduciary agent.[209] Bearer shares with simple voting rights totalling 30 million Reichsmark went to Deutsche and Dresdner Bank, Reichskreditgesellschaft AG, and Berliner Handelsgesellschaft KGaA. With this corporate structure, Konti Öl was to be a model for the future relationship of state and business. The state had a dominating influence but left it to the oil companies and banks involved to handle financing and operations.

Ernst R. Fischer was appointed Chair of the Advisory Council and later the Management Board, the clear eminence grise behind Konti Öl and confidante of Göring. His deputies were Karl Blessing, until early 1939 Director of the Reichsbank, and Hans Brochhaus, Director of Gewerkschaft Elwerath. The 28-member Supervisory Board was subordinate to a Presiding Council that included Reich Economics Minister Walther Funk as Chair and State Secretaries Wilhelm Keppler and Erich Neumann. The other seats on the Supervisory Board went to important representatives of the Wehrmacht, the Four-Year Plan Authority, the oil industry, and the

---

208 Reichswirtschaftsministerium: Aktennotiz, betr.: Kontinentale Öl AG, Berlin, 27.8.1941, RGVA Moscow, 1458-40-160, sheet 1.

209 Cf. Wixforth, *Die Ausbeutung von Ressourcen*, 363.

banks.[210] DEA was represented by its CEO Karl Schirner on the Konti Supervisory Board.

Konti Öl was outfitted with extraordinary powers of attorney. While other monopoly companies simply acted as trustees managing the companies they absorbed and were then dissolved at the end of the war, Konti Öl was planned as a permanent corporation. Its name itself stated what the agenda was – the company was meant to take over all the major oil fields in Europe. It was clear to everyone involved that this would only be possible on the back of further war and a policy of occupation.

Whether the men in the background already had their sights set on the oil fields in the Caucasus when they founded Konti Öl is doubtful, as initially the idea was to bundle German oil interests in Romania.[211] Moreover, Konti Öl GmbH, the company's Romanian subsidiary, signed a deal with Astra Romana, a Royal Dutch Shell subsidiary, on 26 May 1941 for a joint exploration venture. This contract secured Konti Öl GmbH 50 percent of the shares in the concessions Astra held.[212] The Reich Economics Ministry considered the Romanian oil industry as henceforth coming under German majority control.[213]

DEA had not been party to the discussions surrounding the foundation of Konti Öl, and it was only after the company had started operating that the Reich Economics Ministry contacted Schirner and requested assistance with restructuring the Romanian oil industry. He thereupon dispatched Günther Schlicht to Romania, who stated that he set up a joint venture there that improved supplies of materials to the strategically so crucial Romanian oil industry.[214]

---

210 Cf. Eichholtz, *Geschichte der deutschen Kriegswirtschaft,* Vol. 1, 237.

211 Cf. Gottfried Griebel, *Deutsche Mineralölwirtschaft*, VII/7 (unpublished manuscript), Hamburg 1950.

212 Cf. Kasper, *Die Erdölgewinnung Deutschlands*, 95.

213 Cf. Reichswirtschaftsministerium: Aktennotiz, betr.: Kontinentale Öl AG, Berlin, 27.8.1941, RGVA Moscow, 1458-40-160, sheet 1.

214 Cf. Schlicht, *Memoiren*, 87.

To summarize: The foundation of Kontinentale Öl AG marked a rupture in the history of the German oil business. The company was based on the acquisition of foreign assets through seizure and was, a little later, to give way to a policy of plundering other countries. The Four-Year Plan Authority dreamed of Konti Öl becoming the German equivalent of the international oil majors, but the latter had outstanding technological resources and oil experts leading them, while Kontinentale Öl AG was ruled by state officials together with Nazi Party members.

Advancing to the oil fields in the Caucasus

While Kontinentale Öl AG was still being set up, military plans were being hatched in secret for war against the Soviet Union, and Hitler issued a corresponding order regarding "Operation Barbarossa" on 18 December 1940. The plan was to exploit the territory of the Soviet Union in classical colonial manner, and Göring had had detailed guidelines drawn up for this. These stated, above all: "*The exploitation of the territories to be occupied shall primarily focus on the fields of food and the oil industry. Gaining as much food and oil for Germany as possible is the main economic objective of the action.*"[215]

For the planners at the Defence Economics Office, it was clear by May 1941 that the Wehrmacht lacked the fuel for additional major operations. In a report prepared for the head of the OKW, Field Marshal Keitel, they calculated that the monthly shortfall was 400,000 t.[216] Whether the report got as far as Hitler is not known, and he had long since resolved to subjugate the Soviet Union with a second lightning attack.

---

215 Richtlinien für die Führung der Wirtschaft (Grüne Mappe). Teil I. Aufgaben und Organisation der Wirtschaft in den neubesetzten Ostgebieten. Berlin, Juni 1941, in: Der Prozeß gegen die Hauptkriegsverbrecher. Vol. 28, 3–26, here 5f.

216 Cf. Griebel, *Deutsche Mineralölprobleme*, VI.8.

It is not quite clear how the German business elites viewed the planning for "Barbarossa".[217] There is evidence that the I.G. Farben group was planning on plundering the Soviet Union from an early date, but the same cannot be said of DEA, which had nowhere near the same high-ranking contacts and influence. There are no indications that the company was involved in the planning for "Barbarossa", which is not surprising. Even after the beginning of the war, DEA was still a corporation that realized most of its revenue through coal production and processing.

One day after Germany launched its attack on the Soviet Union, Günther Schlicht, who was in Marienbad taking the waters, was informed by DEA Chairman Schirner that he had been ordered back immediately for military work.[218] Schlicht was included in a War Administrative Council with a function corresponding to the rank of a major and was, like other German oil industry experts, attached to the pool of specialists who were expected to take positions in the subsidiaries of Konti Öl or the mineral oil brigades.

On 27 July 1941, around one month after the attack on the Soviet Union, Göring issued his so-called "green folder" containing a series of decrees on business in the occupied eastern territories.[219] German interest in raw materials focussed on grains, oil seeds, light metals – and oil, and Göring assigned Kontinentale Öl AG the exclusive right to produce, distribute, and trade in oil for the period of 99 years.[220] How the Soviet oil industry would be plundered was laid out in detail in a Göring decree of 28 October 1941.[221] The plan

217 Cf. Eichholtz, *Deutsche Ölpolitik*, 400.

218 Cf. Schlicht, *Memoiren*, 90.

219 Cf. Wirtschafts-Führungsstab Ost, Geheim, Richtlinie für die Führung der Wirtschaft in den neubesetzten Ostgebieten (Grüne Mappe), 27.7.1941, RGVA Moscow, 1458-40-38.

220 Cf. Erlass vom August 1941, RGVA Moscow, 700-1-12, sheet 15f.

221 Cf. Wirtschafts-Führungsstab Ost, Geheim, Richtlinie für die Führung der Wirtschaft in den neubesetzten Ostgebieten (Grüne Mappe), 27.7.1941, RGVA Moscow, 1458-40-38.

was to form oil exploration squads, investigation and operational management units, oil command structures, and technical brigades. Konti Öl founded subsidiaries for the various regions: Ost-Öl GmbH, Baltische Öl GmbH, Ostland Öl Vertriebs GmbH, Ukraine Öl Vertriebs GmbH, and Kontinentale Transport AG.[222] Ost-Öl, where Günther Schlicht was a member of the board, was to have a special role, as it was to take over the Caucasian oil fields.

In the late summer of 1941, the military still felt it possible that German armed forces would swiftly occupy the Caucasus. In great haste, the OKW set up a special unit of refinery experts who followed Heeresgruppe Süd to the Crimea. Oil Brigade K (for "Kaukasus") was meant *"directly after the combat troops to secure and occupy the oil fields and area of operations. Moreover, at the same time it should undertake to initiate restoration of the production facilities."*[223]

After the 1941 campaign was thwarted, Oil Brigade K was put on hold near Rostov-on-Don. Hitler wanted to decide the war on the Eastern Front in 1942 with the next major offensive, whereby the main strategic targets were to take Stalingrad and conquer the oil fields around Baku, Maykop, and Grosny. Field Marshal Keitel remarked in this context: *"It is clear that the operations in the year 1942 must get us to the oil fields. If we don't succeed, then we will not be able to conduct further operations the following year."*[224] Hitler concurred with this assessment: *"If I don't get the oil from Maykop and Grosny, then I'll have to terminate this war."*[225]

Annual oil production in the fields round Baku, Grosny, and Maykop totalled, as Bentz of the Four-Year Plan Authority cal-

---

222 Cf. Reichswirtschaftsministerium: Aktennotiz, betr.: Kontinentale Öl AG, Berlin, 27.8.1941, RGVA Moscow, 1458-40-160, sheet 2f.

223 Richtlinie für die Führung der Wirtschaft in den neubesetzten Ostgebieten, 27.7.1941, RGVA Moscow, 1458-40-38.

224 Aktennotiz General Thomas über eine Besprechung bei Keitel, 28.5.1942, BArch Berlin, FS, Film 1829.

225 As cited in: witness hearing of General Paulus, 11.2.1946, Internationaler Militärgerichtshof Nürnberg (IMG), Vol. 7, 290.

Fig. 55 Maykop oil fields (1942)

culated, about 27 million t.[226] Given this scale, Göring pursued the strategy of ruthlessly exploiting the German oil fields and requisitioning a lot of the German experts and drilling equipment for the Caucasus project.

On 13 January 1942, the Konti Öl Supervisory Board convened, with the main item on the agenda being preparation of the "Caucasus deployment".[227] Günther Schlicht played a key role in this context, as he was in charge of planning drilling rig use and purchasing vehicles and materials. The entire programme he developed together with a few members of staff covered an order volume of more than 100 million Reichsmark.[228] Schlicht planned to deploy around 600 rigs. Since German industry was hardly able to

226 Cf. Eichholtz, *Deutsche Ölpolitik*, 437.
227 Cf. ibid., 447.
228 Cf. Schlicht, *Memoiren*, 93f.

provide so much equipment at such short notice, the plan was to involve French companies in the Caucasus project, hence Konti Öl attempted talks with French oil companies.[229] It offered the French a participation in the Caucasian oil wells that would hopefully be tapped, but the French entrepreneurs were indifferent to the offer. Meanwhile, the oil experts had realized what a huge scale the Caucasus project entailed, and Schlicht mentioned that it was a task "*which to date no oil industry in the world has tried to tackle*".[230]

Göring reacted by turning Oil Brigade K into Technical Brigade Oil (TBM) as of 1 April 1942.[231] Luftwaffe General Erich Homburg was made its commanding officer, while DEA board member Schlicht was made head of the specialist section. Homburg moved into an office in the DEA building in Schöneberg, Berlin, and insisted that Schlicht wear his uniform when appearing before him.[232] General Homburg was assisted by oil expert Cavalry Captain (retd.) Erich Will,[233] who had already acted as Special Commissioner for the Oil Industry in the Generalgouvernement.

TBM's equipment was provided by Konti Öl as well as all the large German oil companies and French corporations: more than

229 Cf. Eichholtz, *Deutsche Ölpolitik*, 448.

230 Günther Schlicht, *Grandprobleme des Osteinsatzes auf dem Gebiet der Erdölförderung and -gewinnung*, 16.6.1942, as cited in: Titus Kockel, *Geologie and Krieg. Die Erdölpolitik des Reichsamtes für Bodenforschung and seine Vorläufer*, M.A. Berlin, 1995, document 11.

231 The history of the Mineral Oil Brigade K and the TBM is well researched. Cf. esp.: Günther Schlicht, *Die deutsche Expedition in den Kaukasus*, n.d., Archiv der BGR Hannover, Sign. 58277; Dietrich Eichholtz, *Der Raubzug des faschistischen deutschen Imperialismus zu den Erdölquellen des Kaukasus 1941–1943*, in: Jahrbuch für Geschichte (1976), 445–502; Id., *Deutsche Ölpolitik*; Hermann Häusler/Bruno W. Koppensteiner, *Das Kaukasus-Öl. Ziel der Deutschen Wehrmacht im Zweiten Weltkrieg*, in: Berichte der Geologischen Bandesanstalt (2021), 77–102; Matthias Puchta, *Die Technische Brigade Mineralöl and ihre Kriegsgefangenen. Der wehrwirtschaftliche Einsatz kriegsgefangener Mineralölfachkräfte an der Ostfront*, in: VSWG, 1 (2024), 35–65.

232 Cf. Schlicht, *Memoiren*, 93.

233 For Erich Will cf. the section about the Karpathen Öl AG.

100 deep-drilling rigs, 225 sets of well pumps, 10 mobile distillation units, and 75 blow-out sets. The mass of equipment weighed about 80,000 t and had a value of around 80 million Reichsmark.[234]

TBM was less of a military unit and more of a hodgepodge of civilian experts, some of whom had at best served briefly in the military. Looking back, Schlicht said that total TBM manpower in January 1942 was approx. 6,500,[235] although historians estimate the figure to have been as many as 10,000, several thousand of them Soviet POWs.[236] They were better fed than the Soviet POWs in other camps, where the German strategy was to let hundreds of thousands of men starve to death.

At the end of June 1942, the Wehrmacht again advanced on the Caucasus. Shortly beforehand, Schlicht had presented an exhaustive analysis on the status of technical readiness at TBM and stated the main problem was the lack of skilled experts.[237] He nevertheless expected that after six months of set-up, the first oil would flow in noteworthy quantities in Grosny and Maykop, but the big success would be once the Baku oil fields were taken.

Impressed by the first military successes, on 10 July 1942 Göring convened an "oil meeting", attended by Schlicht, among others,[238] at which Göring demanded the swift resumption of oil production. Schlicht tried to dampen Göring's optimism, pointing to the destruction of the oil wells and the lack of heavy drilling rigs and skilled staff, above all master drillers. Göring also had "solutions" to this:

"*Propaganda material will be dropped by aircraft, informing workers that they should prevent destruction as otherwise their jobs will*

---

234 Cf. Griebel, *Deutsche Mineralölprobleme*, IX.7.

235 Cf. Schlicht, *Die deutsche Expedition in den Kaukasus*, 86.

236 Cf. Puchta, *Die Technische Brigade Mineralöl*, 35–65.

237 Cf. Günther Schlicht, *Grundprobleme des Osteinsatzes auf dem Gebiet der Erdölförderung and -gewinnung*, 16.6.1942.

238 Cf. Stenografischer Bericht über die Öl-Sitzung im Hauptquartier des Reichsmarschalls, 10.7.1942, Ifz Munich, MA 114-3, sheet 5604–5637.

Fig. 56 Destroyed pumping probe nr. Maykop (1942)

be lost and they will share the awful fate of the workers transported to the workshops, factories, etc." He instructed Schlicht: "*Take the oil workers from Romania and Hungary, all the ones who are suitable.*" Schlicht added: "*Including POWs?*" Göring: "*Yes.*"

Schlicht, Bentz, and Neumann then drew Göring's attention to bottlenecks. Schlicht said that the German oil industry had never before conducted such a massive operation, to which Göring responded: "*And we've never waged such a large war.*"[239] He swept the experts' objections aside: "*That doesn't interest me! What is tough has to be achieved all the same!*"[240] Göring insisted on rapid successes and

239 Ibid.

240 Ibid.

Fig. 57 Steel reinforcement system with clamping jaws, nr. Maykop (1942)

wanted to know how much oil TBM could produce in the shortest space of time. Schlicht put the target at 1.5 million t within the first year from the North Caucasus region.

As of August 1942, the Wehrmacht managed to gain control of parts of the western oil fields in the Caucasus. When TBM entered the production zone near Maykop, though, it found most of the wells had been destroyed,[241] with the drilling rigs dismantled and the wells professionally plugged. It proved impossible to jerry-rig them. Schlicht bore even more professional responsibility when, on 9 August 1942, the TBM staff, headed by Erich Will, died in a plane crash.[242]

In early October 1942, the German plans to conquer the fields seemed to be working. The 6th Army reached Stalingrad and the oil fields round Grosny were within tangible distance. Göring had an order prepared for Hitler to command that the Caucasus oil industry be rebuilt as fast as possible,[243] and this "Führer order" would include sufficient provisions for the oil workers.[244] TBM interrogated captured Soviet engineers and master drillers, had them compile maps of the oil fields, and prepared to seize this strategically crucial region. An advance towards Baku saw forward units enter Grosny, but fierce Soviet resistance stopped TBM from entering the oil fields there. In a communication to State Secretary Neumann on 20 October 1942, Schlicht outlined why swift large-scale production in the conquered oil fields could not be expected.[245]

---

241 Cf. Schlicht, *Die deutsche Expedition in den Kaukasus*, 64.

242 Cf. id., *Memoiren*, 96.

243 Cf. Dr. Grönnert an Göring, Notiz für Reichsmarschall für Besprechung beim Führer, 8.10.1942, MA 114-3, sheet 5736, 5766–5776, 5865.

244 Cf. Puchta, *Die Technische Brigade Mineralöl*, 40.

245 Cf. Schlicht to Secretary of State Neumann, 20.10.1942, in: Richard Brachwitz, *Technische Brigade Mineralöl im Kaukasus* in: "Glückauf" Rundbrief der AG Bergbau, Erdöl, Geologie e.V. 78 (1999).

Fig. 58 Günther Schlicht, Alfred Bentz, and others in uniform in the Maykop oil fields (November 1942)

Göring convened the second oil meeting on 21 November 1942.[246] Given the major problems in restoring oil production operations and the uncertain military situation, chief geologist Bentz proposed withdrawing the drilling equipment, which was in such short supply, and concentrating on pumping the newly struck oil in Austria. There was a lack of skilled staff and food, he said, to which Göring responded: "*What do you mean, they are dropping out? Then find ways to keep them.*" Göring even brushed aside Schlicht's reference to the problems on the combat front, saying: "*At the moment*

[246] Cf. Stenografischer Bericht über die Öl-Sitzung, 21.11.42 im Hauptquartier des Reichsmarschalls, MA 114-3, sheet 5661–5699.

everyone is laughing about the oil brigade. If at least you did something! If you only pumped a little oil, it would be something!" Schlicht defended TBM by pointing to the fact there were not enough Soviet staff, and they were unreliable. Göring raged: "*Then hang one of them from an oil rig!*" Schlicht: "*Once it's in place we'll find a few.*" Göring: "*So what oil have you produced? Nothing. [...] That's no OKW unit. You know full well that this entire set of zeros for the whole economy is subordinate to me.*" He fumed: "*If by next spring there's no oil ... may the devil take you.*" Schlicht answered: "*It's all still inside the theatre of operations.*"[247]

Göring's anger reflects the dramatic difficulties of supplying oil to the German troops. Without the oil from the Caucasus, the plans for Germany to be a world power would go up in smoke, and in early 1943 a Soviet counter-offensive promptly scuppered the Caucasus project entirely. TBM suffered massive losses of personnel and material during the retreat,[248] and although no one dared speak of a definitive defeat, with the collapse of the "Caucasus Pincer" the battle for oil was over. Schlicht was aware of this and felt the war was now lost, but in his opinion there was "*no point thinking about such things.*"[249] Instead, he immersed himself in new tasks.

Looking back, Günther Schlicht and other members of TBM only discussed their time on the frontline in the Caucasus in specialist terms or as one great adventure. They suggest that relations with the local inhabitants in the Caucasus were good and that all the German experts had "*behaved impeccably*". Schlicht wasn't prepared to "*say anything bad*" about the SS Panzer Division "Wiking".[250]

Back in Berlin, Schlicht was made a DEA board member. He assumed control of all DEA oil companies, including the wells operating in Heide (Holstein), Wietze (Hannover), Neusiedl (Austria), Pechelbronn (Alsace), and Gbeli (Slovakia), as well as the refineries

---

247 Ibid.

248 Cf. Eichholtz, *Deutsche Ölpolitik*, 459–461.

249 Schlicht, *Memoiren*, 119.

250 Cf. ibid., 110.

Fig. 59 Soviet slave labour preparing a new drill site (end of 1942)

in Heide, Wilhelmsburg, Rositz, Pechelbronn, and Schwechat near Vienna. Furthermore, he succeeded Karl Grosse as head of the "Oil Production" Expert Group attached to the Fuel Industry Business Group.

X. FOREIGN AND FORCED LABOUR AT DEA: VARIANCES IN AN AMBIVALENT SITUATION

(Manfred Grieger)

Applying non-economic force on people for one's own needs and then exploiting those people in order to rely on their labour seemed to be a right that resulted from the racist mindset underpinning the Nazi system of rule – namely that Germans were superior to the groups they disparaged and defamed in racist fashion. In the pre-war period, this initially affected people who were politically and socially ostracized, as well as Jews or Sinti and Roma, who were deliberately squeezed out of the German "people's community" [Volksgemeinschaft]. After the war started, the political leadership and the Nazi state applied their own ethnic[völkisch]-racist categorization to assign members of subjugated nations to a subordinate structure and thus determine how they were treated. This structure condemned Jews and Sinti and Roma to a status completely bereft of any rights and discriminated against people from East Europe such as Poles, Russians, and Ukrainians by relative comparison to West Europeans, such as the French or Walloons, and by stark comparison to Germans.[1]

---

1 Cf. Ulrich Herbert, *Fremdarbeiter. Politik und Praxis des "Ausländer-Einsatzes" in der Kriegswirtschaft des Dritten Reiches*, Berlin 1985, 67ff.; Mark Spoerer, *Zwangsarbeit unter dem Hakenkreuz. Ausländische Zivilarbeiter, Kriegsgefangene und Häftlinge im Deutschen Reich und im besetzten Europa 1939–1945*, Stuttgart 2000, 24ff.; Manfred Grieger, *Extermination and Work under the Nazi System of Forced Labor*, in: Volkhard Knigge et al. (Eds.), Forced Labor. The Germans, the Forced Laborers, and the War, Weimar 2010, 208–220.

The lives of those placed outside the German "people's community" did not really count. The murderous treatment of Soviet POWs in particular resulted from the assumed superiority of the Germans and the conviction that foreign "labour" could be recruited in infinite numbers. The German wartime economic system in the territory of the German Reich was based essentially on labour performed by millions of forced labourers, who in 1944 formed roughly a quarter of the workforce. Companies, meaning entrepreneurs and managers, considered the government-organized provision of foreign substitute labour with fewer civil rights to be an undisputed opportunity to continue their manufacturing operations or businesses – or even expand them, to the extent that in many companies slave labour accounted for at least a third of the workforce.

The system of forced labour was initially intended as a temporary stopgap but was soon adopted as a permanent solution to the labour shortage. The millions of forced labourers constituted a kind of contribution to German wartime society that ensured companies received the labour force they required, institutions of state and local authorities were able to maintain their duties such as providing infrastructure, buildings, or waste disposal services, and German employees and residents moved collectively up the social ladder thanks to the ethnic hierarchy imposed in the workplace. The German population expressed hardly any reservations about this system – with the exception of those whose sympathetic contact with foreign civilian labourers and POWs was prosecuted and punished.

These processes and phenomena are well known and have often been described at the level of society as a whole. Considering them at the level of a company and its different sites with different tasks also means addressing the in-company processes of learning and habituation. It is obvious that the immediate working conditions of mining underground or of construction or loading-bay activities had influenced the situation of those involved, as membership of the different national subsets among the set of foreign workers. The surveillance and disciplining system also had an impact on their circumstances.

Corporate managers initially considered foreigners as substitute labour and, as a rule, as a necessary evil. The exploitation of foreign forced labourers at the DEA Group started in its lignite and hard coal operations, and in May 1940 open-cast mining operations relied for the first time on 240 foreign civilian workers and 600 Polish POWs.[2] In early 1941, there was an increasing shortage of workers for the lignite plants,[3] and recruiting a foreign substitute workforce seemed to be the solution. Management therefore had a camp erected in February 1941, consisting of blocks of huts sited to the north of the "home for single men" [Ledigenheim) for the open-cast mines in the Regis coal fields to "house 300 French POWs and the necessary guard units".[4]

The "labour deployment situation" was considered "difficult" in the hard coal operations, too. The policy of bridging the staffing gaps with foreign workers commenced in May 1940 at the Graf Bismarck colliery, and from 21 May 1940 onwards Polish workers who had been deployed in pitheads II and VII were lodged in a camp DEA had erected in the near of the pit. The mine management was not aware of "complaints", especially as the Poles who had been put to work were "willing". Mine Director Max Grotowsky stated in his report on the mood in June 1940 that their "performance" was

---

2 Niederschrift über die Verhandlungen des Aufsichtsrats der DEA, 25.10.1940, 3, WD-CA, D-PA-0120; see Thomas Urban, *Zwangsarbeit im Tagebau. Der Einsatz von Kriegsgefangenen und ausländischen Zivilarbeitern im mitteldeutschen Braunkohlenbergbau 1939 bis 1945*, Essen 2006, 183ff.

3 Niederschrift über die Verhandlungen des Aufsichtsrats der DEA, 2.4.1941, 6, WD-CA, D-PA-0120.

4 Deutsche Erdöl-AG, Verwaltung der Braunkohlenbetriebe, Regiser Kohlenwerke an Bergamt, 27.2.1941, 1, Bergarchiv Freiberg, Bestand 40128, No. 1–10.

"good". He did not perceive there being any "disagreement" over the food.[5]

The foreign civilian workers recruited in the Netherlands or in Belgium who held a "Hauerschein" or "tusker certificate" and could thus prove they had received preliminary training as foremen, among them Dutch and Belgian men, received only 95 percent of the union-agreed wages in the first few months. After they had been familiarized with their tasks and achieved the same "tusker" output as a German, this group of workers received the same wages as their German counterparts. Many of the German tuskers had reservations about the foreigners, above all when it came to the workers from Poland or other East European countries. There was concern that the foreigners' ostensible inability to achieve the same levels as the Germans would spell financial disadvantages for the German foremen, since the wages paid for the work of miners employed underground often hinged on a pregiven amount of coal to be cut (truck piecework) or progress at the face (meter piecework) that was often calculated as "comrades' piecework" [Kameradschaftsgedinge], meaning everyone got the same share of the wages.[6] The issue of piecework was a matter of continual conflict in the mining sector anyway.

The creation of an underclass of East European workers – a subproletariat of men who had been only partly trained as miners – meant the issue of "just wages" [Lohngerechtigkeit] between the foreigners and Germans and within the different groups of foreigners became more acute.[7] Concerned about seeing their own income dented owing to the lower "team" output, some German workers at Graf Bismarck colliery did not wish to work with the foreigners, so the management at the Graf Bismarck colliery tried putting together

5 DEA, Zechen Graf Bismarck und Königsgrube, Max Grotowsky, an Bergrevier Buer, 29.6.1940, 1f., LAV NRW, dept. Westfalen, Bergämter No. 8049.

6 Seidel, *Ruhrbergbau*, 131ff.

7 Ibid., 294ff.

piecework teams for facework that consisted only of foreigners. Nevertheless a "Russian longwall team" [Russenstreb], consisting of several Soviet POWs or Ukrainian civilian workers, was always under the command of a German foreman, who was responsible for training them in mining and for assigning the tasks within the team.

Polish civilian workers suffered further discrimination at DEA, as their wages were also subject to deduction of the social welfare levy as 15 percent.[8] Added to this, many miners felt – or so the opinion of the Buer Mining Office [Bergrevier] – that the increasing recruitment of foreign workers was "discriminating against the mining profession" and tantamount to de-skilling. Only if the "destructive mixture of peoples" was eliminated and pride in the "most respected profession" and as the "best paid craftsmen" was restored would it be possible, so the officials thought, to ease the tensions in the recruitment of mining apprentices.[9] The mining directors reported to the Supervisory Board that their experiences with the foreigners had been "bad".[10] The Buer Mining Office likewise termed the "deployment of countless untrained and often fairly unwilling foreign workers" a crucial "drag on operations". For all the efforts, the "apprenticeship problem" was getting worse, owing to the sharp drop in the number of youths being hired, which meant companies "would have no other option but to draw on foreign workers more strongly going forwards," the DEA Supervisory Board stated in 1942 with a tone of resignation.[11]

At the pyrolysis plants in Rositz, one of the widespread complaints in most companies was that "no normal work output"

---

8 Herbert, *Fremdarbeiter*, 93f.

9 Jahresbericht des Bergreviers Buer für das Jahr 1940, 17, 33 and 36, LAV NRW, dept. Westfalen, Bergämter No. 8089.

10 Niederschrift über die Verhandlungen des Aufsichtsrats der DEA, 23.10.1941, 5, WD-CA, D-PA-0120.

11 Niederschrift über die Verhandlungen des Aufsichtsrats der DEA, 1.4.1942, 8, ibid.

could be achieved "with the foreign workers allocated to us".[12] Foreign substitute workers were considered the negative version of what would otherwise be positions filled by normal German workers; the only difference was that most of them, to the extent that they were subject to the coercive systems of workforce controls and treatment, could be dealt with as management liked. This was an advantage since, in the course of time, companies learned to use them all the more intensively to their benefit.

The "deployment of foreigners" [Ausländereinsatz] became standard practice from 1941 onwards. In May 1941, the Reich Trustee for Work [Reichstreuhänder der Arbeit] had created the option of cutting the wages of foreigners performing piecework by as much as 40 percent if they "underperformed". Although this occurred "only in the rarest of cases", this measure – whereby the wages deducted from the foreigners were reassigned to the German members of the piecework team in question – evidently led to dwindling "opposition among the German workers to foreigners being assigned to the teams of piecework comrades".[13]

The Graf Bismarck colliery was assigned some contingents of foreign workers in 1941. In January/February 1941, 100 miners from Belgium arrived, followed in April/May 1941 by an additional 250 miners, mainly "of the Polish Volk" from Upper Silesia who were meant to work for three to four months in the Graf Bismarck until they were needed elsewhere.[14] Between June and October 1941, 320 unskilled workers arrived from Croatia, who, as cit-

---

12 Deutsche Erdöl-AG, Mineralölwerke Rositz, Bericht über die Betriebsergebnisse der Schwelwerke im Jahre 1941, März 1942, 2, StA Leipzig, Bestand 20684, DEA-Mineralölwerke Rositz, No. 14.

13 Jahresbericht des Bergreviers Buer für das Jahr 1941, 1 and 14, LAV NRW, dept. Westfalen Bergämter No. 8089.

14 Jahresbericht der Zeche Graf Bismarck der DEA, Werner, für das Jahr 1941, 3, LAV NRW, dept. Westfalen, Bergämter No. 8085; Oberbergamt Dortmund an Bergrevierbeamte des Bezirks, 19.5.1941 betr. 10. Transport, LAV NRW, dept. Westfalen, Bergämter No. 7498.

izens of a state that was a political ally, could expect to be treated the same way as the German workers. Of the men recruited by the German Labour Office [Arbeitsamt], by year-end only about a third remained on site owing to the hard and unfamiliar work at the coalface, as most of them had "gradually and secretly stolen away from the camp".[15] Between October and December 1941, 100 unskilled Ukrainian civilian workers filled the gaps that had thus arisen. In mid-May 1941, the Königsgrube colliery was cleared to receive a contingent of 100 men for several weeks from the transports expected from Upper Silesia, each of which consisted of 850 men of the "Polish Volk".[16] Their activity at the Königsgrube colliery therefore ended as early as August 1941.[17]

As elsewhere, the growing contingents of foreigners were accommodated in specially created mass housing. The management of the Graf Bismarck II colliery had a camp consisting of dormitory blocks erected in 1941.[18] The Königsgrube colliery maintained its "Böhm hut camp" at Bochumer Strasse 285 in Wanne-Eickel, where in mid-August 1943 a total of 243 foreigners and later 465 "eastern workers" [Ostarbeiter][19] were housed. "Maintaining the regulations", such as those governing life in the camp, was enforced by Mine Deputy Heinrich Opitz as the "camp leader" responsible.[20] His permanent deputy was a member of the white-collar staff, Wilhelm Steinmann. The camp held 304 foreigners and was visited on 27 October 1943

15 Jahresbericht der Zeche Graf Bismarck der DEA, Werner, für das Jahr 1941, 3, LAV NRW, dept. Westfalen, Bergämter No. 8085; Herbert, *Fremdarbeiter*, 120f.

16 Oberbergamt Dortmund an Bergrevierbeamte des Bezirks, 19.5.1941 betr. 8. und 12. Transport, LAV NRW, dept. Westfalen, Bergämter No. 7498.

17 DEA, Zechen Graf Bismarck und Königsgrube, Max Fröhlich, an Bergrevier Herne, 19.3.1942 ibid.

18 Jahresbericht der Zeche Graf Bismarck der DEA, Werner, für das Jahr 1941, 4, LAV NRW, dept. Westfalen, Bergämter No. 8085.

19 Stadtarchiv Herne, Jürgen Hagen an Manfred Grieger vom 25.6.2024.

20 DEA, Zechen Graf Bismarck und Königsgrube, Max Fröhlich, an Leiter des Bergamts Herne, 18.8.1943, Nordrhein-Westfälisches Landesarchiv, dept. Westfalen, Bergämter No. 7556.

by a commission from the German Labour Front [Deutsche Arbeitsfront (DAF)] that was looking for new tasks for itself and claimed responsibility for the camp accommodation for workers. The DAF Gau Officer [Gau-Beauftragte] for Camps and the Head of the Public Health Office in Wanne-Eickel ascertained during the inspection that the camp was "generally unclean", with the worst conditions found in the large sleeping hall. If even DAF, which on principle and for racist reasons advocated that East European forced labourers in particular be structurally treated worse than the Germans, complained about conditions, then we can assume they were well below the usual norm. The colliery management said they would rectify things, and DAF, as the self-appointed supervisory office, stated that it would undertake a "second inspection".[21] Three weeks later, the Herne Mining Office noted that additional blocks had been erected in the Böhm camp. In the Graf Bismarck camps, meanwhile, similarly inadequate hygienic conditions prevailed: A set of blocks housing 700 "eastern workers" offered only 18 water taps, one shower, and 28 toilets.[22]

Foreigners were considered indispensable workers and yet, owing to language difficulties that made communication hard, they were also viewed as an accident risk. For that reason, the pithead staff trained those assigned to them in mining work and familiarized them with the safety regulations in order to boost mining output and reduce the danger of accidents such as existed if the men did not heed the absolute prohibition on smoking, as this could cause mine explosions. Such measures resulted less from an overarching sense of responsibility for the forced labourers assigned to the pitheads and rather served mainly to ensure maximum mining output was achieved at the face. In the lignite mines, there were similar efforts

---

21 Pg. Kuth (Gauwaltung), Gaubeauftragter/Medizinalrat Greif (Wanne-Eickel), Gesundheitsamt, Lagerbesichtigungen no date given [October/November 1943], LAV NRW, dept. Westfalen, Bergämter No. 7556.

22 Seidel, *Ruhrbergbau*, 525.

to compile a German-Russian picture dictionary for lignite mining, which was intended not only to help prevent accidents but also to boost output.[23]

The mining industry in the Ruhr region had lengthy experience in handling workers who spoke foreign languages, as it had been hiring large numbers of Polish-speaking miners since the last third of the 19th century. The practice evolved of bilingual teaching panels and imparting a rudimentary knowledge of specialist mining terms.[24] After 1941, mining in the Ruhr region relied on materials tried and tested in the First World War, such as the German-Russian picture dictionaries, in order to enable at least those who spoke Russian to communicate functionally. In the interest of safety in the mines, newly hired miners with no prior knowledge of mining received routine "instruction". To the extent that interpreters were at hand, at the DEA collieries an introduction to accident prevention was conducted for "foreign civilian workers and Russian POWs". "Civilian Russian youths" were familiarized with the operational dangers by means of "pictures of accidents".[25]

The so-called "pit militarism" [Grubenmilitarismus) of German mining officials before and during the First World War had already combined an arrogant sense of social and cultural superiority with a form of authoritarianism that bordered on violence. That said, in the collieries the Nazis' form of racism led to further brutalization

---

23 Urban, *Zwangsarbeit*, 246ff.

24 Christoph Kleßmann, *Polnische Bergarbeiter im Ruhrgebiet 1870–1945. Soziale Integration und nationale Subkultur einer Minderheit in der deutschen Industriegesellschaft*, Göttingen 1978.

25 DEA, Zechen Graf Bismarck und Königsgrube, Max Fröhlich, an Bergrevier Buer, 13.2.1943, LAV NRW, dept. Westfalen, Bergämter No. 8078.

Fig. 60 Instructing Soviet POWs in using lamps
in the mines in Harpen, 1942

of the power relationships within the company.[26] German workers were being drafted into the Wehrmacht, and at the same time the regime was demanding an increase in mining output in the services of the armament effort. This led to greater "deployment of foreigners", with the proportion of foreigners in the workforce rising in the DEA collieries from 22 to 40 percent.[27] The expansion in operations and the thus increased need for operational control and management and a streamlined use of machines and materials prompted DEA's

26 Helmuth Trischler, *Partielle Modernisierung, Die betrieblichen Sozialbeziehungen im Ruhrbergbau zwischen Grubenmilitarismus und Human Relations*, in: Mathias Frese/Michael Prinz (Eds.), Politische Zäsuren und gesellschaftlicher Wandel im 20. Jahrhundert. Regionale und vergleichende Perspektiven, Paderborn 1996, 145–171, here 147ff. and 157.

27 Bergamt Herne an Max Friedrich, 1.4.1943, LAV NRW, Abt. Westfalen, Bergämter No. 7580.

mining operations management to fill the vacant position of operational director as at 1 April 1943.[28] The application for an "exemption for indispensability" (a so-called UK application) was filed on 16 December 1943 with Army District Command VI in Münster via the Senior Mining Office in Dortmund, and was supported by the Herne Mining Office.[29]

In spring 1943, the Königsgrube colliery made no complaints to the Herne Mining Office regarding difficulties in procuring overalls and boots for the "eastern workers" assigned to it. This contrasted with the description of the situation in other mines in Herne, who did not know how to clothe their workers owing to the supply shortfall.[30]

In the interests of both mine safety and to cement the social asymmetry, even informal promotion was to be restricted. In response to a corresponding enquiry from the Herne Mining Office, in mid-June 1944, the DEA collieries replied that "workers speaking a foreign language" were at best deployed as second face workers or deputy truck repair workers. Foreign workers were exclusively used as "auxiliaries" in mechanical provisioning and were active in coal mining itself "only under the supervision of German workers (slide masters)".[31]

In the lignite companies, the lack of workers assumed "ever more serious proportions", although DEA constantly endeavoured

---

28 DEA-Zechen Graf Bismarck und Königsgrube, Max Friedrich, an Bergamt Herne, 22.3.1943, 1, ibid.

29 DEA-Zechen Graf Bismarck und Königsgrube, Max Friedrich, an Wehrkreiskommando VI, 16.12.1943, ibid.; Bergamt Herne an Oberbergamt Dortmund/Wehrkreiskommando, 23.12.1943, ibid.

30 Bergamt Herne an Oberbergamt Dortmund, 19.4.1943, 2, LAV NRW, dept. Westfalen, Bergämter No. 7556; Nörtemann, Pott, 78.

31 DEA-Zechen Graf Bismarck und Königsgrube, Werner, an Bergamt Herne, 13.6.1944, LAV NRW, dept. Westfalen, Bergämter No. 7556.

"to bring foreigners on board".[32] The annual report for 1942 notes that the "foreign workers and POWs" do not constitute "cheap labour" as, in particular, the "housing and care for the eastern workers and other civilian workers require considerable staff input" at a level that was not matched by any "corresponding performance".[33] This led to a rise in the operating and prime costs of mining output in 1941-2 by between nine and ten percent. In Regis, the camp for foreigners was expanded to include three new hut blocks, and in Rositz the company likewise erected dormitory blocks.[34] The Croatian workers had been recruited on a one-year contract in 1941, which expired in mid-1942. As had been the case in Gelsenkirchen, some of them had not returned to Regis from their home vacation; "almost half" of them fled, something communicated to the Supervisory Board to emphasize the insufficient supply of labourers at the end of October 1941.[35] In 1942, by way of substitutes, the lignite operations received 823 "eastern workers" and 25 "female eastern workers"; of that figure, by year-end 1942 only 686 men and 19 women were still on site, many having been released owing to "unsuitability" or because they had "fled". Alongside 1,050 civilian foreigners, 875 POWs (601 French, 269 Red Army members, and five Serbs) were part of the workforce; they constituted 27.3 percent of the total DEA workforce, which ran at 7,041 men and women.[36]

---

32 Niederschrift über die Verhandlungen des Aufsichtsrats der DEA, 1.4.1942, 8, WD-CA, D-PA-0120.

33 Deutsche Erdöl-AG, Verwaltung der Braunkohlenbetriebe, Paul Günther/Lampe, Jahresbericht für das Jahre 1942, 8.3.1943, 3, Bergarchiv Freiberg, Bestand 40144, No. 31.

34 Ibid., 5 and 8.

35 Niederschrift über die Verhandlungen des Aufsichtsrats der DEA, 23.10.1941, 5, WD-CA, D-PA-0120; Urban, *Zwangsarbeit*, 246ff.

36 Deutsche Erdöl-AG, Verwaltung der Braunkohlenbetriebe, Paul Günther/Lampe, Jahresbericht für das Jahre 1942, 8.3.1943, 13, Bergarchiv Freiberg, Bestand 40144, No. 31.

At Mineralölwerke Rositz, the "workforce status" was likewise tense.[37] The Rositz pyrolysis plant used foreign civilian workers for the first time in 1941; the payroll had held steady at 203, and now, alongside a few Czechs, mainly Italian civilian workers were deployed, having been made available by the fascist government in Rome as part of the "Axis" collaboration. Yet most of them returned home in autumn 1941, as they had themselves been called up for military service.[38] The first two blocks of huts for foreigners were erected in 1941 to house the 78 Italians who had remained with the company, while a total of 42 POWs were lodged in a separate block of huts.[39] In 1942, the proportion of foreign workers active in the Rositz pyrolysis plant rose to 15.6 percent, with the workforce in Rositz including Italians, Dutch, French, and Ukrainians.[40] In the Regis I pyrolysis plant, Czech civilian workers were deployed for the first time in 1942, accounting for 19.7 percent of the average workforce of 190. The refinery built two sets of dormitory blocks, a wash hut, and a kitchen hut to accommodate the additional 225 foreign workers.[41] At the end of 1942, at Mineralölwerke Rositz "foreign-

---

37 Niederschrift über die Verhandlungen des Aufsichtsrats der DEA, 2.4.1941, 8, WD-CA, D-PA-0120.

38 Deutsche Erdöl-AG, Mineralölwerke Rositz, Bericht über die Betriebsergebnisse der Schwelwerke im Jahre 1941, März 1942, 2, StA Leipzig, Bestand 20684, DEA-Mineralölwerke Rositz, No. 14; Bruno Mantelli, *Zwischen Strukturwandel auf dem Arbeitsmarkt und Kriegswirtschaft. Die Anwerbung der italienischen Arbeiter für das "Dritte Reich" und die "Achse Berlin-Rom"*, in: Cesare Bermani et al. (Eds.), Proletarier der "Achse". Sozialgeschichte der italienischen Fremdarbeiter in NS-Deutschland 1937–1943, Berlin 1997, 253–391.

39 Deutsche Erdöl-AG, Mineralölwerke Rositz, Hans Hase/Hans Collischon, Jahresbericht für das Jahr 1941, 10.3.1942, 9 and 13, StA Leipzig, Bestand 20684, DEA-Mineralölwerke Rositz, No. 10.

40 Deutsche Erdöl-AG, Mineralölwerke Rositz, Bericht über die Betriebsergebnisse der Schwelwerke im Jahre 1942, März 1943, 3ff., StA Leipzig, Bestand 20684, DEA-Mineralölwerke Rositz, No. 15.

41 Deutsche Erdöl-AG, Mineralölwerke Rositz, Hans Hase/Hans Collischon, Jahresbericht für das Jahr 1942, 10.3.1943, 7, StA Leipzig, Bestand 20684, DEA-Mineralölwerke Rositz, No. 10.

ers" comprised more than one third of the workforce. Alongside 361 "Germans from the Altreich" and 346 German-speakers from the Sudetenland, there were 120 Italian civilian workers, 74 Czechs ("Protectorate members"), 42 French civilians, 47 French POWs, 14 Dutch, two Hungarians, 20 Ukrainians, and one Belgian and one Swiss.[42]

None of that really altered the main situation, namely the major "shortage in workers" ascertained in spring 1942.[43] The DEA Management Board could clearly see that deploying foreign workers would ensure the workforce did not contract further. Yet in a sense this was merely window-dressing the situation, as the downside was the "sharp difference in performance", which caused problems between these new workers and the core workforce.[44]

In early 1943, the number of foreigners at Mineralölwerke Rositz was initially boosted by the arrival of 300 French civilian workers and then, from October 1943 onwards, above all by the allocation of Italian military internees (IMIs, the hundreds of thousands of Italian soldiers who had been captured and deported to Germany in September 1943 after Italy's capitulation) to reach a total of 735.[45] In this context, Mineralölwerke Rositz had four additional dormitory huts built in the "Schelditz work camp", containing a total of 432 beds, and the dormitory camp was also outfitted with two air-raid slit trenches. In the pyrolysis plants' annual report for 1943, we read

42 Deutsche Erdöl-AG, Mineralölwerke Rositz, Hans Hase/Hans Collischon, Jahresbericht für das Jahr 1943, 22.3.1944, 11, ibid.

43 Niederschrift über die Verhandlungen des Aufsichtsrats der DEA, 1.4.1942, 8, WD-CA, D-PA-0120.

44 Niederschrift über die Verhandlungen des Aufsichtsrats der DEA, 4.11.1942, 2, ibid.

45 Oberkommando der Wehrmacht, W Stb, Jnl. 3/V (66 b 2206) an OKM, Skl. Qu A III, 20.3.1943, BA-MA, RW 19, No. 3024, sheet 48; Deutsche Erdöl-AG, Mineralölwerke Rositz, Hans Hase/Robert Hanke, Jahresbericht für das Jahr 1943, 22.3.1944, 10, StA Leipzig, Bestand 20684, DEA-Mineralölwerke Rositz, No. 10; on the deplorable situation of the Italians who were deprived of their rights as prisoners of war as punishment for "treason", see Herbert, *Fremdarbeiter*, 259ff.; Urban, *Zwangsarbeit*, 328ff.

that the "productivity and willingness to work among the workforce as well as their work discipline fell", a development rated as "inevitable with the rising proportion of workers from foreign peoples". The Rositz pyrolysis plant also integrated additional IMIs into the workflow and recruited "women for the first time in the context of the commitment to total war".[46]

Below the line, management was upbeat at having constantly boosted the works' throughput as a result of the installation from 1940 onwards of higher-performance plant components. From the management's viewpoint, the elimination of work by hand reduced the reliance on unskilled substitute staff and foreign slave labour. Irrespective of this, on the refinery grounds "a special dormitory building for female eastern workers" was erected in light of the "increased deployment of women", who now also had to perform hard physical tasks.[47] At year-end 1943, Rositz and Regis together provided dormitories with a total of 1,744 beds, 1,330 in their own camps.[48]

Conditions in Rositz reflected the overall situation in the DEA corporation. The overall DEA workforce rose between 30 September 1942 and 30 September 1943 from 23,719 to 26,661 persons and by year-end 1943 reached 27,943 persons.[49] However, the number of German employees fell over the same period from 20,016 to

---

[46] Deutsche Erdöl-AG, Mineralölwerke Rositz, Bericht über die Betriebsergebnisse der Schwelwerke im Jahre 1943, Juni 1944, 1 and 4, StA Leipzig, Bestand 20684, DEA-Mineralölwerke Rositz, No. 40.

[47] Deutsche Erdöl-AG, Mineralölwerke Rositz, Hans Hase/Robert Hanke, Jahresbericht für das Jahr 1943, 22.3.1944, 8, StA Leipzig, Bestand 20684, DEA-Mineralölwerke Rositz, No. 10; on the use of "Eastern workers" in opencast lignite mining, see Urban, *Zwangsarbeit*, 310f.

[48] Deutsche Erdöl-AG, Mineralölwerke Rositz, Hans Hase/Robert Hanke, Jahresbericht für das Jahr 1943, 22.3.1944, 8f., StA Leipzig, Bestand 20684, DEA-Mineralölwerke Rositz, No. 10.

[49] DEA, Bericht des Vorstands über die Zeit vom 1. Januar 1943 bis 30. September 1943, 1.11.1943, 3f., WD-CA, D-PA-65; DEA, Bericht des Vorstands an den Aufsichtsrat über das Geschäftsjahr 1943, 3, ibid.

17,753 persons. In line with this, the number of members of the payroll conscripted into the Wehrmacht increased from 1,923 to 3,896, which translated into a ratio of 17.9 percent of the total performing military service. In other words, the growth in the workforce can be attributed solely to the strong growth in the number of foreign workers, which more than doubled between September 1942 and December 1943 – from 3,704 to 8,902 persons. In addition to 4,856 foreign civilian workers, 4,046 POWs had to perform forced labour on behalf of DEA. The proportion of foreigners in the total workforce rocketed within the space of one year from 15.6 to 31.2 percent.[50]

By the end of March 1944, the situation changed in the Regis pyrolysis plant in that the 205 foreign workers there accounted for one quarter (24.14 percent) of the workforce. Alongside 24 French and 79 Czechs, there were 33 Poles and Ukrainians as well as 33 IMIs in the workforce.[51] In Rositz, the percentage of foreigners was even higher at 31.59 percent – 245 IMIs, 165 French, 21 Dutch, seven Czechs, 11 Poles, 64 "eastern workers", and 48 French POWs. The total share was thus just under one third, and it was clear, given that 573 German employees had been drafted for the Wehrmacht, that the plants' capacity to operate depended on the allocation of foreign workers. From the perspective of the operations management and the Saxon core staff, the "Germans from outside the Reich" – meaning the German speakers from the Sudetenland and those obligated German employees [Dienstverpflichtete] – were just as alien to the staff as were the foreigners. The situation contradicted their sense of homogeneity. At the Regis coal plants, on 14 August 1944 there were 836 Germans employed; alongside them were 103 foreign civilian workers, 296 "eastern workers", 269 POWs (102 British and 167 French) as well as 100 IMIs; in other words, foreigners

---

50 DEA, Bericht des Vorstands über die Zeit vom 1. Januar 1943 bis 30. September 1943, 1.11.1943, 3f., ibid.

51 Mineralölwerke Rositz, Personal-Abteilung, Dienststelle A, Gefolgschaftsstärke am 3.3.1944, 6.5.1944, StA Leipzig, Bestand 20684, DEA-Mineralölwerke Rositz, No. 49.

accounted for 48 percent of the workforce.[52] This was considerably higher than the 30 September 1944 average for the DEA corporation of 34.1 percent. The figure that DEA itself calculated in 1999 of 9,900 forced labourers merely adds to the figures for 1944. In actual fact, the scale involved was far higher, as there was much fluctuation in forced labourers due to repostings, death, or escape.[53] Moreover, forced labour outside the Reich's borders was completely omitted.

DEA group workforce structure inside the "Altreich", 1939-44[54]

Year	Total workforce	Germans	Slave labour	POWs
1939	19,010	19,010	0	0
1940	20,082	18,659	678	745
1941	21,834	18,911	1,441	1,482
1942	25,209	19,159	3,154	2,896
1943	26,624	17,659	4,541	4,424
1944	26,947	17,064	5,511	4,372

At the end of January 1945, a total of 6,135 people worked in the company's lignite operations at a time when 1,514 Germans had been conscripted into the Wehrmacht. Of the total workforce in the lignite plants, POWs and "war-interned Danes" accounted for 824 of the total, "eastern workers" for 736, and "other foreigners" for 619. Together with the 100 "female eastern workers" employed in mining operations, the 2,279 forced labourers held more than 37 percent of

52 Regiser Kohlenwerke, Dekadenbericht über Arbeitseinsatz im Kohlenbergbau, 18.8.1944, Bergarchiv Freiberg, Bestand 40128, No. 01–16.

53 In the case of H. Bahlsens Keksfabrik KG, the difference between the company data based on the reporting date and the individuals affected by research was 200 to 795 people, Hartmut Berghoff/Manfred Grieger, *Die Geschichte des Hauses Bahlsen: Keks – Krieg – Konsum 1911 bis 1974*, Göttingen 2024, 269.

54 Karlsch/Stokes, *Faktor Öl*, 225; compiled according to Klaus Brüning, *Zwangsarbeit im DEA-Konzern*, 1939–1945, Hamburg 1999, 4, WD-CA, DA-00017; the figures determined in connection with the forced labor compensation under discussion at the time tend to lag behind other key date figures.

the jobs.[55] The average raw coal produced per person per shift was 9.35 tonnes, whereby the figure fluctuated between 4.18 tonnes at the Rositz works and 15.7 tonnes in the Beuna works. Average output per person per shift in briquette production came to 1.67 tonnes.

To boost labourers' motivation, various of the 17 civilians from the Netherlands and seven Czechs in white-collar positions in the administration received 10–14 days "vacation" in the first quarter of 1944 to travel home to their families.[56] However, not all these foreigners, who were relatively privileged compared to the "eastern workers", reacted to these measures, which the corporation had believed showed understanding, in the way it had hoped. A Dutchman named Henricus Ernst, who was working in the Sales section in place of a conscripted German, did not return from the special leave granted him from 30 March to 12 April 1944. Mineralölwerke Rositz complained on various occasions that Dutch citizens did not return to Rositz from their home leave, and as a result well-trained staff were being lost.[57] The expert advisor at the German Labour Office in The Hague announced in mid-June 1944 that once he had been arrested, Ernst would be sent to a penal camp and on release would be sent back to his posting with DEA.[58] Since Ernst had gone underground, the company had to put up with his position not being filled and the work therefore not being done, so by 6 October 1944 the

55 Deutsche Erdöl-AG, Verwaltung der Braunkohlenbetriebe, Belegschafts- und Leistungsnachweisung für Januar 1945, 27.2.1945, WD-CA, RW-139.

56 Mineralölwerke Rositz, Lohnabteilung betr. Urlaub für ausländische Gefolgsleute, 24.1.1944, StA Leipzig, Bestand 20684, DEA-Mineralölwerke Rositz, No. 64.

57 Mineralölwerke Rositz (Pers. 17/Schm.), Hans Hase/Oskar Gerth an Arbeitsamt Den Haag, 28.4.1944, StA Leipzig, Bestand 20684, DEA-Mineralölwerke Rositz, No. 103; Mineralölwerke Rositz (Pers. 17/Schm.), Hans Hase/Oskar Gerth an Arbeitsamt Altenburg, 28.4.1944, StA Leipzig, Bestand 20684, DEA-Mineralölwerke Rositz, No. 103.

58 Deutsche Fachberater beim Arbeitsamt den Haag (Az. 5752 Hk) an Deutsche Erdöl-AG, Mineralölwerke Rositz, 15.6.1944, StA Leipzig, Bestand 20684, DEA-Mineralölwerke Rositz, No. 103.

Altenburg Labour Office approved dissolution of the labour contract since he had placed a burden on the "comrades' staff levels".[59]

A similar case occurred with Hendrik van Pijlen, who postponed his return by weeks and referred to a medical diagnosis of depression and nervous exhaustion. Even if, in the opinion of the Personnel section, van Pijlen was "not an especially valuable worker", the company wanted to prevent "such cases setting an example" and sought to have him return, albeit to no avail.[60] By contrast, Czech Gleb Žekulin was "arrested" on 31 May 1944. The Sales section, which stated that both men "had familiarized themselves well" with their tasks and "to a certain extent" had duly performed the relevant duties, eventually demanded replacements, assuming that neither "would come back" to their workplace.[61]

Forced and slave labour at the various DEA sites also had fatal results for the persons concerned. On 16 February 1945, for example, "eastern worker" Alexei Parshin from Stalino, who had been working in the Regis mines since 23 May 1942, was shot dead by the police while "stealing potatoes".[62] Alexei Kopshinski from Taganrog near Rostov-on-Don died at the age of 19 on 30 Octo-

---

59 Mineralölwerke Rositz (Pers. 17/Schm.), Hans Hase/Oskar Gerth an Arbeitsamt Altenburg, 6.10.1944, ibid.

60 Mineralölwerke Rositz, Personalabteilung, Dienststelle B an Pesonalabteilung, 2.5.1944, ibid.; Mineralölwerke Rositz (Pers. 17/Schm.), Hans Hase/Oskar Gerth an Arbeitsamt Altenburg, 6.7.1944, ibid.

61 Mineralölwerke Rositz, Einkaufsabteilung an Personal-Abteilung B, 2.6.1944, StA Leipzig, Bestand 20684, DEA-Mineralölwerke Rositz, No. 49; see too https://collections.arolsen-archives.org/de/document/74755153 [last retrieved on 20.10.2023]. It was not possible to clarify why the purchasing department issued a positive draft certificate for Žekulin, who wanted to leave the company "at his own request", for his work in the electrical materials and metal department on February 10, 1945, Mineralölwerke Rositz, Einkaufsabteilung Zeugnis-Entwurf betr. Gleb Žekulin, 15.2.1945, StA Leipzig, Bestand 20684, DEA-Mineralölwerke Rositz, No. 49. Žekulin emigrated to Austria with his family in 1950, cf. https://collections.arolsen-archives.org/de/document/69006609 [last retrieved on 20.10.2023].

62 Deutsche Erdöl-AG, Verwaltung der Braunkohlenbetriebe, Regiser Kohlenwerke, an das Arbeitsamt Borna, 22.2.1945, Bergarchiv Freiberg, Bestand 40128, No. 1–18.

ber 1942 of pneumonia and pleurisy and was buried the next day in the "Russian graveyard".[63] There were also those killed in bombing raids. On 14 February 1945 several of the dormitory blocks in the Schelditz camp were destroyed, and one Italian and one Pole met their deaths. Of the men attached to Organisation Todt's Construction Battalion IV deployed in Rositz, 11 French POWs died and nine were injured.[64] In total, the number of deaths in the mining operations came to 28, according to post-war figures.[65] Physical abuse was a daily occurrence, as revealed in the investigation of a DEA staff member at Mineralölwerke Rositz by the Altenburg Criminal Investigation Bureau in the first years after the war.[66]

In September 1944, the 138 foreigners attached to the pyrolysis plants and the refinery in Rositz were housed in the "Gasthof Steinbrecher" camp at the DEA colliery in Zechau. Of the persons housed there, 32 received normal rations with no add-ons, 105 received food for those performing heavy labour, and one got the added rations for extra-heavy labour.[67] The seven-man guard unit lodged in Schelditz, where there was also a camp housing 52 persons,

---

63 Deutsche Erdöl-AG, Verwaltung der Braunkohlenbetriebe, Regiser Kohlenwerke, an das Arbeitsamt Borna, 3.11.1942, ibid.

64 Mineralölwerke Rositz, Werkluftschutzleiter, betr. Bericht über den Luftangriff am 14.2.1945, 21.2.1945, StA Leipzig, Bestand 20684, DEA-Mineralölwerke Rositz, No. 51; Mineralölwerke Rositz an Bürgermeister der Gemeinde Rositz, 22.2.1945, ibid.

65 Deutsche Erdöl-AG, Verwaltung der Braunkohlenbetriebe, Regiser Kohlenwerke, Betriebsfragebogen, 1.1.1946, Bergarchiv Freiberg, Bestand 40128, No. 1–18.

66 Ermittlung der Kriminaldienststelle (K 5) Altenburg, *Bundesbeauftragter* für die Unterlagen des Staatssicherheitsdienstes der ehemaligen DDR – *Außenstelle Leipzig, Bestand KD ABG, No. 1434.*

67 Deutsche Erdöl-AG, Mineralölwerke Rositz, Lagerverwaltung, Antrag auf Erteilung von Sammelbezugscheinen für Arbeitergemeinschaftslager Lager Steinbrecher, 23.8.1944, StA Leipzig, Bestand 20684, DEA-Mineralölwerke Rositz, No. 49.

including French civilian workers, Dutch, Ukrainians, and Poles.[68] Moreover, in Schelditz there was also a separate camp for 66 "eastern workers", of whom applications were lodged for 21 men to get heavy-labour add-ons and 42 men to get extra-heavy labour rations. A total of 128 IMIs who were all performing heavy labour likewise lodged in Schelditz but, unlike the 58 Italian civilian workers, they received only horse meat or meat from injured animals that had to be slaughtered.[69] In Fichtenhainichen there was also the Eisenrieth dormitory camp for nine civilian foreigners and 180 French POWs.

During the course of the war, the wartime society based on subjugation increasingly faced the threat that the upper hierarchies would lose control. Those groups subject to racist exclusion were under particular surveillance and threatened with punishment. Initially, the company introduced in-company penalties as a deterrence against the increasing propensity of "idling at work" [Arbeitsbummelei], something expressed, for example, in people turning up too late for work at the factory gates. In December 1942, ten workers, half of them foreign civilian workers, had between 2.50 and 5 Reichsmark deducted from their wages for "idling at work" or "uncomradely behaviour".[70] "Inattention" or "negligence at work", "violations of works discipline", "undisciplined behaviour", or "gross negligence of one's duties" were other charges brought. "Vio-

68 Deutsche Erdöl-AG, Mineralölwerke Rositz, Lagerverwaltung, Antrag auf Erteilung von Sammelbezugscheinen für Arbeitergemeinschaftslager Wachmannschaften Schelditz, 23.8.1944, ibid.; Deutsche Erdöl-AG, Mineralölwerke Rositz, Lagerverwaltung, Antrag auf Erteilung von Sammelbezugscheinen für Arbeitergemeinschaftslager Schelditz (Zivil. Franz., Ukrainer, Holländer, Polen), 23.8.1944, ibid.

69 Deutsche Erdöl-AG, Mineralölwerke Rositz, Lagerverwaltung, Antrag auf Erteilung von Sammelbezugscheinen für Arbeitergemeinschaftslager Militär-Internierte Schelditz, 23.8.1944, StA Leipzig, Bestand 20684, DEA-Mineralölwerke Rositz, No. 49; Deutsche Erdöl-AG, Mineralölwerke Rositz, Lagerverwaltung, Antrag auf Erteilung von Sammelbezugscheinen für Arbeitergemeinschaftslager Italiener-Lager, 23.8.1944, ibid.

70 Deutsche Erdöl-AG, Mineralölwerke Rositz, Strafbuch 1926–1945, StA Leipzig, Bestand 20684, DEA-Mineralölwerke Rositz, No. 54.

lations of the camp order" or insufficient blacking-out of the camp along with idling at work led to fines being imposed in October 1943 on no fewer than 33 workers, primarily Italians.

Repression and reprisals were something the foreign workers suffered most of all, such as Frenchman René Wandar who received ten months in jail in October 1943 for a statement judged to be inimical to the state. But these also affected German workers such as Johannes Olmstede, who was arrested for the same offence in December 1943. Men such as Dutchman Adrianus Jager, born on 29 October 1919, were transferred to a "work education camp" [Arbeitserziehungslager (AEL)], such as AEL Römhild run by the Weimar Gestapo,[71] which meant they were at the mercy of the state structures of persecution. The Criminal Investigation Bureau [Kriminalpolizei] arrested Pole Otto Grodak in June 1943 for "intercourse with a German woman", and several men received prison sentences for leaving their place of work without permission. On 29 February 1944 the company filed a complaint with the Labour Office that Max Bachmann, who had worked in the pyrolysis plant since 1938, had "refused to work", whereupon Bachmann was sentenced on 8 June 1944 to three months in prison.[72] The workforce was informed of the fact with an announcement on the company notice boards.[73]

In the company's opinion, irrespective of the punishments intended as deterrents, work discipline continued to lag. For on 24 November 1944 no fewer than 176 men arrived at the various factory

---

71 Mineralölwerke Rositz, Verzeichnis der bei uns beschäftigt gewesenen ausländischen Arbeitskräfte, Niederländer no date given [1946] https://collections.arolsen-archives.org/de/document/70930986 [last retrieved on 29.10.2023]; Gert Stoi, *Das Arbeitserziehungslager Römhild 1943–1945. Dokumentation eines Verbrechens*, Leipzig 2010.

72 Betr. Max Bachmann no date given, StA Leipzig, Bestand 20684, DEA-Mineralölwerke Rositz, No. 103; Oberstaatsanwalt bei dem Landgericht Altenburg (1 Js. 2563/44) an Deutsche Erdöl-AG, Mineralölwerke Rositz, 12.7.1944, ibid.

73 DEA-Mineralölwerke Rositz, Hauptverwaltung (Pers. 19/Schm), Robert Hanke, Aushang,15.6.1944, ibid.

gates between 6.45 and 7.00 a.m., and therefore late.[74] Men extending their lunch breaks was another thorn in the side of the supervisors. Director Franz Landwehr was encouraged by a section head on 11 December 1944, for example, to first officially warn those members of the workforce who left their workplaces ahead of time in order to queue for ten minutes in front of the meal distribution point, and then to withdraw their added-rations cards.[75]

Foreign workers increasingly shirked working, something the line managers noted with ever greater concern. Czech members of the 5th Company of Work Battalion (L) 12 tried to leave the works 10-15 minutes early in October 1944. The guard accompanying them indicated to the gate watchman, who was refusing to let them exit, that he was not about to take orders from a watchman, then a Czech named Chalaupka knocked the watchman to the ground and the Czechs pushed their way out. Director Franz Landwehr then called for Chalaupka to be punished "within the bounds of the existing statutory regulations".[76]

The announcement by French POW Pierre Boidin that he was refusing to work, as he felt he was being harassed by being made to walk a detour to another works gate, led on 20 November 1944 to the demand that the "POW be punished for his agitational behaviour".[77] Another painful experience was direct rebellion against German supremacy. When a French POW was not prepared to stand up and give his seat in the break room to a German who had walked in but rather raised his arm and threatened a fight, a brawl ensued. In this case, the plant managers again called for the Frenchman to be

---

74 Mineralölwerke Rositz, IX/26, Gentsch, Aktenvermerk betr. Arbeitsbeginn, 24.11.1944, StA Leipzig, Bestand 20684, DEA-Mineralölwerke Rositz, No. 53.

75 Mineralölwerke Rositz, IX/26, Oberingenieur Hertzberg an Direktor Franz Landwehr, 11.12.1944, ibid.

76 Deutsche Erdöl-AG, Mineralölwerke Rositz an 5./Arb.Batl. (L) 12, 11.10.1944, ibid.

77 Deutsche Erdöl-AG, Mineralölwerke Rositz, Franz Landwehr/Hans Georg Kayser an Kriegsgefangenen-Bau- und Arb. Batl. 4, 21.11.1944, ibid.

punished.[78] In other words, DEA managers actively contributed to the deterioration in the lives of the foreign forced labourers.

The Operation Todt deployment to clear bombing damage led to people being brought on site who, until then, had been spared transportation to the death camps but who, since the late summer of 1944, had been recruited as "special cases performing mandatory service" [jüdische Sonderdienstverpflichtete] and thus condemned to forced labour. These were "Jewish half-breeds" [jüdische Mischlinge] or German Jews who had thus far been protected by virtue of being married to an "Aryan" wife.[79] The pressganging of German Jews and "Jewish first or second-degree half-breeds" led to the first 21 persons forced into working specifically on the construction and clearing of the site at the end of October 1944 initially being lodged in the Gasthaus zur Post tavern in Oberzetzscha. They were placed under the command of a camp head and were only allowed to leave the camp in columns to go to work. Their number swiftly grew until, by the end of November 1944, it had reached a maximum of 413 men.[80] They wore their civilian clothes, and after the Schelditz camp had been expanded they moved there in January 1945.

It was not just the Operation Todt guards but also the company managers who made their lives difficult. On 11 December 1944, Senior Engineer Hertzberg, who had already denounced foreign forced labourers, claimed that the "half-breeds spent a longer

---

78 Ibid.

79 Regierung von Oberbayern, Der Beauftragte des Landesamtes für Wiedergutmachung an International Tracing Service Arolsen, 31.1.1950, https://collections.arolsen-archives.org/de/document/87767530 [last retrieved on 20.10.2023]; see Wolf Gruner, *Die NS-Führung und die Zwangsarbeit für sogenannte jüdische Mischlinge. Ein Einblick in die Planung und Praxis antijüdischer Politik in den Jahren 1942 bis 1944*, in: Manfred Weißbecker/Reinhard Kühnl (Eds.): Rassismus, Faschismus, Antifaschismus, Köln 2000, 63–79.

80 Mineralölwerke Rositz, VII/79/Gr./Ko., Wirth, Eingesetzte Arbeitskräfte am 30. November 1944, 4.12.1944, StA Leipzig, Bestand 20684, DEA-Mineralölwerke Rositz, No. 53; see also Ingolf Strassmann, *Altenburg in Thüringen. Stadt und Landkreis unterm Hakenkreuz 1933–1945*, Altenburg 2003, 45 and 61.

period (up to ¼ hour) in the tent after the end of the lunch break". To prevent this happening, he proposed a gong be installed in the meals tent, which the supervisor from the construction companies would then strike at the end of the lunch break.[81] There is no certain information about the situation of the Jews on site but, according to recollections by one of those concerned, there were "several instances of suicide".[82]

The separation of the foreigners from the Germans and the isolation of the Jewish "half-breeds" from the other groups of forced labourers was upheld even during the increasing bombing raids: Italians, Dutch, Russians, and French had been told to use the split trenches in the Schedlitz camp in the event of the air raid warning sounding; the Jewish forced labourers had to use split trenches 2–6 along Schelditzer Hohlweg. The safe mine shafts in Schedlitz used as air raid shelters were the privilege of the German staff and local inhabitants.[83] Hertzberg, as head of the company guard unit, demanded on 17 March 1945 that the chief guards under his command should "distinguish between Germans and foreigners" when performing their duties. Thus, only Germans were allowed to leave the works grounds during the lunchbreak. POWs were only allowed to enter the works in "closed groups or with a Wehrmacht guard" and were not permitted to leave the grounds "without a guard or special papers".[84]

---

81 Mineralölwerke Rositz, IX/26, Oberingenieur Hertzberg an I/93, 11.12.1944, StA Leipzig, Bestand 20684, DEA-Mineralölwerke Rositz, No. 53.

82 Regierung von Oberbayern, Der Beauftragte des Landesamtes für Wiedergutmachung an International Tracing Service Arolsen, 31.1.1950, https://collections.arolsen-archives.org/de/document/87767530 [last retrieved on 20.10.2023].

83 Werk Rositz, Werkluftschutzleiter, Hertzberg betr. Einteilung der Ausländer für die Deckungsgräben bei Fliegeralarm, 23.2.1945, StA Leipzig, Bestand 20684, DEA-Mineralölwerke Rositz, No. 53.

84 Werk Rositz, Werkluftschutzleiter, Hertzberg an Wachführer Ziegengeist. Kropfgans und Heinke, 17.3.1945, ibid.

On 31 March 1945, among the 1,552 workers at Mineralölwerke Rositz there were still 499 who were foreigners, the majority of them French and Italian.[85] A further 1,669 men worked on site, mainly skilled construction workers and unskilled labour, either for outside companies or for Organisation Todt, so the total number of people active on DEA projects totalled 3,230. Of that figure, 691 were foreign civilian workers, 569 POWs, and 331 "half-breeds", i.e. German Jews who were discriminated against. In other words, at DEA's Rositz site foreigners and forced labourers accounted for around 50 percent of the workforce, even during the closing days of the war.[86]

As a result of the damage to the tar processing lines and the transportation facilities, the company had to reject the offer from the Labour Office for the provision of additional foreign forced labourers at the end of February 1945. The production restrictions it now faced meant that for the foreseeable future, despite the company being part of the Geilenberg Programme, it was only possible to deploy about two thirds of the previous workforce, which is why weekly work hours were reduced as of early March 1945 to 56 hours for alternate shifts and 48 hours on day shifts. Furthermore, in the case of conscriptions to the "Volkssturm", the pyrolysis plants wanted to show "good will" and make personnel available to the Nazi Party district leaders.[87] A total of 40 of the 90 German women employed in the plant were also to be placed at the disposal of the Labour Office to enable them to be deployed in other jobs. Finally, the company also wanted to release 50-100 foreign workers in order

---

85 Mineralölwerke Rositz, Hauptverwaltung (19/Sr.) betr. Ausländische Arbeitskräfte des Werkes Rositz, Stand vom 31.3.1945, 24.4.1945, StA Leipzig, Bestand 20684, DEA-Mineralölwerke Rositz, No. 92.

86 Werk Rositz, VII/79/Gr./Ko., Wirtz betr. Eingesetzte Arbeitskräfte am 31.3.1945, 11.4.1945, ibid.

87 Aktenvermerk betr. Besprechung am 28.2.1945 beim Arbeitsamt Borna mit Herrn Regierungsrat Sachse, 1.3.1945, StA Leipzig, Bestand 20684, DEA-Mineralölwerke Rositz, No. 34.

to scale the workforce back to an economically meaningful size. To a certain degree, even before the end of the war the Rositz facility was starting to cut payroll, masking its entanglement in the Nazi system of forced labour.

Eight of the German Jewish forced labourers, who were called "prisoners" in the company jargon but were "special cases performing mandatory service" to the command of Organisation Todt, were handed over in the early hours of 27 March 1945 to the Works Guards Unit II to be kept under stringent guard. The Jews were not allowed to talk to one another and, should they try to escape, the guards were told to "make use of your weapons without recourse".[88] At about 3.45 a.m. two of the men, including "Prisoner Stein", succeeded in escaping.[89] The camp for the Jewish forced labourers was emptied during the night of 12 April 1945 and the early morning of the next day. The men were marched the 17 kilometres to Gössnitz, where the plan was for them to be loaded onto a train.[90]

The DEA corporation, with its different divisions and activities, formed a microcosm of the Nazi war economy. This also applied to the different types of forced and slave labour, whereby it was only in exceptional cases that the differences had any bearing on how the administrative sections acted. In the mining segment in particular, both in the coal mines in the Ruhr region and in Central Germany and in the oil sand mine in Wietze and the oil pastel mine in Heide, specifically the Soviet POWs, but also the IMIs and "eastern workers" were forced to perform the physically toughest and most onerous tasks. Given that they generally did not receive sufficient nutrition and the dormitories were overcrowded, they faced

88 Konrad Heinig, Vernehmungsniederschrift, 28.3.1945, StA Leipzig, Bestand 20684, DEA-Mineralölwerke Rositz, No. 53.

89 Iwan Fiedler, Vernehmungsniederschrift, 28.3.1945, ibid.

90 Bayerisches Hilfswerk für die durch die Nürnberger Gesetze Betroffenen, Außenstelle Oberfranken, Guttmann an International Tracing Service, 6.6.1950, https://collections.arolsen-archives.org/de/document/87767532 [last retrieved on 20.10.2023].

massive health risks, added to which they were exposed to various forms of violence by the German foremen and guards. In addition, they were subject to special disciplinary measures, so they tended to get caught in the cogs of the Nazi dictatorship's repressive apparatus to an above-average extent.

DEA was reliant on foreign workers from 1941 onwards at the latest. With foreigners accounting for over one third of staff in the production operations, the ratios at DEA resembled the average for German industry. To this extent, it profited like other German corporations from forced labour capacity being made available to it. DEA adopted the racist hierarchization of work in its everyday company operations and in this way participated faithfully in the exploitation of a violently created foreign subproletariat. DEA profited as company, and many of its employees also enjoyed a collective rise in social status and were thus among those minions who benefited from a racist regime of forced and slave labour. This explains why, after the end of the Second World War, the omnipresence of forced and slave labour at the DEA facilities and the suffering of those affected was for a long time repressed and forgotten in both East and West Germany.

XI. FROM UNCONDITIONAL SURRENDER TO THE CURRENCY REFORM (1945–1948)

(Rainer Karlsch)

Consequences of war

On 8 May 1945, the Second World War in Europe unleashed by the Third Reich ended with Germany's unconditional capitulation. Only a few weeks earlier, DEA had prepared for the inevitable, left only skeleton staff in its Berlin head office, and started transferring staff, materials, and documents to Wietze and Celle. The management of Karpathen Öl AG likewise relocated in spring 1945 to Garbsen, near Hanover.

For DEA, the war had on balance been a disaster. Hundreds of staff members had died, were wounded, or were classified as missing. Moreover, a considerable part of the group's fixed assets had been destroyed or impaired, with the refineries in Rositz, Wilhelmsburg, and Heide sustaining the worst war damage. Less severely affected were the hard coal collieries, with the exception of the severely hit coking plant attached to the Graf Bismarck Colliery. The oil fields in Wietze had been spared any major bombing but had suffered from rampant exploitation as part of the war effort.

What hit DEA hardest was the complete loss of its lignite operations, now located in the Soviet Occupation Zone (SOZ). Starting with the financial statements for the year 1944, the war and post-war losses were carried at the following book values, figures that were in part well below the net asset values:

Book values of DEA war and post-war losses – 1944 to June 1948[1]

Asset item	Book value (in million Reichsmark)
Plants and participations in the SOZ	86.4
Plants in Austria	26.6
Participations elsewhere outside Germany	5.2
Special write-downs for bombing damage	12.7
Write-offs of claims for war damage	17.1
Write-offs for Reich treasury notes	3.0
Write-offs for other receivables	3.9
Total	**155.1**

The DEA lignite works, briquette factories, carbonization plants, and refineries in Saxony and Thuringia were in part disassembled and confiscated by the Soviet occupying forces in 1945-6. From mid-1946 onward, ownership of these works was transferred to the Soviet Union by way of reparations and administered henceforth by the "Brikett" and "Topliwo" stock corporations.[2] In the years 1952-3, they were handed over to the East German government and nationalized.

DEA had certain hopes for a time that it would be able to retain its influence in the coal trading business in the SOZ. Brikett- und Kohlenhandel AG (Briko) in Leipzig had not been confiscated by the Soviet occupying forces, nor was the company one of those on the list for the referendum in June 1946 in Saxony on expropri-

1 Compiled according to: Geschäftsberichte 1944 bis 1948, WD-CA, D-GB, DEA.

2 Cf. For the importance of the Sowjetischen Aktiengesellschaften SAG (Soviet Stock Corporations) in the economy of the Sowjetische Besatzungszone Deutschland SBZ (Soviet Occupation Zone (SOZ) / Deutsche Demokratische Republik DDR (German Democratic Republic (GDR): Rainer Karlsch/Johannes Bähr, *Die sowjetischen Aktiengesellschaften (SAG) in der SBZ/DDR*, in: Karl Lauschke/Thomas Welskopp (Eds.), Mikropolitik im Unternehmen, Essen 1994, 214–255.

ating Nazi and war criminals.[3] Nevertheless, Lothar Ritter, CEO of Briko, had come under pressure.[4]

The works council considered him a "representative of the corporate group" and on 24 November 1945 forced the company to fire him.[5] Ritter had not been a member of the Nazi Party and explained in vain that during the Third Reich he had helped colleagues who had been under threat. Only three days before he was fired, Johannes Dieckmann[6] had offered him a top management position on the Saxon Coal Board (Kohlen-Kontor), which the state administration, as the predecessor to the state government, had just founded. Dieckmann was head of the Saxon Coal Board and in the SOZ was one of the co-founders of the Liberal Democratic Party of Germany (LDPD), of which Ritter was also a member. After he had been fired, he turned to his party friend and asked for support. His case was thereupon discussed at the highest level, namely by the Saxon Minister President Rudolf Friedrichs (Social Democrat), Vice President Fritz Selbmann (Communist) and Johannes Dieckmann (LDPD). After the matter had been examined, Ritter was vindicated, but he did not return to Briko, instead becoming managing director of the Leipzig division of the Saxon Coal Board.[7]

---

3 Cf. note, 12.11.1946, WD-CA, B 182/130.

4 Cf. Lothar Ritter, Niederschrift über meine Entlassung, no date (end of december 1945), WD-CA, D-RW-39.

5 Cf. note: Re.: "Briko", 16.9.1946, WD-CA, D-RW-40.

6 Johannes Dieckmann was one of Gustav Stresemann's closest collaborators after the First World War (DVP) (German People's Party) and had been a member of the Saxon state parliament as a DVP delegate from 1929 to 1933. From 1933 to 1939 and from 1941 to the end of the war, he worked as managing director of several coal industry associations. He was a co-founder of the LDPD in Saxony. From 1948, he served as Minister of Justice and Deputy Prime Minister of Saxony. (Cf. Jürgen Frölich, *Johannes Dieckmann (1893–1969)*, in: Torsten Oppenland (Ed.), Deutsche Politiker 1949–1969. 17 biographische Skizzen aus Ost und West, Vol. 1, Darmstadt 1999, 60–71.

7 Cf. Ritter an DEA, Vorstandsabt. Berlin-Schöneberg, 27.2.1946; WD-CA, Personalakte Lothar Ritter.

DEA released him on leave for the duration of his new activity, whereby he assured the company that he would continue to support its interests.[8] DEA granted Ritter full pay until the end of June 1946 and left it open whether he would later be restored to his position.[9] But before long, Ritter came into conflict with the Communist Party (and later the Socialist Unity Party, SED), which dominated works council at the Saxon Coal Board, too. He wrote of the matter in a letter to DEA CEO Hugo Griebel: "*Probably things will never calm down as they simply want to install a socialist in my stead.*"[10]

By this time, Briko still existed, albeit no longer in Leipzig. Its liquidation had been set in motion by the Saxon state government in 1946,[11] and the staff and furnishings had been transferred to the Saxon Coal Board.[12] Before that happened, the old Briko management had tried to have ownership of their firms transferred to DEA and had initiated a relocation of the company head office to Schöneberg in Berlin,[13] but the district courts in both Leipzig and in Schöneberg rejected the relevant applications. The district court in the Hanseatic city of Hamburg indicated it would help, and Briko moved its registered office there in August 1948. The company was as good as penniless and led a shadow existence in the hope that a divided Germany would not be long-lived.

The parent company had for some time hoped that the division of Germany would swiftly be overcome, and hopes were bolstered in the short term by the upheaval in conditions in East Germany in the wake of the death of Soviet dictator Stalin in March 1953 as well as the popular uprising of 17 June 1953. It was still unclear what thrust the new Soviet leadership policy on Germany

8 Cf. Ritter an DEA, Vorstandsabt. Berlin-Schöneberg, 19.4.1946, ibid.

9 Cf. Ritter/Grages an Ritter, 22.8.1946 sowie Ritter/Grages an Lothar Ritter, 9.9.1946, ibid.

10 Ritter an Hugo Griebel, 16.4.1946, ibid.

11 Cf. Notiz, 12.11.1946, WD-CA, B 182/130.

12 Cf. Mätzschker an Vorstand DEA, Berlin-Schöneberg, 28.11.1946, ibid.

13 Cf. Bezirksgericht Berlin-Schöneberg: Beschluss vom 8.7.1948, WD-CA, B 182/131.

Fig. 61 Lothar Ritter, Chairman of the Briko Management Board 1924–46

would take, but DEA senior management wanted to be ready for reunification. DEA board member Schlicht concerned himself closely with plans for how the group would need to act in such an event. He assumed that DEA would have its plants in East Germany returned to it, and at "reunification discussions" in Hamburg, as late as 1956 management debated the staffing charts for the East German works and setting up mixed East-West workforces.[14] The brief period of the thaw in the Cold War ended in autumn 1956 when Soviet troops put down the popular uprising in Hungary; it would be many years before anyone could return to considering an easing in relations between East and West Germany, let alone reunification.

14 Cf. Notiz: Wiedervereinigungsbesprechung, Hamburg 25.7.1955, WD-CA, D-RW-194.

As a result, DEA in Hamburg gradually lost interest in its former sites in East Germany.

Not only Germany, but the Republic of Austria was also divided into four occupation zones following the end of the Second World War. The largest proportion of the DEA assets were located in the Soviet Occupation Zone, and the Soviet military government claimed it was entitled to take possession of both the "Nova" refinery in Vienna and the mining rights that DEA had acquired in 1938 as reparation payments. Only the underground refinery in Ebensee, built in the closing months of the war, lay in the American Occupation Zone. The directors of the Ebensee facility applied on 25 May 1945 to be permitted to resume oil production,[15] and their petition was approved by the US military administration, especially as the plant was the only crude-oil processing facility in Upper Austria.

In summer 1945, the US Military Administration commenced investigations into the DEA executives in Austria.[16] Erich Greiser, who was the only director who had not been a Nazi Party member, stated that he had not been involved in the maltreatment of slave labourers and prisoners in Ebensee and Schwechat, near Vienna.[17] Herbert Kamptner,[18] who had at the end of the war been the Works Commissioner in the Geilenberg staff office and responsible for repairing the refinery in Schwechat, issued a declaration of hon-

---

15 Cf. Staiger und Greiser an Kapitän Kelly, 25.5.1945, ibid.

16 Aufstellung und Protokoll über die bei der DEA-Nova Raffinerie Ebensee beschäftigten Parteimitglieder, 21.8.1945, ibid.

17 Cf. Erich Greiser: Erklärung, 25.9.1945, ibid.

18 Herbert Kamptner: graduate engineer, 1931 doctorate, 1927–1936 assistant at TH Wien (Technical University Vienna), 1936–38 management of the Ebano road construction laboratory in Harburg, 1938–43 operations manager Gelsenberg hydrogenation plant, 1943–44 Karpathen Öl AG, Lemberg (Lviv), from June 1944 reconstruction of Schwechat refinery, from 1945 Donau Öl AG, after the end of the war Ebensee refinery (Dr. Kamptner: Ubrik über meine Ausbildung und meine Tätigkeit, WD-CA, D-RW-96).

our covering the Nova executives.[19] No staff members were relieved of their positions.

In spring 1946, a decision needed to be taken on whether to continue oil production at Ebensee. Given high transportation costs and the risks of underground production that were hard to gauge, DEA elected to discontinue operations. Thus ended the short history of the only underground plant operated as a business in Austria both during and after the war. On 15 February 1946, the German DEA executives in Ebensee were released and replaced by an Austrian fiduciary agent. The DEA managers were obliged to spend two months instructing the trustee on how to run the plant and then returned to Germany. In 1947, Fritz Staiger[20] was appointed head of the refinery in Heide and was a member of the DEA Management Board from 1955 to 1964.[21] When he was assessed for denazification, his former fellow directors and the works council at the "Nova" refinery supported his cause.[22] His case is a perfect example of how the DEA refinery experts both in West Germany and in Austria were able to continue their careers without interruption, either with their old employer or with other companies.

Old professional networks remained intact. Thus, Kurt Glöckner, who had worked at the "Nova" refinery outside Vienna and from 1940 to 1945 at Beskiden-Gesellschaft GmbH as well as at Karpathen Öl AG, was appointed public administrator of the remaining sections of Kontinentale Öl AG, as well as Preussag and

---

19 Cf. DEA-Nova, Raffinerie Ebensee: Bestätigung, 16. August 1945, WD-CA, D-RW-96.

20 After studying chemistry at the University of Freiburg, Staiger began working as an employee at DEA in 1935. He worked as an industrial chemist in Rositz before he was appointed head of the "Nova" refinery in Vienna in 1941. Staiger joined the NSDAP in October 1937. (Cf. Military Government of Germany: Fragebogen Fritz Staiger, 7.5.1946, Schleswig-Holsteinisches Landesarchiv, dept. 460.7, No. 447.)

21 Cf. Dr. Hugo Griebel: Trauerrede, Fritz Staiger (13.5.1908–6.6.1964), WD-CA, 3000–0514.

22 Cf. Staiger an Greiser, 10.3.1947; Erich Greiser: Zeugnis für Dr. Fritz Staiger, 16.3.1947, ibid.

Winterhall AG, by the Austrian government in early 1951.[23] Glöckner asked his former boss Karl Grosse for support, who, for his part, kept the DEA Management Board in Hamburg abreast of events in Austria.

Expedient alliances were even formed with former opponents. For example, British businessman van Sickle asked Karl Grosse of all people for help bringing his ownership claims to bear in Austria. Their talks led to an agreement being reached in April 1949 between DEA and van Sickle. The Republic of Austria Act on Restitutions of July 1946 envisaged that the legal validity of contracts signed after 13 March 1938 could be questioned. In such a case, the 20 sets of exploration rights van Sickle had had to sell to DEA would not have been considered German, but British assets. While Soviet occupying forces expropriated German assets by way of reparations, it was not entitled to do so for British property.[24]

Both parties to the contract declared that the 20 sets of exploration rights had not been sold by van Sickle to DEA and waived mutual claims.[25] DEA declared that it was willing to support van Sickle's claims to restitution, and if they proved successful, the German group would in return receive a 50-percent share of the profits from van Sickle's oil production.[26] The legal situation remained very complicated, however, as the region in question was part of the Soviet occupation zone in Austria. Things remained confused even after the Austrian State Treaty of 1955 and the withdrawal of the Soviet military presence, and it was not until October 1961 that van Sickle's claim to compensation was heard and approved.[27] A dispute between his heirs prevented the activation of the agreement

23 Cf. Große an DEA-Vorstand, 6.1.1951, WD-CA, "Österreich"-Ordner.

24 Cf. Aktennotiz Griebel, WD-CA, 3.5.1949, D-PA-0114.

25 Cf. Vereinbarung, 28.4.1949, Vertraulich, ibid.

26 Cf. Griebel: Aktennotiz, Streng vertraulich, 4.5.1951, ibid.

27 Cf. Rechtsanwalt Gerhard Stoiber an DEA-Vorstand, 12.10.1961, ibid.

reached with DEA in 1949, which was of dubious legal validity anyway.

"Denazification" and a new Management Board

In December 1945, the DEA Supervisory Board extended the Management Board contracts of Karl Schirner and Albert Ritter for a further three years,[28] with Schirner to continue as CEO. Only one month later, however, the Supervisory Board resolution looked set to wobble. In January 1946, the Allied Control Council in Berlin had issued its famous Directive no. 24 setting out the criteria for denazification, and the document was also to have consequences for the DEA Management Board.[29] The directive established that members of the Nazi Party "who have been more than nominal participants in its activities" should be removed from public and semi-public offices and from responsible positions in "important private undertakings". Immediately after Directive no. 24 was issued, the British Military Government dismissed three DEA Management Board members Karl Schirner, Günther Schlicht, and Max Grotowsky from their positions. The trio had to present themselves for assessment by the local German denazification tribunals now set up under the March 1946 Law for Liberation from National Socialism and Militarism.[30]

As a result, in March 1946 Erich Grages and Hugo Griebel were appointed proxy members of the Management Board.[31] The DEA Management Board sought to make a eliminate any possible weak flanks by choosing both Grages and Griebel, neither of

---

28 Cf. Aufsichtsratsbeschluss, 19.12.1945, WD-CA, PA-0120.

29 Cf. Clemens Vollnhals, *Entnazifizierung. Politische Säuberung unter alliierter Herrschaft*, in: Hans-Erich Volkmann (Ed.), Ende des Dritten Reiches – Ende des Zweiten Weltkrieges, Munich 1995, 372.

30 Cf. Cornelia Rauh-Kühne, *Die Entnazifizierung und die deutsche Gesellschaft*, in: Archiv für Sozialgeschichte 35 (1995), 35–70, here 44.

31 Cf. Geschäftsbericht 1944, 1945, 1946, WD-CA, D-GB-DEA Geschäftsberichte, 3.

whom had been Nazi Party members. Erich Grages was a lawyer who joined DEA in 1935 and had been head of the legal sections in the Wilhelmsburg and Rositz refineries. Griebel was likewise a lawyer and had since 1939 been one of the staff members closest to CEO Karl Schirner. Schirner felt his dismissal to be a "*severe shock and unjustified*",[32] and stated in the hearing before the denazification tribunal that he had not been a member of the Nazi Party. Schirner cited in his favour, amongst other things, that he had "*consciously prevented any expansion of DEA thanks to the wartime economy and had rejected any raiding of occupied territories during the war, too*". He also stated that he had helped people who were persecuted for racist reasons: "*I did whatever was in my powers to protect and assist people who were persecuted by the Nazi system.*"[33] He cited as his witness the Managing Director of Chemische Fabrik Eisenbüttel GmbH, Wilhelm Neumann, who had been dismissed by DEA in 1938 but received a pension that enabled him to survive.

With his statements, Schirner played down DEA's active involvement in the war economy and suggested that he himself had had no truck with the Nazi system. The denazification tribunal judged him to be "*completely exonerated*", and in March 1947 he resumed his function as Chair of the Management Board. He also acted as a member of the German Coal Board, i.e., the committee representing mining in the Ruhr region to the military government, and held various Supervisory Board positions, including one at VIAG.[34] In December 1951, Schirner retired from the DEA Management Board and took a seat on the Supervisory Board.

The denazification proceedings against Günther Schlicht also ended leniently, although he had joined the Nazi Party in 1937

---

32 Karl Schirner, Curriculum Vitae, 1946. Biographische Notizen für den Entnazifizierungsausschuss. WD-CA, D-14-2/1381.

33 Ibid.

34 Cf. Pohl/Schneider, *VIAG-Aktiengesellschaft*, 243.

and in 1942 had been appointed a "War Economy Leader".[35] He was classified as a "follower" and was able to return to the Management Board in the early summer of 1947. In the years that followed, DEA had his efforts to thank primarily for the fact that it was successfully reestablished.

The denazification proceedings took longest for Max Grotowski.[36] He and his commercial director, along with other Ruhr region mining directors, were incarcerated for about two years.[37] After he was released at the end of 1947, Grotowski was able to return to his function as a DEA Management Board member.

Karl Grosse, whose employment contract with DEA had been played on hold, hoped that a new agreement would be forthcoming. Given his prominent position in the war economy as the former Chairman of the Management Board of Karpathen Öl AG and member of the Nazi Party since 1933, the Interim Management Board of DEA had no interest in taking such a step. Schirner and Griebel intimated to Grosse that he should terminate his contractual relationship with DEA with effect from 31 December 1946,[38] and that was the route he then chose.

The DEA Supervisory Board membership also had to be changed in part. In September 1945, Supervisory Board Chairman Karl Kimmich died and was succeeded by Hans von Flotow, who himself passed away in October 1947. Mining Assessor Albert Ritter, long-standing Director of the Graf Bismarck Colliery, was thereupon made the new Chairman of the Supervisory Board. The interim period at DEA came to a close with the company head office relocating from Berlin to Hamburg in November 1947.[39]

---

35 Cf. NSDAP-Gaudatei: Günter Schlicht, BArch Berlin, R 9361-IX Kartei/37700385.

36 Cf. NSDAP-Gaudatei: Max Grotowski, BArch Berlin, R 9361-IX Kartei/12201441.

37 Cf. Schlicht, *Memoiren*, 171f.

38 Cf. Schirner und Griebel an Große, 29.11.1945, WD-CA, Direktor Karl Große, Personal-Abteilung DEA.

39 Cf. DEA-Geschäftsbericht 1947, WD-CA, D-GB, 1947 new.

Under British supervision

After 1945, DEA owned facilities only in the British Occupation Zone. These were placed under supervision by "North German Coal Control" (NGCC) and "North German Oil Control" (NGOC), the relevant departments of the British military government. The hard coal collieries in the Ruhr region were confiscated as per the SHAEF Military Government Law no. 52 on Blocking and Control of Property,[40] and it was unclear what would happen to these operations in future.

During the first phase of British military government, policies were based on the view that German industry needed to be further weakened through the dismantling of industrial plant in order to prevent any feared resurgence of Germany. The nationalization of key industries, in particular coal mining, was intended to put an end to the concentration of economic power in just a few hands. By nationalizing the coal industry, the British wanted to strengthen the Social Democrats and at the same time drive a wedge between them and the Communists. At the end of November 1946, a plan got underway for installing trustees for the coal mines in the Ruhr region.

The Allies in West Germany focused less on the small German oil industry, but it was still subject to strict controls. For DEA, the fact that the North German Oil Control (NGOC) HQ was located in Hamburg with a satellite in Celle was to prove favourable, and countless files had been moved to Celle from the Oil section at the Reich Office for Georesearch. One figure who played an important role at NGOC was Major Albert Everard Gunther (1903–1998), who had studied geology and from the mid-1920s onwards had pursued a career as a petroleum geologist that had taken him, amongst

---

40 Cf. Amtsblatt der Militärregierung Deutschland (SHAEF – Supreme Headquarters Allied Expeditionary Force), No. 3, 18.

other places, to South America. Gunther was pragmatic and had the senior executives at DEA and Karpathen Öl AG compile extensive material on the development of the German oil industry, in particular in the territories occupied during the war. He used these papers for a major series of articles on the wartime activities of the German oil industry, which he then published in "Petroleum Times". Here, he adopted the narrative put forward by his German colleagues, who considered themselves exclusively experts who had no dealings with politics, whereas it was the "Party offices" that were solely responsible for plundering the occupied territories and exploiting the oil resources there. This narrative could be perfectly backed up by the history of Kontinentale Öl AG, as government representatives had held sway at that company. German oil companies had, so the line went, had little with which to oppose them and had only reluctantly followed the stipulations set by the Four-Year Plan Authority. Gunther also defended Karl Grosse as the most important representative of the German oil industry. Why should that expert, Gunther asked, have refused to take the tempting post of General Director of Karpathen Öl AG?[41] If even Grosse, as head of the Oil Industry Expert Group and decisively responsible for the take-over of oil companies in Austria, France, Poland, and Slovakia, need not take the stand for his actions in the Nazi war economy, then why should anyone else in the oil industry?

The importance of Gunther's rejection of all nationalization plans for DEA should also not be underestimated. The opinion that the military government should not intervene in the ownership structure swiftly gained sway at NGOC, for in the German oil industry there was, he argued, neither an excessive concentration of capital nor any thoroughbred oil companies. Added to this, the operations of the German oil corporations were focussed only on the domestic market. British policy in its occupation zone revolved

41 Cf. Gunther, *Der deutsche Krieg um Erdöl*, Chapter XI.

around three constitutive elements anyway: overt pragmatism, an anti-Soviet stance, and primarily conservative staff members in the occupying authorities. This left little scope for social structural reforms from the very outset.[42]

Among the trade unions, the Social Democrats and some of the Christian Democrats (conservatives) there was strong anti-capitalist sentiment given the disastrous experiences of Nazi dictatorship, and criticism was levelled in particular at the big industrialists for having too much economic and political influence. As in the years after the First World War, the Social Democrats resorted to the concept of a social economy. This entailed the nationalization of key industries, above all the coal and steel industry, a step that was meant to serve as a lever for macroeconomic control.[43] In Hessen and North Rhine Westphalia, the Social Democrats even succeeded in gaining parliamentary majorities for the model of a social economy.

The most radical demands were raised by the Communists who, with a view to the expropriations they undertook in the Soviet Occupation Zone in Germany with Soviet guidance, sought to "break the power of the monopolies" in the three western zones. A well-informed member of the Communist Party in Hanover published an article on the situation in the West German oil industry at the end of 1946 in East Berlin magazine "Die Wirtschaft". He pointed the finger at the four "major conglomerates" in the oil industry. After the end of the war, the old "*general directors and War Economy Leaders, Schirner and Schlicht, had established a new corporate headquarters in Wietze.*"[44] He also mentioned the Karpathen Öl AG liquidation office in Celle, where there were around 40 employ-

[42] Cf. Werner Plumpe, *Wirtschaftsverwaltung und Kapitalinteresse im britischen Besatzungsgebiet 1945/46*, in: Dietmar Petzina/Walter Euchner (Eds.), Wirtschaftspolitik im britischen Besatzungsgebiet 1945–1949, Düsseldorf 1984, 121–152, here 131.

[43] Cf. Werner Abelshauser, *Deutsche Wirtschaftsgeschichte seit 1945*, Munich 2004, 102–105.

[44] Cf. n.n., in: Die Wirtschaft 8 (1946).

ees, some of them clearly incriminated as Nazis. The author called for extended codetermination rights for the employees and for the nationalization of the entire oil industry.

In 1946-7, the newly nominated State Parliament of Lower Saxony hotly debated what the best approach should be to the oil industry.[45] On 26 March 1947, shortly before the first elections to the state parliament in Lower Saxony on 24 April 1947, the Social Democrats parliamentary party tabled a motion for the "*operations of the primary industries (coal, ore, oil), the iron and steel industry, and the operations of supply industries and transportation enterprises that rely on tracks and catenary lines and are still in private hands, and cement production to be transformed into public property.*"[46] The Communist Party took things even further and called in an amendment to the gazetted motion no. 206 for the aforementioned industries to be expropriated without compensation,[47] although the West German Communist Party had no prospect of actually getting this achieved. In the debate, State Minister Hans-Christoph Seebohm took the floor as the most determined opponent of any nationalization of the oil industry.[48] Seebohm was a member of the right-wing Deutsche Partei (DP) and was head of Wirtschaftsverband Erdölgewinnung (the Oil

---

45 Cf. Betriebsrat und Direktor der Karpathen Öl AG an Albert Köhler Stellv. Oberbürgermeister von Celle, 24.1.1947, WD-CA, D-43-13-19.

46 Cf. Antrag der SPD-Fraktion auf die Überführung der Betriebe der Grundstoffindustrie, der Eisen- und Stahlerzeugungsindustrie und der noch in Privathand befindlichen Betriebe der Versorgungsunternehmungen und Verkehrsunternehmungen, die an Schienen und Oberleitungen gebunden sind, und der Zementproduktion in den Besitz der Allgemeinheit, Archiv des Niedersächsischen Landtages Hannover, ENLT2019/012.

47 Cf. Memorandum (der KPD) über die deutsche Erdölproduktion, 1947; Flugblatt der KPD zu den Landtagswahlen in Niedersachsen vom April 1947, WD-CA, D-43-13-19.

48 Cf. Stenographischer Bericht über die Sitzung des Niedersächsischen Landtages am 26.3.1947, Archiv des Niedersächsischen Landtages Hannover, ENLT2019/012.

Industry Business Association) in the British Occupation Zone.[49] The Social Democrats' motion for nationalization (gazetted motion no. 206) only just failed in a roll-call vote – by 40 to 43 votes.[50]

The restitution demands brought against Karpathen Öl AG, now domiciled in Celle, were also controversial. The head of the Polish Military Mission in Berlin, Major General Pravin, called for the dissolution of the company and the return of the industrial plant and equipment that had been transported to West Germany to the Polish government.[51] Faced with such public attacks, Karpathen Öl AG requested an appointment with the Lord Mayor of Celle, Albert Köhler. Köhler was a dyed-in-the-wool Social Democrat who had worked at DEA in Wietze from 1919 to 1924 and had then been Managing Director of the "Celler Volkszeitung" until 1933, as well as a member of the city council from 1929 onwards. During the Third Reich, Köhler was twice arrested and imprisoned in a concentration camp.[52] Parallel to the meeting with Köhler, Hermann Petri, as the new director of Karpathen Öl AG, conducted talks with State Minister Seebohm in Hanover in January 1947, and the immediate dissolution of Karpathen Öl AG was averted.

While the motion to nationalize the oil industry fell short of a majority in the Lower Saxon Parliament, in August 1947 the State Parliament in Schleswig-Holstein had, with the votes of the Social Democrats, resolved the nationalization of the Heide Erdölwerke, the Portland cement factories, and the blast furnaces in Lübeck, as

49 Cf. Petri: Re.: "Angriffe auf die Karpathen Öl AG", WD-CA, 23.1.1947, WD-CA, D-43-13-19.

50 Cf. Der Direktor beim niedersächsischen Landtag, Entwurf, 1.4.1947, Archiv des Niedersächsischen Landtages Hannover, ENLT2019/012.

51 Cf. n.n., "Plünderer verwalten polnisches Gut", in: Neues Deutschland, 14.1.1947.

52 Cf. Barbara Simon, *Abgeordnete in Niedersachsen 1946–1994. Biographisches Handbuch*, Hanover 1996, 204.

well as some of the larger transportation companies.[53] To the great relief of the DEA board, the British military government nevertheless prevented the nationalization from taking place.[54] The merger of the American and British zones from 1 January 1947 onwards to form the "United Economic Area" or "Bizone" brought about a change in British policy on Germany and laid the foundations for Anglo-American cooperation henceforth in Germany and Europe.[55] Nationalization disappeared completely from the agenda following the Economic and Currency Reform of June 1948.

Reconstruction

The Chairman of the DEA Management Board felt the corporation was in a catastrophic state, given the capital losses and the destruction of assets incurred during the war. The technologies to produce tar and oil from lignite were completely valueless, and now control of hard coal mining came under the aegis of the North German Coal Control (NGCC), meaning the DEA executives had no direct influence on operations any longer. The greatest problem was the lack of staff and falling output per shift owing to poor nutrition.[56]

The oil operations were also subject to various restrictions, with any new exploratory drilling having to be authorized by the NGOC. DEA's oil trading companies were relocated to Wietze,

---

53 Cf. Holger Martens, *Die Geschichte der Sozialdemokratischen Partei Deutschlands in Schleswig-Holstein 1945 bis 1959*, PhD thesis Hamburg 1997; Uwe Danker, *"Raus aus dem Elend". Selbstverortung und Programmatik schleswig-holsteinischer Nachkriegspolitik in sozialdemokratischer Regie*, in: Demokratische Geschichte 19 (2008), 315–328.

54 Cf. Niederschrift über die Sitzung des Aufsichtsrats, 5.11.1947, WD-CA, PA-0120.

55 Cf. Rolf Steininger, *Reform und Realität. Ruhrfrage und Sozialisierung in der anglo-amerikanischen Deutschlandpolitik 1947/48*, in: Vierteljahrshefte für Zeitgeschichte 27 (1979), 167–241.

56 Cf. Geschäftsbericht 1945, WD-CA, D-GB DEA-Geschäftsberichte 1944, 1945, 1946.

while those of the DEA subsidiaries that were located in the west continued to function.[57] In 1946, Gebhardt & König Deutsche Schachtbau AG, Nordhausen, set up a subsidiary in the British Occupation Zone and in 1947 relocated its registered office there. Edeleanu GmbH likewise had to relocate and moved from Berlin to Frankfurt/Main.

Given that DEA had neither any major oil fields of its own nor its own filling station network, Schirner had little hope of restoring the group to a leading position among the German oil companies. He feared that the international oil corporations whose representatives were also to be found among the ranks of the occupying forces would largely seek to squeeze their weak German rivals out of the market once and for all.[58] The British Military Government had initially forbidden DEA to rebuild its lubricants refinery in Wilhelmsburg, something that seemed to justify Schirner's pessimism, and he was also wary of rebuilding distillation capacities in Wietze. This led to conflict with Schlicht, who did not share his CEO's pessimistic view.[59]

Reconstruction at DEA was somewhat facilitated by the dormant reserves it had established during the war economy and the option of repaying the bond floated in 1938 before the Currency Reform in the summer of 1948.[60] In the first few years after the war, DEA dedicated itself to restoring output in the field of hard coal as swiftly as possible to the levels achieved before the war, while the oil operations in Wietze and Heide first needed to overcome the impact of having been over-exploited during the war.

In the late 1940s, approximately two thirds of DEA sales and revenues stemmed from its hard coal operations, as in 1947 the situation in mining had started to improve slightly. Care packages and a

57 Cf. DEA-Geschäftsbericht 1947, WD-CA, D-GB, 1947 new.

58 Cf. Karl Schirner, *Gutachten*, Wietze 1946.

59 Cf. Schlicht, *Erinnerungen*, 169f.

60 Cf. Niederschrift über die Sitzung des Aufsichtsrats, 5.11.1947, WD-CA, PA-0120.

points system for miners created incentives to work harder, and this contributed decisively to a gradual boost in performance per shift. However, operating costs still remained very high, while sales prices remained regulated irrespective of this, and so operations needed to be subsidized. While the workforce at the end of 1947 was almost back on a par with the pre-war level, output per shift and thus mine productivity was still well below the pre-war levels, primarily owing to the poor nutrition of the miners.

DEA hard coal output – 1939 to 1947 (in million tonnes)[61]

Year	Output (in million t)	Workforce
1939	3.58	9,647
1944	3.13	10,271
1947	1.85	9,150

Things were even worse when it came to crude oil production, which by mid-1948 had fallen to even below the low level of 1946. Schirner did not believe that DEA would be able to tap any notable new deposits with its follow-up drilling,[62] but Schlicht nevertheless insisted that it should give itself a strong profile as an oil company again. The success tapping new oil fields near Heide and Hohne ultimately proved him right.

DEA oil output – 1932 to 1947 (in tonnes)[63]

Year	Total production	Wietze	Heide	Austria
1932	53,415	53,415	0	0
1939	152,626	64,688	77,107	10,831
1944	685,410	72,435	125,817	487,158
1947	113,230	57,030	56,200	-

61 Cf. ibid.

62 Cf. Schlicht, *Erinnerungen*, 224.

63 Cf. Aufsichtsratsprotokoll, 5.11.1947, WD-CA, PA-0120.

After the drastic reduction in oil output, DEA suffered a massive hit when it had to relinquish the Vienna refinery and absorbing the destruction of the one in Wilhelmsburg. Now, in total a little more than 100,000 tonnes of crude oil could be refined – and only in Heide and Wietze. DEA therefore concentrated on manufacturing specialty products.

Schlicht's optimism rested above all on his trust in the well-qualified team of oil workers and the future earning power of the new oil fields in Schleswig-Holstein, which he felt would enable profitable oil wells. This was the context to the 1948 resolution to set up a lubricants plant in Grasbrook, a district in the Hamburg Free Port, and to acquire a majority interest in Ernst Schliemann's Ölwerke GmbH.[64]

The Economic and Currency Reform in the summer of 1948 improved macroeconomic conditions and enabled DEA to rebuild and re-emerge on a level no one could have imagined at the end of the war.

DEA nevertheless faced structural difficulties. The era of German hard coal mining was drawing to a close, so it was foreseeable that in the medium-term hard coal mining only promised modest earnings. Domestic oil production therefore seemed the main key to the company's success, but DEA did not manage to set up a strong sales arm of its own, while its rivals had widespread filling station networks.

Given the structural problems merely touched on here, it was foreseeable that DEA would not be able to survive in the long term as an independent coal and oil company in the fiercely contested, liberalized German market. This state of affairs was little altered by efforts to invest in petrochemicals and thus establish a new field of

64 Cf. Hasso von Wedel, *Die Entwicklung der Deutsche Erdöl-Aktiengesellschaft/ Deutsche Texaco Aktiengesellschaft 1952 bis 1974*, Ms., Hamburg 1975.

operations.[65] In the early 1960s, DEA was, to all intents and purposes, dead in the water as an independent enterprise.

65 Cf. ibid., 22ff.

ARCHIVES AND BIBLIOGRAPHY

Archives

Archiv der BEB Hannover

Archiv der Bundesanstalt für Geowissenschaften und Rohstoffe (BGR) Hannover

Archiv des Instituts für Zeitgeschichte München (IfZ)

Archiv des Niedersächsischen Landtages

BASF-Archiv

Bayer-Archiv Leverkusen

Bundesarchiv Berlin (BArch Berlin)

Bundesarchiv Freiburg (BArch Freiburg)

Bundesarchiv Ludwigsburg

Bundesbeauftragte für die Unterlagen des Staatssicherheitsdienstes der ehemaligen DDR – Außenstelle Leipzig (part of the BArch Berlin)

Deutsches Erdölmuseum Wietze

GeoSphere Austria-Archiv Rohstoffe Wien

Historisches Archiv der Deutschen Bank (HADB)

ITS Archive Bad Arolsen

Landesarchiv Berlin (LAB)

Landesarchiv Nordrhein-Westfalen (LAV), dept. Westfalen

Landesarchiv Saarland

Landesarchiv Sachsen-Anhalt (LASA)

National Archives Washington

Österreichisches Staatsarchiv Wien (ÖStA)

Rheinisch-Westfälisches Wirtschaftsarchiv (RWWA)

Russisches Staatliches Militärarchiv Moscow (RGVA)

Sächsisches Staatsarchiv, department Bergarchiv Freiberg und Staatsarchiv Leipzig (StA Leipzig)

Schleswig-Holsteinisches Landesarchiv

Staatsarchiv Bremen (StAB)

Wintershall Dea Corporate Archive (WD-CA)

Literature

Abelshauser, Werner, *Deutsche Wirtschaftsgeschichte seit 1945*, Munich 2004.

Aly, Götz, *Hitlers Volksstaat. Raub, Rassenkrieg und nationaler Sozialismus*, Frankfurt a.M. 2005.

Bachmann, Karl, *Dr. Friedrich Fetzer von Schloss Moos. Ein verdienter Lindauer unserer Zeit*, in: Jahrbuch des Landkreises Lindau (1993), 17–24.

Bähr, Johannes, *Die Dresdner Bank in der Wirtschaft des Dritten Reiches*, Munich 2006.

Bähr, Johannes/Köhler, Ingo, *Verfolgt, „arisiert", wiedergutgemacht? Wie aus dem Warenhauskonzern Hermann Tietz Hertie wurde*, Munich 2023.

Bajohr, Frank, *„Arisierung" und wirtschaftliche Existenzvernichtung im Nationalsozialismus*, in: Andrea Bambi/Axel Drecoll (Eds.), Alfred Flechtheim. Raubkunst und Restitution, Berlin 2015, 29–36.

Banken, Ralf, *Edelmetallmangel und Großraubwirtschaft. Die Entwicklung des deutschen Edelmetallsektors im „Dritten Reich" 1933–1945*, Berlin 2009.

Baranowski, Frank, *Rüstungsprojekte in der Region Nordhausen, Worbis und Heiligenstadt während der NS-Zeit*, Duderstadt 1998.

Barkai, Avraham, *Vom Boykott zur „Entjudung". Der wirtschaftliche Existenzkampf der Juden im Dritten Reich 1933–1943*, Frankfurt a.M. 1988.

Bauer, Eugen, in: Baltisches Biografisches Lexikon digital, bbld.de/GND1195506732 [last retrieved on 10 October 2023].

Baumert, Martin, *Autarkiepolitik in der Braunkohlenindustrie. Ein diachroner Systemvergleich anhand des Braunkohlenindustriekomplexes Böhlen-Espenhain 1933 bis 1965*, Berlin 2022.

Bavendamm, Dirk, *1899–1999. Die Geschichte des Unternehmens. 100 Jahre RWE-DEA*, in: RWE-DEA AG (Ed.), 100 Jahre RWE-DEA. 1899–1999, Hamburg 1999, 171–278.

BEB Erdgas und Erdöl GmbH, Hannover (Ed.), *Die Gewerkschaft Elwerath. Chronik eines Erdölunternehmens 1866–1969*, Hanover 1987.

Beck, Hermann, *Konflikte zwischen Deutschnationalen und Nationalsozialisten während der Machtergreifungszeit*, in: Historische Zeitschrift 3 (2011), 645–680.

Becker, Hubert S., *Die deutschen Erdölgebiete, ihre Entwicklung und Rentabilität*, PhD thesis Vienna 1933.

Benz, Wolfgang, *Gewalt im November 1938. Die „Reichskristallnacht". Initial zum Holocaust*, Berlin 2018.

Berg, Thomas von, *Korruption und Bereicherung. Politische Biografie des Münchener NSDAP-Vorsitzenden Christian Weber (1883–1945)*, Munich 2003.

Berghoff, Hartmut/Grieger, Manfred, *Die Geschichte des Hauses Bahlsen: Keks – Krieg – Konsum 1911 bis 1974*, Göttingen 2024.

Birkenfeld, Wolfgang, *Der synthetische Treibstoff 1933–1945*, Göttingen 1964.

Bischoff, Ursula, *Der Einfluss der bergbaulichen Traditionen und großindustriellen Entwicklungen auf das soziale Gefüge und die Mobilität der Braunkohlenwirtschaft von Borna*, PhD thesis Berlin 2000.

Blaich, Fritz, *Der „Standard-Oil-Fall" vor dem Reichstag. Ein Beitrag zur deutschen Monopolpolitik vor 1914*, in: Zeitschrift für die gesamte Staatswissenschaft 126 (1970), 663–682.

Bleidick, Dietmar, *Die Energieregion Ruhrgebiet. Eine historisch-statistische Studie*, Baden-Baden 2023.

Bohrtechniker Zeitung 10 (1938).

Brachwitz, Richard, *Technische Brigade Mineralöl im Kaukasus*, in: Glückauf. Rundbrief der AG Bergbau, Erdöl, Geologie e.V. 78 (1999).

Brechtken, Markus et al., *Die Nürnberger Gesetze – 80 Jahre danach. Vorgeschichte, Entstehung, Auswirkungen*, Munich 2017.

Brinkmann, Sabine, *Das Dritte Reich und der synthetische Treibstoff. Eine Kritik der Forschung aus chemietechnischer Sicht*, in: Akkumulation 15 (2001), 16–23.

Bruder, Franziska, *„Den ukrainischen Staat erkämpfen oder sterben!" Die Organisation Ukrainischer Nationalisten (OUN) 1928–1948*, Berlin 2007.

Brunswig, Hans, *Feuersturm über Hamburg. Die Luftangriffe auf Hamburg im 2. Weltkrieg und ihre Folgen*, Stuttgart 2003.

Bütow, Tobias/Bindernagel, Franka, *Ein KZ in der Nachbarschaft. Das Magdeburger Außenlager der BRABAG und der Freundeskreis Himmler*, Weimar 2003.

Combined Intelligence Objectives Sub-Committee (CIOS) (Ed.), *File No. XXVIII – 57. Deutsche Erdöl A.G. Erdölwerke "Nova" Dachs II Plant, Ebensee, Austria*, London 1945.

Danker, Uwe, *„Raus aus dem Elend". Selbstverortung und Programmatik schleswig-holsteinischer Nachkriegspolitik in sozialdemokratischer Regie*, in: Demokratische Geschichte 19 (2008), 145–170.

Dapprich, Gerhard, *Leitfaden des Bergrechts und anderer für den Bergbau wichtiger Rechtsgebiete mit Gesetzestexten*, Essen [4]1955.

Dehnke, Reinhold, *Nachruf Ernst Middendorf*, in: Glückauf 41 (1933), 980.

Deist, Wilhelm et al., *Das Deutsche Reich und der Zweite Weltkrieg*, Vol. 1:. *Ursachen und Voraussetzungen der deutschen Kriegspolitik*, Stuttgart 1979.

Deutsche Erdöl-Aktiengesellschaft (Ed.), *Denkschrift zum 25jährigen Bestehen der Deutschen Erdöl-Aktiengesellschaft Berlin 1899–1924*, Berlin 1924.

Die Zukunft 32 (1919).

Dürkop, Hinrich, *Die Erdölwerke bei Heide in Dithmarschen 1856–2006*, Hamburg 2007.

Eichholtz, Dietrich (Ed.), *Deutsche Ölpolitik im Zeitalter der Weltkriege, Studien und Dokumente*, Leipzig 2010.

Eichholtz, Dietrich, *Geschichte der deutschen Kriegswirtschaft 1939–1945,* Vol. 1: *1939–1941,* Berlin 1969.

Eichholtz, Dietrich, *Geschichte der deutschen Kriegswirtschaft 1939–1945,* Vol. 3: *1943–1945,* Berlin 1996.

Eichholtz, Dietrich, *Das Versailler System. Verlust der deutschen Erdölressourcen in Europa und in Mesopotamien*, in: id. (Ed.), Deutsche Ölpolitik im Zeitalter der Weltkriege. Studien und Dokumente, Leipzig 2010, 96–187.

Eichholtz, Dietrich, *Der Raubzug des faschistischen deutschen Imperialismus zu den Erdölquellen des Kaukasus 1941–1943*, in: Jahrbuch für Geschichte (1976), 445–502.

Eisenblätter, Gerhard, *Grundlinien der Politik des Reiches gegenüber dem Generalgouvernement 1939–1945*, PhD thesis Frankfurt a.M. 1969.

Eminger, Stefan et al., *Nationalsozialismus in Niederösterreich. Opfer. Täter. Gegner*, Innsbruck 2021.

Emme, Erich, *Deutschlands Mineralölindustrie und Handel. Eine Untersuchung unter Berücksichtigung des Standorts- und des Konzentrationsproblems*, PhD thesis Hamburg 1924.

Essner, Cornelia, *Die „Nürnberger Gesetze" oder die Verwaltung des Rassenwahns 1933–1945*, Paderborn 2002.

Fahrion, Helmut, *Die Gewerkschaft Elwerath. Chronik eines Erdölunternehmens 1866–1969*, Hanover 1987.

Feichtinger, Friedrich/Spörker, Hermann, *ÖMV-OMV. Die Geschichte eines Österreichischen Unternehmens*, Vienna 1994.

Feldman, Gerald D., *Die Deutsche Bank vom Ersten Weltkrieg bis zur Weltwirtschaftskrise. 1914–1933*, in: Lothar Gall et al., Die Deutsche Bank 1870–1995, Munich 1995, 138–314.

Flachowsky, Sören, *Das Reichsamt für Wirtschaftsausbau als Forschungsbehörde im NS-System*, in: Technikgeschichte 3 (2015), 185–224.

Frenkel, Erich, *Die preußische Mutungssperre für Kalisalze und Steinkohlen (Die "Lex Gamp"). Ein Beitrag zur Frage der Aufhebung der Bergbaufreiheit*, Berlin 1913.

Freund, Florian, *Arbeitslager Zement. Das Konzentrationslager Ebensee und die Raketenrüstung*, Vienna 1989.

Freund, Florian, *Konzentrationslager Ebensee. Ein Außenlager des KZ-Mauthausen*, Vienna 2015.

Freund, Florian, *Das Konzentrationslager Ebensee. Raketenrüstung im SS-Arbeitslager „Zement"*, Innsbruck 2006.

Freund, Florian, *Die Toten von Ebensee. Analyse und Dokumentation der im KZ Ebensee umgekommenen Häftlinge 1943 – 1945*, Vienna 2010.

Frölich, Jürgen, *Johannes Dieckmann 1893–1969*, in: Torsten Oppelland (Ed.), Deutsche Politiker 1949–1969. 17 biographische Skizzen aus Ost und West, Darmstadt 1999, 60–71.

Gall, Lothar, *Die Deutsche Bank von ihrer Gründung bis zum Ersten Weltkrieg*, in: id. et al., Die Deutsche Bank 1870–1995, Munich 1995, 1–137.

Ganzer, Christian, *Die Karpato-Ukraine 1938/39. Spielball im internationalen Interessenkonflikt am Vorabend des Zweiten Weltkriegs*, Hamburg 2001.

Gebhardt, Gerhard, *Ruhrbergbau. Geschichte, Aufbau und Verflechtung seiner Gesellschaften und Organisationen*, Essen 1957.

Genschel, Helmut, *Die Verdrängung der Juden aus der Wirtschaft im Dritten Reich*, Göttingen 1966.

Gilbert, Martin, *Endlösung: Die Vertreibung und Vernichtung der Juden. Ein Atlas*, Frankfurt a.M. 1983.

Gotto, Bernhard, *Adaption und Kooperation. Neue Geschäftspraktiken im Dritten Reich*, in: Johannes Bähr et al., Der Flick-Konzern im Dritten Reich, Munich 2008, 295–378.

Grieger, Manfred, *Extermination and Work under the Nazi System of Forced Labor*, in: Volkhard Knigge et al. *(Ed.), Forced Labor. The Germans, the Forced Laborers, and the War*, Weimar 2010, 208–220

Grieger, Manfred, *In-company social welfare policies and forced labour. The two sides to the Nazi "Betriebsgemeinschaft" (works community) at Wintershall*, in: id. et al., Expansion at all costs. Studies on the Wintershall AG between Crisis and War, 1929–1945, Frankfurt a.M. 2020, 160–225.

Gröbel, Hans, *Menschen in Erle. Schriftenreihe zur Ortskunde*, Erle 1994.

Grundmann, Erich, *Chemie und Technologie des Braunkohlenteers*, Berlin 1964.

Gruner, Wolf, *Die NS-Führung und die Zwangsarbeit für sogenannte jüdische Mischlinge. Ein Einblick in die Planung und Praxis antijüdischer Politik in den Jahren 1942 bis 1944*, in: Manfred Weißbecker/Reinhard Kühnl (Eds.), Rassismus, Faschismus, Antifaschismus, Cologne 2000, 63–79.

Gunther, Albert E., *Der deutsche Krieg um Erdöl in Europa 1934–1945*, Arbeitsübersetzung der DEA, n.d.

Gunther, Albert E., *The German War for Crude Oil in Europe 1934–1945*, in: The Petroleum Times, 3.1.1948, 22–26.

Hachtmann, Rüdiger, *Industriearbeit im „Dritten Reich". Untersuchungen zu den Lohn- und Arbeitsbedingungen in Deutschland 1933–1945*, Göttingen 1988.

Hachtmann, Rüdiger, *Vom Wilhelminismus zur neuen Staatlichkeit des Nationalsozialismus. Das Reichsarbeitsministerium 1918–1945*, Göttingen 2023.

Häusler, Hermann/Koppensteiner, Bruno W., *Das Kaukasus-Öl. Ziel der Deutschen Wehrmacht im Zweiten Weltkrieg*, in: Berichte der Geologischen Bundesanstalt (2021), 77–102.

Harrington, Dale, *Mystery Man. William Rhodes Davis. American Nazi Agent of Influence*, New York 2001.

Herbert, Ulrich, *Eine „Führerentscheidung" zur „Endlösung"?*, in: Neue Züricher Zeitung, 14./15.3.1998.

Herbert, Ulrich, *Fremdarbeiter. Politik und Praxis des „Ausländer-Einsatzes" in der Kriegswirtschaft des Dritten Reiches*, Berlin 1985.

Hermann, Walter, *Das Kapital im mitteldeutschen Braunkohlenbergbau*, PhD thesis Leipzig 1930.

Hoffmann, Dietrich, *Acht Jahrzehnte Gefrierverfahren nach Poetsch. Ein Beitrag zur Geschichte des Schachtabteufens in schwierigen Fällen*, Essen 1962.

Hoffmann, Dietrich, *Die Erdölgewinnung in Norddeutschland. Von den Anfängen vor über 400 Jahren bis heute*, Hamburg 1970.

Hüttenberger, Peter, *Düsseldorf. Geschichte von den Ursprüngen bis ins 20. Jahrhundert,* Vol. 3: *Die Industrie- und Verwaltungsstadt (20. Jahrhundert)*, Düsseldorf 1989.

Humann, Detlev, *„Arbeitsschlacht". Arbeitsbeschaffung und Propaganda in der NS-Zeit 1933–1939*, Göttingen 2011.

Iber, Walter M., *Die sowjetische Mineralölverwaltung in Österreich. Zur Vorgeschichte der OMV 1945–1955*, Innsbruck 2011.

Ibing, Günther, *Über die Extraktion von Steinkohle in Kombination mit der Druckhydrierung von Pech. Arbeitsweise der Ruhröl GmbH von 1938 bis 1944*, in: Deutsche Gesellschaft für Mineralölwissenschaft und Kohlechemie (Ed.), Compendium 1974/75, Leinfelden-Echterdingen 1975, 311–318.

Internationaler Militärgerichtshof Nürnberg (Ed.), *Der Prozess gegen die Hauptkriegsverbrecher vor dem Internationalen Militärgerichtshof. Nürnberg 14. November 1945 – 1. Oktober 1946*, Vol. 7/8, Munich 1985.

James, Harold, *Die deutsche Bank und die Diktatur*, in: Lothar Gall et al., Die Deutsche Bank 1870–1995, Munich 1995, 315–408.

James, Harold, *Georg Solmssen. Eine biographische Annäherung*, in: id./Martin L. Müller (Eds.), Georg Solmssen. Ein deutscher Bankier. Briefe aus einem halben Jahrhundert 1900–1956, Munich 2012, 11–52.

Käppner, Joachim, *Berthold Beitz. Die Biografie*, Berlin 2010.

Karlsch, Rainer, *Die Aktiengesellschaft Sächsische Werke (ASW) und das Hydrierwerk der Braunkohlen-Benzin AG (Brabag) in Böhlen*, in: Konstantin Hermann (Ed.), Führerschule, Thingplatz, „Judenhaus". Orte und Gebäude der nationalsozialistischen Diktatur in Sachsen, Dresden 2014, 190–193.

Karlsch, Rainer/Bähr, Johannes, *Die Sowjetischen Aktiengesellschaften (SAG) in der SBZ/DDR*, in: Karl Lauschke/Thomas Welskopp (Eds.), Mikropolitik im Unternehmen, Essen 1994, 214–255.

Karlsch, Rainer, *Ein vergessenes Großunternehmen. Die Geschichte der Karpaten Öl AG*, in: Jahrbuch für Wirtschaftsgeschichte 1 (2004), 95–138.

Karlsch, Rainer/Stokes, Raymond G., *„Faktor Öl". Die Mineralölwirtschaft in Deutschland 1859–1974*, Munich 2003.

Kasper, Hanns-Heinz, *Die Ausplünderung polnischer und sowjetischer Erdöllagerstätten im Gebiet der Vorkarpaten durch den deutschen Imperialismus im Zweiten Weltkrieg*, in: Jahrbuch für Wirtschaftsgeschichte 4 (1978), 41–64.

Kasper, Hanns-Heinz, *Die Erdölgewinnung Deutschlands*, PhD thesis Freiberg 1977.

Kettenacker, Lothar, *Nationalsozialistische Volkstumspolitik im Elsass*, Stuttgart 1973.

Kleßmann, Christoph, *Polnische Bergarbeiter im Ruhrgebiet 1870–1945. Soziale Integration und nationale Subkultur einer Minderheit in der deutschen Industriegesellschaft*, Göttingen 1978.

Kockel, Titus, *Deutsche Ölpolitik 1928–1938*, Berlin 2005.

Kockel, Titus, *Geologie und Krieg. Die Erdölpolitik des Reichsamtes für Bodenforschung und seine Vorläufer*, M.A. Berlin 1995.

Kockel, Titus, *Eine Quelle zur Vor- und Gründungsgeschichte der Kontinentale Öl AG aus dem Jahr 1940*, in: Jahrbuch für Wirtschaftsgeschichte 1 (2003), 176–208.

Kockel, Titus, *Zickzackkurs in den Krieg. Deutsche Ölpolitik von Achnacarry Castle bis Karinhall (1928–1938)*, in: Dietrich Eichholtz (Ed.), Deutsche Ölpolitik im Zeitalter der Weltkriege, Studien und Dokumente, Leipzig 2010, 188–279.

Köhler, Ingo/Ziegler, Dieter, *Heirats- und Verkehrskreise als Instrument wirtschaftsbürgerlichen Aufstiegs. Die Familie Andreae*, in: Genealogie. Deutsche Zeitschrift für Familienkunde 1/2 (1997), 385–402.

Kratzsch, Gerhard, *Das wirtschaftspolitische Gauamt. Der Gauwirtschaftsberater*, in: Jürgen John et al., Die NS-Gaue. Regionale Mittelinstanzen im zentralistischen „Führerstaat“, Munich 2007, 218–233.

Krau, Ingrid, *Kohle, Öl und Krieg. Eine Biographie*, Berlin 2015.

Kroener, Bernhard R. et al., *Das Deutsche Reich und der Zweite Weltkrieg, Organisation und Mobilisierung des deutschen Machtbereichs. Teilband 2: Kriegsverwaltung, Wirtschaft und personelle Ressourcen 1942 bis 1944/45,* Stuttgart 1999.

Kwiet, Konrad, *Nach dem Pogrom. Stufen der Ausgrenzung*, in: Wolfgang Benz (Ed.), Die Juden in Deutschland 1933–1945. Leben unter nationalsozialistischer Herrschaft, Munich 1988, 545–659.

Lausitzer und Mitteldeutsche Bergbauverwaltungsgesellschaft mbH (Ed.), *Braunkohlenveredlung in Mitteldeutschland. Teil II (Süd)*, Senftenberg 2019.

Lausitzer und Mitteldeutsche Bergbauverwaltungsgesellschaft mbH (Ed.), *Mitteldeutsches Braunkohlenrevier*, Senftenberg 2013.

Lehmann, Gottfried, *Das Mitteldeutsche Braunkohlensyndikat in Leipzig*, PhD thesis Greifswald 1930.

Lindner, Stephan H., *Das Reichskommissariat für die Behandlung feindlichen Vermögens im Zweiten Weltkrieg. Eine Studie zur Verwaltungs-, Rechts- und Wirtschaftsgeschichte des nationalsozialistischen Deutschlands*, Stuttgart 1991.

Linne, Karsten, *Die Gründung der Kontinentale Öl AG*, Hamburg 2023.

Linne, Karsten, *Der Krieg als Chance. Ein deutscher Manager auf „Expedition“ in den Kaukasus*, in: Zeitschrift für Geschichtswissenschaft 5 (2024), 398–418.

Loose, Ingo, *Die Juden in der Wirtschaft Schlesiens von der Reichsgründung 1871 bis zur Schoah*, in: Werner Brämer et al., Jüdisches Leben zwischen Ost und West. Neue Beiträge zur jüdischen Geschichte in Schlesien, Göttingen 2014, 156–217.

Loose, Ingo, *Das Reichswirtschaftsministerium und die nationalsozialistische Judenverfolgung 1933–1945*, in: Albrecht Ritschl (Ed.), Das Reichswirtschaftsministerium im Dritten Reich, Berlin 2016, 357–532.

Lütgert, Stephan A., *„Ein Bergmann ging ins Öl“. Zur Erinnerung an Bergassessor Dr. Ing. E. h. Günther Schlicht (1901–1962)*, in: EEK 9 (2022), 34–46.

Madajczyk, Czeslaw, *Die Okkupationspolitik Nazideutschlands in Polen 1939–1945*, Cologne 1988.

Magistrate Liegnitz, Goldberg, Schönau (Eds.), *Liegnitz, Goldberg, das schöne Katzbachtal*, Berlin 1925.

Mai, Gunther, *Die Nationalsozialistische Betriebszellen-Organisation. Arbeiterschaft und Nationalsozialismus 1927–1934*, in: id./Detlev Heiden (Eds.), Nationalsozialismus und Thüringen, Weimar 1995, 165–188.

Mallis, Ullrich, *Zur Geschichte der Nordhäuser Aktiengesellschaften*, in: Beiträge zur Geschichte aus Stadt und Kreis Nordhausen 40 (2015), 143–186.

Mantelli, Bruno, *Zwischen Strukturwandel auf dem Arbeitsmarkt und Kriegswirtschaft. Die Anwerbung der italienischen Arbeiter für das „Dritte Reich" und die „Achse Berlin-Rom"*, in: Cesare Bermani et al., Proletarier der „Achse". Sozialgeschichte der italienischen Fremdarbeiter in NS-Deutschland 1937–1943, Berlin 1997, 253–391.

Marschner, Erhard, *Liebieg, Theodor Freiherr von*, in: Neue Deutsche Biographie, Vol. 14, Berlin 1985, 495–497.

Martens, Holger, *Die Geschichte der Sozialdemokratischen Partei Deutschlands in Schleswig-Holstein 1945 bis 1959*, PhD thesis Hamburg 1997.

Meier-Dörnberg, Wilhelm, *Die Ölversorgung der Kriegsmarine 1935 bis 1945*, Freiburg 1973.

Milert, Werner/Tschirbs, Rudolf, *Die andere Demokratie. Betriebliche Interessenvertretung in Deutschland 1848 bis 2008*, Essen 2015.

Militärgeschichtliches Forschungsamt (Hg.), *Das Deutsche Reich und der Zweite Weltkrieg. Organisation und Mobilisierung des deutschen Machtbereichs*, Stuttgart 1999.

Münch, Ingo v., *Die deutsche Staatsangehörigkeit. Vergangenheit, Gegenwart, Zukunft*, Berlin 2007.

Münzel, Martin, *Die jüdischen Mitglieder der deutschen Wirtschaftselite*, Paderborn 2006.

Mullay, Dieter, *Von der NSBO zur Deutschen Arbeitsfront (DAF)*, in: Heinrich Berger et al., Politische Gewalt und Machtausübung im 20. Jahrhundert. Zeitgeschichte, Zeitgeschehen und Kontroversen, Vienna 2011, 193–214.

Mulot, Tobias, *Von der Betriebszelle zur Arbeitsfront. Die Hamburger NSBO auf dem Weg in die „Leistungsgemeinschaft" des „Dritten Reiches"*, in: Frank Bajohr/Joachim Szodrzynski (Eds.), Hamburg in der NS-Zeit. Ergebnisse neuerer Forschungen, Hamburg 1995, 203–230.

Nietzel, Benno, *Die Vernichtung der wirtschaftlichen Existenz der deutschen Juden 1933–1945. Ein Literatur- und Forschungsbericht*, in: Archiv für Sozialgeschichte 49 (2009), 561–613.

Nussbaum, Manfred, *Wirtschaft und Staat in Deutschland während der Weimarer Republik*, Berlin 1978.

N.n., *Plünderer verwalten polnisches Gut*, in: Neues Deutschland, 14 January 1947.

Petzina, Dietmar, *Autarkiepolitik im Dritten Reich. Der nationalsozialistische Vierjahresplan*, Stuttgart 1968.

Peukert, Detlev, *Die KPD im Widerstand. Verfolgung und Untergrundarbeit an Rhein und Ruhr 1933–1945*, Wuppertal 1980.

Plumpe, Gottfried, *Die I.G. Farbenindustrie AG. Wirtschaft, Technik und Politik 1904–1945*, Berlin 1990.

Plumpe, Werner, *Wirtschaftsverwaltung und Kapitalinteresse im britischen Besatzungsgebiet 1945/46*, in: Dietmar Petzina/Walter Euchner (Eds.), Wirtschaftspolitik im britischen Besatzungsgebiet 1945–1949, Düsseldorf 1984, 121–152.

Pöhlmann, Rainer, *Mein Leben. Gedanken und Erinnerungen*, Jena 2015.

Pohl, Dieter, *Nationalsozialistische Judenverfolgung in Ostgalizien 1941–1944*, Munich 1997.

Pohl, Manfred/Schneider, Andrea H., *VIAG-Aktiengesellschaft 1923–1998. Vom Staatsunternehmen zum internationalen Konzern*, Munich 1998.

Priamus, Heinz-Jürgen, *Meyer. Zwischen Kaisertreue und NS-Täterschaft. Biographische Konturen eines deutschen Bürgers*, Essen 2011.

Priemel, Kim Christian, *Flick. Eine Konzerngeschichte vom Kaiserreich bis zur Bundesrepublik*, Munich 2013.

Puchta, Matthias, *Die Technische Brigade Mineralöl und ihre Kriegsgefangenen. Der wehrwirtschaftliche Einsatz kriegsgefangener Mineralölfachkräfte an der Ostfront*, in: Vierteljahrschrift für Sozial- und Wirtschaftsgeschichte 1 (2024), 35–65.

Randhahn, Walther, *Der Wettbewerb der deutschen Braunkohlenindustrie gegen die Einfuhr der böhmischen Kohle*, PhD thesis Jena 1908.

Rasch, Manfred, *Alfred Pott*, in: Neue Deutsche Biographie, Vol. 20, Berlin 2001, 658–659.

Rasch, Manfred, *Zur Mineralölpolitik der Kriegsmarine*, in: Militärgeschichtliche Mitteilungen 1 (1985), 71–101.

Rauh-Kühne, Cornelia, *Die Entnazifizierung und die deutsche Gesellschaft*, in: Archiv für Sozialgeschichte 35 (1995), 35–70.

Reiter, Martin, *Das Arbeitserziehungslager Wilhelmsburg. Aktuelle Forschungen zu einem kaum bekannten NS-Lager*, in: Christine Eckel et al., Stigmatisierung – Marginalisierung – Verfolgung, Berlin 2015, 184–202.

Röper, Burkhardt, *Die drei Abwertungen in Großbritannien*, in: Econstor Wirtschaftsdienst 29 (1949), 9–15.

Rössler, Mechthild/Schleiermacher, Sabine (Eds.), *Der „Generalplan Ost". Hauptlinien der nationalsozialistischen Planungs- und Vernichtungspolitik*, Berlin 1993.

Rothauer, Doris, *Das Tiefbohrunternehmen van Sickle. Seine Entwicklung und Tätigkeit im Rahmen der gesamten österreichischen Mineralölindustrie*, Vienna 1985.

Ruthammer, Gerhard, *Öldorado Weinviertel. Zur Geschichte des Erdöls im Weinviertel*, Schleinbach 2013.

Sächsisches Landesamt für Umwelt und Geologie (Ed.), *Der Braunkohlenbergbau im Südraum Leipzig*, Dresden 2003.

Sandkühler, Thomas, *„Endlösung" in Galizien. Der Judenmord in Ostpolen und die Rettungsinitiativen von Berthold Beitz 1941–1944*, Bonn 1996.

Scherner, Jonas, *Die Logik der Industriepolitik im Dritten Reich*, Stuttgart 2008.

Seibold, Eugen/Seibold, Ilse, *Alfred Bentz. Erdölgeologe in schwieriger Zeit 1938–1947*, in: International Journal of Earth Sciences 6 (2002), 1081–1093.

Seidel, Hans, *Österreichs Wirtschaft und Wirtschaftspolitik nach dem Zweiten Weltkrieg*, Vienna 2005.

Seidel, Hans-Christoph, *Der Ruhrbergbau im Zweiten Weltkrieg. Zechen – Bergarbeiter – Zwangsarbeiter*, Essen 2010.

Siemens, Daniel, *Sturmabteilung. Die Geschichte der SA*, Berlin 2019.

Simon, Barbara, *Abgeordnete in Niedersachsen 1946–1994. Biographisches Handbuch*, Hanover 1996.

Spoerer, Mark, *Zwangsarbeit unter dem Hakenkreuz. Ausländische Zivilarbeiter, Kriegsgefangene und Häftlinge im Deutschen Reich und im besetzten Europa 1939–1945*, Stuttgart 2001.

Stadler, Gerhard A., *Das industrielle Erbe Niederösterreichs. Geschichte – Technik – Architektur*, Vienna 2006.

Steensen, Friederike, *Ein Latecomer macht sich auf den Weg. Ein Firmenjubiläum als Katalysator für den Archivaufbau*, in: Archiv und Wirtschaft 1 (2024), 16–22.

Steinbach, Peter, *Die Gleichschaltung. Zerstörung der Weimarer Republik – Konsolidierung der nationalsozialistischen Diktatur*, in: Michael Kißener (Ed.), Der Weg in den Nationalsozialismus 1933/34, Darmstadt 2009, 66–99.

Steininger, Benjamin, *Die Sammlung Rohstoff Geschichte. Ein Findbuch*, Vienna 2016.

Steininger, Rolf, *Reform und Realität. Ruhrfrage und Sozialisierung in der anglo-amerikanischen Deutschlandpolitik 1947/48*, in: Vierteljahrshefte für Zeitgeschichte 27 (1979), 167–241.

Stiller, Alexander, *Die ideologische Instrumentalisierung des Wettkampfes im Nationalsozialismus zur Erziehung der männlichen Jugend. Selbstinszenierungen und Praktiken des Regimes zwischen 1933 und 1945*, Hamburg 2017.

Stoi, Gert, *Das Arbeitserziehungslager Römhild 1943–1945. Dokumentation eines Verbrechens*, Leipzig 2010.

Strassmann, Ingolf, *Altenburg in Thüringen. Stadt und Landkreis unterm Hakenkreuz*, Altenburg 2003.

Tennstedt, Florian, *Wohltat und Interesse. Das Winterhilfswerk des Deutschen Volkes. Die Weimarer Vorgeschichte und ihre Instrumentalisierung durch das NS-Regime*, in: Geschichte und Gesellschaft 2 (1987), 157–180.

Terres, Ernst, *Edeleanu, Lazăr*, in: Neue Deutsche Biographie, Vol. 4, Berlin 1959, 307–308.

Tittelbach-Helmrich, Wolfgang, *Arnstadts jüdische Bürger*, Arnstadt 1995.

Tooze, Adam, *Ökonomie der Zerstörung. Die Geschichte der Wirtschaft im Nationalsozialismus*, Munich 2006.

Toprani, Anand, *Germany's Answer to Standard Oil. The Continental Oil Company and Nazi Grand Strategy 1940–1942*, in: Journal of Strategic Studies 6–7 (2014), 949–973.

Toprani, Anand, *"The Navy's success speaks for itself". The German Navy's Independent Energy Security Strategy 1932–1940*, in: Naval War College Review 68 (2015), 91–118.

Treue, Wilhelm, *Dokumentation. Hitlers Denkschrift zum Vierjahresplan 1936*, in: Vierteljahrshefte für Zeitgeschichte 2 (1955), 184–210.

Trischler, Helmuth, *Partielle Modernisierung, Die betrieblichen Sozialbeziehungen im Ruhrbergbau zwischen Grubenmilitarismus und Human Relations*, in: Mathias Frese/ Michael Prinz (Eds.), Politische Zäsuren und gesellschaftlicher Wandel im 20. Jahrhundert. Regionale und vergleichende Perspektiven, Paderborn 1996, 145–171.

Ulbrich, Bernd, *Geschichte der Industrie- und Handelskammer Halle-Dessau 1844–2019*, Halle 2019.

Urban, Thomas, *Zwangsarbeit im Tagebau. Der Einsatz von Kriegsgefangenen und ausländischen Zivilarbeitern im mitteldeutschen Braunkohlenbergbau 1939 bis 1945*, Essen 2006.

Vollnhals, Clemens, *Entnazifizierung. Politische Säuberung unter alliierter Herrschaft*, in: Hans-Erich Volkmann (Ed.), Ende des Dritten Reiches. Ende des Zweiten Weltkrieges, Munich 1995, 369–392.

Walther, René, *Pechelbronn. A la source du pétrole 1735–1970*, Strasbourg 2007.

Weber, Erhard, *Der staatseigene Industriekonzern in Sachsen*, Leipzig 1928.

Weisz, Franz, *Die personelle Zusammensetzung der Gestapo Wien 1938 – 1945*, Vienna 2019.

Welsch, Fritz, *Geschichte der chemischen Industrie. Abriss der Entwicklung ausgewählter Zweige der chemischen Industrie von 1800 bis zur Gegenwart*, Berlin 1981.

Werberg, Dennis, *Der Stahlhelm - Bund der Frontsoldaten. Eine Veteranenorganisation als politischer Akteur und ihr Verhältnis zum Nationalsozialismus*, Berlin 2023.

Wiggershaus, Norbert Theodor, *Der deutsch-englische Flottenvertrag vom 18. Juni 1935 und die geheime deutsche Aufrüstung 1933–1935*, Bonn 1972.

Wildt, Michael, *Generation des Unbedingten. Das Führungskorps des Reichssicherheitshauptamtes*, Hamburg 2002.

Wir wollten den Wega-Hagi-Konkurs verhindern, in: FAZ, 3 August 1983.

Wischnath, Johannes Michael, *Bauer, Walter Albert*, in: Bernd Ottnad (Ed.), Baden-Württembergische Biographien, Vol. 2, Stuttgart 2009, 16–19.

Wisotzky, Klaus, *Der Ruhrbergbau im Dritten Reich. Studie zur Sozialpolitik im Ruhrbergbau und zum sozialen Verhalten der Bergleute in den Jahren 1933 bis 1939*, Düsseldorf 1983.

Wixforth, Harald, *Die Ausbeutung von Ressourcen im Zeichen der Kriegswirtschaft. Die Kontinentale Öl AG*, in: Johannes Bähr (Ed.), Die Dresdner Bank in der Wirtschaft des Dritten Reiches, Munich 2006, 360–370.

Włodarczyk, Tamara, *Aus der Geschichte der Juden in der Region Liegnitz*, Warschau 2016.

Wojak, Irmtrud/Hayes, Peter (Eds.), *„Arisierung" im Nationalsozialismus. Volksgemeinschaft, Raub und Gedächtnis,* Frankfurt a.M. 2000.

Wolter, Rolf, *Werdegang des ehemaligen Erdölbergwerkes Wietze in der Gemeinde Wietze, Landkreis Celle*, Wietze 2001.

Wulf, Peter, *Die Auseinandersetzungen um die Sozialisierung der Kohle in Deutschland 1920/1921*, in: Vierteljahrshefte für Zeitgeschichte 1 (1977), 46–98.

Yelton, David K., *Hitler's Volkssturm. The Nazi Militia and the fall of Germany, 1944–1945*, Lawrence 2002.

Zetzsche, Hans-Jürgen, *Logistik und Operationen. Die Mineralölversorgung der Kriegsmarine im Zweiten Weltkrieg*, PhD thesis Kiel 1986.

Ziegler, Dieter, *Kriegswirtschaft, Kriegsfolgenbewältigung, Kriegsvorbereitung. Der deutsche Bergbau im dauernden Ausnahmezustand (1914–1945)*, in: id. (Ed.), Rohstoffgewinnung im Strukturwandel. Der deutsche Bergbau im 20. Jahrhundert, Münster 2013, 15–182.

Zilch, Reinhold, *Schwabach, Paul Hermann von*, in: Neue Deutsche Biographie, Vol. 23, Berlin 2007, 776–777.

PICTURE CREDITS

Archiv der Bundeanstalt für Geowissenschaften und Rohstoffe (BGR):
Fig. 55, 56, 57, 58, 59

Bergbrüderschaft Meuselwitz-Rositzer Braunkohlenrevier e.V./ Archiv Rehfeld:
Fig. 25, 28, 29, 30, 37, 38 and Cover

Deutsches Erdölmuseum Wietze (DEW):
Fig. 1, 18, 22, 33, 34, 40, 41, 42, 43, 44, 45, 46, 48, 49

Historisches Archiv der Deutschen Bank (HADB):
Fig. 16, 32

Montanhistorisches Dokumentationszentrum (montan.dok) beim Deutschen Bergbau-Museum Bochum (BBA):
Fig. 19, 60

Wintershall Dea Corporate Archive (WD-CA):
Fig. 2, 3, 4, 5, 6, 7, 8, 9, 10, 11, 12, 13, 14, 15, 17, 20, 21, 23, 24, 26, 27, 31, 35, 36, 39, 47, 50, 51, 52, 53, 54, 61

THE AUTHORS

Photo: Gerrit Mumme

Manfred Grieger, born. 1960, honorary professor at Institute for Economic and Social History of Georg-August-University Göttingen, last publications: „Rebstock“ und „Rebstock (Stephan)“ – zwei Außenlager im Konzentrationslager-System bei Marienthal und Dernau, August bis Dezember 1944 (Mainz 2021); Die Geschichte des Hauses Bahlsen: Keks – Krieg – Konsum 1911–1974 (Göttingen 2024) mit Hartmut Berghoff.

Photo: private

Dr. Rainer Karlsch (Institute of Contemporary History Munich-Berlin), born 1957, studied economic history at Humboldt-University of Berlin. In 1996, he won the first prize of the Stinnes Stiftung for his book "Allein bezahlt? Die Reparationsleistungen der SBZ/DDR 1945–53". His past publications include: Faktor Öl. Die Mineralölwirtschaft in Deutschland 1859–1974, Munich 2003 (along with Raymond Stokes); Wirtschaftsgeschichte Sachsens im Industriezeitalter (along with Michael Schäfer), Leipzig 2006; Uran für Moskau, Die Wismut eine populäre Geschichte, Berlin 2007; Leuna – 100 Jahre Chemie, Löbejün 2016.